INTRODUCING CATHOLIC THEOLOGY

Thinking about God

INTRODUCING CATHOLIC THEOLOGY

General editor: Michael Richards

This series, for theology students in colleges, universities and seminaries, offers comprehensive guides to the source material and to the research and reflection needed for a thorough understanding of Christian theology within the Catholic tradition. It provides reliable information and stimulates personal inquiry. The authors, who are drawn from a variety of countries and schools of thought within the English-speaking Catholic world, have constantly borne in mind the relationship of Christianity with other religions and the need to reconcile the faith of divided Christendom.

Father Michael Richards, formerly lecturer in church history, ecclesiology and pastoral theology at Heythrop College, London and editor of *The Clergy Review* from 1967 to 1985, is now a parish priest in central London.

INTRODUCING CATHOLIC THEOLOGY

Thinking about God

Brian Davies

GEOFFREY CHAPMAN
LONDON

A Geoffrey Chapman book published by
Cassell Ltd
1 Vincent Square, London SW1P 2PN

First published 1985

ISBN 0 225 66476 3

Nihil obstat: Anton Cowan, *Censor*
Imprimatur: Monsignor John Crowley, *V.G.*
Westminster, 3 July 1985

The *Nihil obstat* and *Imprimatur* are a declaration that a book or pamphlet is considered to be free from doctrinal or moral error. It is not implied that those who have granted the *Nihil obstat* and *Imprimatur* agree with the contents, opinions or statements expressed.

British Library Cataloguing in Publication Data

Davies, Brian, 1951—
Thinking about God.—(Introducing Catholic
theology; 5)
1. God   2. Catholic Church—Doctrines
I. Title   II. Series
231   BT102

Phototypesetting by Georgia Origination, Liverpool

Printed and bound in Great Britain at
Billing & Sons Ltd, Worcester

Contents

Foreword

Introducing Catholic Theology has been conceived and planned in the belief that the Second Vatican Council provided the Church with a fundamental revision of its way of life in the light of a thorough investigation of Scripture and of our history, and with fresh guidelines for studying and reflecting upon the Christian message itself. In common with every other form of human enquiry and practical activity, the Christian faith can be set out and explained in ways appropriate to human intelligence: it calls for scientific textbooks as well as for other forms of writing aimed at expressing and conveying its doctrines.

It is hoped that these volumes will be found useful by teachers and students in that they will supply both the information and the stimulus to reflection that should be taken for granted and counted upon by all concerned in any one course of study.

Conceived as expressions of the Catholic tradition, the books draw upon the contribution to the knowledge of God and the world made by other religions, and the standpoint of other patterns of Christian loyalty. They recognize the need for finding ways of reconciliation where differences of understanding lead to human divisions and even hostility. They also give an account of the insights of various philosophical and methodological approaches.

In *Thinking about God*, Brian Davies has provided an introduction to the attempts made by Christian thinkers to express the understanding of God and his relationship with the world that they consider to be accessible to human reason without explicit reference to the special self-revelation that he has in many different ways made available, above all in Christ and through the history of salvation. The affirmations made by the Christian faith about the nature of God are, they would say, at least compatible with what we are able to work out for ourselves concerning the nature of the universe. Readers will find themselves being led to think along with the author as he expounds, explores and discusses the arguments in the case. They will be helped to reflect for themselves as well as finding themselves clearly informed about the positions taken up in this vital area of human investigation, after many centuries of debate.

Michael Richards

For C. J. F. W. from the Same Man

Several people have kindly read and commented on material which has ended up in this book. I am especially grateful to P. T. Geach, Herbert McCabe, OP, Denis Minns, OP, H. P. Owen, Illtyd Trethowan, and Simon Tugwell, OP. Much of the text was completed while I enjoyed a research fellowship at Yale University, where I was greatly assisted and nurtured by the Prior and Community of St Mary's Priory, New Haven. Fr Michael Richards first invited me to write the book and proved thereafter to be a continual help and support.

Blackfriars,
Oxford

April 1985

Introduction

Some people say that there is a God and that it is reasonable to believe in him. Others deny this and hold that belief in God is unreasonable.

Some people think that there is no God, but that there could be one. Others, however, say that the very notion of God is somehow meaningless or contradictory.

For some people, all our knowledge of God must be based on faith. We can know nothing of him apart from Revelation. But others take the view that we can discover some truths about God apart from Revelation.

Christians say that Christ is God and that God is Father, Son, and Spirit. Yet opponents of Christianity deny this, and they sometimes insist that the doctrines of the Trinity and the Incarnation are somehow disprovable.

So what is the answer? Is there any reason to believe in God apart from Revelation? Can reason tell us anything about God? Can it undermine the specifically Christian doctrine of God?

The traditional Catholic answer to these questions, which you can find in the documents of Vatican I, is clear, but also unhelpful. A distinction is drawn between what can be known by natural reason apart from Revelation, and what can be known only through Revelation. Then it is said that by natural reason we can know that God exists, and by Revelation that he is One in Three and Incarnate. But we are not told exactly how natural reason can know of God's existence. Nor are we told what precisely is to be said to those who suppose that the Trinity and the Incarnation are impossible. These matters are not so far resolved in terms of Catholic doctrine. There are no views about them which can claim to be *de fide*.

The following questions therefore arise. *How* can we know of God's existence apart from Revelation? *What* can reason tell us about God? *How* does reason fare with respect to Christianity? And these are the questions with which I am concerned in this book, which consequently differs from other volumes that have so far appeared in this series. I do not here assume that God exists. I ask whether there is reason for supposing that he does. Then I try to consider what reason can tell us about him, and what it cannot tell us. In this sense the book is not so much a work of theology as a discussion of matters which theology can take for granted.

At one level, therefore, you can read what follows as an essay on fundamentals. But it is also intended to be more than a statement of personal opinion. *Introducing Catholic Theology* is a series intended to help readers to find their way around in areas of debate in which much has already been said and written. So I have tried to place my views in the context of an account of major arguments and conclusions. At another level, therefore, the book can be read as an introduction to its subject matter designed to explain what has been said about it by others than myself. Each chapter is factual as well as argumentative, so even if you do not like my views, you will find plenty of others recorded. And, to make things as clear as possible, I proceed on the assumption that the reader has no specialist knowledge. Much of the book is about what is sometimes referred to as 'philosophy of God', but it is not aimed chiefly at professional philosophers or those with a philosophical training. Its primary target is anyone who wants to understand something about the debates alluded to at the beginning of this Introduction.

The first of these is the reality of God. So our topic at the outset is reasons for belief in God. The centuries have thrown up many of these, and I cannot look at all of them. But I do turn to the major ones, which can be roughly divided into three kinds.

Examples of the first hold that it is reasonable to believe in God because of what he has brought about or produced. Under this heading come what are commonly referred to as the Cosmological Argument and the Argument from Design. There is also an argument based on the miraculous.

Examples of the second kind hold that God somehow makes his presence directly felt, or that some aspect of human experience is evidence for him. Under this heading come arguments for God based on what is taken to be experience of him, and arguments based on morality.

Examples of the third hold that God's existence can be established by reflecting on the concept of God. The chief candidate for consideration here is the so-called Ontological Argument for the existence of God.

These arguments will concern us in Part One. In Part Two I turn directly to the question of God's nature or attributes. To begin with I consider some general questions about the way we talk of God. Then I move on to specific topics concerning what we say about God. It is commonly asserted that God is eternal, omnipotent, omniscient, omnipresent, and good. I therefore consider this assertion, along with a variety of conclusions that have been offered concerning it.

Finally, I look at some matters of specific concern to Christianity. In Part Three I consider the relationship between what we can know of God apart from Revelation and what we believe about God in the light of Revelation. Various topics call for mention at this point, including, for example, the doctrine of the Incarnation and the doctrine of the Trinity. So, among other things, I have observations to make about these. At the end of the book I turn to an issue relevant to the practice of Christianity. Christians are told to pray. In Chapter 11 I consider this advice.

A few points to end with.

First, though I write as a Catholic, the text which follows is designed to be accessible to people of any religious persuasion or none. Much of my concern is with questions that have been widely debated well beyond the confines of the Catholic Church, and what I have to say about them can be treated as an entry and contribution to that debate.

Second, though my own views will become clear as the book proceeds, its format is intended to enable readers to arrive at a position where they can usefully reach conclusions of their own. To this end I have included a lot of discussion questions and a substantial amount of bibliographical notes.

Third, the reader will quickly discover that I often refer to St Thomas Aquinas and that I clearly think highly of him. Some will find this frustrating or outdated, for in many quarters Aquinas is quickly dismissed. To some extent this is understandable, but it is also, I think, enormously regrettable. In my opinion Aquinas is one of the greatest thinkers ever produced by the Catholic Church (in spite of the fact that he was condemned in Oxford by a Dominican Archbishop), and what he has to say is often of permanent relevance – as, quite ironically, many secular philosophers now concede, often in curious contrast to Catholic writers and to theologians who are not Catholics, who seem frequently concerned simply to do Aquinas down, often without evidence of having studied him seriously (cf. Kenny 1980, pp. 27ff.). For this reason, therefore, I do not hesitate both to quote from Aquinas at some length and to consider his arguments in some detail.

Fourth, and rather lamely, almost all the major questions of philosophy arise when one turns to many of the issues discussed in this book, and all of them deserve treatment which is prohibited by the nature of the series to which the book belongs. That is unfortunate, but unavoidable. Nevertheless, I hope that what I say shows some philosophical rigour and can be recognized as a philosophical contribution in its own right.

Finally, since the Church has not committed itself to any definite conclusion on many of the matters which I discuss, it should be clearly realized at the outset that what I have to say about them can no more be taken as Catholic teaching than can anything said about them by others. This, of course, means that Catholics are as free as anyone to disagree with me at length and to try to offer different or better conclusions than mine. It is therefore to be hoped that those of them who read this book will be stimulated to reflections of their own and that the title of the book can serve as a description of what they will find themselves doing.

Part One
The Existence of God

1

The Things That Have Been Made

It has been said that, in matters of religion, belief cannot argue with unbelief; it can only preach to it. On this view, those who believe that there is a God need offer no particular defence of their position other than a statement of the position itself. On this view, belief in God stands in no need of anything that we might regard as rational justification. It is proclaimed, not argued for. Either you believe in God, or you do not, and there is not much more to be said.

But people, of course, often do want some rational justification for believing in God. It has been observed that at the foundation of our reasoning lie beliefs which are not themselves arrived at by means of argument or rational justification (cf. Wittgenstein 1974, paras 174ff.), and perhaps it is true that belief in God, as in anything else, must always rest somehow on faith. In any argument one has to begin by accepting certain premises. But few of us would accept every belief without question, and belief in God's existence is a classic example of a belief which for many people requires rational justification. These people ask why one should believe in God, and, in asking this question, they are heirs to an ancient tradition not only of sceptics but also of believers. The reality of God has not always been taught as an object of belief to be swallowed with the eyes shut. It has been seen as something open to rational support. As one writer puts it: 'Theism, to those who ask about its beliefs, is not offered for consumption in a large anti-rational gulp. It has been *argued* by Christian theologians since St Paul, and by Islamic theologians at least as early as al-Kindi' (Gaskin 1984, p. 30).

A problem

So is there any reason for believing in God which does not presuppose that there is indeed a God? Can belief in God be rationally defended without presupposing its truth at the outset?

The question has been answered in different ways, some of which I shall turn to later. Among believers, however, perhaps the most popular line of thinking comprises the suggestion that the existence of God can be reasoned to or known in the light of God's effects. As St Thomas Aquinas (1224/5-74) puts it:

Now any effect of a cause demonstrates that that cause exists, in cases where the effect is better known to us, since effects are dependent on their causes, and can only occur if the causes already exist. From effects evident to us, therefore, we can demonstrate what in itself is not evident, namely that God exists (*Summa Theologiae* Ia, 2, 2).

The point is repeated thus by Vatican I in chapter 2 of its *Dogmatic Constitution on the Catholic Faith*:

God, the beginning and end of all things, may be certainly known by the natural light of reason by means of created things.

On this account, belief in God is reasonable in the light of what God has produced or brought about.

But how can we know that he *has* produced anything? Why should we speak at all of his *effects*? The argument that has dominated discussions of these questions is generally referred to as the Cosmological Argument (the name derives from Immanuel Kant [1724–1804] but can be used to cover more arguments than the one for which Kant devised the name). We can therefore begin with that. It has two main forms, the first of which concentrates on the relationship between God and the beginning of the universe.

THE COSMOLOGICAL ARGUMENT – I

GOD AND THE BEGINNING OF THE UNIVERSE: THE KALĀM COSMOLOGICAL ARGUMENT

Many things exist which we know to have come into being. People are a case in point. And their existence prompts a perfectly natural question. What brought them into being? What got them going? When we are dealing with things which began to exist, we do not assume that they just 'happened'. We suppose that something produced them, and we go on to ask what that could be.

This familiar way of reasoning brings us to the first notable version of the Cosmological Argument. It is particularly associated with a group of writers working in the Middle Ages and earlier, a group which belonged to the Islamic Kalām tradition of philosophy, so we can call it 'the Kalām Cosmological Argument'. But, though the name may sound unfamiliar, the argument is not. It is, on the contrary, exceedingly common. It is the Kalām Argument that people are basically offering when they say, as they often do, that they believe in God because 'something must have started it all' or because 'things cannot have got going by themselves'. The fundamental idea here is that God must exist because the universe must have had a beginning and because only God could have brought this about. Together with this idea goes the belief that everything that has a beginning of existence must have a cause. In the words of one of the Kalām Argument's most recent defenders:

Since everything that begins to exist has a cause of its existence, and since the universe began to exist, we conclude, therefore, the universe has a cause of its existence . . . Transcending the entire universe there exists a cause which brought the universe into being . . . But even more: we may plausibly argue that the cause of the universe is a personal being . . . If the universe began to exist, and if the universe is caused, then the cause of the universe must be a personal being who freely chooses to create the world . . . The kalām cosmological argument leads to a personal Creator of the universe (Craig 1979, pp. 149ff.).

The Kalām Cosmological Argument can therefore be stated as follows:

(1) Everything that has a beginning of existence must have a cause.
(2) The universe began to exist.
(3) Therefore, the beginning of the universe's existence must have been caused by God.

Beginnings

But is it really true that whatever has a beginning of existence must have a cause? The Kalām Argument relies on the assumption that it is true, but the assumption has been challenged, most notably perhaps, by the Scottish philosopher David Hume (1711–76), according to whom the ideas of cause and effect are distinct so that there could, in principle, be something which we take to be an effect but which is really no such thing. As Hume himself puts it:

As all distinct ideas are separable from each other, and as the ideas of cause and effect are evidently distinct, 'twill be easy for us to conceive any object to be non-existent this moment, and existent the next, without conjoining to it the distinct idea of a cause or productive principle. The separation, therefore, of the idea of a cause from that of a beginning of existence, is plainly possible for the imagination; and consequently the actual separation of these objects is so far possible, that it implies no contradiction or absurdity; and is therefore incapable of being refuted by any reasoning from mere ideas; without which 'tis impossible to demonstrate the necessity of a cause (*A Treatise of Human Nature*, pp. 79ff.).

Yet, though many have found this an attractive argument, it is really rather poor. Hume is saying one of two things (which of these he is arguing is not clear from what he writes):

(a) We can imagine a beginning of existence without some

particular cause; therefore there can be a beginning of existence
without a cause.

(b) We can imagine a beginning of existence without any cause;
therefore there can be a beginning of existence without a cause.

But both these arguments are open to question.

Can we imagine a beginning of existence without a particular cause?
Apparently we can. We can, for instance, imagine that the Mona Lisa was
painted by someone other than Leonardo. But this does not entail that there
can be a beginning of existence without a cause. All that follows is that a
particular beginning of existence can be supposed to have happened without a
particular cause, as, for example, *this* painting can be supposed to have come
about without *that* painter.

So if (a) is Hume's argument, it is misguided. And if (b) is what he intends,
then there is this problem. I can draw a picture of something and write under
it 'Something coming into existence without a cause'. But this does not
prove that there is no absurdity in the idea of something coming into
existence without a cause since it presupposes that what I have drawn *is* a
picture of something coming into existence without a cause. And, though
one may suppose that something can arise without a cause, how is one to
show that what one is thinking of as beginning to exist without a cause *is*
something that has begun to exist without a cause?

One might say, as Hume is possibly saying, that one can imagine something coming into existence at some time and place and there being no cause
of this. But how does one know that the thing in question has come into
existence at this time and place and not at any other? One has to exclude the
possibility of it having existed elsewhere and by some means or other come to
be where one says that it has begun to exist. Yet how is one to do that without supposing a cause which justifies one in judging that the thing came to be
at one particular time and place? Here is where (b) seems to break down. For
we say that things begin to be at such and such a time and at such and such a
place because we have the notion of them being brought about by various
identifiable objects or operations. 'We can observe beginnings of new items
because we know how they were produced and out of what . . . We know
the times and places of their beginnings without cavil because we understand
their origins' (Anscombe 1981, vol. II, p. 62). In other words, recognizing
that we are dealing with a genuine beginning of existence is something we
are capable of because we can identify causes. To know that something began
to exist seems already to know that it has a cause or that it has been caused. In
that case, however, it seems odd to suppose that there really could be a
beginning of existence without a cause. Nor, in fact, do we generally suppose
otherwise.

So the Kalām Argument is evidently on to something. We do have reason to suppose that beginnings of existence arise from causal activity. And if the universe began to exist, perhaps we should conclude that the same is true of it. But this, of course, brings us to another question. Did the universe have a beginning?

The beginning of the universe

There would seem to be two possible ways of trying to decide this question. One would be to consider the available scientific evidence and to ask whether that favours the conclusion that the universe had a beginning. Another would be to inquire whether or not there are any good philosophical arguments in favour of the conclusion. Both methods have found supporters.

The scientific arguments which have been offered for supposing that the universe began to exist are much too complex and technical to discuss here. Nor am I competent to discuss them. But it does seem clear that those familiar with the issues involved are prepared to allow that on the basis of scientific considerations the possibility of the universe having had a beginning is a very real one. Some put it more strongly than this. According to one writer: 'Scientific evidence concerning the expansion of the universe and the thermodynamic properties of closed systems indicates that the universe is finite in duration, beginning to exist about fifteen billion years ago' (Craig 1979, p. 140; = 15,000 million years). According to another: 'There is no doubt that the models best substantiated today are ones which show the Universe expanding from a "big bang" some 14,000 million years ago. These models successfully predict not merely the density and rate of recession of the galaxies, but the ratios of the various chemical elements to each other and to radiation in the universe, and above all the background cosmic radiation' (Swinburne 1981b, p. 258).

What, then, of the philosophical arguments? Unlike the modern scientific ones, these have a long history. Ancient Greek thinkers, who had much to say about change and beginnings, regularly denied a beginning to the material world. But later writers contested this conclusion and tried to show that there were good arguments for doing so. A notable example of such writers was the sixth-century Christian philosopher John Philoponus, who in 529 turned to the issue now in question in *De Aeternitate Mundi Contra Proclum*. Here he offers at least three major arguments for the universe having had a beginning. First, he says, if the universe had no beginning, then an infinity of years or generations will actually have been traversed, which is impossible. Second, if the universe never began, then, since the universe carries on, infinity is constantly being added to, which is impossible. Third, if the universe had no beginning, then we could have a multiplication of infinity, which is, again, impossible. If, say, Saturn has undergone an infinity of revolutions, then other heavenly bodies will have revolved many times that infinite number, which is absurd.

Arguments like this have proved very popular with those anxious to prove a beginning of the universe apart from scientific considerations (cf. Craig 1979). But they have drawbacks. Consider those just mentioned. If, for example, there were a first day plus an infinity of days to cram in between then and today, an infinity of days would have to have been traversed before today, which seems impossible. But if we actually believe that the universe never began, then we deny that there is any infinity of years or generations which have been traversed. In other words, the first of Philoponus's arguments merely 'expresses a prejudice against an actual infinity' (Mackie 1982, p. 93). And, with respect to the second and third arguments, one has to reply that if the universe had no beginning, then there is no reason for supposing either that infinity is being added to in any objectionable sense, or that it is multiplied in any objectionable sense (cf. Sorabji 1983, ch. 14). If the universe had no beginning, then no definite number of infinite past moments is being added to as time goes on, for there is no definite number to which addition is thereby made. And if the universe had no beginning, though it may be true that in any given period one thing may have done such and such more times than some other thing has done such and such, there need be no final count in the light of which we end up with two things doing such and such from infinity one of which does such and such more times than the other. Between time 1 and time 10, say, a planet may have revolved more times than some other (specifiable) planet. But in an infinite time, and with an infinite number of revolutions on the part of both planets, it will be false that one has revolved more times than the other.

Does this, then, mean that one cannot prove by purely philosophical argument that the universe had a beginning? Some would say 'Yes', but others would raise doubts. If an infinity of days had to pass before the arrival of today, so some would argue, then today would never arrive. Others would add that if the history of the universe goes backward infinitely, then something is happening which cannot happen in reality – viz. an actually infinite number of events is being added to. But even so it is hard to see how one can demonstrate that the universe must have begun to exist. Beginnings of existence are commonly recognized for what they are as things which take place by virtue of the activity of agents within the world operating at definite times and places. But the beginning of the universe cannot be like this since it is that which must be prior to things within the world acting at times and places. Furthermore, as many would say, there seems no conceptual impossibility in the assertion that for any time past it might have been true then to say 'There was a universe before now'. In other words, there seems to be nothing in the notion of the universe existing at any time which entails that there was no universe before that time.

So one may be justly sceptical of the view that philosophy can establish that the universe must have had a beginning. This, at any rate, is certainly the position adopted by some notable writers on the subject, and not only those who have no belief in God. A good example is Aquinas, who discusses the beginning of the universe in several works. Aquinas believed for biblical reasons that material things began to exist. He took this to be the sense of Genesis 1:1. But, having considered a range of philosophical reasons for and against a beginning, he concludes that the issue cannot be settled either way.

God and the beginning

Let us, however, suppose that the universe really did have a beginning. Does it follow that this must have been brought about by God? Here we come to a third major question raised by the Kalām Argument. Defenders of the Argument suppose that only the existence of God could account for the universe beginning to exist. But is that really so?

Islamic supporters of the Kalām Argument dealt with the question by appealing to a particular principle. They held that prior to the existence of the universe it was possible for the universe either to be or not to be, and that only a personal choice could have determined that it should be. And others have argued in the same manner. It has been said that when one of two equally possible states of affairs comes to pass, explanation must be sought in the action of a personal agent who freely chooses one rather than the other. And, on the basis of this principle, it has been argued that in trying to account for the beginning of the universe it is natural to appeal to something like God. For he is traditionally said to act in freedom. He is also traditionally said to have brought about the beginning of the universe.

There are several difficult features of this argument. One is its assumption that when one of two equally possible states of affairs comes about that must be because someone has decided that it shall come about. But may there not be genuine indeterminacy in nature such that something can happen which does not, in some absolute sense, have to happen? And may not something happen which does not have to happen when there are no personal agents involved in the thing happening? The argument also seems to assume that there was time before the existence of the universe. But can we attach any sense to the notion of time passing prior to the existence of any universe at all? And can we attach any sense to there being possibilities prior to the existence of the universe? One can readily grant that something may or may not happen; but one always does so as an individual already part of the universe's history. One says that things could go one way or the other; but only when there are things to start with. Yet how is one to understand it being true in the absence of any universe that something may or may not happen? Does it mean anything to speak of it being true before the existence of any universe that things could go one way or the other? What things?

Nevertheless, the argument is not entirely without merit. It would be widely agreed that in accounting for what happens there seem to be available only two intelligible alternatives. On the one hand we can invoke an explanation of a scientific kind, thereby appealing to natural necessities within the world. On the other we can appeal to personal explanation in terms of the free choices of rational agents. It has, of course, been said that all explanation of events is ultimately in terms of natural necessity. On this view there is no such thing as freedom, understood as the ability to act in a way that is undetermined by prior conditions in the world. But if we agree that we can, in this sense, be free, then we agree that personal explanation is in order. And it seems to be the only alternative to scientific explanation. If we need to account for something that happens, therefore, and if we cannot account for it in scientific terms, personal explanation would seem to be a rational alternative. So something at least like it would seem to be legitimate with regard to the beginning of the universe. That cannot be said to depend on natural necessities since the reality of these depends on there being a world. If, then, we agree that the beginning of the universe was caused, it seems sensible to appeal to personal explanation.

But this move would be contested by various philosophers for reasons not so far mentioned. We may put the most important ones in the form of a set of questions.

(1) Is non-embodied personality possible?
(2) Is all non-worldly personality divine?
(3) Is God a personal explanation?

The first of these questions has been very much pressed, especially in the twentieth century. Some philosophers, notably the French philosopher Descartes (1591–1650), have held that persons are really identical with their minds, not their bodies, and that non-bodily personal existence is not only possible but really a fact of life. Classical philosophers such as Aristotle (384–322 B.C.), however, have placed more emphasis on the importance of the body in an account of what it means to be a person. In the Middle Ages such philosophers were supported by the writings of authors like Aquinas, and their general position – that to be a person in the full sense depends on being bodily – is now very widespread among those who write on the matter, especially those influenced by writers such as Ludwig Wittgenstein (1889–1951), whom many would hail (quite rightly) as one of the most important philosophers of modern times. For this reason, therefore, many would reject the conclusion of the Kalām Argument. That refers to a personal choice, but it is clearly no choice of a bodily agent. Can it therefore really be a personal choice? Many would say that it cannot be.

Others would note that, even if it could be, this would not have to mean that it was the choice of God. That is the point behind the second of the above questions. The idea here is that, though the beginning of the universe might have been caused by a personal choice, the choice in question could have been that of something which does not match traditional views of God.

The point behind question three can, perhaps, be expressed in the slogan 'God is not a person'. When we invoke personal explanation, we normally suppose the activity of a person. But, so many have argued, God ought not to be thought of as a person. According, for example, to the theologian Paul Tillich (1886–1965), God is not a being but 'Being-itself' and the object of our 'ultimate concern'. A related view can be found in the writings of thinkers like St Anselm (1033–1109) and Aquinas. According to them, God defies classification and description. He is not just another individual alongside everything else.

I shall have more to say about such views later. For the moment, however, we can note some possible replies to them, replies which could be made by a defender of the Kalām Argument.

(1) In deciding what is and what is not possible, we must often pay attention to arguments given for supposing that some assertion or other is true. We may feel that a given assertion could not possibly be true. We may feel that there is some kind of contradiction or absurdity buried in it. But we may have to banish such feelings in the face of a solid argument to the effect that the assertion is true. Proof that such and such is the case, we may say, is proof that such and such is possible. So in reply to the claim that persons are bodily and that there cannot therefore be a personal choice behind the beginning of the universe, the defender of the Kalām Argument might say that what he has argued is evidence to the contrary. He might, that is, say that non-bodily personality is possible because its existence is the only thing that could account for the existence of the universe. An objector might reply that persons as we understand them are bodily agents, and that non-bodily personality is therefore impossible. But, given that the universe began to exist, and given that its beginning cannot be accounted for by scientific explanation, there is still some point in supposing that it ought to be accounted for in personal terms. In supposing that this is so, one will implicitly concede certain differences between persons as we normally understand them and whatever it is whose choice accounts for the beginning of the

world. But that will only be because of the nature of the overall argument. If the Kalām Argument has any cogency, then we would expect there to be differences between what the Argument refers to as God and what we normally refer to as persons. By the same token, however, we would also expect there to be similarities.

(2) While it may be true that persons, as we understand them, are bodily, it does not follow that everything rightly called personal is nothing but a body. And some such things seem plainly not to be bodily. Take, for example, thinking. That can be referred to as something personal, but if it were just a bodily process then it would make sense to describe it as having physical location and as taking a certain time to occur. Yet it is odd to suppose that when, for example, I think that John and Mary are well matched, I am doing anything that could in principle be observed, or that I am engaging in a process that can be timed. It may be true that my being a thinking person goes with my being a bodily individual in the material world. But that is another matter.

(3) One may feel that in arguing for God as a personal explanation of the universe one is arguing for something which is not all that those who believe in God suppose him to be. And for this reason one may doubt that the God to which the Kalām Argument concludes ought rightly to be called divine. But one may have reason to suppose that something exists without having reason to suppose that everything believed about it is true. You may be thought to be musical, for example, but I can have reason to believe that you exist without having reason for supposing that you are indeed musical. In principle, therefore, it is not necessarily absurd to hold that the Kalām Argument is a defence of belief in the existence of God even though it may not be a defence of such belief as understood by those who believe more about God than the Kalām Argument might justify one in doing. And, in any case, it is a traditional part of much belief in God that God is indeed responsible for the universe having begun. It is also commonly held that he is personal and that he acts freely. So defenders of the Kalām Argument might well say that their argument at least suggests a presumption in favour of what many understand by belief in God.

God the Creator

And yet, of course, most people understand belief in God to involve a belief in the existence of a Creator, and this brings us to what is certainly a drawback in the Kalām Argument. For, even if we allow that the Argument has merit, it does not show that there exists a Creator.

We shall be returning to the notion of creation at various points in this book, but at the moment it is important to stress one significant fact about it.

This is that, in the full theological sense of the word, 'creating' must be distinguished from 'bringing about the beginning of the existence of'. Traditionally speaking, the doctrine of creation teaches that everything apart from God, everything created, depends entirely for its existence on God *for as long as it exists*. In other words, the theological notion of creation is traditionally bound up with the notion of sustaining or conserving, not just starting. As H. P. Owen puts it: 'God is the Creator of everything at every moment of its existence. If he withdrew his creative presence from an entity for a second it would immediately cease to be. Although we find it natural to distinguish between creation and preservation, they are in reality identical' (Owen 1984, p.9).

Consider the case of Abraham begetting Isaac. Here Isaac depends on Abraham for his birth, but not necessarily for what subsequently happens to him. Abraham could die while Isaac is a baby.

But now consider the milk in a pot on a stove which is heating the pot and the milk in it. The milk is being heated, but if the stove is turned off the heating of the milk ceases.

The point to grasp now is that the relationship implied in the case of God creating something is like that of the stove/milk example. It is not that God first creates and then leaves things alone, as Abraham may copulate and then die before his child. The full theological notion of God creating holds that if X exists, then if 'God is the Creator of X' is true, it is true of X that it *is being created*, i.e. it is true of X that its continued existence is due to God. On this view, creation is not just a matter of God bringing about the *start* of something. It is a matter of created things owing their existence to God *all the time that they exist*. As Aquinas classically puts it, God, as Creator, 'is the cause not only of becoming but of being' (*De Potentia*, III, 7).

Now we can see why the Kalām Argument fails to show that there is indeed a Creator. The point is that the Argument does nothing to indicate that the universe *now* depends for its existence on God. The most it shows is that its beginning was brought about. So, even if we are convinced that personal choice, or something analogous to this, must account for the beginning of the universe, we still need to be offered a reason for belief in a Creator in the full traditional sense.

THE COSMOLOGICAL ARGUMENT – II

GOD AND THE EXISTENCE OF THE UNIVERSE: CONTINGENCY AND FIRST CAUSE

Yet now consider not the fact that many things began to exist, but the fact that they exist at all, the fact that they are there rather than not there (regardless of how long they have been there, or whether they ever had a beginning). Should we not try to account for this? Should we not, indeed, try to account for the fact that the whole universe exists? Maybe the universe had a beginning. Maybe it did not. But it is certainly there. What, then, accounts for this?

These questions bring us to the second main form of the Cosmological Argument, though this itself can be divided into two distinct arguments. I shall refer to them respectively as 'the Argument from Contingency' and 'the First Cause Argument'. The proponents of these two arguments have been legion, and they have stated their case in different ways. But the basic line of reasoning of each argument can be simply given.

A. THE ARGUMENT FROM CONTINGENCY

The nature of the Argument

In order to appreciate what this argument is driving at one needs to note a certain distinction made by some philosophers, a distinction between what is contingently true and what is true of necessity.

Consider the statement 'There are roses in my garden'. As it happens, this is true. There are roses in my garden. But the statement could have been false. I am lucky enough to have roses in my garden, but they do not have to be there in some absolute sense. Someone who denied that there were roses in my garden would not necessarily be guilty of contradiction.

Let us therefore say that 'There are roses in my garden' is contingently true. On this understanding, other examples of contingently true statements would be 'There are towns in Austria', or 'President Lincoln was murdered'. Both these statements are true, but one cannot determine their truth or falsity just by hearing them being made. They could be either true or false, and one may have to do some investigation to determine which, in fact, they are. They are, as we might put it, not self-evidently true, and to deny them is not to say something self-evidently false or meaningless.

But now consider the statement 'All bachelors are unmarried'. This is clearly rather different from 'There are roses in my garden'. And this is because there is no possibility of the statement being false. It is not just a happy (or unhappy) accident that all bachelors are unmarried. They could not be anything else. And if one were to deny that all bachelors are unmarried one would clearly contradict oneself. 'All bachelors are unmarried', unlike 'There are roses in my garden', *is* self-evidently true. Let us put this by saying that statements like 'All bachelors are unmarried' are true of necessity, or are necessarily true.

So we can distinguish between statements that are contingently true (e.g.

'There are roses in my garden') and statements which are true of necessity (e.g. 'All bachelors are unmarried'). And in the light of this distinction we can now go straight to the heart of the Argument from Contingency. For that holds that 'The universe exists' or 'There is a universe' is only contingently true and that 'There is a God' or 'God exists' is therefore true of necessity.

Consider the fact that there is a universe. This, says the Argument from Contingency, is a contingent matter. That is to say, 'There is a universe', though true, might have been false. In other words, according to the Argument from Contingency there does not have to be a universe. There is one, but its being there, its existence as opposed to its non-existence, is not necessary in the way that being unmarried is necessary in the case of bachelors. According to the Argument from Contingency, 'The universe exists' is not self-evidently true, or true of necessity.

But in that case, so the Argument continues, there must be a reason for the universe being there. If 'There is a universe' does not have to be true, then something must make it true just as, if you like, someone must plant the roses in my garden. In other words, there must be a cause of the universe being there. And, says the Argument, this something cannot merely exist contingently like the universe itself. If that were the case, then it too would have to be caused to exist. It too would need a reason outside itself for its existence.

The Argument therefore concludes that there must be something which exists of necessity and which is somehow responsible for there being any universe at all. And this something, says the Argument, is God. According to the Argument from Contingency, therefore, God must exist as cause of the universe if 'There is a universe' is indeed only contingently true. Furthermore, he must exist as something with which there is no possibility of non-existence. To say that he exists is to make a statement which is true of necessity. On this account, 'God exists' is self-evident just as 'All bachelors are unmarried' is self-evident.

How successful is the Argument?

If the Argument from Contingency is correct, then, it would seem that we can show not only that God exists, but that he must exist, i.e. that his non-existence is strictly impossible. And, for many people, this is one of the chief virtues of the Argument. God, they will say, cannot be something which just *happens* to exist. His existence must be something ultimate or non-accidental, which is just what the Argument from Contingency says that it is. The Argument also insists that where there is the possibility of something not existing, but where the thing actually exists, then one will finally account for its existence only when one arrives at something with which there is no possibility of non-existence. And this, too, is for many people an attractive assumption. They will say it allows us to give full rein to our desire that everything should be accounted for completely, and they would defend the Argument by noting that it satisfies this desire with respect to one of the most obvious facts of experience. There is no escaping the existence of the universe, and, so it has been urged, the Argument from Contingency accounts for this in a way that seems to tidy things up nicely since it ends with a truth which just cannot be other than it is.

But even if we are swayed by these considerations, it must also be admitted that, as it stands, the Argument from Contingency contains what looks like a fatal weakness. And the difficulty lies in just what many have found to be the Argument's most attractive feature: its concept of God as a being who exists of necessity so that we cannot deny his existence without contradiction.

If the Argument from Contingency is sound, then there is something the defintion of which entails that it exists. The point of the argument is to show that since in the case of contingent things *what* they are does not entail *that* they are, there must be something which is not in such an embarrassing position. There must, in fact, be something of which it makes no sense to say 'This thing does not exist/might not have existed'. If the Argument from Contingency is sound, then, as some philosophers would put it, 'God exists' is logically necessary. But if 'God exists' is logically necessary (i.e. if it is true of necessity like 'All bachelors are unmarried'), then existence must enter into the definition of God. The whole point about logically true statements is that once you understand the meaning of the terms contained in them, you can see that the statements cannot be false. If 'God exists' is true of logical necessity, therefore, 'exists' must belong to the meaning of 'God' as 'unmarried' belongs to the meaning of 'bachelor'. But can this really be true?

This question brings us, in fact, to issues which will concern us at greater length in Chapter 4. So I do not propose to deal with it in detail here. Nevertheless, and anticipating what I shall try to argue for later, I think it has to be said that the answer to the question is 'No'. For to define something is not to say that it exists. It is to say what it would be like if it did exist. To define something is to say *what* it is, not *that* it is. If this were not the case, there would be some property difference between two things definable in the same way one of which exists and the other of which does not. Yet this does not seem to be so. I can seriously say 'I have two cats which are different because one has a tail and the other has none'. But I cannot seriously say 'I have two cats which are different because one of them exists and the other does not'. Existence is not some kind of property that things may have or lack. In that case, however, it cannot enter into their definition. And that means that it cannot be part of the meaning of any word that what is signified by the word exists.

This, however, is just what the Argument from Contingency is finally denying. According to the Argument, God must exist just as bachelors must be unmarried. But, while it is true that being unmarried enters into the definition of 'bachelor', existing does not enter into the definition of anything. In that case, however, it does not enter into the definition of 'God', from which it would seem to follow that 'God exists' cannot, as the Argument from Contingency claims, really be true of necessity. If there is reason to believe in the existence of God because of the existence of the universe, it cannot be that 'God exists' must be true since 'The universe exists' is true only contingently.

B. THE FIRST CAUSE ARGUMENT

The nature of the Argument

Many well-known authors have offered versions of the First Cause Argument, but perhaps the classic statement of it comes in the work of Aquinas, in texts such as the second of his so-called Five Ways of proving the existence of God (*Summa Theologiae* Ia, 2, 3). Thus, for example, according to Aquinas:

In the observable world causes are found to be ordered in series; we never observe, nor ever could, something causing itself, for this would mean it preceded itself, and this is not possible. Such a series of causes must however stop somewhere; for in it an earlier member causes an intermediate and the intermediate a last (whether the intermediate be one or many). Now if you eliminate a cause you also eliminate its effects, so that you cannot have a last cause, nor an intermediate one, unless you have a first. Given therefore no stop in the series of causes, and hence no first cause, there would be no intermediate causes either, and no last effect, and this would be an open mistake. One is therefore forced to suppose some first cause, to which everyone gives the name 'God'.

One thing about the First Cause Argument needs to be stressed immediately. This is that, though the Argument can be confused (and has been confused) with the Argument from Contingency, it is really a different argument – not just in Aquinas, but also in other writers. For it does not maintain that only what exists of logical necessity can account for what exists contingently. Its main point is that things are caused to exist by other things within the universe and that, since there is a universe, there must be something on which the universe as a matter of fact depends for its existence. Here God is said to exist in something like the way we would speak of people having to exist as sources of certain things we encounter and which we recognize as standing in need of causal explanation. If we heard a song being sung, we would naturally try to account for the noise in terms of a singer. According to the First Cause Argument, we can make a somewhat similar inference with respect to the whole universe. This, says the Argument, has many things in it which owe their existence to other things. But, so the Argument concludes, there must be something which accounts for the existence of everything in the universe. Notice that for the purposes of this argument it is irrelevant whether or not the universe had a beginning (as we have already seen, Aquinas, for example, did not think there is any philosophical proof that the universe began to exist). The Argument is concerned with the fact that there is any universe at all, not with what might or might not be true of something by virtue of which the universe got going. The point of the Argument is to suggest that it is now true that the universe depends for its existence on God. Something which accounts for the beginning of something might cease to exist while what it has produced carries on. According to the First Cause Argument, however, if it were false now that God exists, then there would not now be any universe. On this account God is introduced as Creator, i.e. as holding the universe in being for as long as the universe lasts. We can therefore state the First Cause Argument as follows:

(1) Things within the universe depend for their existence on other things.
(2) The universe as a whole depends for its existence on something other than itself.
(3) The universe as a whole depends for its existence on something other than itself all the time that it exists.
(4) The universe as a whole depends for its existence on God.

How successful is the Argument?

The First Cause Argument, as well as having had many different defenders, has also been subject to much discussion and, consequently, to much criticism. But the most common objections to it reduce to two major arguments.

According to the first, the First Cause Argument erroneously supposes that in accounting for the existence of things within the universe we cannot suppose an endless series of things the activity of which accounts for what we now find to exist.

According to the second, the First Cause Argument erroneously supposes that the existence of the universe must be caused. On the contrary, says the objection, the existence of the universe is just a brute fact and there is no need to ask what, apart from itself, accounts for its existence.

The first objection here denies that there need be any first cause. So we can call the objection the 'Endless Series of Causes' objection.

The second objection denies that the existence of the universe raises any causal questions of the kind implied by the First Cause Argument. So we can call this objection the 'No Causal Questions' objection.

An endless series of causes?

According to the First Cause Argument we can ask what accounts for the existence of things within the universe and what accounts for the existence of the universe itself. But the Endless Series of Causes objection rejects this assumption. It holds that there can be an infinite or never-ending series of things within the universe accounting for what exists in the universe, and that there is therefore no reason to speak of any cause distinct from the universe.

In one sense that is surely correct. Suppose we try to account for the existence of something – dogs, say. We may then be led on to discover that there is something else on which they all depend somehow. And so we may go on indefinitely. In other words, it seems hard to see how we can rule out the possibility that however far we go in seeking to account for things within the universe, we may still go yet further. When we try to account for things scientifically, there may be no end to our inquiries. Suppose thing A depends for its existence on thing B, and B on C, and C on something else. Suppose someone now says: 'But if A does not ultimately depend on something which does not owe its existence to anything, then A would not exist at all'. We can reply as follows: 'What if the causes that account for A being there are infinite? Then your conclusion does not follow. For then there is always something accounting for what in the end accounts for the existence of A'.

This has been denied on the ground that it expresses the same kind of reasoning as that shown by someone who thinks that you can take away a table without removing the books which lie on it. According to this objection, one who believes in the possibility of endless series of causes is saying that you can remove a first cause and still have the things which depend on it. As one writer puts it, the supporter of the possibility of an infinite series of causes is 'asking us to believe that although each link in a suspended chain is prevented from falling simply because it is attached to the one above it, yet if only the chain be long enough, it will, taken as a whole, need no support, but will hang loose in the air suspended from nothing' (Joyce 1923, p. 82).

But this objection is misguided. Someone who believes that any given thing can have an endless series of causes behind it need not be trying to take away a first cause in the way imagined. Such a person might well agree that if you remove a first cause, then you remove what depends on it as well. But he may add that this is neither here nor there since what he is challenging is the assumption that there is any first cause. He may then say that anything in the universe you care to mention may depend for its existence on something else, and so on without end.

Yet this, in fact is no real answer to the First Cause Argument. Let us suppose that we can indeed account for the existence of anything in the universe and that we can do so in terms of something else within the universe. And let us suppose that we can account for that in terms of another thing. Let us also suppose that there need be no end to the number of things in the universe to which we can appeal once we have started the game of accounting for the existence of things. There still remains the question of how it is that we can embark on this game at all. In other words, we can still ask 'What accounts for there being any universe at all?'

A common reply to this point is that if we can indeed account for the existence of anything in the universe in terms of something else within the universe, then no further question arises about the universe itself. Suppose that ten people are at a party and that someone asks how they come to be there. Each of the ten people tells his or her story. But suppose someone says when the tales are over 'Yes, but what about the group as a whole? Why is *it* at the party?' (cf. Edwards 1959). We would, presumably, be puzzled. We have accounted for the members of the group at an individual level, so why should we suppose that there is any more to be said?

But this is not an objection to the point it is trying to challenge. It may indeed be silly to ask why a group is at a party once each member of the group has accounted for his or her presence. But asking about the presence of people at parties is not to ask what the First Cause Argument is asking when it comes to the universe. For the Argument is asking not for a history of the bits of the universe, but for an account of the fact that the universe as a totality exists at all. Furthermore, it is false that if we can account for something in terms of something else, no further questions arise about all that we consequently speak about. Imagine a tyrant who orders that nobody can eat food unless it has been obtained by begging. In that case, everyone who has food will have it by virtue of someone else. But this does not mean that no question arises as to how everyone comes to have food. By the same token, even though it may be true that any given thing in the universe can be accounted for in terms of something else, it does not follow that no question arises as to why there is any universe at all. As the German philosopher Leibniz (1646–1716) puts it:

Let us suppose the book of the elements of geometry to have been eternal, one copy always having been written down from an earlier one; it is evident that, even though a reason can be given for the present book out of a past one, nevertheless out of any number of books taken in order going backwards we shall never come upon a full reason; since we might always wonder why there should have been such books from all time – why there were books at all, and why they were written in this manner. What is true of books is also true of different states of the world . . . And so, however far you go back to earlier states, you will never find in those states a full reason why there should be any world rather than none, and why it should be as it is (*On the Ultimate Origination of Things*).

One need not be diverted here by the fact that Leibniz concentrates on a causal series infinite in past time. Nor, for the moment, need we concern ourselves with the question of why things should be as they are. The important point to note at present is that Leibniz is asking us to distinguish between two different questions. The first is 'What within the universe accounts for such and such?' The second is 'What accounts for there being any universe at all?' And, as Leibniz implies, we do not answer the second question simply by answering the first.

Nor, of course, do we answer it by referring to something which is itself part of the universe. If we are prepared to ask what accounts for there being any universe at all, then we will only be able to give an answer by breaking out of the universe altogether and by supposing that there is something which does not itself depend on anything for its existence in the way that things do within the universe.

In other words, given that the universe as a whole depends for its existence on something, it can only depend on something which does not depend in the same way on anything else for its existence. In this sense, therefore, the First Cause Argument is right. The existence of something within the universe might always be accounted for in terms of something else within the universe. In this sense there may be no first cause lying behind the existence of anything we care to mention. But if the existence of the universe as a whole is to be accounted for, it cannot be accounted for by anything within the universe. The answer must lie in something outside it, something distinct from it, something, furthermore, of which we cannot sensibly ask 'On what does its existence depend?' as we can ask this question of the universe considered as a totality.

No causal questions?

Asking questions

At this point, however, we come to the No Causal Questions objection. For why suppose that we ought to ask what accounts for the existence of the universe? Plenty of people, in fact, would not suppose any such thing. Perhaps they never give the question any thought. But why should they? And what can be said if someone should observe that he has given the question some thought, but that he sees no reason to suppose that it needs to be asked? This is certainly the view of many. They will ask why we cannot just suppose that the existence of the universe is something ultimate, something which has no causal explanation. They will say, as Bertrand Russell (1872–1970) once bluntly put it: 'The universe is just there, and that's all' (cf. Hick 1964, pp. 167ff.).

On the other hand, if anything counts as a reasonable assumption, then it is reasonable to assume that we should ask what accounts for things, what brings them about. And it is reasonable to suppose that the question has an answer.

Think for a moment about Hamlet. In Act 1, scene IV, he is on the platform when his father's ghost appears. What does he say?

He could have said something like 'Oh look. Another boring old ghost. Let's go and have a cup of tea' – or something like that, perhaps in blank verse.

But, of course, he does not say that. He wonders how the thing comes to be there. He says: 'What may this mean? . . . Say, why is this?' He does not suppose that there is no explanation for the ghost being there. And neither would we.

To bring the example down to earth a bit, suppose you live in an English country village and that you come across an elephant on the village green. If you have been drinking, you will probably ignore it. But you are much more likely to ask why it is there. What you will not do, at any rate, is suppose that there is no explanation for the elephant being there.

Now what does that prove? Not very much by itself, perhaps. But it does draw attention to the fact that confronted by things in the world we naturally ask how they come to be there. This is something that we just do. Of course, we take plenty of things for granted. But we still suppose that things can be accounted for in some way. We are inquisitive animals who recognize the need to ask why things are there – meaning, what accounts for them being there, what brings them about. We are most likely to ask why they are there when their presence is *unexpected*, and that is why we would quickly start asking questions about elephants on village greens. But we concede the relevance of asking what accounts for things even when we are dealing with what is wholly *familiar*. Elephants on village greens are rare. But grass is not. Yet no one would think it silly to ask how the grass on some village green comes to be there. We do not suppose that the grass of village greens is some kind of brute fact. We do not suppose that it is just there and that nothing accounts for it being there. And that, indeed, is why we come to have science.

So we naturally ask what accounts for things being there. We do not just note that they are there; we ask why they are there. And this, of course, can lead to different answers.

There are, for example, answers which refer to particular things which acted in certain ways in the past. If someone asks how I come to be here, I can tell him about my parents. I can refer him to my mother and father. And that will be one kind of answer.

But there are also answers which refer us to facts about the natures of things. In asking how I come to be here you may be interested not in me *qua* Brian Davies, but in me *qua* human being. Then you will be asking how there comes to be the sort of thing that I am. And that can be accounted for in terms of the way people function. You can have something like me because my parents were things of the sort which tend to produce things of the sort to which I belong – human beings rather than penguins, say. And that will be another kind of answer.

And so one might go on for quite a long time. I am here because of my parents. I am here because my parents were human beings. But how do human beings come to be there? Questions like this are also asked, so we have scientists trying to account for a whole range of things in terms of explanations which may become more and more complicated. Asking why I am here may lead one beyond my parents and the human race, and on into facts about the solar system or whatever.

Why is there a universe?

But in asking how things come to be there, do we have to stop short at answers that are recognizably scientific? What about the fact that there is any universe at all?

This is not a scientific question. It is not just asking why something in particular is there. Nor is it asking why anything in particular first came to be there. The question takes in anything that could be called a scientific explanation. It asks why there is a world of things over and against there being no world at all.

But should we not ask this question? As I have said, many would say that we should not. The trouble, however, is that it seems arbitrary not to. For we do ask why things are there. We do ask what brought them about. We do this again and again, and it would be hard to imagine what things would be like if we did not. Presumably, we would still be groping around in caves. And for this reason it seems reasonable to press our questions until they become silly. And that, I think, means that we ought indeed to ask why there is any universe at all. This question is not silly, so it seems sensible to ask it. And if it is sensible to ask the question, it is sensible to suppose that the question has an answer.

An objector, of course, might reply that there is no way of proving that we have to ask what accounts for there being a universe. And this, I suppose, is right in a sense. If someone insists with Russell that the universe is just there, it is hard to know what we can appeal to that he would be bound to accept in some absolute sense. Someone who refuses to ask questions can remain solidly uninquisitive. Most people would not see anything odd in asking, for example, 'Why are there people in Europe?' But someone can always insist that the European population is just there, and that nothing more remains to be said. In the same way, someone can always dig in his heels and insist that the universe is just there. And he might be in a stronger position than the one who finds no puzzle in the existence of people in Europe. From what we know of non-European populations we can suggest that the European one is no brute fact, while we have no knowledge of other universes in the light of which we can ask questions about this one.

Yet this does not mean that we should not ask such questions. And, in particular, it does not mean that we should not ask what accounts for the universe being there. It is, of course, true that asking, for example, why human beings are there seems a proper thing to do since we have made ourselves familiar with some answers in this area. We talk, for example, of evolution. We have not, on the other hand, made ourselves familiar with an answer to the question of why there is any universe. But asking why human beings are somewhere would have been perfectly reasonable at any time, long before we knew about genetics and so on. And my suggestion now is that it is reasonable to ask why there is a universe. After all, the universe is perfectly real. Why should we not therefore suppose that something accounts for its reality? An objector might reply that we have no reason to think that something accounts for every real thing. But we are not now talking about 'every real thing'. We are talking about the universe. And, as Peter Geach puts it, this, if nothing else, 'shares with its parts attributes that give rise to causal questions: it is a complex whole of parts in process of change' (Anscombe and Geach 1961, p. 115). So why should we not ask what brings its existence about? Why should we not ask what accounts for it continuing to exist? Could it be that if we ask these questions we will find ourselves going beyond the existence of the universe? Could it be that these questions suggest that there is something other than the universe? But that is just another way of saying that there is no need to account for there being any universe. And, in any case, if we are right to ask what accounts for the universe being there, we would expect to find ourselves going beyond it; we would expect there to be something other than the universe. Could it be that the universe is too big to be accounted for? But why should size be of relevance here? How big does something have to be before it becomes legitimate for us to treat its existence as something ultimate?

The fact of the matter is that the existence of the universe is puzzling. If we can ask why things within it are there, we can ask why the universe itself is there. In this sense, therefore, the First Cause Argument is perfectly right. The Argument insists that the universe's existence raises causal questions. It insists that we are entitled to ask what accounts for the universe as a whole being there. And that seems to me to be true. It would, I think, be odd to suppose otherwise. People like Russell would, of course, deny this. They would insist again that the universe is just there. But then people sometimes insist on the oddest things.

Objections

It has, however, been urged that there are further positive reasons for not supposing that we should ask what accounts for the existence of the universe. Some, for example, have said that it makes no sense to suppose that there might not have been a universe and that there is therefore no reason to ask what accounts for the fact that there is one. Others have said that there is just no reason to believe that, though we naturally ask what accounts for things, there is actually something accounting for everything that we can think of as part of the universe.

But is it really absurd to suppose that there might have been no universe? There not being any universe is certainly not something that can be pictured. In other words, the alternative to there being a universe is not a possibility like the possibility of something within the universe being replaced by something else – as, say, one person might replace another in the same chair. Nor can it be a possibility like the possibility of something in the universe being different from what it is – as, say, I might grow grey hair rather than brown hair. But there is no reason to suppose that the universe has to exist. If it did not exist there would be nobody around to comment on the fact. But that is not to say that the existence of the universe is absolutely inevitable. And, unless we have positive reason for supposing that it is inevitable, then why should we not ask what accounts for it?

One reply might be the second of the objections just noted, which we can, perhaps, express by saying that things do not have to be as we expect them to be. Someone might say: We may be unable not to wonder what accounts for there being a universe, but maybe nothing does account for this. The objector might then go on to ask: What if our intellectual curiosity compels us to ask why there is any universe at all? Why not write this off as a fact about our psychology? Why suppose that there is anything on which the universe depends for its existence?

Yet there is surely something peculiar in this position, as one might see by considering the claim that nothing at all might account for something like the Grand Canyon. At one level we might agree that the Grand Canyon could have no cause, for we might be unable to think of anything bringing the Canyon about. But if the word 'reasonable' means anything, it is just not reasonable to suppose that massive geological formations have no cause. Nor is it reasonable to suppose that geologists who seek causes for geological formations are merely displaying a psychological trend which gives us no ground for thinking that their questions really have answers. By the same token, if someone says that it is reasonable to suppose that the universe exists uncaused, it is hard to know what he can mean by 'reasonable'. It is unreasonable to suppose that the Grand Canyon should be something uncaused. Why should it be any less unreasonable to suppose that the universe exists uncaused? One might reply by saying that in the case of the Grand Canyon we are inquiring after causes which are themselves part of the universe. Our questions here are scientific. But this is not to show that all our causal questions must be scientific, and, in the case of the universe considered as a totality, we can still ask what it is that accounts for it.

The First Cause Argument and God

So we are entitled to say that something or other accounts for there being a universe. Even if we concede that the universe had no beginning, there remains the question of why there should be any universe at all. Can we, however, build on this conclusion? More specifically, can we now suggest that thinking along the lines of the First Cause Argument gives us reason to believe in the existence of God? Here, I think, we need to note three basic points.

To begin with, in terms of traditional theology to say that God exists is to say that there is a Creator. If the First Cause Argument gives us reason to believe in the existence of a Creator, therefore, it can be regarded as a reasonable argument for the existence of God. An objector might reply that, for traditional theology, 'God' means more than 'a Creator'; but this response need not now detain us. For, as I noted earlier, one can reasonably suppose that something exists without having reason to suppose that everything believed about it is true.

Secondly, the First Cause Argument does give us reason to believe in the existence of a Creator. As we have seen, to say that something is created (in the full theological sense) is to say that its continued existence is brought about. But we can now suggest that the continued existence of the universe is brought about, for we can suppose that something accounts for there being any universe at all.

Thirdly, even waiving the point just made, we are effectively supposing that there is a Creator in supposing that something or other accounts for there being a universe. This follows from another point which theologians have traditionally made concerning the notion of creation. It follows, in fact, from their assertion that creation is *ex nihilo*, out of nothing.

Suppose I want to make a rum punch. In that case I will take various ingredients which I shall mix together. What I cannot, alas, do is 'wish' the punch into existence. Unfortunate, but true. I must bring the punch about by working on things which are already there. Before ever the punch reaches the mouth, its ingredients have a biography.

But suppose I could produce a punch simply by wishing one into existence. In that case there would be no putting together of ingredients, and this could be expressed by saying that the punch would come to be from nothing or out of nothing. And it is this coming to be that theologians are talking about when they speak about creation *ex nihilo*. The idea is that God causes things to be, or that he makes them to be, but not by working on ingredients and not by setting afoot a process in the world out of which things come to be. For God to create is for him to bring it about that there are things, but not things produced by tinkering around with any pre-existent materials. As St Augustine (354–430) puts it: 'But by what means did you make heaven and earth? What tool did you use for this vast work? You did not work as a human craftsman does, making one thing out of something else as his mind directs . . . It was you who made the craftsman's body and the mind which controls his limbs. It was you who made the material from which he makes his goods' (*Confessions* XI, 5).

But now consider what we are saying if we say that we ought to ask what brings it about that there is any universe at all. Could we be asking what made the universe in the sense that I can make a rum punch? No. Why not? Because the question is concerned with everything that could be regarded as ingredients and with everything that could be regarded as the bringing about from ingredients that something exists at the end of a process in the universe. To ask what accounts for there being a universe is to ask why there are *any* ingredients and why there are *any* processes by means of which ingredients get turned into end products. And this means that in asking the question seriously we are already, so to speak, talking the language of theology. For to ask the question seriously is already to concede the possibility of creation *ex nihilo*. And, by the same token, to suppose that the question has an answer is to suppose that creation *ex nihilo* is a fact. If something accounts for there being any universe at all, then the universe must be created *ex nihilo*.

Conclusion

So if the First Cause Argument is acceptable at all, it is acceptable as an argument for the conclusion that the universe is created. And that, I think, means that the answer to the question raised above is 'Yes'. If we think along the lines of the First Cause Argument, we do have reason to believe in the existence of God. To believe in God is to believe in the existence of a Creator. To follow the reasoning of the First Cause Argument is to concede that the universe is created. So to follow the reasoning of the First Cause Argument is to concede the existence of God. I have suggested that we may indeed follow the reasoning of the First Cause Argument. So now I suggest that we have reason to believe in the existence of God.

Yet not all arguments offered in defence of belief in God have been based on the existence of the universe. Some famous and popular ones have proceeded with reference to general characteristics exhibited by things which go to make up the universe, or with reference to things which have come to pass in the history of the universe. These will be our concern in the next chapter.

QUESTIONS FOR DISCUSSION

1 Should people who believe in the existence of God be able to provide some intellectual support for their position? If so, why? If not, why not?
2 What do you understand by the word 'atheism'? How prevalent is atheism today? Is there any single cause of it? Does it have any religious significance?
3 Can you think of any decisive reasons for or against supposing that the universe began to exist?
4 Is inquiry into the beginning of the universe relevant to the question of God's existence?
5 'Whatever has a beginning of existence must have a cause.' Discuss.
6 Is 'God exists' contingently true, or true of necessity? What implications does each possibility have for belief in God?
7 Under what conditions does it make sense to ask for the cause or causes of something?
8 'The universe is just there.' Discuss.
9 Might there have been no universe at all?
10 How much must an argument establish before it can be taken to have established the existence of God?

FURTHER READING

The question of God's existence, and many of the questions touched on in this book, are commonly discussed in general introductory textbooks on the philosophy of religion, including my own *An Introduction to the Philosophy of Religion* (Oxford, 1982). Particularly worth recommending are the following:

J. C. A. Gaskin, *The Quest for Eternity* (Harmondsworth, Middx, 1984). This is chiefly concerned with the existence of God and is lively and very readable, as well as philosophically sophisticated. Agnostic in conclusion.

John Hick, *Philosophy of Religion* (3rd ed., Englewood Cliffs, N.J., 1983). A much used and evidently popular book. It covers basic issues in a very lucid way.

Anthony O'Hear, *Experience, Explanation and Faith* (London, 1984). This is agnostic in conclusion, but philosophically challenging and much more informed about theology than most books of its kind.

William L. Rowe, *Philosophy of Religion* (Encino, Cal./Belmont, Cal., 1978). This is short, lively, informative, and well-reasoned. It includes discussion topics.

Books on reasons for belief in God are legion. For an historical survey of views, see Hans Küng, *Does God Exist?* (London, 1980). Shorter and more elementary is Christopher B. Kaiser, *The Doctrine of God* (London, 1982). See also M. J. Charlesworth, *Philosophy of Religion: The Historic Approaches* (London, 1972) and Patrick Masterson, *Atheism and Alienation* (Harmondsworth, Middx, 1973). For an impressive and full-length recent attempt to defend the rationality of belief in God, see Richard Swinburne, *The Existence of God* (Oxford, 1979). For a comprehensive discussion of belief in God written from the position of an unbeliever, see J. L. Mackie, *The Miracle of Theism* (Oxford, 1982). A useful selection of texts on the topic of God's existence is John Hick (ed.), *The Existence of God* (London/New York, 1964). For a selection of texts attacking belief in God, see Peter Angeles (ed.), *Critiques of God* (Buffalo, N.Y., 1976). Both Hick and Angeles have good bibliographies.

The reader should realize that, though we tend to speak of belief in God as if everyone who believes in God believes the same thing, there are actually many concepts of God. For a clear and informative summary of forms taken by belief in God, see H. P. Owen, *Concepts of Deity* (London, 1971).

For a very good, though largely uncritical, survey of versions of the Cosmological Argument, see William Lane Craig, *The Cosmological Argument from Plato to Leibniz* (London, 1980). The following works are also of particular interest for discussions of the Argument in one form or another:

Germain Grisez, *Beyond the New Theism* (Notre Dame/London, 1975), chs 4–5.

Hugo Meynell, *The Intelligible Universe* (London, 1982).

Bruce R. Reichenbach, *The Cosmological Argument: A Reassessment* (Springfield, Illinois, 1972).

William Rowe, *The Cosmological Argument* (Princeton/London, 1975).

Richard Taylor, *Metaphysics* (3rd ed., Englewood Cliffs, N.J., 1983), ch. 10.

For a useful reader on the Argument, see Donald R. Burrill (ed.), *The Cosmological Arguments: A Spectrum of Opinion* (New York, 1967).

One of the most discussed versions of the Cosmological Argument comes in the text of Aquinas's five ways. For an influential, though philosophically complicated, discussion of these, see Anthony Kenny, *The Five Ways* (London, 1969). There is a very clear and helpful treatment of Aquinas on the existence of God in G. E. M. Anscombe and P. T. Geach, *Three Philosophers* (Oxford, 1961).

For a lengthy exposition and defence of the Kalām Cosmological Argument, see William Lane Craig, *The Kalām Cosmological Argument* (London, 1979). On the question of the beginning of the universe, there is a very lively and well informed discussion of classical arguments in Richard Sorabji, *Time, Creation and the Continuum* (London, 1983). For Aquinas on the beginning of the universe, see *De Aeternitate Mundi Contra Murmurantes* and *Summa Theologiae* Ia, 46. For a further defence of the Kalām Argument in response to recent criticism, see William Lane Craig, 'Professor Mackie on the Kalām Cosmological Argument', *Religious Studies* 20 (1984).

I have suggested that asking what accounts for the universe goes with the frame of mind on the basis of which it is possible to do serious science. For a most informed and interesting development of this thesis, written with an eye on belief in God, one can strongly recommend the work of Stanley L. Jaki. In particular, see the following:

The Road of Science and the Ways to God (Edinburgh, 1978).

Cosmos and Creator (Edinburgh, 1980).

The first of these volumes comprises the Gifford lectures of 1974–76 and is more technical and detailed than the second volume, which is an attempt by Jaki to state his position in terms more accessible to the general reader.

2
The Way the World Goes

Those who believe in God have given many arguments for his existence based on the way things happen in the universe, or on particular things that have happened, as opposed to the fact that there is any universe at all. Some, for example, have said that the emergence of beauty is evidence for God. This was the view of F. R. Tennant (1866–1957), who has proved a very influential figure in philosophical theology. Others, such as the English philosopher John Locke (1632–1704), have held that the same is true of the emergence of consciousness. But two arguments of the general type now in question have been especially popular. These are the Argument from Design and the Argument from Miracles. So in this chapter it is to these that I shall turn.

THE ARGUMENT FROM DESIGN

Like the Cosmological Argument, the Argument from Design (sometimes called the 'Argument to Design' for reasons which will soon become obvious) comes in different forms. A useful way of dividing them up is to distinguish between arguments based on the notion of purpose, and arguments based on the notion of regularity.

The first kind of argument typically notes that something, or that various things, show every sign of being designed to achieve some goal. And, in the light of this, the conclusion drawn is that one can infer the existence of God in much the same way as one would infer the existence of intelligence at work when confronted by the existence of something like a radio or a typewriter.

The second kind of argument is rather different. The emphasis here falls not so much on purpose as on predictability or temporal order. Suppose you come across something which seems to have no particular function or purpose, but which does go through a whole lot of movements in such a way that you can quickly work out what it is going to do next. Suppose, in short, that you encounter something which exhibits a high degree of regularity in its behaviour or even, perhaps, in its construction (assuming it to be relatively immobile). Then, according to the second kind of Argument from Design, you have something which suggests intelligent agency. The Argument then goes on to suggest that in nature one encounters such regularity-displaying things, and that one may therefore infer the existence of intelligent agency, but not of such a kind as to be part of nature itself.

Examples

(1) Design qua *purpose*

The classical statement of the first kind of argument (though there are some other famous statements of it) is probably best agreed to be the argument found in the first three chapters of William Paley's work of 1802 called *Natural Theology; or, Evidences of the Existence and Attributes of the Deity, Collected from the Appearances of Nature.* Paley (1743–1805) notes that if one encountered a watch on a heath one would not assume that the thing came to be there by chance, as one might assume in the case of a stone. In fact, says Paley, one would infer that the watch came about by virtue of a watchmaker. And yet, Paley adds, the universe is very like a watch. In nature, says Paley, we find numerous things which seem to be made up of parts which work together to achieve a final goal or end. And so, Paley suggests, just as we would invoke a watchmaker to account for the watch, we can invoke God to account for what we discover in nature. 'Every indication of contrivance', says Paley, 'every manifestation of design, which existed in the watch, exists in the works of nature; with the difference, on the side of nature, of being greater and more, and that in a degree which exceeds all computation' (*Natural Theology*, p. 12). He continues:

I mean that the contrivances of nature surpass the contrivances of art, in the complexity, subtilty, and curiosity of the mechanism; and still more, if possible, do they go beyond them in number and variety: yet, in a multitude of cases, are not less evidently mechanical, not less evidently contrivances, not less evidently accommodated to their end, or suited to their office than are the most perfect productions of human ingenuity (*Natural Theology*, p. 12).

(2) Design qua *regularity*

There are traces of the regularity argument in classical authors like Cicero, as well as in subsequent writers. But in our own time the argument has been most notably championed by Richard Swinburne, to whom we can now refer for a statement of the second kind of Argument from Design.

Swinburne offers what he calls a 'teleological argument from the temporal order of the world'. That there *is* temporal order is, says Swinburne, very evident.

Regularities of succession are all-pervasive. For simple laws govern almost all succession of events. In books of physics, chemistry, and biology we can learn how almost everything in the world behaves. The laws of their behaviour can be set out by relatively simple formulae which men can understand and by means of which they can successfully predict the future. The orderliness of nature to which I draw attention here is its conformity to formula, to simple, formulable, scientific laws. The orderliness of the universe in this respect is a very striking fact about it. The universe might so naturally have been chaotic, but it is not – it is very orderly (Swinburne 1979, p. 136).

And from all this Swinburne concludes that some explanation is called for. He asks why the universe is characterized by the order to be found in it, and his answer is that if the universe's temporal order requires explanation, it can be reasonably explained by something analogous to human intelligence imposing order. This is because, in Swinburne's view, there are only two kinds of explanation for phenomena: scientific explanation (in terms of scientific laws) and personal explanation (in terms of the free, conscious choices of a person). According to Swinburne, scientific explanation of the universe's temporal order is out of the question, for 'in scientific explanation we explain particular phenomena as brought about by prior phenomena in accord with scientific laws; or we explain the operation of scientific laws (and perhaps also particular phenomena) . . . (yet) from the very nature of science it cannot explain the highest-level laws of all; for they are that by which it explains all other phenomena' (Swinburne 1979, pp. 138f.). And so, Swinburne concludes, if we are to account for the fact that there are such laws, we will have to appeal to personal explanation. Someone has brought it about that the universe exhibits a high degree of temporal order.

PALEY'S ARGUMENT

Goals and purposes

Paley's argument rests on the assumption that there is purpose in nature since the universe contains behaviour or operations which occur in order that certain ends or goals should be realized. In objection to this supposition it has been said that all such behaviour or operations can be differently described without reference to ends or goals in that they can be said to come about not *in order that* something may be achieved, but only *as a result of* what has already occurred. And this has been thought of as a damaging objection to Paley since, so it has been said, there is therefore no need to think of things in the universe operating in the light of any kind of purpose, and therefore no reason to suppose that any kind of intelligence needs to be invoked to account for their operation.

On the other hand, however, there is an obvious truth in what Paley seems to be saying. When we ask why something happens we can be asking not just what it results from, but also what goal is being aimed at or what end is being served. If John walks along a tightrope, we may say that he does so because he has been hypnotized or because he has been drinking; but we might be justified in saying that he does so because he wants to show off or because he wants to earn his living. And the same sort of account can be given of the behaviour of things other than human beings considered as acting intentionally. It would be strange to suppose that non-human things necessarily act with anything like a conscious purpose; but it is, for example, natural to say that eyes function in order that people and animals might see, or that the heart functions as it does in order that the blood might circulate. One might, of course, only say that people see as a result of the ways their eyes function, or that the blood circulates only as a result of the way the heart beats. But that does not seem to capture the whole of it, and it sounds rather like saying that John is showing off or earning his living only because he is walking along the tightrope.

Let us put this by saying that when something occurs in order that an end or goal may be achieved, then the occurrence can be accounted for *teleologically* (Gk. *telos* = 'end' or 'goal'). Let us also say that something is a *teleological system* when it operates so as to achieve a goal. In that case, it seems natural to suppose that there are occurrences in nature which can be accounted for teleologically, or that there are teleological systems in nature. And this is what Paley seems to be saying. He supposes that the universe provides examples of happenings geared to an end or goal, and he supposes that certain things in nature act so as to produce ends or goals. And, in that case, we can agree with him.

Nature and explanation

But Paley is saying more than this. His final point is that teleological systems in nature cannot have been produced by anything other than something analogous to a machine maker. In other words, he is ruling out any non-intentional explanation of their presence and opting for a personal one. And this move has been disputed on scientific grounds, and especially in the wake of notions like that of natural selection as explained by writers like Charles Darwin (1809–82). The argument here is that teleological systems in the organic world arise because of conditions favouring the development of certain species, which, in turn, arise due to chance factors at a genetic level.

And, if this argument is accepted, then it seems that we can account for at least many teleological systems without invoking intelligent planning. As Darwin himself put it in his *Autobiography*:

The old argument of design in nature, as given by Paley, which formerly seemed to me so conclusive, fails, now that the law of natural selection has been discovered. We can no longer argue that, for instance, the beautiful hinge of a bivalve shell must have been made by an intelligent being, like the hinge of a door by man. There seems to be no more design in the variability of organic beings and in the action of natural selection, than in the course of the wind which blows (Darwin 1984, pp. 50f.).

According to the theory of natural selection, which has, in fact, been developed since Darwin, teleological systems in the organic world have come about because things well suited to their environment have been produced and have survived through reproduction and in competition with other things less adapted to their environment. Applied to arguments like that of Paley, the theory has then been held to offer a credible alternative to any personal explanation of the existence of organisms in the world of our experience. Paley notes purposefulness in nature and invokes conscious purpose or design on the part of God. With reference to natural selection, so it has been argued, one can concede the purposefulness in nature while explaining it in non-personal terms.

On the other hand, however, there are problems with saying that the appeal to natural selection is enough to discredit Paley's argument entirely. Such an appeal evidently goes some way to accounting for ostensible teleology in the natural world. We can now account for much of it in terms of development through time and in the light of certain conditions. But there is reason for denying that all ostensibly teleological mechanisms in organic life can be explained by natural selection. On the theory of natural selection, there is similarity and difference as between parents and offspring. And the differences arise in a random way. The long-term consequences are the teleological systems we now observe in the organic world. Yet the origin of species, as opposed to a chaos of monsters, requires strong resemblance between parents and offspring in each generation. This is as important as the variation, and it comes about by an intricate and ostensibly teleological mechanism. And since it is required in order that there should be any origin of species by natural selection, its own origin and ostensibly teleological character logically cannot be explained by natural selection. As F. R. Tennant once put it: 'The survival of the fittest presupposes the arrival of the fit' (Tennant 1930, II, p. 85). Paley can therefore agree that natural selection provides some account of particular teleological systems now confronting us. But he can add that there is still teleology not itself accounted for by natural selection. And then he can ask how we propose to account for this.

But he can also express puzzlement without having to appeal to any attack on natural selection considered as a theory accounting for the way things are now. Let us suppose that teleological systems of the kind envisaged by Paley have evolved by natural processes. Let us also allow for a certain element of chance in all this. We would still have to recognize the operation of a whole lot of natural laws of the kind summarized by chemists and biologists and physicists. The theory of natural selection is, after all, a scientific theory, and, as such, it presupposes that nature behaves with a high degree of uniformity, or that its processes display a large degree of intelligibility. So are we to say that the laws which allow theories like that of natural selection to get going are the most that we can appeal to in attempting to account for the emergence of the phenomena used by Paley as the basis of his argument? Are we to say that these laws are the end of the story? Or might we not speak in terms of intention, as Paley clearly wishes to do?

People are likely to differ in their responses to these questions. And some would certainly say that there is no clear way of deciding whether or not they ought to be answered as Paley would evidently suppose that they should be. Yet it is surely striking that things should behave over time in accordance with laws that can be scientifically formulated. Furthermore, the attempt to account for such regularity in terms of decision is intrinsically more satisfying than the attempt to account for it in terms of itself – by saying, that is, that the regularity is a brute fact which does not call for explanation beyond itself. The point I have in mind here is usefully brought out by Peter Geach, who reports a story of how a Tsar sought to account for the fact that a soldier stood always on guard in the middle of a lawn in the palace grounds. The Tsar was told that it had always been that way. This explanation did not satisfy him. Finally, he discovered that a Tsaritsa had put the man on guard to prevent a snowdrop from being trampled on, and the order was never countermanded. As Geach observes, 'The Tsaritsa's capricious will was a satisfying explanation beyond which we need not look' (Geach 1977b, p. 74).

THE ARGUMENT FROM REGULARITY

If, then, some teleological systems are not to be accounted for in terms of natural selection, and if those which we know of can, at least partly, be accounted for in terms of regularities in nature, the attempt to account for them also in terms of choice is a plausible one. But this mention of regularities brings us more directly to the second major type of the Argument from Design, the one illustrated by the work of Swinburne. So let us now consider that in some detail.

Objections and replies

According to the present argument, the temporal order in the universe – the fact that there is regularity of the kind recorded by scientists – calls for explanation. In response to this suggestion some would reply by citing three major objections which have proved very influential in discussions of the Argument from Design. These can be summarized as follows:

(1) The order in the universe is not surprising since human beings could not find anything else.

(2) We have no good reason to believe that the universe will continue to behave in an orderly way.

(3) Since the universe is unique, we can make no reasonable inference about the reason why it operates in an orderly manner.

Let us consider these objections straight away.

(1) The first has a certain plausibility. If there were not a high degree of order in the universe, then people would not be around to comment on the fact since the existence of human beings requires a high degree of regularity in themselves and in other things. Furthermore, as many have argued, it belongs to human nature to impose patterns on things so as to try to make sense of them. Perhaps we would be disposed to find temporal order in any world we inhabited, even one which was objectively pretty disorderly.

But, though we may impose patterns on things, it seems strange to suggest that the vast temporal order in the universe is simply in our minds. If we really believed that, then we would have to regard scientific discovery as nothing but a report of how we happen to see things. Yet few of us would want to do that. We would say that here we have an opening for genuine discovery. We would say that temporal order is a fact, and that it would still be a fact even if nobody was around to recognize it. That, of course, is why we feel able to talk about what took place before the emergence of human beings.

Nor is it reasonable to suppose that the order in the universe requires no explanation just because human beings could not find anything but an orderly universe. Swinburne brings this point out by means of a devastating analogy.

Suppose that a madman kidnaps a victim and shuts him in a room with a card-shuffling machine. The machine shuffles ten packs of cards simultaneously and then draws a card from each pack and exhibits simultaneously the ten cards. The kidnapper tells the victim that he will shortly set the machine to work and it will exhibit the first draw, but that unless the draw consists of an ace of hearts from each pack, the machine will simultaneously set off an explosion which will kill the victim, in consequence of which he will not see which cards the machine drew. The machine is then set to work, and to the amazement and relief of the victim the machine exhibits an ace of hearts drawn from each pack. The victim thinks that this extraordinary fact needs an explanation in terms of the machine having been rigged in some way. But the kidnapper, who now reappears, casts doubt on this suggestion. 'It is hardly surprising', he says, 'that the machine draws only aces of hearts. You could not possibly see anything else. For you would not be here to see anything at all, if any other cards had been drawn.' But of course the victim is right and the kidnapper is wrong. There is indeed something extraordinary in need of explanation in ten aces of hearts being drawn. The fact that this peculiar order is a necessary condition of the draw being perceived at all makes what is perceived no less extraordinary and in need of explanation. The teleologist's starting point is not that we perceive order rather than disorder, but that order rather than disorder is there. Maybe only if order is there can we know what is there, but that makes what is there no less extraordinary and in need of explanation (Swinburne 1979, p. 138).

(2) The second objection raises well-known philosophical difficulties. We regularly suppose that, on the basis of past experience, we can reasonably predict the future in certain ways. We suppose, for example, that if we drink poison, we will be harmed. We suppose that if we jump from tall buildings, we will be killed. We suppose that if we stay under water without oxygen, we will drown. But the future, after all, is future and not present or past. So may not our expectations one day come to nothing even with regard to suppositions like those just mentioned? Are we really justified in our claims about the future? Might they not be proved wrong, however incredible that may seem? Some philosophers have regarded these questions as serious ones, and some have said that there is no way of answering them so as to leave us sure that the future will indeed turn out in many of the ways we expect. And this is the point behind the present objection. The Argument from Regularity refers to temporal order; but, so the objection goes, we have no guarantee that this order will continue.

Nevertheless, we do frequently reason that such and such will happen given what has happened already. This kind of reasoning is part of what is known as 'inductive' reasoning, and the fact is that we do reason inductively for a great deal of the time. You are doing it now as you read this book on the assumption that it is not going to turn into a banana before you turn the next page. And we even discriminate between inductive arguments from the viewpoint of soundness or cogency. If someone tells me that since the bus arrived at the bus stop at eight yesterday, it is reasonable to believe that it will arrive at this time today, then I should be sceptical, and so, I imagine, would most people. But if I know that the bus has arrived at eight each day for the last twenty years, then, in the absence of any further information (e.g. to the effect that there is a bus strike on), it would be quite reasonable for me to act on the assumption that the bus will indeed arrive at eight today. It may not arrive at this time, of course. But it is reasonable, in the absence of any additional information about the bus, to suppose that the bus will come at eight.

And, returning to our present concern, it is surely reasonable to believe that the temporal order in the universe is something that will continue, at least for a long time. It is, perhaps, logically possible that this order should suddenly cease. We might not contradict ourselves in saying that it will soon be gone. But we have no reason to suppose that it will soon be gone, and we have good reason based on past experience to suppose that it will not. And even if this order were to cease, we still have the fact that it now exists and that it has done so for millions of years. Merely pointing out that there might in the future be nothing for the Argument from Regularity to account for does not abolish the fact that there is now something, or that there has long been something, which the Argument tries to explain.

(3) But should we now concede that the uniqueness of the universe counts against the Argument? The case for saying that it does can be illustrated like this.

Suppose you get a letter through the post. You know that it was written by someone using various materials, probably specifiable, and going through various operations. And you know something about the sender. The letter may be from a complete stranger, but from the evidence of the letter alone you can infer that he has a certain skill or degree of intelligence, that he can write and spell and so on.

But how do you know all this? It is because you already have experience of letters and letter-writers. You would normally make inferences about senders of letters based on what you know of letter writing in general.

The present objection focuses on this kind of point. It observes that the universe, so to speak, is not like a letter. We know how letters come about because we have experience of letters and their manufacture. But, so it is said, we have no experience of the origin of universes and we are therefore in no position to say that the features displayed by this one – including temporal regularity – point to any kind of origin or source. 'When two *species* of objects have always been observed to be conjoined together', says David Hume, 'I can *infer* by custom, the existence of one wherever I *see* the existence of the other' (*Dialogues Concerning Natural Religion*, p. 149). 'But', Hume adds, 'how this argument can have place, where the objects, as in the present case, are single, individual, without parallel, or specific resemblance, may be difficult to explain. And will any man tell me with a serious countenance, that an orderly universe must arise from some thought and art, like the human; because we have some experience of it? To ascertain this reasoning, it were requisite that we had experience of the origin of worlds; and it is not sufficient surely, that we have seen ships and cities arise from human art and contrivance' (*Dialogues*, pp. 149f.).

Yet this objection is also defective. Its force can be seen from the example given above concerning the letter. It is a fact that we regularly make inferences about what accounts for what on the basis of what we have already observed. But it is wrong to assume that no question about the origin of something unique can reasonably be raised. Nor is this something that we should normally suppose. Scientists certainly try to account for various things which are unique. The human race and the universe itself are two good examples. Are they wrong to do this? We may have no experience of the origins of universes, but we do have knowledge of this one. Should we not therefore seek to account for the way in which it operates? Why should the legitimacy of such an effort be ruled out in advance? And, in any case, is it so obvious that the universe is totally unique? The Argument from Regularity is pointing to the fact that, considered as a whole, the universe is not totally unique. For the Argument draws attention to the fact that the universe as a whole resembles at least some of its constituents. As defenders of the Argument would put it: the universe, like things within it, operates in an orderly way.

Another point worth noting is this. Even if we observe that the universe is unique, just what would we have established? Would we thereby have drawn attention to some characteristic of the universe which prohibits one from raising questions of explanation? Some have spoken as if we would have done this, as if the uniqueness of the universe somehow distinguishes it from other things and puts it in a class of its own. Hume seems to be doing this. But that is to misconstrue the nature (or, if you like, the logic) of uniqueness. To say that there is only one universe is not to *describe* the universe. 'The universe is unique' or 'There is only one universe' does not draw attention to some *property* of the universe. What it does is to say that the notion of something with certain properties is one that matches no more than one thing, that the concept 'universe' has no more than one instance. In reply to this it might be said that the universe falls under no concept that anything else falls under. But this is false. The universe, for example, resembles human beings in being changeable. And, as the Argument from Regularity supposes, it also behaves in an orderly way as other specifiable things do. In other words, the universe shares characteristics with some of its parts.

Regularity and explanation

But should we now say that the Argument from Regularity is a cogent one? The objections just noted may not succeed in ruling the Argument out; but can anything definite be said on its behalf?

One evident point in its favour must surely be its starting point: regularity or temporal order. For there does appear to be considerable temporal regularity in the universe, and, on the basis of this, we make inferences concerning past, present, and future, and we formulate laws of nature. This is not to say that such and such must always follow given certain conditions.

But it is to say what we generally assume: that there are many objects behaving in a generally uniform way.

Why, then, should this be so?

We could say that the question ought not to be asked. We could say that the regularity is just there and nothing more needs to be said. And that is what many have said.

But this reaction also seems rather arbitrary. We can easily entertain the thought of there being no order like that displayed by the universe. So the order does not have to be there regardless. Why, then, should we not seek to account for it? Where one of two possibilities has been realized in the world we would normally ask why the one realized has been realized. Consistency would therefore seem to require that we ask why the universe displays temporal order in the way that it does.

And once we do this we also have reason for saying that the answer must be one that invokes the notion of intelligence or mind, that it must, in Swinburne's terminology, belong to the area of personal explanation. This is so for two reasons. The first is that in accounting for temporal regularity it will not do to appeal to scientific considerations – in terms of regularities recorded in scientific laws. The second is that there is an analogy between temporal regularity and the result of intelligent activity.

The first point is really a logical one. It is just that in asking what accounts for temporal regularity one is already ruling out an answer which appeals to the regularities displayed by things in the universe. Trying to account for temporal regularity in terms of scientific laws is to invoke as an explanation an example of the very thing to be explained, for explanation in terms of scientific laws draws attention to temporal regularity in nature, and this is precisely what we are trying to account for.

A possible reply to this is that science may be able to account for temporal regularity as something due to chance. It may, for example, be said that the temporal order we observe can be shown to be just a local apparent regularity that we should expect to occur in a perfectly random way. But, given the regularity, we are certainly not obliged to ascribe it to chance and we actually have good reason for regarding it differently. Suppose we have many packs of cards some of which on inspection prove to be arranged in suits and seniority. We would reasonably infer that the unexamined packs are similarly arranged, and we would account for the grouping observed and inferred not in terms of chance but in terms of intention. By the same token, we have reason for inferring that, given the observed temporal order in the universe, an order on the basis of which we infer further unobserved order, we again have something for which intentional explanation is legitimate.

This brings us to the second point. According to the Argument from Regularity, the temporal regularity in the universe may be accounted for in terms of intelligence. Now, given that it is not to be accounted for with reference to scientific laws, with reference to what are we to account for it? Here we need to remember that as well as accounting for temporal regularity in terms of laws of nature (which can, indeed, be done – as when we account for the operation of certain laws in terms of the operation of other laws), we also account for it in terms of intention. The natural inference just mentioned concerning the cards illustrates our tendency to do this, but there are other examples. Geach's story about the Tsaritsa is a case in point. Then again, we would account intentionally for the behaviour of machinery, for the regularity in a piece of music, for an ordered garden, for the statement of a complex deductive argument, for the motions of a dance, or for the features observed in the playing out of a piece of ritual. These are examples of order which depend on there being general order in nature which is not, so far as we can tell, brought about by human beings. But they also require personal explanation, i.e. explanation with reference to intelligence or purpose. And, since this is so, one has some reason for supposing that personal explanation should be invoked in accounting for regularities in nature, given that an appeal to such regularities is not a sufficient explanation of them, and given that such explanation of them is required.

A standard objection to this is that agents to which we appeal in offering explanations of regularity in terms of intention (i.e. people) are themselves part of the spatio-temporal world the regularity of which the Argument from Regularity is trying to account for. How, then, can the Argument succeed? Will it not inevitably conclude to the very kind of thing for which it is seeking to account? This kind of point was forcefully raised by Hume. According to him, an argument for God based on design or order is an argument from analogy whose proponents are therefore committed to embarrassing consequences. If we say, for example, that the universe, like machines, requires intelligent production, we should also say that, like machines, its producer has a body, for machines are produced by people with bodies. And, since many machines are produced not by one person but by groups of people, we should also say that order in the universe may be produced by a pantheon of gods. 'A great number of men', says Hume, 'join together in building a house or ship, in rearing a city, in framing a commonwealth: Why may not several Deities combine in contriving and forming a world? . . . And why not become a perfect anthropomorphite? Why not assert the Deity or Deities to be corporeal, and to have eyes, a nose, mouth, ears, &c?' (*Dialogues*, pp. 167f.).

These arguments, however, seem to miss the point. The argument from temporal regularity is indeed an argument from analogy. It holds that since in some respect the universe resembles what we try to account for by personal explanation, it can itself be accounted for in terms of something like (in terms of something analogous to) what we recognize as personal explanation. But not all arguments from analogy hold that because one thing is postulated to account for another, then something exactly like this one thing must be postulated to account for something else. In scientific reasoning a common pattern of argument is as follows:

As are caused by Bs. A*s are similar to As. Therefore – given that there is no more satisfactory explanation of the existence of A*s – they are produced by B*s similar to Bs. B*s are postulated to be similar in all respects to Bs except in so far as shown otherwise, viz. except in so far as the dissimilarities between As and A*s force us to postulate a difference (cf. Swinburne 1968, p. 205 and Swinburne 1979, p. 148).

Thus, for example, if John displays symptoms A, B, and C, which are known to reflect the presence of virus X, and if Mary displays symptoms A, B, and D, the origin of which is unknown, then, given that there is no more satisfactory explanation of Mary's symptoms, one might postulate that she is affected by something like X (call it X*) except insofar as the differences between her symptoms and those of John force us to think otherwise. And, in the light of this reasoning, we can say why at least one of Hume's proposed inferences is unacceptable. If we account for temporal regularity in terms of a bodily agent, or in terms of several bodily agents, we simply do not account for temporal regularity. We can deny that the universe's temporal order is to be accounted for in terms of a body obeying this or that natural law. For bodies obeying natural laws are part of what the Argument from Regularity is trying to account for.

This does not dispose of the objection that many gods should be postulated to account for the order in the universe. But here we can say this: we have positive evidence that much temporal order is the result of many people working together with an end in view. But we have no evidence that the same is true of the temporal order in the universe as a whole. Yet it is reasonable to postulate intention with respect to this temporal order. Let us therefore do this, leaving the question of numbers open until decided by further evidence.

This is the pattern of reasoning called 'Ockham's razor', according to which 'Entities are not to be multiplied beyond necessity'. And it is a pattern of reasoning which it is both common and natural to invoke. Consider an example. I enter a room and find a man with ten stab wounds. Obviously, he has been stabbed! On the available evidence I can infer that someone stabbed him (we will suppose that the wounds cannot have been self-inflicted). But, obviously, it is *possible* that each wound was inflicted by a different person. It is *possible* that ten people stabbed him. Yet, confronted with nothing but the body, it would be gratuitous to conclude that ten people stabbed the victim.

One person would suffice, and there is no evidence of more than one. So I may reasonably conclude that only one person was involved, or that there is no evidence for more than one person being involved. I may, of course, be wrong. Things may be as they are in Agatha Christie's novel *Murder on the Orient Express* where a number of people turn out to be responsible for what looks at first to be the work of an individual. But when the detective realizes this, he has more evidence than the victim on his own. He has positive evidence that several people were present at the time of the crime, and that they all had a motive for murder.

The Argument from Design and God

So I suggest that the temporal order in the universe is puzzling, and that it would be reasonable to account for it in terms of something analogous to human intention or intelligent agency. But how far can this be taken as evidence for the existence of God? Might it not be taken only as evidence for something less than God?

One's answer to these questions will doubtless depend on what one takes God to be. But, insofar as the Argument is acceptable in the way that I am urging that it is, it must surely be taken to provide support for belief in God as traditionally understood, even if it does not show that God is all that believers might wish to say that he is. For God is traditionally said to act in nature so that the natural world operates in accordance with his will, while the conclusion of the Argument from Design is that the order we observe in the universe is to be accounted for by intelligent agency distinct from that which we find in the universe itself. To put it at its weakest, the Argument from Design would seem to provide some confirmation of belief in God as traditionally understood.

But people, of course, can confer order on things which exist before they get to work on them. A sculptor, for example, can mould clay into patterns, or an electrical engineer can arrange sound to produce a tune. And, with examples like these in mind, one may wonder whether the Argument from Design is of any use as an argument for God since God is commonly said to be responsible not merely for the way the universe operates, but also for the fact that there is a universe in the first place. As we saw in the last chapter, belief in God includes belief in God as Creator. Some religious thinkers have distinguished between a Creator, who accounts for the existence of matter, and a designing power, who confers order on it. Might it not therefore be said that the Argument from Design is at best an argument for One conferring order, and not for a Creator?

Some have here appealed to Ockham's razor. They would reply that identifying what creates the universe with what originates order in it is a more economical hypothesis than supposing that there is both a Creator and something conferring order. And there is surely something in this suggestion. If we postulate both a designer and a Creator, we introduce complications arising from obvious questions like 'Why have the two of them collaborated as they have?', or 'Why are there just two of them? – Why not, for example, a myriad of designers?'. To assume that the designer and what creates the universe are identical is to make an assumption which has more explanatory power than the assumption that they are really distinct.

But there is a better reason for speaking of identity here. And this has to do with what we must be saying in asserting that there is an orderly universe. For in saying this, we are also saying that there is a universe.

Think for a moment (if you do not find it too disedifying) of somebody who works in a strip-club. Think, that is to say of the stripper. Such a person earns money by removing his or her clothes before an audience prepared to watch. The audience assembles. The stripper arrives. And the clothes disappear (accompanied by various gyrations which readers of books about God might prefer not to think about).

But the stripper, of course, does not disappear as the clothes fall by the wayside (which is, of course, supposed to be the object of the exercise). Here, if at no other time, the stripper obeys a law of nature. You cannot take off your clothes and turn into something different from what you are. The naked stripper is still a human being.

Let us now suppose that someone invites us to what is claimed to be the greatest strip show of all time. At this, so we are told, the universe will strip. It will, in fact, take off its order and display its true and delightful naked self. At the end of the show we will see the bare universe divested of its orderly behaviour.

Should we feel any inclination to attend this promised delectation? A moment's reflection ought to persuade us that, whatever our taste in entertainment, we are going to be sorely disappointed if we act on any inclination we might feel to respond to this dubious suggestion as to how we should spend our time. For the plain fact is, of course, that the order in the universe is just not like the clothes that the ordinary stripper can remove while still remaining what he or she was before the stripping began. Take, for example, the humble chicken's egg. That has parts arranged in order, and we know what will happen to it in various specifiable circumstances. We can indulge in inductive arguments with respect to chicken's eggs, as any good cook knows. A chicken's egg is part of the orderly world from which writers such as Swinburne argue that we have reason to give credence to the Argument from Design. But if such an egg could strip itself of its order, then it would, of course, cease to be what it is. It would, in short, cease to exist (though this, perhaps, would result in something else coming to exist).

In other words, the fact that there is a universe is not something over and above the fact that the universe is the way that it is. And, given that the universe operates in an orderly way, therefore, we are obliged to say that for the universe to exist includes its behaving in an orderly way. The order displayed by the universe is not like a coat which covers some independently existing thing which we can call 'the universe'. It is the form taken by the universe as existing; it is what we are referring to when we talk about the universe. For the universe to exist is for the universe to exist as orderly. But that must mean that our previous question about there being a universe at all (the question held to give substance to the First Cause version of the Cosmological Argument) incorporates our present question about the order displayed by the universe. Whatever it is that accounts for there being a universe must be that which accounts for the order in the universe, for the existence and order of the universe cannot be torn apart.

In other words, if we speak of the universe being created, we can speak of its Creator as being responsible for the temporal order that the universe displays. At this point the Cosmological Argument and the Argument from Design come together. If both arguments are good ones, they support the belief that there is a designing Creator when they are taken together.

THE ARGUMENT FROM MIRACLES

Yet both the Cosmological Argument and the Argument from Design proceed with reference to what we might call extreme generality. The first begins from the fact that there is any universe at all. The other starts from the way in which it behaves over huge areas of space and time. Might it not be said, however, that particular events are evidence for the existence of God? Can we not argue for God on the basis of happenings which can be specified and singled out from the great backdrop of the universe as a whole?

The Argument from Miracles is one of the most popular forms of reply to these questions offered by those who think that the way things have gone is evidence for the existence of God. The Argument can be stated fairly simply. Miracles, so it is said, have occurred. They could not have occurred without the action of God. Therefore, God exists. But in order to grasp the nature of this argument we need to consider what is meant by 'miracles', and why God is supposed to be their necessary condition.

What is a miracle?

Miracles have sometimes been defined as unexpected and fortuitous events in the light of which people are disposed to give thanks to God. They have also been identified with any event leading people to wonder or surprise. In the context of arguments for the existence of God, however, the usual line taken is that miracles are evidence for God because they are events which come about but which could not have come about if nature had been left to itself. On this view nature is conceived of as operating in a fixed or predictable way which can be understood and referred to in order to say what must happen given certain conditions. Miracles are then presumed to be examples of things which happen but which are different from what must happen. This is sometimes expressed by saying that miracles are violations of the laws of nature, or that a miracle is a violation of a natural law. On this account, a miracle is a happening which is different from what was bound to happen given the state of the universe prior to the occurrence of the miracle (and maybe during its occurrence also). And miracles, on this account, are taken to be evidence for God because it is assumed that only God can override laws of nature, and because it is assumed that if something happens which, given the laws of nature, could not happen, then the happening in question must be brought about by what is able to override the laws of nature.

Arguments against miracles

An obvious question raised by all this is whether or not there ever could be a miracle. A second question is whether or not we could ever be justified in supposing that one had occurred. And both these questions have frequently been given negative answers.

(1) Some have said that miracles are just flatly impossible because the laws of nature just cannot be violated. On this account, if something occurs it can always be regarded as what had to occur given the way nature operates and given the state of nature up to and including the occurrence in question.

(2) Others, however, have taken a less stringent line and have merely argued that we could never be rationally justified in supposing that miracles have occurred. A famous defender of this position is Hume, who turns to the topic of miracle in chapter X of his *Enquiry concerning Human Understanding*, which is commonly taken to be the classic philosophical discussion of miracles. There are passages in this text which have been interpreted as an absolute denial that miracles are possible (the exact nature of Hume's position on miracles is a matter of debate); but the bulk of its discussion seems to be directed to arguing that, whether or not miracles are possible, we could never have reason to suppose that one had occurred. And, in this connection, Hume makes three main points.

(a) *Given the meaning of 'miracle' we could never have reason to believe in one.* By this Hume means that since a miracle is a violation of a natural law (or a violation of natural laws), the evidence against a miracle occurring must always be taken to outweigh any evidence to the contrary. Hume is here thinking of the way in which we come to determine what are laws of nature. In his view, this consists in our having observed in a vast number of cases that things behave thus and so in given conditions. Our justification for calling L a law of nature is that L describes what has happened in innumerable instances. Therefore, Hume concludes, the evidence against a miracle happening must always be greater than the evidence for it having occurred. The point about a miracle is that it is something that happens contrary to what is commonly observed to happen. But, says Hume, for that very reason the claim that it has happened must always be thought to be called into question by what is commonly observed to happen.

(b) *Those who report the occurrence of miracles are unreliable.* In his discussion of miracles Hume maintains that no miracle comes with the testimony of enough people who can be regarded as sufficiently intelligent, learned, reputable, and so on, to justify us in believing reports of miracles. Hume also observes that human nature is naturally uncritical and credulous when it comes to the miraculous, and that religious people are predisposed to report miracles and are subject to disreputable motives in doing so. 'It forms', says Hume, 'a strong presumption against all supernatural and miraculous relations that they are observed chiefly to abound among ignorant and barbarous nations' (*Enquiry*, p. 119).

(c) *Miracles reported by different religious traditions cancel each other out.* Suppose that twenty witnesses say that Jones was in London yesterday. Also suppose that twenty others say that he was in Glasgow. With no other evidence to go on, we would almost certainly agree that we cannot decide where Jones was yesterday, for the evidence is conflicting and equally balanced. In a similar way, Hume's third point is that miracles reported by one religion face a conflicting claim in reports of miracles coming from other religions. He therefore concludes that none of the reports should be believed.

How cogent are the objections?

Are miracles impossible?

In dealing with this question our answer, of course, is bound to depend on how we conceive of the possible and the impossible. By 'impossible' one could mean 'what cannot happen in the course of nature'. This is not an easy notion, but is presumably what we have in mind when we say, for example, that it is not possible for people to fly like birds, or that it is not possible for dogs to give birth to elephants. Whether or not miracles are impossible in this sense is a question I shall turn to in a moment. There is, however, a second sense of 'impossible' where it means 'logically impossible' and where it is applied to assertions or statements. The idea here is that these are impossible if they are contradictory, or if they entail or are entailed by contradictory assertions or statements. And in this sense of 'impossible' it is hard to see that miracles are impossible when considered as violations of the laws of nature. Those who accept the violation theory of miracles would, for example, commonly agree that the following events, if they occurred, would be violations of the laws of nature: 'levitation; resurrection from the dead in full health of a man whose heart has not been beating for twenty-four hours and who was, by other criteria also, dead; water turning into wine without the assistance of chemical apparatus or catalysts; a man getting better from polio in a minute' (Swinburne 1968, p. 323). We might perhaps doubt whether things like this have happened. But it is hard to see that there is any contradiction involved in saying that they have happened. Where would the contradiction lie?

Miracles and evidence

But could we ever have sufficient evidence that a law of nature has been violated? Here there are several points to make.

One is that it is by no means clear that we ought to accept what seems to be the assumption of those who reject the occurrence of a miracle with reference to the notion of a law of nature. For in what sense can nature be said to obey laws such that we can confidently suppose that laws of nature have not been broken? This is a difficult question that quickly takes us into an already much discussed range of philosophical issues which cannot be treated in detail here. Nevertheless, those who are sceptical of miracles in the name of laws of nature usually seem to presume that things that happen in the natural world cannot fail to happen given the state of the universe considered apart from the happenings themselves. In other words, they commonly suppose that things happen by virtue of necessity, and they think of laws of nature as telling us what must come to pass because of this. But an objector can wonder how anyone can know that there is any necessity in nature, or (perhaps better) that some particular happening is necessitated. One may grant that certain conditions usually lead to certain happenings. One may grant that in the absence of certain conditions then certain happenings are not to be expected. But it is hard to see how it can be proved that certain conditions must lead to certain happenings, or that without certain conditions then certain happenings absolutely could not come to pass.

In reply to this point one might observe that one can specify events which, if they occurred, would reasonably be called violations of the laws of nature. The examples given in the last paragraph but two would seem to be cases in point. Let us, for instance, suppose that a person recognized by all the doctors as long dead were to be restored to life. Would this not constitute a violation of a law of nature?

Perhaps the strongest argument to the effect that it would is our past experience of human bodies. We have overwhelming grounds for supposing that when people die, their bodies embark on an irreversible process of corruption. And, for this reason, we must surely say that the first of Hume's arguments is a very powerful one. The evidence from experience against the occurrence of something like a dead person rising is very strong. But it is one thing to say this, and another to suppose that a case of resurrection would be a cancelling of what must happen of necessity, that it would be a case of something which, given the way the universe is apart from itself, could not come to pass. This is not to say that things do not have characteristic properties or that their operation does not lead to products or operations that can be accounted for scientifically. But it is to say that the onus of proof rests on someone who thinks that given the way things are in the universe then all that happens within the universe must happen.

Let us, however, waive this point. Let us now suppose, as many would, that there are laws of nature and that we can say that unless something outside the universe interferes, then certain events are ruled out. An example here would again be the case of resurrection. Let us suppose that we have excellent reason for supposing that corpses do not return to life. Could we then have reason to think that one had?

Hume evidently agrees that we could not, and his arguments against miracles have been very influential. Even so, they can be challenged. The last argument, for a start, begs a very important question. Hume takes it for granted that reported miracles must be viewed as evidence against the truth of religions in which other miracles are reported. But this would only be true of miracles which were indubitably evidence for contradictory religious assertions, and it needs to be shown that all reported miracles are like this. According to Hume, 'every miracle . . . pretended to have been wrought in any . . . [religion] . . . as its direct scope is to establish the particular system to which it is attributed; so has it the same force, though more indirectly, to overthrow a rival system, it likewise destroys the credit of those miracles, on which that system was established' (*Enquiry*, pp. 121f.). But, as Swinburne has observed, 'evidence for a miracle "wrought in one religion" is only evidence against the occurrence of a miracle "wrought in another religion" if the two miracles, if they occurred, would be evidence for propositions of the two religious systems incompatible with each other' (Swinburne 1970, p. 60).

Then again, must we say that all reported miracles come from people whose honesty and reliability is always open to question? Maybe many or most reports of miracles come from unreliable sources, but it is surely going too far to say that we could never conclude that those who report a miracle do speak truly about what actually came to pass. And, even if we doubt the testimony of people, there are other ways of determining that something probably happened. Hume says nothing about traces of past events open to inspection in the present, as ruined castles may be traces of ancient battles. Can we rule out in advance the possibility that by means of what we may come to observe we can reasonably infer that something happened which, other things being equal, we have good reason to think somehow impossible?

One answer to questions like this appeals to the weight of past experience in support of what is taken to be a law of nature. It has been said that this might always make it most reasonable to doubt the occurrence of a miraculous event. But, as others have replied, if we act on this principle we may be forced unreasonably to revise our conception of the way things work. Suppose an event happens which conflicts with what we take to be a law of nature. Suppose also that we then insist that this event merely fits in with a hitherto unknown law. Would that necessarily be the most reasonable response? It might be if what we take to be our new law allowed us to predict under what conditions further events like our present one would occur, and if it allowed us to account for the event itself in relation to what we already take to be laws of nature. But not if that were not the case, and if our first supposed law continued to allow us to make successful predictions. Given that we can talk about laws of nature in the first place, it might be more rational (because more explanatory and economical) to conclude that our event is the violation of a law of nature. Later observations may, of course, also make it reasonable to change one's verdict here. But that need not mean that the verdict was not a reasonable one at the time it was made.

Still, it ought, perhaps, to be agreed that there is a difficulty for someone who insists that a law of nature has been violated. This arises from the fact that laws of nature are indeed taken to be based on enormous evidence. The point can be put like this: if someone believes that a miracle has occurred, and if he concedes that this means that what is vastly improbable has, in fact, happened, then he concedes that what he claims to have occurred is vastly improbable, in which case he ought to doubt that it has, in fact, occurred. 'This event must, by the miracle advocate's own admission, be contrary to a genuine, not merely a supposed, law of nature, and therefore maximally improbable. It is this maximal improbability that the weight of the testimony would have to overcome. . . . Where there is some plausible testimony about the occurrence of what would appear to be a miracle, those who accept this as a miracle have the double burden of showing both that the event took place and that it violated the laws of nature. But it will be very hard to sustain this double burden. For whatever tends to show that it would have been a violation of a natural law tends for that very reason to make it most unlikely that it actually happened' (Mackie 1982, pp. 25ff.). In Hume's words: 'Nothing is esteemed a miracle, if it ever happen in the common course of nature. . . . There must, therefore, be a uniform experience against every miraculous event, otherwise the event would not merit that appellation' (*Enquiry*, p. 115). This is not to say that one never could have reason to suppose a law of nature has been violated. It is not even to say that there are such things as laws of nature. But it is to say that there is always a reasonable presumption against laws of nature being violated, and such a presumption may be hard to overthrow.

The evidential value of miracles

It seems, then, that miracles may be possible in principle (logically possible), and that those who believe in them can fairly require their opponents to prove that they cannot occur since laws of nature determine what must happen. Nor is it obvious that there could not be circumstances in which one might reasonably conclude that a law of nature has been violated. But, in the nature of the case, one will need very good grounds indeed to be justified in concluding on the basis of evidence that there has been such a violation. And this, to say the least, must mean that any argument from a miracle, or from miracles, to God will have to be treated with great caution. There can be no really cogent argument to God from the miraculous if there is serious doubt about the miraculous itself.

But does this mean that the Argument from Miracles cannot serve to show that we have good reason to believe in God? As the reader may realize by now, this is a question that cannot be adequately answered here. For what is required is a detailed examination of particular purported miracles, and that would take me way beyond the limits of this book. Nevertheless, a few general points can be made.

Those who argue from miracles to the existence of God sometimes talk as if once the miracle is granted, then the existence of God follows automatically. In other words, they suppose, as I noted earlier, that God is a necessary condition of the occurrence of miracles, that if there were no God then there could be no miracles. But why should we believe that this is really so?

A case might be made for doing so if we already have good reason to believe in God. And it has, in fact, been said that if God exists he can be expected to bring about the occurrence of miracles, or even that he can be expected to bring about the occurrence of certain sorts of miracles. At the moment, however, we are asking about the force of the Argument from Miracles as an independent argument for the existence of God, and an objector could reply that we cannot therefore begin by supposing that there is a God. And if we do not suppose that God exists, then the possibility arises of accounting for the miraculous in terms of something other than God. Might it not be said, for instance, that miracles could be produced by something like what Christians and others have referred to as angels? Might their origin not lie in something outside the scientifically discoverable universe, but in something less than God?

In view of what I have said about the Cosmological Argument and the Argument from Design, one may, perhaps, anticipate a possible answer to these questions. For if we can account for the existence of an orderly universe in terms of God, then we must ultimately appeal to God in accounting for all that happens in the universe. For this will be what we mean by there being a universe. In other words, it might be said that if God accounts for the existence of the universe, then he must account for any miraculous event that takes place in it, for this will be part of the universe.

Yet this move is not really much use to the Argument from Miracles considered as an independent argument for the existence of God. For the Argument from Miracles would now be simply equivalent to the assertion that the existence of the universe can be accounted for by God, which is not what the Argument is holding. Granted that the existence of the universe is to be accounted for by God, it follows that the same goes for miracles. But what do we have evidence for if we only have the miracles?

Some have argued that we could have evidence for God because a miracle could occur in circumstances which would make it reasonable to account for it in terms of God rather than something else. We already know that events can come about as a result of human intention. And some of these may be regarded as responses to requests made by people. Suppose then that somebody called on God to silence disbelievers by performing a specified miracle. Suppose also that the miracle occurred and that we are justified in regarding it as an event produced in violation of the laws of nature. Suppose in addition that the miracle were followed by a voice heard by everyone to say: 'Now that I've shown I exist, I hope you will all start believing in me!' Would that be evidence for the existence of God? Some would say that it could be and they would describe themselves as arguing by analogy. They would say that the strength of their case would lie in the similarities between the supposed miracle and other non-miraculous happenings rightly accounted for as intentional responses to requests. If I am locked in a room and if someone outside says 'If there's someone in there called Davies, then let him rap on the door', and if he heard the rapping as well as my voice, he might reasonably conclude that I am there – though even so he could be wrong. In a similar way, so it has been argued, we might reasonably be led to conclude on the basis of the miraculous that God is there.

But even if there occurred events like those now imagined (and one needs quite a good imagination at this point) one might surely still take leave to doubt that what we are dealing with is evidence for God. Why not an evil spirit anxious to lead us to a belief in God based on error? Why not something good and worth knowing about, but still not divine? In the circumstances just imagined perhaps most of us would incline to the view that we have evidence for God no matter how sceptical we might be in the frigidity of an academic debate. But sceptical questions do intrude here, and they can be more or less academic depending on one's concept of God. They will not, perhaps, be all that troublesome if we think of God as an invisible being who is very like a human person and who can seriously be thought to behave in the way envisaged by those who would take happenings like those just imagined as evidence for the existence of God. But God has also been said, for example, to be all-powerful and all-knowing. Some have also thought of him as totally changeless and as existing outside time. I shall be returning to such views in later chapters, but even here we can ask why the evidence of our imagined miracle should be taken as evidence for God as they depict him. If someone protests that it should so be taken, there is, after all, an obvious reply. This is that human beings intentionally bringing about events in response to requests are not all-powerful and the rest of it. Here there seems little ground for an argument by analogy.

So if the Argument from Miracles is to be of any use as part of a case for belief in God, it looks as though it might have to be supplemented by another which gives us reason to suppose that what happens in the universe is rightly attributed to God. We have already considered two arguments (or versions of two such arguments). In the next chapter we can turn to yet another.

QUESTIONS FOR DISCUSSION

1   How would you decide whether or not something is designed?
2   How would you decide whether something has a purpose?
3   If purpose must account for a watch on a heath, should it account for a stone?
4   'The universe might so naturally have been chaotic, but it is not – it is very orderly.' Discuss.
5   What is natural selection? What would count as evidence for it?
6   Have we any reason to suppose that the past resembled the present or that the present resembles the future?
7   If temporal order is to be accounted for, is there any reason to account for it in terms of God?

8 'We can offer a natural explanation for anything that happens, and, if we can't, there must still be one to offer.' Discuss.

9 What exactly is Hume's view on miracles? Or does he have no consistent view?

10 If a violation of a law of nature occurred, must we attribute it to God? If not, how should we account for it?

FURTHER READING

A classic philosophical critique of the Argument from Design is to be found in David Hume, *Dialogues Concerning Natural Religion* (ed. Norman Kemp Smith, Edinburgh, 1947; repr. Indianapolis, 1977). Many subsequent discussions of the Argument, including most of those mentioned below, consider Hume's discussion, but for detailed and exegetical treatments of it two books in particular are to be recommended. These are Antony Flew, *Hume's Philosophy of Belief* (London, 1961) and J. C. A. Gaskin, *Hume's Philosophy of Religion* (London, 1978). Both these books are also excellent on Hume on miracles.

For good full-length treatments of the Argument from Design, see Thomas McPherson, *The Argument from Design* (London, 1972) and R. H. Hurlbutt, *Hume, Newton and the Design Argument* (Lincoln, Nebraska, 1965). McPherson's book is probably best for beginners and is intended for such. It clearly traces some of the Argument's history, and it highlights the major questions raised by it.

A notable modern defence of the Argument, one to which my discussion is much indebted, has been offered by Richard Swinburne. See the following: *The Existence of God* (Oxford, 1979), ch. 8; 'The Argument from Design', *Philosophy* 43 (1968); 'The Argument from Design – A Defence', *Religious Studies* 8 (1972); 'Mackie, Induction and God', *Religious Studies* 19 (1983). The last of these articles is a reply to John Mackie's *The Miracle of Theism* (Oxford, 1982), which has a lively critique of the Argument from Design in ch. 8. I have defended Swinburne against Mackie in 'Mackie on the Argument from Design', *New Blackfriars* (September 1983).

A good source-book to consult with reference to Paley and Darwin is Tess Cosslett (ed.), *Science and Religion in the Nineteenth Century* (Cambridge, 1984). This contains important texts and background information. For an informative but brief introduction to Darwin, see Jonathan Howard, *Darwin* (Oxford, 1982). The full text of Paley's *Natural Theology* can be found in vol. IV of *The Works of William Paley* (Oxford, 1838).

For an intriguing version of the Argument from Design see Richard Taylor, *Metaphysics* (3rd ed., Englewood Cliffs, N.J., 1983), ch. 10. Taylor holds that if we rely on our senses as bearers of information, we ought to suppose that they have a purposeful origin. Taylor's argument, and other versions of the Argument from Design, is explained and discussed by John Hick in chs 1 and 2 of *Arguments for the Existence of God* (London, 1970). Hick's book, I should point out, has helpful introductions to many other arguments for God's existence.

Perhaps the most useful, recent study of miracle is Richard Swinburne, *The Concept of Miracle* (London, 1970). Some of the material in this book can also be found in Swinburne's article 'Miracles', *The Philosophical Quarterly* XVIII (1968). With reference to Hume on miracles, and in addition to the above mentioned books by Flew and Gaskin, mention should be made of R. M. Burns, *The Great Debate on Miracles* (Lewisburg, Pa., 1981). This is a fine introduction both to Hume on miracles and to the historical context of Hume's discussion.

Many works could be recommended on the topic of nature and necessity, but as good a book as any to start with is Richard Sorabji, *Necessity, Cause, and Blame* (Ithaca, N.Y., 1980). This is ostensibly a discussion of Aristotle, but it is of much more than exegetical interest. It has important things to say on its subject matter and is a good way into the whole topic.

3
The Experience of God and the Moral Life

With the exception of the Argument from Miracles, the arguments for God's existence so far considered proceed with reference to the universe in general. But an important and popular line of reasoning holds that God can be discovered by reflection on data provided only by human beings, or directly in such data. Here we can distinguish two main arguments which I shall call the 'Argument from Experience' and the 'Argument from Morality'. The first holds that we have reason to believe in God because God can be known as an object of experience. The second argument holds that there is something about the reality of morality which shows that God exists. In this chapter, therefore, I want to consider these arguments.

THE ARGUMENT FROM EXPERIENCE

Sometimes we learn that something exists because we infer or deduce its existence on the basis of something other than itself. Thus, for example, I might infer that there is a bear in the area because of the trail of destruction which I can observe without actually meeting the bear.

But we often also discover that things exist because, as we put it, we have 'first-hand experience' of them. Thus, for example, I might simply leave the house and walk right into the bear.

In the same way, so it is said, God can be directly and non-inferentially encountered as an object of experience, and on the basis of an experience of God one has reason to say that God exists. The idea here is that there is such a thing as an awareness of God's presence which must be recognized as evidence for God's existence just as the awareness of the presence of other things can be recognized as evidence for their existence.

And this argument is sometimes developed into an argument based on testimony. What if you have no consciousness of having had any experience of God's presence? Then, so it is said, you can rely on the evidence of those who have been conscious of an experience of God's presence. I may never have been to China, but I would be inclined to believe someone from China who told me that he had seen various things there. By the same token, so it has been argued, those with no consciousness of having experienced God can appeal in defence of belief in God to the experience of him reported by others. This, so it is claimed, is very impressive evidence.

How successful is the argument?

God and experience

A.   What is an experience of God?

Many people have said that they have had or that they do have experience of God, and it would be absurd to deny that this is evidence that something has indeed happened to them. We can put this most uncontroversially by saying that there is no reason to doubt that many people have thought that they have had experience of God, or that many people think that they have it. This is not something that anyone denies.

But nobody denies that people also think that they have had experience of things which others would assert to be no object of anyone's experience. Some people think that they have seen fairies or extra-terrestrials and nobody denies the fact. But they do, of course, often deny that there are any fairies or extra-terrestrials. And this suggests an obvious question with respect to the supposed existence of God. Is it reasonable for anyone to believe in God because God can be known as an object of experience?

One problem here lies in the use of the word 'experience'. If God is an object of one's experience, of what is God supposed to be an object? A common answer is that God is an object of something akin to sensory experience, that experiencing God, or experiencing the presence of God, can be compared to experiencing, say, a table or a mountain. An analogy is also sometimes drawn between the experience of God and our everyday experience of people considered as conscious selves transcending the limitations of materiality. People, so it is said, are more than just material. Yet we can recognize their presence directly. In a similar way, so it is added, we can recognize the presence of God. As H. P. Owen puts it: 'Our direct knowledge of God takes the form of an intellectual intuition which is analogous to our intuition of other human persons in so far as, firstly, it is mediated by signs, and, secondly, it terminates in a spiritual reality' (Owen 1969, p. 307).

Yet there are difficulties with all of this. Take, to begin with, the analogy between experience of God and sensory experience. Is that really illuminating? Can it help us to understand what an experience of God could be? Up to a point, yes. We all have experiences of coming across things in the material world, and we might try to explain what is involved in them by talking about things impinging on us, forcing themselves on our attention, crowding into our consciousness, and so on. And God, it might be said, makes his presence felt in this kind of way. That, at any rate, is what many people do say. But one must also be struck by the differences between sensory experience and what must be involved in an experience of God, assuming, that is, that this is really an experience with God as its object. For things whose presence is detected by means of the senses are physical, while God is normally said to be non-physical. To detect something by means of the senses is to locate it as *here* and not *there*, as *now* and not *then*. Yet God is commonly said to be present everywhere and always. To say that one has perceived an object by means of the senses is to say that there is something (or that there was something) whose presence is (or was) in principle confirmable by a whole range of familiar tests. We can check on the presence of physical objects by means of eye-witness reports, by the analyses of physicists and chemists, and by reference to the evidence of photographs and recordings. Yet these tests are not applicable when it comes to checking the presence of God. They are ruled out by God not being material.

Similar difficulties can be noted with respect to the proposed analogy between experience of God and direct experience of people. Some philosophers have held that people are essentially incorporeal. Others have rejected this conclusion as unintelligible. But, whichever party is right here, it still remains that we recognize the presence of people because they are physically present, or, if you like, because their bodies are physically present. If God is non-material, however, his presence cannot be detected like this. In other words, there must be a genuine and considerable disanalogy between any putative experience of God and our familiar experience of people. It is as things with a bodily history, or, if you like, as things tied to things with a bodily history, that people are recognized to be present. One may therefore wonder what can be the point of comparing the presence of God with the presence of people, and of saying that both can be known in the same kind of way. Far from making it clear what the experience of God amounts to, the comparison between knowledge of God and knowledge of people only serves to raise problems. And these increase the more that one stresses the difference between God and people. On some views of God they seem enormous. Take, for example, the Christian assertion that God is really three persons. We shall return to that later, but even here we can note that it is not an assertion to the effect that God is three persons in one human being. In the case of the doctrine of the Trinity, one is struck more by what is claimed to be the difference between God and people than by any possible similarity.

B.   Mistrusting experience of God

Yet remarks like these would be answered by defenders of the Argument from Experience. They will probably say that, while there are analogies between familiar experiences of things and experience of God, these are no more than analogies and it is hardly surprising that they break down. And that, indeed, may be a legitimate response. If God did enter into people's experience, one would, presumably, expect there to be differences between the experience of God and the experience of other things. Nor, perhaps, would it be surprising to find people talking of one in terms of the other. For we naturally try to fit what occurs to us into a frame of reference that already makes some sense to us or which is familiar to other people.

But, even though they might accept this point, others would now observe that there are still some insuperable objections to the view that one might reasonably believe in God on the basis of an experience of him, or on what one takes to be an experience of him. Among those objections which have been most frequently expressed, three in particular are recurrent:

(1) Experience is often deceptive.
(2) We may never be perceiving what we think we are perceiving.
(3) One can always account for supposed experience of God in naturalistic terms.

(1)   Experience and deception

The idea behind the first objection hardly needs explaining and evidently calls for serious consideration. We all know what it is like to be 'sure' that we saw someone or something, only to discover that we did not. And we all know that there are such things as hallucination and misinterpretation of available evidence. Experience is indeed frequently deceptive, and anyone who supposes that he has had an experience of God will clearly need to consider whether or not what he has had is any such thing. We can put this by saying that he will need to consider whether the experience is truly veridical.

But it would also surely be wrong to be over-dogmatic here. We are often mistaken in what we take ourselves to be aware of, but it cannot be inferred from this that all claims to a knowledge of God by experience must therefore stand discredited or that nobody can suppose that his supposed experience of God is really veridical. For, though we are sometimes wrong in our judgements about what is there, we are also sometimes right. And we can have good reason on many occasions for insisting that we are right. In other words, a general argument from illusion, from the possibility of mistaken identification or misinterpretation of evidence, cannot always be rationally used in assessing the correctness of all assertions based on experience that something is the case. Context is extremely important here. You may often have proved to be an unreliable witness, but what if I have proved to be a very reliable one? Might that not give me reason for thinking that what seems to me to be so is so? You may say that you saw the Empire State Building standing in the middle of Parliament Square in London, and I may reasonably suppose that you are mistaken. But should I say the same of someone who says that he saw Big Ben by Parliament Square? What if something of which I seem to be aware is something that one would expect to be where it seems to me to be?

In this connection, also, we need to remember the implications involved in our notions of mistaken identity, misinterpretation of evidence, and hallucination. Mistakenly to identify X is to have an experience of X and erroneously to believe that it is something other than X. It must therefore be possible to have an experience of X and correctly to believe that it is X. To misinterpret evidence is to be aware of something and to draw mistaken conclusions about it. It must therefore be possible to be aware of something and to draw correct conclusions about it. To have an hallucination is mistakenly to believe that something is present to one. It must therefore be possible correctly to believe that something is present to one.

Some would reply to these points by saying that as long as there is even the remotest possibility of being mistaken, then judgements based on experience should always be regarded as suspicious. But this principle itself is surely suspicious. Once one determines to doubt all that might possibly be doubted, one will find oneself virtually unable to assert that anything is true. For someone with a suitably lively imagination can always persist in thinking up some story to cast doubt on what we take to be true, and he can do this with reference to almost any judgement based on experience. But, as philosophical critics of absolute scepticism have observed, that does not mean that his procedure is truly rational. When I seem to see a book it might be that I am momentarily the victim of some demonic illusionist. But that does not mean that I must always suppose that I am such a victim. It does not even mean that I must ever suppose this. And sometimes, indeed, it will not even make sense to suppose it. Imagine someone telling a group of tourists in India that they are not actually looking at the Taj Mahal. What would it even mean to say this? The Taj Mahal could, of course, be destroyed at any time. People could also mistakenly take one building like the Taj Mahal to be the Taj Mahal itself. But we are now to imagine someone seriously suggesting to one of those many groups who visit the building that they are not really looking at it. Yet if that suggestion makes sense, why should we suppose that there is even such a place as India? Why should we suppose that any of our perceptions are any such thing? And why should sceptics suppose that they have anyone to argue against?

(2) Perception and error

These points are also relevant to the second of the above objections. For this holds that we can never take the fact that we seem to perceive something as evidence to the effect that we do perceive it. If that is true, however, then we are in no position to say that when, for example, we go to the Taj Mahal and seem to see it we are actually seeing it. Yet that is surely absurd. Nor does it take account of the fact that it is generally reasonable to suppose that we do indeed perceive what we seem to perceive. Unless I have particular grounds for supposing otherwise, the fact that it seems to me that I am holding a book, say, is reason for me to suppose that there is a book there. In many circumstances we would indeed hold ourselves reasonably to believe that such and such is the case because it seems to us to be the case. If we did not do this, it is hard to see how we would manage to get anything done. And if the belief is not rational, then it is hard to know what it is rational to believe. One may, indeed, reply that it can seem to us that something is there and the thing not be there. But that is not now being denied. What is being denied is that its seeming to me that something is there is not *prima facie* evidence for the thing being there.

(3) Experience of God and naturalistic explanation

The third objection is familiar to us in the light of work by psychologists and sociologists or philosophers of history. Those who think that they have had experience of God naturally presume that their belief in God is finally to be accounted for in terms of the reality of God. But the present objection precisely denies this and offers an alternative account of the formation of belief in God, an account in terms of the nature of things or the operation of things within the universe. Thus, for example, it has been argued that belief in God is to be accounted for in terms of some psychological abnormality. Others have seen it as arising not from abnormal psychology so much as common aspects in people's psychological make-up or development. According, for instance, to Freud (1856–1939), the solution lies in feelings of helplessness coupled with experience of parenthood. We find ourselves in a hostile world and we defend ourselves by creating out of our wishes a belief in a God who is able to satisfy our needs. According to Marx (1818–83), the solution is to be found in the influence on people of economic and political exploitation. On this account, people are religious because they are constricted by the conditions of their society and by their place in it. The result is that they are led to seek consolation in what is illusory.

But these positions too are insufficient if taken as ruling out the claim that God can be known as an object of experience. Even if many who report an experience of God are psychologically abnormal so that we might reasonably doubt their capacity to perceive correctly, it does not follow that all are like this. And, as many have pointed out, some of those who report that they have or have had experience of God seem to be as judicious as the next person and a great deal more judicious than many of those whose judgements in general we would not call into question. And, even if they are not, there remains the possibility that experience of God might require psychological abnormality just as an aerial view of Paris requires that one be abnormally elevated. A common objection to this is that those who are psychologically abnormal display evidence of misperception with respect to matters other than God, and that this creates a presumption against what they take to be their perception of God. As Russell once put it: 'From a scientific point of view, we can make no distinction between the man who eats little and sees heaven and the man who drinks much and sees snakes' (Russell 1935, p. 188). But this simply assumes that what leads us to misperception with respect to what is not God must also lead us to misperception with respect to God. Here the psychological critic of those who claim experience of God must be able to give independent reason for supposing that they are indeed misperceiving. And the same applies to those who challenge the claim to experience of God with reference to social or economic pressure. Maybe such things do account for much that is taken to be experience of God. Maybe it would be surprising if they did not. But we are not entitled to presume that they account for all of this unless we already have reason to reject the veridicality of all supposed experience of God. It is, indeed, significant that writers like Freud and Marx were convinced of atheism before they offered their accounts of the origin of religion.

C. Recognizing God by experience

There is, however, a more telling difficulty with the assertion that one can know that God exists because he is an object of experience. And this can be introduced by the question 'How can anyone know that it is God that he perceives and not something else?' The problem here lies in understanding how one could come across an object of experience and recognize it as God.

Consider, for a moment, how one does recognize that one has come across certain things. Is it by simply coming across them, by being in contact with them, by them impinging on one? The answer, of course, is 'No'. If that were the case, then new-born infants would recognize things in their environment as soon as they are born, for they are close to many things from the outset. But, though babies undoubtedly respond to things around them, though they register their presence, we do not suppose that they recognize

them. I mean by this that they are not, for example, able to say to themselves
'That's a doctor' or 'That's a cot' or 'That's a woollen blanket'. It takes time
for human beings to be able to do this. It also depends on them having an
understanding of things to which what is perceived can be related. I can
recognize that something is a tap, say, because I already understand what taps
are, and because the thing in question matches this understanding.

So now consider the position of someone who thinks that as well as
coming across taps and the like, he also comes across God. In that case he
must be able to recognize that what he has come across corresponds to what
God is understood to be. Yet how is one to recognize that any object of one's
experience is God?

If 'God' were merely said to be another name for material objects, or a
name for a physical object within the universe, this question would not pose
any obviously insuperable difficulty. For we can specify how many of these
things can be identified. But God is not traditionally taken to be any such
thing. Nor do those who make much of experience of God ask us to suppose
otherwise. God, so they regularly say, is the non-material Creator of the
universe. Yet, as soon as one accepts this, one is back with the question at the
end of the last paragraph. How is one to recognize that any object of one's
experience is God?

Some have said that one can perceive oneself and the universe to be
dependent on God for existence, and they have therefore added that God can
be perceived as that on which people and the universe are dependent. But,
though that might be true, it cannot be that being dependent or depended on
can be recognized as qualities of any object of one's experience. If they could,
then we should be able to recognize them as objective and distinguishing
features of things, which we cannot. While I am in the plane I am dependent
on it in all sorts of ways. And the plane stands to me as something on which I
depend. But nothing in me or the plane disappears when I leave it. Nor is
there some new way of distinguishing both of us from each other and from
anything else when I climb aboard again. What here corresponds to being
dependent or depended on is a relationship between things that have
identities of their own apart from the relationship. People, indeed, are
sometimes said to be dependent on others, meaning that there is something
about them that distinguishes them in some way. In this sense a child might
be said to be dependent on its mother while another child might be said to be
very self-sufficient. In this sense we can distinguish between dependent and
independent children. But 'dependent' here refers to ways in which
individuals behave, while those who talk about the dependence of themselves
and the universe on God are not supposing that a universe dependent on God
would behave any differently from a universe independent of God. With
reference to God, the notion of dependence is an absolute one; as in the case

with the dependence of passengers on a plane, it does not imply any distinguishing feature in an object of one's experience. It has to do with something that is true of all such features.

The general difficulty here can, perhaps, be put by saying that there seems to be no distinguishing property or activity that something must have or display if it is, indeed, the Creator of the universe. To call God the Creator of the universe is to assert a relationship between God and the universe. It is not to specify a distinguishing feature of God, for that would imply what no traditional believer wants to assert: that God would have been a different kind of thing if he had not created. In this sense, being the Creator can no more be an identifiable property of God than being the baker of a cake can be an identifiable property in a baker. Nor can it involve an activity which can be recognized simply by the awareness of it, as one might, indeed, recognize the activity of baking by perceiving someone engaged in it, or as one might recognize the activity of singing when coming across a singer in action. This is because for God to create the universe is for him to bring it about that everything in the universe exists, and one cannot recognize that he is doing this without also knowing that the existence of everything in the universe is brought about by God. Yet one cannot know this simply by somehow observing God. One must also observe everything in the universe. And, even if one could do this, there remains the problem of knowing what one could be aware of as constituting God's creating. Is it, for instance, that one could be aware of some operation undergone by God? Some have spoken as if creating is for God as, say, singing is for people: a process to be distinguished by changes gone through by God. But this would seem to imply that it takes time for God to create, which is a very dubious notion. If for God to create something is for God to bring it about that the thing exists, how can his creating take any time? Or are we to imagine two stages in God's creating something: one where he is creating and the thing created is not there, and another where he is creating and the thing created is there? In any case, it is also traditional teaching that God is changeless, and many of those who appeal to experience of God as reason for believing in him accept this teaching. They, at any rate, cannot countenance the suggestion that for God to create is for God to undergo a process distinguished by changes.

Similar difficulties arise from other things that God is traditionally said to be. He is, for example, said to be infinite and omniscient (all-knowing). Yet how can one recognize, just by virtue of the experience, that some object of one's experience is either of these things? It is easy to see how one might recognize that someone is bald or fat. It is easy to see how something – the Atlantic Ocean, for example – can be looked upon and justly be pronounced to be immense, huge, vast, and so on. But 'infinity' signifies boundlessness or endlessness, and it is exceedingly hard to see how anything can be known to be infinite just through experience of it as an object of experience. What feature of anything could serve to mark it off as boundless or endless? What feature of anything could allow one to recognize it as such? And, with regard to omniscience, surely only what is omniscient can recognize omniscience as a reality in something it comes across. This is not to say that in order to know that an object of one's experience is thus and so one has to be thus and so oneself. I can know that you are drunk without being drunk also. But if omniscience can be recognized as a reality in an object of one's experience, it can only be recognized by one who understands just what is there before him, just as drunkenness can only be recognized by one who understands what it means to be drunk. In this sense it seems that anyone who claims that he can recognize omniscience in something he comes across is committed to claiming omniscience for himself. This would not be so if he merely claimed to infer that something is omniscient. For one can infer that something is thus and so without necessarily having any understanding of what it is to be thus and so. Someone who has never even heard of alcohol can infer that Fred is drunk because he is told that if Fred is in the pub, he is drunk, and because he knows that Fred is in the pub.

D. Encountering God by experience

In reply to problems like these, it has been said that some things have to be discovered for the first time, and that God is one of them. It has also been said that when God is encountered he is experienced as defying description or, as it is sometimes put, as being 'ineffable' or 'wholly other'. But these replies do not really engage the fundamental difficulty. Of course I may come across something for the first time. But if I am to know that it is one thing and not something else, I must be able to say that it satisfies a certain description and that I can be aware of it as an object which does this. And the problem is seeing how anyone can say this of God considered simply as an object of experience. And if the answer is that God is ineffable or wholly other, the difficulty is only made worse. How does one ineffable reality differ from another? How can anything wholly other be distinguished from anything at all or from any other wholly other? The very significance of terms like 'ineffable' and 'wholly other', in so far as they are intelligible at all, makes such questions impossible to answer.

Nor will it do to say, as many do, that God can be known simply because he is an object of experience in which the knowledge of God that is given is 'self-authenticating'. This, again, is a common response. The idea is that there just is the experience of being certainly aware that God is there, and that this is enough to warrant one's claim to know that God is there. But we need to distinguish between feeling certain and being right. And the experience of certainty cannot by itself allow us to do this. We often feel certain that something is the case. Sometimes we are right, and sometimes we are wrong. But it is not the feeling certain that tells us how things are in any given case. This is not to say that feeling certain and being right cannot go together. I may feel certain that I am looking at Smith, and I may be right. But I cannot conclude that I am right from my feeling of certainty. The feeling, as such, is not evidence of anything. If it were, then we should have to allow that all sorts of things which we know to be false are actually true. Thus, if 'Fred feels certain that such and such is the case' is enough to warrant 'Such and such is the case', it follows that if the drug addict feels certain that there is a purple cow in the room, then there is a purple cow in the room.

Yet if all this is accepted, one might ask how it is that we come to know anything at all by experience. Are we committed to a self-refuting scepticism, as some have claimed? There is a book in front of me on the table. Can I not know this just by being aware of the book? And must this not be taken into account with reference to the suggestion that God is known by experience?

Well, indeed it is true that I am entitled to say that I know the book is there because I can see it. But this does not mean that I have some infallible faculty of 'knowing-a-book-by-experience'. The fact, of course, is that I already know something of books when I find myself in the situation of saying things like 'I know there's a book there because I can see it'. And not only that. I know something of my situation when I say such things. I know, for example, that I am not short-sighted, or drunk, or hypnotized, or liable to hallucinations. And it is by appealing to some or all of this that I can reasonably say 'I know of the book by experience'. In other words, the evidential value of an experience depends on the context of the experience and cannot be determined by the experience itself. Imagine me saying 'I just know' when asked how I know that there is a book in front of me. You would assume I meant something like 'I'm not drunk, and books have that kind of appearance and texture, and the light is good', and so on. But suppose I say: 'I don't mean that at all. I just mean that I just know'. The reply makes no sense. Whether or not one knows is determined by what it is one says one knows and the reasons that can be adduced for saying that one knows in any particular case. There is no need to deny that one can be certain of things. There is no need to deny that one can be rationally justified in saying that something is there because it seems to be there. But one can deny that knowing is a special state of mind that can be recognized in the having of it and treated as something that guarantees that things are as one says they are. Recognizing that something is the case is a complex business which depends on what one already takes to be the case and on what others already take to be the case. And knowing that something is the case means being in a position to identify what is there, which, in turn, is not something that can be brought about by one's state of mind at the time when one says that such and such is the case.

Experience of God and testimony

It would seem, then, that one may indeed doubt whether God can be known to exist simply because he is an object of experience. Experience is something we can generally rely on, perhaps. But one may question whether it can serve to tell us that it is God we experience. And this point now allows us to comment on the view that even those with no experience of God have reason to believe in God because of the testimony of others. For if one may doubt that anyone can recognize God as an object of experience, one may doubt whether many people can, and hence one may doubt that their testimony is indeed to be taken as evidence of God's existence.

But it would also, perhaps, be reasonable to add a qualification to this point. For one may surely be aware of what one cannot recognize for what it is. In that case, however, though God may not be recognizable for what he is as an object of experience, it does not follow that one cannot be aware of him or that he cannot be an object of experience. One might therefore wonder whether agreement between those who report experience of God should not be considered relevant support for belief in God.

An objection sometimes made to this suggestion is that there is not, in fact, a notable agreement among those who report experience of God. Others have said that such agreement as there is need not prove anything since there may be slight differences between the experiences on which it is based, and these might be all-important. And one can sympathize with these points. Many reported experiences of God are described in terms which are notably vague. And slight differences between what looks or sounds the same can, indeed, be crucial. There is different significance, but much visual similarity, in the printed words 'No talking' and 'No walking'. The sentences 'He adored his wife' and 'He abhorred his wife' sound similar, but mean different things. Yet there is still enough *prima facie* agreement among those who talk about experience of God to convince at least some who have studied the matter that similar elements can be detected in reports of those who claim experience of God. A case for agreement here can be made. And, though small differences can matter, it would normally be conceded that when many people agree in their reports concerning what they have come across, we have some reason to suppose that what is said to have been encountered was actually there. So why not suppose that agreement between reports of experience of God is evidence for God? Some would bluntly reply that God is non-material and what is non-material cannot be an object of experience. But one may ask whether this response simply expresses a prejudice against non-material objects of experience. We distinguish between objects of experience in the physical world with reference to their materiality, but it does not therefore follow that there is no possible non-material object of experience. All that follows is that one would not be able to pick it out as material.

On the other hand, one is still left with the problem of being able to know that it is God who has been encountered when one thinks that one has experience of God, or when others say that they have had this. And this problem does not disappear because of an increase in numbers on the part of those who claim to know God by experience. Nor does it disappear if we concede that there can be non-material objects of experience. Even if there are such things, we can still ask how any of them can be recognized by people as divine.

So perhaps the best thing to say is that, though there may be experience which indeed has God as its object, we cannot know that there is such experience in a way that would allow us to argue that because of the experience it is more reasonable than not to believe in God. In other words, the Argument from Experience is not a conclusive argument for the existence of God.

THE ARGUMENT FROM MORALITY

But what of the Argument from Morality? Like other arguments we have looked at, it takes different forms. The most famous or popular of them, however, propound three theses:

(1) Morality needs God to achieve its end.
(2) If there is no God, there is no point in being moral.
(3) Moral experience implies the existence of God.

Let us consider each thesis in order.

(1) God and the end of morality

The most famous philosophical defender of our first view is Immanuel Kant, who develops his case in the *Critique of Practical Reason* (1788). There is some controversy concerning the true nature of Kant's position, for some of his remarks suggest that he is not so much saying that morality gives us any knowledge of God as that we cannot help but bring in the idea of God when we reflect on morality. But, whatever the truth of the matter, Kant does offer a recognizable argument for God's existence based on what he takes to be the end of morality.

According to Kant, as moral beings we must strive to act morally. And this, he says, means that we must strive for the highest good (the *summum bonum*). 'The achievement of the highest good in the world is the necessary object of a will determined by the moral law', says Kant (p. 134). 'The moral law', he adds, 'commands us to make the highest possible good in a world the final object of all our conduct' (p. 134).

But what is this 'highest good'? Some might say that the highest possible good would be for each person to aim at what is morally desirable. And, at one level, Kant does not disagree. As he puts it in his *Foundations of the Metaphysics of Morals* (1785): 'Nothing in the world . . . can possibly be conceived which could be called good without qualification except a *good will*' (p. 11).

But Kant also thinks that things will not be really right until those who aim at what is right are themselves happy. For, he says, 'to be in need of happiness and also worthy of it and yet not to partake of it could not be in accordance with the complete volition of an omnipotent rational being' (p. 115). If one deserves to be happy, one will, Kant thinks, naturally strive to ensure one's happiness. For Kant, therefore, the highest good, properly so called, implies happiness proportionate to moral rectitude. And he thinks that we are morally bound to strive for this. We must will the *summum bonum*.

Yet the trouble, of course, is that we cannot by ourselves ensure that virtue and happiness will coincide as they ought. We are part of a world which we cannot fully control and which does not ensure that virtue is properly rewarded. And, for this reason, says Kant, we can postulate the existence of God. Morality requires the realization of the supreme good, but that can only be brought about by God.

The acting rational being in the world is not at the same time the cause of the world and of nature itself. Hence there is not the slightest ground in the moral law for a necessary connection between the morality and proportionate happiness of a being which belongs to the world as one of its parts and as thus dependent on it. Not being nature's cause, his will cannot of its own strength bring nature, as it touches on his happiness, into complete harmony with his practical principles. Nevertheless . . . in the necessary endeavour after the highest good, such a connection is postulated as necessary: we *should* seek to further the highest good (which therefore must at least be possible). Therefore also the existence is postulated of a cause of the whole of nature, itself distinct from nature, which contains the ground of the exact coincidence of happiness with morality. . . As a consequence the possibility of a highest derived good (the best world) is at the same time the postulate of the reality of the highest original good, namely, the existence of God. . . Therefore, it is morally necessary to assume the existence of God (pp. 129–30).

Is Kant right?

Those who find something to commend Kant's argument usually focus on its major assumption – that virtue must be rewarded. How intolerable, they say, that a lack of justice should prevail in the end. Surely, we can and must believe that those who are truly virtuous will enjoy happiness in proportion to their virtue. Would life not be ultimately absurd otherwise?

But though questions like this may move us at an emotional level, though we might indeed find ourselves unable to accept that the end for the righteous is not what they deserve, there is an obvious difficulty to be faced. For, unless we already have reason to believe in God, why should we suppose that there will be a final balance of virtue and happiness? If this is indeed going to come about, one might naturally expect to find signs of it in what has already happened. One might suppose that history will give reason to expect an eventual balance of virtue and happiness. The trouble, however, is that we just do not find this. For many morally admirable people have simply been crushed. And many of those who can fairly be regarded as morally vile have lived to flourish over them. As the author of the book of Job puts it:

It is all one; therefore I say,
  he destroys both the blameless and the wicked.
When disaster brings sudden death,
  he mocks at the calamity of the innocent.
The earth is given into the hand of the wicked (Job 9:22–24).

One may, of course, find this situation unbearable. And one may, perhaps, be less pessimistic than the author of the book of Job. But there is truth in what he writes, and one may, with some reason, rhetorically ask what reason there is, apart from any belief in God that we may have, to suppose that disaster is not indeed the end of the story for many.

This, however, is not a decisive objection to Kant. For he does, after all, allow that 'the acting rational being in the world is not at the same time the cause of the world and of nature itself'. And he recognizes that 'not being nature's cause, his will cannot of its own strength bring nature into complete harmony with his practical principles'. It is, one must concede, part of Kant's argument that virtue is not always properly rewarded in the world.

But can we now accept Kant's reasoning for supposing that it must be rewarded in spite of the way the world goes?

Here we come to a major difficulty in Kant's position. For, according to him, the fact that the highest good is possible implies that it will come about. Yet that, surely, is false. All sorts of things which could have come to pass have not come to pass. Why, then, should we suppose that the highest good will come about just because it is possible?

A likely reply to this question would focus on the notion of obligation. For what do we imply when we say that someone should do something? It looks as though we imply that the person could do what we specify. There is a famous philosophical slogan (accepted by Kant) which runs: 'Ought implies can'. And this slogan seems to express a truth. It would, for example, be odd to suggest that people should fly like birds, or that infants should write books on nuclear physics. And, with this point in mind, someone might try to defend Kant by noting that people ought to try to bring about the highest good. In that case, however, it would seem that they can bring it about. And Kant would seem justified in postulating something that will help them to do this.

But the argument is mistaken. For from 'We ought to try to bring about the highest good' it only follows that we can try to bring about the highest good. It does not follow that we can actually bring it about. An objector can therefore maintain that Kant's argument suffers from a fatal weakness. It assumes that the highest good can be brought about by us since we should seek the highest good. But what it ought to be saying is that the highest good is something we can seek.

Even so, if we really should be seeking the highest good, does it not follow that the highest good is something more than a thing that we can simply seek to bring about? Suppose I say: 'You should seek to learn French'. Would that make sense if I have good reason to suppose that nothing you can do will result in you speaking or understanding French? If I say that you should seek to learn French, must I not presume that you can learn French as well as that you can seek to learn French? And is not that what Kant is basically saying? What if we have reason to think that we cannot bring about the highest good without God? Ought we not therefore to conclude that it makes no sense to think that we should even try to bring it about? And, if we think that we should try to bring it about, must we not therefore suppose that we can bring it about with God?

Yet this line of reasoning is also of little help as a defence of Kant's argument. For it does make sense to suppose that people should try to do what we know that they cannot do. I may know, as many teachers do, that my pupil will never master French. Yet I may rationally suppose that he should try to master the language since I may rationally suppose that this will help him in some way, or that it may be of some use to others. And, by the same token, I may rationally suppose that we should try to bring about the highest good even though I know that we cannot actually bring it about, or even if I doubt that we can. What if aiming to bring about the highest good will bring about all sorts of other goods? Would that not give us a reason for supposing that we ought to try to bring it about? Again, it seems, we are back to where we were two paragraphs ago. Maybe we should aim for the highest good, but whether we can bring it about is another matter. And if someone insists that we ought not to aim for it if we cannot bring it about, there is, of course, another obvious answer. Perhaps we ought not to aim for it. Kant, indeed, assumes that this is false, but his own argument can clearly be turned against him at this point. He maintains that only if God exists can we bring about the highest good, that we can bring about the highest good since we ought to bring it about, and that God therefore exists. But why not argue that only if God exists can we bring about the highest good, that God does not exist, and that therefore we cannot bring about the highest good and it is false that we ought to bring it about?

And even if we do not argue like this, there is a further and final difficulty with Kant's own argument. For let us suppose that we ought to bring about the highest good, that we can bring it about, and that we can only bring it about if we are helped to do so by what is able to rectify or nullify the unjust course of events that history apparently reveals to us as the lot of many virtuous people. Why should we also suppose that nothing but God can enable us to bring about the highest good? Why not something both anxious and able to help us, but also less than divine? Why not something akin to the concept of an *eldil* as introduced in those novels of C. S. Lewis that make up his famous Silent Planet Trilogy? Why not something akin to the traditional notion of an angel? Why not an angel of great power and of highly developed sympathy to Kantian principles?

Kant, in fact, makes an enormous leap here. For even if we concede that God could ensure that the highest good is achieved by us on condition that we go for it, it does not follow that only God could ensure it. As philosophers might say, Kant is here confusing a sufficient condition with a necessary condition. He is supposing that what *could* bring about, or help to bring about, the highest good, is *needed* to bring about the highest good. And, even if we are generous to Kant, we have no grounds in his argument for supposing anything other than 'the possible existence of a wholly good and all-powerful governor of the world' (Mackie 1982, p. 109). And the question that arises is whether or not that is enough to allow us to conclude that God exists.

The answer is surely 'No'. Someone who believes in God can certainly say that by 'God' he means a wholly good and all-powerful governor of the world. That is at least part of what 'God' has meant in the mouths of those who have professed to believe in God. The believer may therefore say that Kant's argument provides some support for belief in God. But belief in God traditionally includes the belief that God is the Creator. And there is nothing in Kant's argument that shows that we need to believe in the existence of a Creator. Being able to govern something does not necessarily involve being able to account for its existence. It does not necessarily involve being its maker. In this respect, therefore, Kant's argument stands together with the Argument from Design. It may support belief in God, but it cannot, by itself, establish the truth of this belief.

(2) Why be moral?

Although Kant thought that morality needs God if what it requires is ultimately to be achieved, he did not think that moral requirements lack force without God. It is, he says, 'not to be understood that the assumption of the existence of God is necessary as the ground of all obligation in general' for there are obligations which rest 'solely on the autonomy of reason itself' (*Critique of Practical Reason*, p. 130). But the second form of the Moral Argument takes a different line. Friedrich Nietzsche (1844–1900) once implied that in the absence of God everything is permitted (*The Genealogy of Morals*, Third Essay, XXIV), and, though they might not agree with the details of Nietzsche's position, others have said something similar. It has, for example, been argued that it only makes sense to be moral on the assumption that one will finally be rewarded. Then, so it is argued, since one's reward cannot be guaranteed without God, the presumption of atheism leaves morality without ultimate justification. If the world is really godless, so it is urged, we do not have sufficient reason for acting morally. In this connection some have appealed especially to the possibility of total self-sacrifice. There have been atheists who have been prepared to sacrifice everything they have, including their lives, on behalf of others. But, so the argument goes, such absolute self-sacrifice is fundamentally irrational if there is, indeed, no God.

Morals without God?

But is it? And is it in general true that one only has reason to be moral if one shall be rewarded in some way?

At least one influential tradition of moral thinking would quickly reply in the negative. And it would justify itself on the ground that the contrary verdict simply misconceives the nature of moral motivation. According to this tradition, which one especially associates with Kant, the reason for acting morally is that one ought to act morally. It is a question of duty for the sake of duty. Someone may do his duty because it will, in some way, pay him to do so. He may do it, for instance, because he knows that someone will reward him. But, according to writers like Kant, he will not be doing his duty for the right reason. For that he would have to do his duty for the sake of doing his duty. On this account, therefore, it would be quite wrong to suppose that one can only justify adherence to moral principles on the assumption that God exists as a rewarder of moral behaviour. That would be to look to something beyond moral requirements, something to give one a reason for paying attention to them, while the truth of the matter is that recognizing a moral requirement for what it is cannot be distinguished from recognizing that one already has a reason for paying attention to it. In short,

'You ought because you ought, and whether or not God exists is beside the point'. Or, as Kant put it: 'The first proposition of morality is that to have moral worth an action must be done from duty' (*Foundations of the Metaphysics of Morals*, p. 19).

Yet, as others have pointed out, this line of thinking is profoundly unsatisfactory. Why should I accept that I *just ought* to do or not do something? What is the force of the appeal to duty for the sake of duty? Suppose I run a club in which one of the rules is that one should always wear a flower pot on one's head. Someone asks me why he should bother with this rule, and I reply 'Because the rule says so'. Cannot my interlocutor fairly reject my reply? Can he not ask for a reason beyond the rule which will make it sensible for him to obey it? And cannot one do the same when people tell us that we should do our duty just because it is our duty?

It can, indeed, be conceded that there is an important distinction between someone who is, say, genuinely charitable, and someone who only practises a show of charity in order to win a reputation. But do we have to express truths like this by saying that, for example, one should only be charitable because one should be charitable? And, if the answer is 'Yes', what do we do if someone feels obliged to do something which we regard as morally despicable? What if he thinks it his duty to massacre innocent people because he has received a military order to do so? What if he says 'You just ought to obey your leader's commands'? Is it enough for us to say 'You just ought not to obey certain commands'? Is that the best we can say?

In fact, of course, it is not. For if someone asks why he should or should not do something it makes perfectly good sense to appeal to something that the questioner needs. And this is precisely what yet another major tradition of moral thinking has argued. I refer here to what we may loosely call the Aristotelian tradition of moral thinking, whose spokesmen look back to or are influenced by patterns of argument found in the ethical theory of Aristotle (384–322 B.C.). In terms of this, we should concentrate not on any supposed sense that one *just must* or *just must not* do certain things; we should concentrate instead on what people need to flourish or function well, on what they need to be happy, on what they need considered as human beings. And since people do need various things, since they cannot function well without certain things and since certain things help them to function well, this proposal for thinking about morality is eminently reasonable. To follow the line of duty for the sake of duty leaves us in the end with a mysterious and arbitrary judgement: 'You just ought'. And matters are different if one pays attention to what people need.

But not only that. For by paying attention to what people need one is able to give them reasons for their behaviour, or for the behaviour one recommends to them, which do not necessarily involve reference to God.

This brings us back to our immediate concern. For, even if we reject the appeal to duty, we can still make sense of acting morally independently of belief in God. And we can do so with regard to what people need.

Take, for example, the view that we should strive to be just. That is a common enough moral principle, but do we need to refer to God to see that it is worth adhering to? No. Unjust societies are a threat to their members, who have good reason to be just if they want to survive and enjoy the many benefits that we know to be possible only in a just society. Quite apart from any truth about God, therefore, people have reason to be just. And they also have reason to be other things that are recognizably moral. Two traditional virtues are temperance and courage, but we do not need to refer to God in order to give people good reason to be temperate and courageous. If they are not temperate, they are likely to damage their health, either by excessive indulgence or by excessive abstinence. If they have no courage at all, they are likely to find themselves notably constricted in their day-to-day lives. 'Courage is constantly needed in the ordinary course of the world. . . For a start . . . people would often not be born but for the courage of their mothers. . . Nobody who was thoroughly cowardly would play physically demanding games, or climb a mountain, or ride a horse or a bicycle' (Geach 1977a, pp. 151ff.). One can always, of course, observe that being, for example, just or courageous may not in some particular case benefit the person who is trying to be just or courageous. Justice can lead one to death, and the same is conceivable with temperance and courage. But this is not to say that people do not need to be just, temperate, or courageous. 'An individual bee may perish by stinging, all the same bees need stings; an individual man may perish by being brave or just, all the same men need courage and justice' (Geach 1977a, p. 17). People do need these virtues and we do not have to be particularly learned to see why. In this sense, therefore, we can indeed give reason for behaving morally which makes no reference to belief in God. And, for this reason if for no other, we are therefore bound to reject the second form of the Moral Argument. Even if God does not exist, there is reason to be moral.

(3)   The nature of moral experience and the existence of God

We come, then, to the last form of the Moral Argument – that the nature of moral experience implies the existence of God. This argument has itself taken different forms, but these are usefully brought together by H. P. Owen in his book *The Moral Argument for Christian Theism*, to which we can therefore now refer. In this book Owen offers four distinct arguments for the existence of God based on moral experience.

(a) *Moral claims are not self-explanatory*. According to Owen, claims ordinarily imply a claimant, and laws ordinarily imply a lawgiver. If this is not the case with moral claims and laws, they are totally enigmatic. 'Either we take moral claims to be self-explanatory modes of impersonal existence or we explain them in terms of a personal God' (p. 50). Owen allows that 'the first of these alternatives cannot be ruled out'. But, he continues, the second alternative is more satisfactory given the personal source of ordinary claims and commands (p. 50).

(b) *Moral obedience implies God*. In responding to the claims of morality, says Owen, we respond to claims which 'transcend every person and every personal embodiment' (p. 53). Yet 'we value the personal more highly than the impersonal; so that it is contradictory to assert that impersonal claims are entitled to the allegiance of our wills' (p. 53). We may therefore suppose, Owen concludes, that 'the order of claims, while it appears as impersonal from a purely moral point of view, is in fact rooted in the personality of God' (p. 53).

(c) *People and their worth*. According to Owen, people have intrinsic worth. They exert absolute claims, and we owe them unlimited respect. But they are not infinitely good. They are often quite sinful. 'We are therefore', says Owen, 'driven to suppose that human persons exert their distinctive claim on account of their relation to a moral Absolute' (p. 55). And this relation must be interpreted in terms of God. The worth of human persons, Owen suggests, 'consists in the fact that they are created, loved, and destined for eternal life by God' (p. 56).

(d) *Reverence, responsibility, and guilt*. According to Owen's last argument, reverence and responsibility to the moral law, together with the sense of guilt at transgressing it, can be made intelligible if it is supposed that in responding to the moral law we are responding to what is fundamentally personal. As Owen himself puts it:

One cannot (morally) devote oneself to an object that is less than personal. . . . To be responsible involves the idea of a person or persons to whom responsibility is due. . . . If in the finite and visible sphere our sense of guilt is proportionate to our betrayal of human persons, and if in this sphere we never find the same sense engendered by reflection on our treatment of mere 'things', we may reasonably conclude that our shame at having violated the moral law is due to the fact that we are in the presence of a holy lawgiver (pp. 57ff.)

In defence of Owen

But can we only make adequate sense of moral experience on the assumption that God exists? Much will clearly depend here on how we conceive of moral experience, but if we conceive of it as Owen does, then the interpretation of it that he recommends is surely not implausible. Let us just concentrate on two reasons for saying this.

The first has to do with what we can infer on the basis of moral claims or laws. According to Owen, we find ourselves confronted by moral claims or laws which are not created by us, but which still warrant our respect or obedience. Not everyone would accept that, but suppose, for the moment, we do. In that case, it seems reasonable to seek some explanation for the fact. And once we try to do that, it makes sense to argue as Owen does. For it is true that claims and laws generally do imply claimants and lawgivers, and if moral experience presents us with moral claims and moral laws, it therefore seems natural and reasonable to take them as evidence of a moral claimant or a moral lawgiver. There is nothing esoteric or complicated about this. It is just that claims and laws do imply claimants and lawgivers, in which case it seems sensible to argue that moral claims and laws imply the same.

Then again, there is the issue of obedience and the recognition of guilt. When a ball falls to the ground it could be said to obey the law of gravity. So we can speak of obedience where its object is not personal. But it does not make sense to speak in this way where what is in question is conscious obedience. We would not talk of being consciously obedient to the law of gravity or to any other law of nature. For this reason, therefore, Owen's second argument has some force. Conscious obedience naturally implies one to whom one is obedient. If we insist that in trying to be moral we are consciously trying to be obedient, it looks as though we ought to concede that we are *ipso facto* trying to be obedient to somebody. And a similar point can be made with respect to the notion of moral guilt. The notion of guilt is a juridical one and someone who accepts that he is guilty would normally be understood as conceding that he has transgressed a law or rule laid down by someone or by many people. If someone accepts that he is morally guilty, therefore, it seems natural to say that he ought also to accept that he is guilty before someone. One may, of course, deny that the word 'guilty' has any proper place when what is in question is moral wrongdoing. One may, as many do, say that doing what is morally bad is not in any meaningful sense to be guilty. But, insofar as one concedes that it does involve guilt, it looks as though one concedes what Owen is arguing. To agree that people are morally guilty seems to suggest that there is someone before whom they are guilty. If one does not wish to imply that, then why use a word like 'guilty' in this context? How can you be guilty before anything less than a personal source of laws or commands?

Another view

In this sense, then, Owen's position has some merit. Given that in being moral we are responding to real laws and claims, and given that we do not create these ourselves, we have reason to infer that moral experience depends on a personal source of moral laws and claims. Given, too, that moral failure involves real guilt, it seems natural to suppose that the moral life is one lived in the constant presence of one before whom we are guilty. But should we concede these crucial assumptions? Is moral experience what Owen takes it to be?

A standard answer that some have adopted (you can find it in Hume, but also in the work of subsequent moral philosophers such as the Emotivists and the Prescriptivists) and that it is not, since moral judgements basically only express or reflect our personal tastes or attitudes. On this account, there are no real moral claims or laws; there are simply people saying what they approve of or what they dislike. And if this view is right, then of course it will follow that no such case as Owen's can hope to get off the ground. If morality is finally a matter of taste, then it is clearly best accounted for in terms of what it is that makes people feel about things in the way that they do. And it is by no means obvious that any such account will lead us to infer the existence of God.

But even if we reject this alternative we can still make sense of morality without recourse to notions like 'law' and 'claim', and without supposing that to fail from the moral point of view is indeed to be guilty in any recognizably juridical sense. For instead of saying that there is a moral law to which we are bound, we can say that some ways of acting are ones which we have more reason to adopt than others. And instead of referring to moral claims, we can speak of what it makes sense for us to do or not to do. And instead of alluding to moral guilt, we can speak of our failure to do what we have reason to do.

It should, in fact, be clear to the reader already that Owen's whole position rests on an approach to morality reminiscent of Kant. Owen begins from the supposition that there just are moral requirements and that we just are bound to act in accordance with them. But this is something we can rationally call into question. Why should we simply accept the existence of moral claims or requirements? Why should we accept that we are confronted by moral demands or obligations? Owen's answer is that we simply recognize their existence. Yet, as we know very well, people differ widely over what they take to be morally binding and the like. The Sense of Duty has led to remarkably divergent conclusions about what is morally right and wrong. So how are we to determine truth in this area? Must we rely only on our private convictions about what morality requires? Or can we appeal to rational con-siderations which do not just amount to a reiteration of how we, as individuals, happen to see things morally speaking?

I have already indicated how I think we can set about answering these questions. As writers like Aristotle have urged, in talking about how people ought to behave we can talk about virtues. And we can justify our judgements about the need for these by appealing to what people need. Here there need be no final reference to laws or claims which are just recognized to be mysteriously hanging over us and which then need to be accounted for in terms of lawgivers or claimants other than human beings. There need, at bottom, be nothing more than the recognition that if we wish to achieve certain goals, if we wish, in fact, to be virtuous, we will need to act in such and such a way, or we will need to avoid acting in such and such a way.

And in that case, of course, moral requirements need no such explanation as that proposed by Owen. If you want to be a good athlete, there are activities you will need to pursue and others you will need to avoid. You will need, for example, to exercise regularly and to refrain from smoking and overeating. Do we then have to account for this fact in terms of God? Not unless we have independent reason for believing in God and for supposing that it is by virtue of him that athletes need what they need. Once you understand what being an athlete involves, you can see why athletes should do or not do certain things, and you can account for this fact in terms of the nature of athletes. And the same sort of thing applies when it comes to morality. We can give people reasons for being moral, and we can do so in terms of what they need. I therefore suggest at this point that one can indeed make sense of moral experience without recourse to God. In reply to arguments like those of Owen one can say this. The arguments have some force if one accepts the approach to moral experience on which they are based. But we do not have to accept this approach, and we can make sense of moral judgements not in terms of God but in terms of virtue. People need virtues, and we can see that they do without also seeing that God exists.

God and morality

The upshot would therefore seem to be that the Argument from Morality is unsuccessful. But it is, perhaps, also worth noting that this does not entail that God is irrelevant to our concerns as moral individuals. Morality may not give us reason to believe in God, but it still remains possible that there would be no morality without God.

There is a famous question derived from a problem posed by Plato (c. 428–348 B.C.) in his dialogue *Euthyphro*. The question runs: Is X morally good because God wills it, or does God will X because it is morally good? This is meant to constitute an embarrassing dilemma for someone who wishes to assert that morality somehow follows from God and might therefore be evidence of his existence. The dilemma consists in this. If one says that X is morally good because God wills it, that would seem to make moral truth arbitrarily dependent on mere *fiat*. Surely, so it is argued, what is morally good cannot be constituted by someone's will, not even by God's. What if God willed us to massacre people indiscriminately? Would that make the action right? On the other hand, so the argument continues, if God wills X because it is morally good, moral standards are independent of God's will and God is therefore irrelevant to moral concerns.

Now if what I have argued is correct, we cannot hold that moral judgements depend on there being a God. That is to say, we do not need to suppose that God exists in order to see that there is reason to be moral. But this does not entail that God must be irrelevant to moral concerns or that it is false that X is morally good because of God's will. Consider the following analogy.

A scientist is trying to discover how best to cure a certain illness. He discovers a cure and therefore declares that God is irrelevant to the concerns of the scientist. Would he be right? Yes, in that one can do science without presupposing the existence of God. But no if it is true that God exists as Creator of the universe. For if that is the case, then science depends on God in at least two ways. The data studied by scientists will owe their existence to God. And the same will be true of the scientists who study the data.

Now consider the case of morality. With no assumption that God exists, a moralist may urge, for example, that people should be just. But if God exists as Creator of the universe, it will be by virtue of him that people are there to debate about justice. And it will also be by virtue of him that their arguments will have any force. Reasons for being just will have to refer to what justice in reality amounts to, and, if God is the Creator, that will again depend on God – at any rate, insofar as it is human justice that we are talking about. Here God would be relevant to moral concerns in two ways. The data studied by moralists will owe their existence to God. And the same will be true of those who study the data.

The point to grasp is that even though moral judgements need not by themselves presuppose or imply the existence of God, it may only be because of God that moral judgements are possible. Someone can therefore accept what I have said against the Argument from Morality, and still concede that morality is not independent of God. And that is worth noting since it has, indeed, been assumed that if morality is not evidence for the existence of God, it is also independent of God. Yet that conclusion does not follow. Nor could it be true if God is the Creator. For, in that case, what we are and what we do will depend on God as the cause of the fact that we are able to do things.

Yet with reference to the Argument from Morality we are still left with a negative note. Like the Argument from Experience, the Argument from Morality is not enough to show that it is more reasonable than not to believe in God. And this is, perhaps, inevitable. For morality, of course, has very largely to do with how we should behave or what ought to be the case. And it is hard to see how knowledge of this (supposing that there is such a thing) can yield information about how things are. From 'Every man ought to be just' and 'Fred is a man' I may conclude that Fred ought to be just. But I cannot conclude that Fred is just or that he will be just. Why, then, should one suppose that we can conclude that God exists given how people ought to behave or given what ought to be the case? If all men should worship God, and if Fred is a man, then Fred ought to worship God. But this argument will not show that God exists. Either it will assume God's existence, or it will show what is true of men, including Fred, if God exists. And so on with regard to other arguments about how one ought to behave. 'To use a conjunction of practical judgements to try to establish what the facts are would be to put the cart before the horse. We must rely on speculative reasoning to determine what is the case, and then frame our practical and moral beliefs and attitudes in the light of these facts' (Mackie 1982, p. 113). What morality requires may depend on God, but whether God exists may not be discovered simply by a knowledge of what morality requires unless it is known to require what cannot be required unless God exists. The Argument from Morality holds that morality requires the existence of God, and that may in some sense be true. But whether or not it is true remains unproved by the Argument itself and must, at best, be assumed by the Argument. At this point, therefore, we can leave it and turn to other matters.

QUESTIONS FOR DISCUSSION

1 Can one distinguish between knowing by inference and knowing by experience? If so, is one of these ways of knowing superior to the other?
2 What kind of difference must there be between knowing of the existence of God by experience, and knowing of the existence of anything else?
3 How would you determine whether you seem to experience what is really there? How would you determine the same for somebody else?
4 What explanation would you offer in accounting for someone's conviction that God is an object of his or her experience?
5 How could one recognize God as an object of one's experience?
6 Must justice prevail in the end?
7 Can an atheist be moral?
8 Why should I do my duty?
9 Could there be ethics without God?
10 Must God be bound by moral considerations?

FURTHER READING

Those approaching the topic of experience of God for the first time will find an excellent introduction to relevant issues and writers in Peter Donovan, *Interpreting Religious Experience* (London, 1979). This is a short book, but it is also informative and cogent. The same goes for T. R. Miles, *Religious Experience* (London, 1972), which is also intended as introductory. Both Donovan and Miles provide helpful bibliographical information.

There are several good collections of writings each of which contains useful material relevant to the topic of experience of God. Richard Woods (ed.), *Understanding Mysticism* (New York, 1980) comprises a variety of extracts by important authors some of whom offer philosophical and theological appraisals of the claim that God can be known as an object of experience. Also worth noting are: S. Hook (ed.), *Religious Experience and Truth* (New York, 1961), Steven T. Katz (ed.), *Mysticism and Philosophical Analysis* (London, 1978) and *Mysticism and Religious Traditions* (Oxford, 1983), and William L. Rowe and William J. Wainwright (eds), *Philosophy of Religion: Selected Readings* (New York, 1973), section IV.

Two classic discussions of God and experience of God are William James, *The Varieties of Religious Experience* (London/Glasgow, 1960), and Rudolf Otto, *The Idea of the Holy* (Oxford, 1923). More recent and philosophically orientated treatments of the topic include the following:

John Baillie, *Our Knowledge of God* (London, 1949).
H. D. Lewis, *Our Experience of God* (London, 1959).
H. P. Owen, *The Christian Knowledge of God* (London, 1969).
Illtyd Trethowan, *Mysticism and Theology* (London, 1975).

These volumes are largely in favour of the notion that it is reasonable to believe in God because God is an object of experience. And this is the position of parts of two other books worth mentioning: Richard Swinburne, *The Existence of God* (Oxford, 1979), ch. 13, and Gary Gutting, *Religious Belief and Religious Skepticism* (Notre Dame/London, 1982), ch. 5. Swinburne places particular emphasis on what he calls the 'principle of credulity', which he defends with reference to arguments of R. M. Chisholm's *Perception* (Ithaca, N.Y., 1957). Gutting is critical of Swinburne, but he defends the Argument from Experience with reference to several standard critiques including those derived from psychology and sociology.

For recent criticisms of the Argument from Experience, see the following:

Antony Flew, *God and Philosophy* (London, 1966), ch. 6.
Anthony O'Hear, *Experience, Explanation and Faith* (London, 1984), ch. 2.
R. Hepburn, *Christianity and Paradox* (London, 1958).
John Mackie, *The Miracle of Theism* (Oxford, 1982), ch. 10.
W. Matson, *The Existence of God* (Ithaca, N.Y., 1965).

Many useful articles on the subject of experience and God could be cited, but particularly worthy of note are:

H. J. N. Horsburgh, 'The Claims of Religious Experience', *Australasian Journal of Philosophy* 35 (1957).
C. B. Martin, 'A Religious Way of Knowing' in A. Flew and A. MacIntyre (eds), *New Essays in Philosophical Theology* (London, 1955).
Simon Tugwell OP, 'Faith and Experience I–XII', *New Blackfriars* (August 1978–February 1980).

It should go without saying that the issue of experience and God also needs to be discussed with some attention to general issues in the field of the theory of knowledge. Beginners in this area can profit from the articles and bibliography in A. P. Griffiths (ed.), *Knowledge and Belief* (Oxford, 1967). Also worth consulting are standard general introductions to philosophy, such as A. R. Lacey, *Modern Philosophy* (Boston/London/Henley, 1982). Very much worth pondering on the whole question of knowledge and justification is Ludwig Wittgenstein, *On Certainty* (Oxford, 1974).

For general and not too technical discussions of the Argument from Morality, see in particular the following:

John Hick, *Arguments for the Existence of God* (London, 1970), ch. 4.
W. D. Hudson, *A Philosophical Approach to Religion* (London, 1974), ch. 3.
H. P. Owen, *The Moral Argument for Christian Theism* (London, 1965).
John Mackie, *The Miracle of Theism* (Oxford, 1982), ch. 6.
W. G. Maclagan, *The Theological Frontier of Ethics* (London, 1961).

For a particularly famous development of the argument based on conscience, see John Henry Newman, *A Grammar of Assent* (Notre Dame/London, 1979). For a defence of the view that moral experience is an awareness of God (and hence that the Moral Argument and the Argument from Experience come together), see Illtyd Trethowan, *Absolute Value* (London, 1970).

There are two good collections of essays or extracts on the question of the relationship between morality and religion, especially belief in God. These are Ian T. Ramsey (ed.), *Christian Ethics and Contemporary Philosophy* (London, 1966), and Paul Helm (ed.), *Divine Commands and Morality* (Oxford, 1981). The second of these volumes has an excellent bibliography.

Serious treatment of the Moral Argument naturally leads to discussion of the nature of moral judgement. Beginners in moral philosophy can here profitably consult such introductions to the subject as the following:

D. D. Raphael, *Moral Philosophy* (Oxford, 1981).
Richard Brandt, *Ethical Theory* (Englewood Cliffs, N. J., 1959).
Bernard Williams, *Morality: An Introduction to Ethics* (London, 1972).
J. L. Mackie, *Ethics* (Harmondsworth, Middx, 1977).

Each of these volumes is clearly written and represents a way into its subject matter that can be recommended. But the volumes taken together also represent some very different points of view. In addition to them, a particularly good introduction to moral philosophy, one which, as it happens, has much to say in defence of positions I have adopted in the preceding chapter, is John Finnis, *Fundamentals of Ethics* (Oxford, 1983).

For a brief, but solid, survey of ethical theories over the centuries, see Alisdair MacIntyre, *A Short History of Ethics* (New York, 1966).

I have tried to indicate the value of approaching morality via the notion of virtue. Four recent texts are particularly helpful on this notion. All of them are notable contributions to ethical thinking, though, with the exception of the book by Geach, I suspect that beginners might have to work hard with them. They are:

G. E. M. Anscombe, 'Modern Moral Philosophy' in *The Collected Philosophical Papers of G. E. M. Anscombe*, vol. III (Oxford, 1981).
P. T. Geach, *The Virtues* (Cambridge, 1977).
Philippa Foot, *Virtues and Vices* (Oxford, 1978).
Alasdair MacIntyre, *After Virtue* (2nd ed., Notre Dame, 1984).

To understand how moral reasoning can be conducted by a notable religious writer without the suggestion that morality intrinsically depends on God, the reader can usefully turn to the ethical writing of Thomas Aquinas. A good, short introduction to this is Ralph McInerny, *Ethica Thomistica: The Moral Philosophy of Thomas Aquinas* (Washington, D.C., 1982).

4

The Existence of God and the Concept of God

Imagine someone telling you that people exist because 'non-existent person' is a contradiction in terms. You would probably suppose that some kind of joke was being made. At any rate, you would almost certainly reject the argument. As we know very well, people have not always existed. And a suitably organized nuclear war could see to it that they will not exist in the future.

Yet one of the most famous and most discussed arguments for the existence of God goes rather like the argument just imagined. Since the time of Kant, the Argument has commonly been called 'the Ontological Argument', and it resembles the above argument about people because it holds that 'non-existent God' is a contradiction in terms and, therefore, that God exists. As the reader will also note, it resembles the Argument from Contingency discussed in Chapter 1. Here I shall first try to introduce the Argument in some of its better-known versions. Then I shall note without comment some of the standard objections which have been levelled against it. Finally, I shall offer some discussion of the Argument myself.

VERSIONS OF THE ONTOLOGICAL ARGUMENT

As I have said, the Ontological Argument has been one of the most discussed arguments for God's existence. This has led to the Argument being stated and defended in different ways and it means that in trying to introduce the Argument one is forced to be selective. Almost everyone agrees that the first clear statement of the Argument comes in the work of St Anselm of Canterbury (1033–1109). Its next most eminent defenders are Descartes and Leibniz. In the twentieth century it has been notably revived and recommended by Norman Malcolm (1911–), Charles Hartshorne (1897–   )

and Alvin Plantinga (1932–   ). So I shall simply concentrate on the
Argument as it appears in the work of these individuals.

(1) Anselm

Anselm's argument can be found in chapter 2 of his *Proslogion* (1077–78),
where he expressly declares his intention to be that of trying to explain why it
is that God exists as he is believed to do so by people like Anselm himself. It
has been suggested by some that in the *Proslogion* Anselm is not so much
trying to prove God's existence as to indicate what is involved in believing in
God (cf. Barth 1960), and it is true enough that Anselm begins as a believer
and even presents his *Proslogion* in the form of a prayer. Yet the text of
Proslogion 2, together with a reply that Anselm later wrote in response to a
critic of the text (*Reply to Gaunilo*), make it abundantly clear that Anselm is
also trying to offer what we can regard as a philosophical demonstration of
God's existence. And, like all versions of the Ontological Argument, it is one
that turns on the meaning of the word 'God'.

What do we mean by the word? Any serious reader of Anselm will
quickly discover that, for him, the word is rich in meaning. He thinks, for
example, that God is knowing, omnipotent, merciful, impassible (not
subject to pain, change, sorrow, suffering), and eternal. And that, of course,
is a very traditional way of thinking about God. But in *Proslogion* 2 Anselm
begins with a minimal understanding of 'God'. In fact, he takes his cue from
the formula 'something than which nothing greater can be thought' (*aliquid
quo nihil maius cogitari possit*). Whatever else we mean by 'God', Anselm
implies, we can at least agree that God is indeed something than which
nothing greater can be thought. And from this notion or concept of God
Anselm's argument begins.

Consider the case of the atheist. He says that there is no God. But does it
make sense to say 'There is no God'? The nerve of Anselm's argument is that
it does not make sense to say this. The idea here is not just that 'There is no
God' is, as a matter of fact, false. Anselm's view is that it is not even *possibly*
true. Why? Because, so Anselm seems to be saying, 'There is no God' is
contradictory and therefore no more true or false than, say, 'Coal is entirely
black and entirely white' or (perhaps better) 'John is a married bachelor'.

But why should one suppose that this is so? Anselm's argument goes like
this.

Suppose we say 'There is no God'. Then we (even if we are unbelievers) at
least have some notion of God. Or, to put it another way, there is an idea of
God.

But must not God be more than an idea? After all, there are plenty of ideas
of things that do not exist. We can, for example, entertain the notion of there

being such a person as Superman (the American comic hero), even though nobody, except perhaps children, actually believe that he exists. Should we not say, then, that God may be no more than an idea in people's minds?

We might, of course, say that. In fact, that is what an atheist might say. But at this point Anselm moves on to the offensive. For, in his view, while you can consistently say, for example, 'I have an idea of Superman but there is no real Superman', you cannot consistently say 'I have an idea of God, but there is no real God'.

But why not? Here is Anselm's reply.

Surely that-than-which-a-greater-cannot-be-thought cannot exist in the mind alone. For if it exists solely in the mind even, it can be thought to exist in reality also, which is greater. If then that-than-which-a-greater-cannot-be-thought exists in the mind alone, this same that-than-which-a-greater-*cannot*-be-thought is that-than-which-a-greater-*can*-be-thought. But this is obviously impossible. Therefore there is absolutely no doubt that something-than-which-a-greater-cannot-be-thought exists both in the mind and in reality.

In other words, according to Anselm a mere idea of God would not match the minimal understanding of God already given by Anselm. The understanding takes God to be something than which nothing greater can be thought, and Anselm's point seems to be that we can think of something greater than a mere idea. And thus, so Anselm concludes, God must be more than a mere idea. He cannot, as Anselm puts it, exist only in the mind (*in intellectu*). He must really exist apart from people's thoughts. He must, as Anselm puts it, exist actually (*in re*).

For Anselm, then, God must really exist if 'God' means 'Something than which nothing greater can be thought'. In the case of God, so Anselm seems to be saying, definition implies existence, i.e. to say what 'God' means commits one to saying that when we use the word God with understanding we really succeed in referring to something actual. Thus, so Anselm argues, 'God does not exist' has to be false, or, rather, cannot be true. It is not just that God exists; his non-existence is inconceivable. Or, as Anselm puts it right at the beginning of *Proslogion* 3 (of which more below):

And certainly this being so truly exists that it cannot be even thought not to exist. For something can be thought to exist that cannot be thought not to exist, and this is greater than that which can be thought not to exist. Hence, if that-than-which-a-greater-cannot-be-thought can be thought not to exist, then that-than-which-a-greater-cannot-be-thought is not the same as that-than-which-a-greater-cannot-be-thought, which is absurd. Something-than-which-a-greater-cannot-be-thought exists so truly then, that it cannot be even thought not to exist.

(2) Descartes

Descartes's version of the Ontological Argument (found in the fifth of his

Meditations on First Philosophy, the second edition of which appeared in 1642) resembles Anselm's except for two points. Anselm argues that God must really exist (or cannot be thought of as not existing) since he is something than which nothing greater can be thought. Descartes, on the other hand, works from a simpler-sounding formula. For his argument, God is 'a supremely perfect being'. And, while Anselm gives no examples of arguments similar to his own, Descartes provides two, thereby making the logic of his reasoning thoroughly explicit.

So by 'God', then, says Descartes, we mean 'a supremely perfect being'. Yet, Descartes adds, existence is 'a certain perfection'. So Descartes immediately concludes that God must exist. Why? Because if God is supremely perfect, and if existence is a perfection, God must have the perfection of existence (otherwise he would not be supremely perfect). This argument, says Descartes, resembles two others. The first holds that, given the meaning of 'triangle' it follows that the three angles of a triangle are equal to two right angles. The second is that given the idea of a hill, one is forced to think of a valley.

Existence can no more be taken away from the divine essence than the magnitude of its three angles together (that is, their being equal to two right angles) can be taken away from the essence of a triangle, or than the idea of a valley can be taken away from the idea of a hill. So it is not the less absurd to think of God (that is, a supremely perfect being) lacking existence (that is, lacking a certain perfection), than to think of a hill without a valley. . . . I am not free to think of God apart from existence (that is, of a supremely perfect being apart from the supreme perfection) in the way that I can freely imagine a horse either with or without wings. . . . Whenever I choose to think of (*cogitare de*) the First and Supreme Being, and as it were bring out the idea of him from the treasury of my mind, I must necessarily ascribe to him all perfections. . . . This necessity clearly ensures that, when later on I observe that existence is a perfection, I am justified in concluding that the First and Supreme Being exists.

(3) Leibniz

Leibniz's discussion of the Ontological Argument occurs in his *New Essays on Human Understanding* (1765), which is a critical commentary on Locke's *Essay Concerning Human Understanding* (1690). And it begins by expressing firm agreement with Descartes, whose version of the Ontological Argument Leibniz refers to and describes as 'not fallacious' (Book IV, ch. X, 437).

However, Leibniz adds, Descartes's argument 'is an incomplete demonstration'. Leibniz agrees that 'existence is itself a perfection', and he concedes that 'this degree of greatness and perfection . . . which consists in existence is in that wholly great and wholly perfect supreme being [i.e. God] for otherwise he would be lacking in some degree, which is contrary to the definition [sc. of 'God' as 'the most perfect of beings']. And so it follows that

this supreme being exists' (*ibid.*). But first, says Leibniz, it must be acknowledged that the idea of a supremely perfect being is the idea of a *possible* being,
i.e. that there could be something corresponding to Descartes's definition of
God. In other words, according to Leibniz, Descartes's argument 'tacitly
assumed that this idea of a wholly great or wholly perfect being is possible
and does not imply a contradiction' (*ibid.*).

With this reservation made, however, Leibniz then repeats his approval of
Descartes (which he also, incidentally, takes to be an approval of Anselm,
whom he also mentions). And he thinks that the reservation is none too
serious since he does, indeed, believe that Descartes's concept of God is the
concept of something possible. In Leibniz's view, there are good grounds for
belief in God quite apart from the Ontological Argument (cf. Chapter 1). In
his view, therefore, defenders of that argument are entitled to assume that
there could be a God. Leibniz also argues that all perfections can exist in the
same subject (cf. Parkinson 1965, pp. 81f.) and, for this reason too he allows
that the notion of a wholly perfect being implies no contradiction. In any
case, so Leibniz adds:

We are entitled to assume the possibility of any being, and above all of God, until someone
proves the contrary; and so the foregoing metaphysical argument [sc. of Descartes] does
yield a demonstrated moral conclusion, namely that in the present state of our knowledge
we ought to judge that God exists and to act accordingly (*New Essays*, Book IV,
ch. X, 438).

(4) Norman Malcolm

As I have so far reported matters, Anselm's version of the Ontological
Argument basically occurs in chapter 2 of his *Proslogion*. This argument has
been subject to much criticism and Malcolm's approach to the Ontological
Argument begins by accepting some of this. A famous objection to *Proslogion*
2 (one to which we will return shortly) is that it treats existence as a
perfection. Malcolm accepts this objection and therefore thinks that
Proslogion 2 fails as an argument for God's existence. According to Malcolm,
however, a study of Anselm reveals a different argument from that of
Proslogion 2, and this argument, though in some ways similar to that of
Proslogion 2, is, in fact, a successful version of the Ontological Argument. It is
found, says Malcolm, in *Proslogion* 3 (from which I have already quoted), and
it turns on the notion of necessary being.

As we have seen, in *Proslogion* 3 Anselm states not only that God exists,
but also that his non-existence is inconceivable. 'And certainly', says Anselm,
'this being so truly exists that it cannot be even thought not to exist'. But
why not? Here we come to Malcolm's reading of the argument of *Proslogion*
3, which can be stated as follows:

(1) 'God' means 'something than which nothing greater can be thought'.

(2) Necessary existence is a perfection.

(3) 'God' therefore also means 'a being with necessary existence'.

(4) It is self-contradictory to say 'A being with necessary existence does not exist'.

(5) Therefore, God exists if 'God' can be used to refer to something the existence of which is possible.

(6) 'God' can be used to refer to something the existence of which is possible.

(7) Therefore, it is self-contradictory to deny God's existence and God cannot even be thought of as not existing, i.e. the non-existence of God is inconceivable.

In this argument, necessary existence is understood to be a mode of existence belonging to what does not depend on anything for its coming into existence or for its continuing to exist. In this argument also, a being with necessary existence cannot be prevented from existing by anything. In Malcolm's view therefore, if 'God' means 'a being with necessary existence' it follows that 'God' means 'a being whose existence is not brought about or threatened by anything'. Or, perhaps to be more accurate, it means 'a being whose existence cannot be brought about or threatened by anything'. And hence, so Malcolm concludes, God must exist.

If God, a being a greater than which cannot be conceived, does not exist, then He cannot *come* into existence. For if He did He would either have been *caused* to come into existence or have *happened* to come into existence, and in either case He would be a limited being, which by our conception of Him He is not. Since He cannot come into existence, if He does not exist His existence is impossible. If He does exist He cannot have come into existence . . . nor can He cease to exist, for nothing could cause Him to cease to exist nor could it just happen that He ceased to exist. So if God exists His existence is necessary. Thus God's existence is either impossible or necessary. It can be the former only if the concept of such a being is self-contradictory or in some way logically absurd. Assuming that this is not so, it follows that He necessarily exists (Malcolm 1960, pp. 59ff.)

(5) Charles Hartshorne

Hartshorne, in fact, has offered many discussions of the Ontological Argument, so in referring to his approval of it one needs to decide which of his accounts to mention. His fullest exposition of the Argument comes in his book *The Logic of Perfection* (La Salle, Ill., 1962), so perhaps we can concentrate on what we find there. And what we do find is an argument which again hinges on the notion of necessity.

Let us suppose that God exists. What must be true of him? Hartshorne's reply is that if God exists then he exists necessarily, i.e. that there can be no possibility of his non-existence. Here 'possibility' means 'logical possibility'. If God exists, Hartshorne thinks, then his non-existence is logically impossible just as, say, the truth of a contradiction is logically impossible. So, says Hartshorne, we can begin by saying that if God exists, then necessarily he exists. Or, to put it another way, we can say that perfection could not exist contingently (i.e. such that there is any logical possibility of it not existing).

But what, if anything, follows from this? It follows, says Hartshorne, that either necessarily there is a God, or necessarily there is no God. Why does this follow? Because if there could be a God then there must be a God, and all that could rule out there having to be a God would be some independent impossibility of there being a God. Thus, Hartshorne concludes, if God is possible, his existence is necessary, i.e. there could not fail to be a God if it is possible that God exists.

In short, according to Hartshorne existence is built into the notion of God so that only two possibilities are left. Either the notion of God is the notion of something impossible, in which case it will be true that necessarily there is no God. Or the notion of God is the notion of something possible, in which case the existence of God is absolutely or logically necessary.

(6)   Alvin Plantinga

Statements of Plantinga's version of the Ontological Argument can be found in at least two places: his books *The Nature of Necessity* (Oxford, 1974) and *God, Freedom and Evil* (London, 1975). In both of these Plantinga offers the same argument, which, in turn, is a development of the arguments of Malcolm and Hartshorne.

Let us agree that if God exists, his non-existence is impossible. Let us agree with Malcolm and Hartshorne that God's existence is necessary existence. One way of putting this – and this is how Plantinga chooses to put it – is to say that if God exists, then he exists *in all possible worlds*.

What is a 'possible world'? The expression is one that has been employed in derivation from Leibniz by philosophers chiefly concerned with notions such as 'possible' and 'necessary'. It is also both hard to elucidate and philosophically controversial. But, for Plantinga, a possible world is, roughly speaking, a complete way things could be. Suppose we knew all that was, is, or will be. Then we would, according to the present terminology, have full knowledge of a possible world. We would, in fact, have full knowledge of the real or actual world. Plantinga would say that the actual world is certainly a possible world, for what is actual must also be possible (which is, of course, correct: if I do exist, then my existence is possible). But conceivably things could be different from the way they are or have been. And conceivably what will happen might be such that it need not have happened. Suppose, for instance, you and I had never been born. In that case, a knowledge of the world in which we did/do not exist might be described as knowledge of a different possible world from the real or actual world. For Plantinga, then, in thinking of possible worlds we are supposed to think of complete world histories, or complete ways in which things could possibly be. In thinking like this we will also, of course, concede that only one possible world could be actual. (For a fuller account, see Plantinga 1974, ch. IV.)

Now as I have said, Plantinga begins by agreeing with Malcolm and Hartshorne. And his agreement consists in accepting that God's existence (if God exists) is necessary existence. Using the expression 'possible world', he then suggests that if some being is possible and if its existence is necessary, then it exists in all possible worlds. The reason why Plantinga puts things this way is that he supposes that if something must be, if something is necessary, then it cannot not be (not, at any rate, if it must be in the sense that its non-existence is strictly impossible). In other words, according to Plantinga, if something exists necessarily, then there is no possible world in which it fails to exist. If there is a necessary being, this being exists in all possible worlds.

But what would this being be like in all possible worlds? Here Plantinga's argument goes beyond those of Malcolm and Hartshorne. For in his view, though they have shown that there is a necessary being, they have not shown that *God* really exists.

Why not? Basically because in Plantinga's view something might be a necessary being, and therefore exist in all possible worlds (including this one) without in all possible worlds having the properties commonly ascribed to God. For this reason, says Plantinga, the Ontological Argument needs to employ something in addition to the suggestion that God's existence is either necessary or impossible. It needs, in fact, to show that God exists (a) as necessary, (b) as having properties commonly ascribed to him, and (c) as having these properties in all possible worlds.

At this point Plantinga asks us to draw a distinction between what he calls being 'maximally great' and having 'maximal excellence'. Let us say that a being is maximally great if it exists in all possible worlds and if it is also maximally excellent in all possible worlds. Let us also say that if it is maximally excellent in all possible worlds, then in all possible worlds it is omniscient, omnipotent, and morally perfect. Here, then, being maximally great is understood as being omniscient, omnipotent and morally perfect in all possible worlds. So if anything is maximally great, it exists in all possible worlds, and in all possible worlds it is omniscient, omnipotent, and morally perfect.

But now, so Plantinga concludes, this gives us what we are looking for. Let us define God as having maximal greatness. Could anything have maximal greatness? Plantinga thinks that it could. So, for him, the existence of maximal greatness is possible. But if maximal greatness is possible (or, to put it another way, if in some possible world there is a being with maximal greatness) then it seems to follow that in all possible worlds there is a being who is omniscient, omnipotent, and morally perfect. Since our world (the real world) is a possible world, it therefore seems that in this world there exists a being who is omniscient, omnipotent, and morally perfect. And thus, so Plantinga concludes, we may truthfully assert that God exists. If maximal greatness is possible, then God exists. Maximal greatness is possible. So God does exist.

OBJECTIONS TO THE ARGUMENT

As one might expect, the Ontological Argument has been met with a range of criticisms. Some of them are better than others, but their cogency will not, for the moment, concern us. To begin with, let us simply note some of the more famous ones, or the ones most frequently held justly to call the Argument into question. There are basically six of these.

(1) There could not be a God

Suppose I say that I have a car which is entirely red and entirely black. You will assume that I am contradicting myself, and you will dismiss what I say as not even possibly true. This is how some have responded to the Ontological Argument, and the response is directed against the Argument's conclusion. The claim here is that the Argument cannot be successful since it concludes to the existence of God while the assertion 'God exists' or 'There is a God' could not even be possibly true. We will see more of this claim later.

(2) We know there is no God

Others have taken a different line from the one just mentioned. Their position is that the Ontological Argument cannot be successful since we have good reason to maintain that there just is no God. This is the line taken, for example, by Jonathan Barnes in his book *The Ontological Argument* (London, 1972). As he puts it:

Under what generic sortal is it plausible to put God? In the religious atmosphere that inspires the Ontological Argument there is only one reasonable suggestion, namely 'person'. Now the notion of a person is hotly controversial; but it is, I think, becoming clear that persons are essentially corporeal. . . . If this is so, then if Gods are persons, then Gods are corporeal. Allow this and it is reasonable to assert as an empirical truth that no Gods exist (Barnes 1972, p. 84).

Barnes is saying here that if anything is a God, it is a person; if anything is a person it is corporeal, and, since we have reason to disbelieve in bodily Gods, we have reason to reject the conclusion of the Ontological Argument.

(3)   Understanding 'God'

All versions of the Ontological Argument begin with what is taken to be some understanding of the word 'God'. Indeed, all versions of the Argument turn on what 'God' is taken to mean. But what if we cannot really understand the import of the word 'God'? It might then be thought that no argument which begins from the meaning of the word can get under way. And this is more or less what some have said with respect to the Ontological Argument. A classic example of someone taking this line is Aquinas. In the *Summa Theologiae* he notes what looks like the argument of *Proslogion* 2, but he rejects it on the ground that the meaning of 'God' is not clear to us. In Aquinas's own words:

The proposition 'God exists' is self-evident in itself . . . since God is his own existence. But, because what it is to be God is not evident to us, the proposition is not self-evident to us, and needs to be made evident. This is done by means of things which, though less evident in themselves, are nevertheless more evident to us, by means, namely, of God's effects (*Summa Theologiae* Ia, 2, 1).

Aquinas agrees that if we could understand what 'God' meant, we would be able to see that existence belongs to him in some necessary way just as we can see that being an animal is what must be true of all human beings since the meaning of 'human being' includes what we mean by 'animal'. But, Aquinas insists, while we know what 'human being' means, we do not in the same sense (at any rate) know what 'God' means. Aquinas therefore concludes that we cannot base an argument for God's existence on the meaning of the word 'God'. In Aquinas's view, arguments for God must be causal arguments based on what God has brought about (i.e. his effects).

(4)   What does 'God' mean?

Aquinas also has another criticism of the Ontological Argument which turns on the meaning of 'God'. For what if someone rejects the definition of 'God' used by writers like Anselm in *Proslogion* 2? Then again the Argument will not work, at least with the person we now imagine. Or, as Aquinas puts it:

Someone hearing the word 'God' may very well not understand it to mean 'that than which nothing greater can be thought', indeed some people have believed God to be a body (*Summa Theologiae* Ia, 2, 1 ad 2).

(5) Existence is not a perfection

Anselm, Descartes, and Leibniz hold that, given a certain understanding of 'God', God must exist since existence (or, for Anselm, existence *in re*) is some kind of perfection or great-making quality that nothing matching the given understanding of 'God' could lack. To put it another way, they hold that anything that is God has the perfection of existence. But another famous objection to the Ontological Argument denies this supposition. This objection holds that existence is *not* a perfection or a great-making quality. Indeed, so it is sometimes said, existence is no kind of property at all. Thus, for example, Pierre Gassendi (1592–1655) replied to Descartes by saying:

Existence is a perfection neither in God nor in anything else; it is rather that in the absence of which there is no perfection.... In enumerating the perfections of God, you ought not to have put existence among them, in order to draw the conclusion that God exists, unless you wanted to beg the question (Haldane and Ross 1912, vol. 2, p. 186).

Perhaps the most famous defender of this point is Kant, who states it in what must be one of the most quoted pieces of philosophical literature. The relevant part runs thus:

'*Being*' is obviously not a real predicate; that is, it is not a concept of something which could be added to a thing. It is merely the positing of a thing, or of certain determinations, as existing in themselves. Logically, it is merely the copula of a judgement.... If, now, we take the subject (God) with all its predicates (among which is omnipotence), and say 'God is' or 'There is a God', we attach no new predicate to the concept of God, but only posit the subject in itself with all its predicates, and indeed posit it as being an *object* that stands in relation to my *concept*. The content of both must be one and the same.... Otherwise stated, the real contains no more than the merely possible. A hundred real thalers do not contain the least coin more than a hundred possible thalers (Kant, *Critique of Pure Reason*, pp. 504f.).

This is not altogether an easy set of remarks to interpret, but Kant's general drift can, perhaps, be teased out. His main point seems to be that in saying that something exists we do not ascribe any property to an object. Rather, we say that there is some object with certain properties, the assumption being that existence is not among them. To return to the example I gave in Chapter 1, Kant's position would seem to be this: I can seriously say 'I have two cats which are different because one has a tail and the other has none'. But I cannot seriously say 'I have two cats which are different because one of them exists and the other does not'. On this view, existence is not a property that things can have or lack, so it cannot enter into their definition as property terms can enter into definitions. As Norman Malcolm puts it:

A king might desire that his next chancellor should have knowledge, wit, and resolution; but it is ludicrous to add that the king's desire is to have a chancellor who exists. Suppose that two royal councilors, A and B, were asked to draw up separately descriptions of the most perfect chancellor they could conceive, and that the descriptions they produced were identical except that A included existence in his list of attributes of a perfect chancellor and B did not.... One and the same person could satisfy both descriptions. More to the point, any person who satisfied A's description would *necessarily* satisfy B's description and *vice versa*! This is to say that A and B did not produce descriptions that differed in any way but rather one and the same description of necessary and desirable qualities in a chancellor. A only made a show of putting down a desirable quality that B had failed to include (Malcolm 1960, pp. 43f.).

(6) You cannot define things into existence

Suppose I say 'A Martian is an inhabitant of the planet Mars'. You might accept this as a definition of sorts, but you will not take it to show that there are any Martians. For, quite generally, we do not suppose that one can guarantee the existence of things simply by defining them. Yet all forms of the Ontological Argument seem to be denying this supposition. They seem to be saying that in the case of God we can move from definition to assurance of existence. Yet for many critics this is one of the Argument's most lamentable features. Again we can quote Aquinas. As he puts it:

Even if the meaning of the word 'God' were generally reckoned to be 'that than which nothing greater can be thought', nothing thus defined would thereby be granted existence in the world of fact, but merely as thought about. Unless one is given that something in fact exists than which nothing greater can be thought – and this nobody denying the existence of God would grant – the conclusion that God in fact exists does not follow (*Summa Theologiae* Ia, 2, 1 ad 2).

Others have made the same point, and one of the Ontological Argument's earliest critics applies it to try to show that if the logic of the Argument is accepted, then the absurdest consequences follow. The critic in question here is Gaunilo, a monk of Marmoutiers near Tours, and a contemporary of St Anselm. According to him, if Anselm is right, then you can define anything into existence, including items belonging to fables.

For example: they say that there is in the ocean somewhere an island which, because of the difficulty (or rather the impossibility) of finding that which does not exist, some have called the 'Lost Island'. And the story goes that it is blessed with all manner of priceless riches and delights in abundance, much more even than the Happy Isles, and, having no owner or inhabitant, it is superior everywhere in abundance of riches to all those other lands that men inhabit. Now, if anyone tell me that it is like this, I shall easily understand what is said, since nothing is difficult about it. But if he should then go on to say, as though it were a logical consequence of this: You cannot any more doubt that this island that is more excellent than all other lands truly exists somewhere in reality than you can doubt that it is in your mind; and since it is more excellent to exist not only in the mind alone but also in reality, therefore it must needs be that it exists. For if it did not exist, any other land existing in reality would be more excellent than it, and so this island, already conceived by you to be more excellent than others, will not be more excellent. If, I say, someone wishes thus to persuade me that this island really exists beyond all doubt, I should either think that he was joking, or I should find it hard to decide which of us I ought to judge the bigger fool – I, if I agreed with him, or he, if he thought that he had proved the existence of this island with any certainty, unless he had first convinced me that its very excellence exists in my mind precisely as a thing existing truly and indubitably and not just as something unreal or doubtfully real (*A Reply on Behalf of the Fool* 6).

In other words, so Gaunilo is saying, if Anselm's definition of God entails God's existence, then it will follow that the most excellent of islands exists. But this is absurd.

Much the same point seems to be made by Kant, who puts it like this:

If, in an identical proposition, I reject the predicate while retaining the subject, contradiction results; and I therefore say that the former belongs necessarily to the latter. But if we reject the subject and predicate alike, there is no contradiction. . . . To posit a triangle, and yet to reject its three angles, is self-contradictory; but there is no contradiction in rejecting the triangle together with its three angles. The same holds true of the concept of an absolutely necessary being. If its existence is rejected, we reject the thing itself with all its predicates; and no question of contradiction can then arise. . . . I cannot form the least concept of a thing which, should it be rejected with all its predicates, leaves behind a contradiction (*Critique of Pure Reason*, pp. 502f.).

Here again is a passage of Kant which raises problems of interpretation. But we can still get a fair grasp of what Kant is saying. This seems to be that while 'God' might indeed mean 'being who exists of necessity', this does not entail that there is a God any more than the fact that 'triangle' means 'three-sided figure' entails that there are any triangles. On Kant's view, to define something is to say that if anything matches the definition, then it will be as the definition states. But whether anything does match a given definition is a further question. In this sense, so Kant seems to be saying, statements of existence can be denied without contradiction.

DOES THE ARGUMENT WORK?

So much, then for some of the standard objections to the Ontological Argument. The question to consider now is whether they are decisive, or whether the Ontological Argument can be defended in spite of them. We can begin with those objections that seem weakest.

Weak objections to the Argument

Perhaps the weakest objections of all are (1)–(4), in reply to which one can argue as follows.

(1) It is certainly true that many philosophers have argued that 'God exists' or 'There is a God' is somehow contradictory. But defenders of the Ontological Argument are surely within their rights to respond to such philosophers by appealing to a point which I made in Chapter 1. This is that in deciding whether an assertion is possibly true we must often pay attention to arguments given for supposing that the assertion is actually true. This, of course, is what defenders of the Ontological Argument are asking us to do. And if their Argument is a good one, then its conclusion will not, after all, be contradictory. In other words, so one might suggest, whether or not the Ontological Argument is unsuccessful because its conclusion is contradictory is not to be decided in advance of considering the Argument itself. Suppose the Argument is really a good one? Then its conclusion will not be contradictory. So it seems reasonable to give the Argument a hearing and to decide on its merits as an argument before dismissing its conclusion.

(2) The same point applies to those who reject the Argument on the ground that they have independent reason for disbelieving in the existence of God. It is, of course, true that if I have grounds for believing that something is not the case, this may justly influence my reading of an argument holding that the thing is, in fact, the case. But it is equally true that considering new arguments may justly lead me to revise my earlier conclusions. Again, so it seems, defenders of the Ontological Argument have a right to a hearing. Maybe the Argument is a bad one. But maybe it is not. How are we to decide on the matter? An obvious reply is 'By considering it'. An objector such as Barnes (who has, in fact, considered the Argument in some detail) might counter this suggestion by saying that the evidence for the non-existence of bodily Gods is strong enough to allow us reasonably to ignore the Ontological Argument altogether (or any other argument for God's existence for that matter). But here we need to ask whether Barnes's argument quoted above is itself a good one. One reason for rejecting it is its assumption that those who believe in God are committed to the formula 'God is a person'. I shall return to this assumption later only saying, at this point, that it is highly questionable. The same goes for Barnes's assertion that the question of God's existence is a question about the existence of something bodily. As we saw in Chapter 1, if there is a Creator, then the Creator cannot be bodily. For this reason, if for no other, defenders of the Ontological Argument have reason for complaining if their Argument is dismissed in advance on the ground that there is evidence against the existence of bodily Gods. Some of the Ontological Argument's defenders might accept that there is indeed evidence against the existence of a bodily God, but they might then add that this is beside the point as far as they are concerned since they do not suppose that God is bodily. Barnes will reply that if they accept that God is a person, then they must suppose this. But it remains to be seen that 'God

is a person' is an assertion that those who believe in God need to feel wedded to in any sense that renders their final position untenable.

(3) If 'God' is taken to mean (as in Anselm) 'Something than which nothing greater can be thought', then it makes sense to say that God will somehow defy our understanding. For the expression 'Something than which nothing greater can be thought' can hardly be regarded as a description picking out something whose nature will be clear to us from the description. The expression, in fact, seems largely negative. If it refers to anything at all, it does so only by drawing attention to what what it refers to is *not* – viz. something than which anything greater can be thought. In this sense, then, the third of our standard objections has a point. And the same can be said with respect to the objection as formulated by Aquinas. As I shall argue later, there are good reasons for accepting that, as Aquinas says, 'what it is to be God is not evident to us' or that 'God' cannot be defined as, for example, can 'human being'.

But even if we agree with all this, not all defenders of the Ontological Argument need be unduly perturbed. Take, for example, Anselm. He might ask 'Can one make any sense at all of the expression "Something than which nothing greater can be thought"?'. Then he might say: 'If one can, then whatever one believes about how hard it is to say what "God" means, enough has been conceded to allow my argument to get started'. And, surely, one can indeed make some sense of Anselm's formula. It is not, after all, a piece of gibberish, like the nonsense verses in Lewis Carroll. One can also use it to construct valid and intelligible arguments. Consider, for instance, the following:

There is something than which nothing greater can be thought. Anything than which a greater can be thought cannot be something than which nothing greater can be thought. Therefore, something than which nothing greater can be thought cannot be anything than which a greater can be thought.

That is a valid argument. It does not seem nonsensical to me, and I think it allows us to say that sense can be made of Anselm's formula even if we are less happy with formulae occurring in versions of the Ontological Argument other than Anselm's. In the light of this point, therefore, it seems to me that Anselm, for one, can reject the third standard objection to the Ontological Argument. He, at any rate, can agree that though in some sense we may fail to understand the import of the word 'God' we can still make enough sense to be going on with of the definition of 'God' used in his argument. And he can, of course, add a further point if the proponent of the present objection to the Ontological Argument is someone who believes in the existence of God as, for example, Aquinas does. For cannot Anselm say that, whatever the believer holds to be true of God, he can hardly deny that nothing can be thought to be greater than God? Aquinas, at any rate, would not have denied that. So one may therefore complain that the first of his objections to the Ontological Argument is rather unfair. And that is surely what one must also do regarding his objection that there are people for whom 'God' does not mean anything like what it is taken to mean in the context of the Ontological Argument. Aquinas notes that some people believe God to be a body. But Anselm can reply quickly enough to this observation. He can say: 'Yes, but so what? Plenty of people do not believe God to be a body, and I am taking an expression which many of those who believe in God can accept as expressing a truth about him. I am then arguing that this expression is one which, when reflected on, allows me to conclude that there must be something to match it if it is considered as a definition'.

In fairness to critics of the Ontological Argument, however, perhaps one ought to add that the objection to it which we are now considering has some force against what Descartes and Leibniz take 'God' to mean. According to Descartes, God is 'a supremely perfect being'. Leibniz uses the expression 'a being whose greatness or perfection is supreme'. But could anything possibly match these definitions? Arguably not. Suppose we have a being which has an enormous number of perfections. Might there not always be one more perfection it could have? Or might not one aspect in which it is perfect be intensified somehow, thereby making it yet more perfect? In other words, is perfection something that admits of a maximum? (Cf. Plantinga 1974, pp. 90f.)

Then again, there is this problem. Can we understand that something is perfect without knowing what the thing is that is said to be perfect? Suppose I announce to you out of the blue: 'It's perfect'. You will not understand me until you know what I am describing as perfect. Perfection in chocolate puddings, for instance, is something different from perfection in Chinese vases. So perhaps we can agree with the present criticism of the Ontological Argument in this sense: the formulae used by Descartes and Leibniz are not by themselves intelligible since they do not specify in what respect or respects God is supposed to be perfect. And a critic of Anselm might level the same criticism against his definition of God as 'Something than which nothing greater can be thought'. The critic might ask: 'Greater in what respect?'.

But Descartes and the others can still defend themselves here. For they can say that 'perfect' is not a meaningless word and that if there is a God he cannot be less than perfect even if we do not know what it takes to make God perfect. That is surely an intelligible presumption, and it can even be accepted by someone with no belief in God. And if it is true that existence is a perfection, if God is perfect he must have the perfection of existence if he is to be perfect in any other way. Otherwise he will not be there to start with. So defenders of the Ontological Argument might therefore hold that, though there is a sense in which what the Argument takes 'God' to mean is hard to understand, it is intelligible enough for the Argument to get started.

More difficult objections

A.   Is existence a perfection?

If existence cannot be regarded as a perfection or great-making quality, however, then it would appear that the Ontological Argument is not going to work in the versions of Anselm, Descartes, and Leibniz. For the claim that existence is a perfection seems to be a key stage of the Argument in all these versions. Can we, then, accept this claim?

Those who maintain that we cannot somehow express themselves by saying that 'existence is not a predicate'. But what does this mean? There seem to be at least two clear possibilities:

(i)   The verb 'to exist' cannot in any form function as a grammatical predicate.

(ii) The verb 'to exist' cannot in any form function so as to ascribe a logical or real predicate to a subject.

The meaning of (i) should be clear enough, and, though it seems that grammarians have some problems deciding how sentences are to be divided into subject and predicate (cf. Lyons 1968, pp. 334ff.), we can, perhaps, readily concede that (i) is not plausible. It looks as though we certainly can place forms of the verb 'to exist' in sentences where they are rightly to be described as grammatical predicates. At any rate, people teaching children to master English grammar will often explain that in, say, 'Mountains exist in China', 'Mountains' is the grammatical subject, and 'exist in China' is the grammatical predicate.

But what of (ii)? The idea here is that to say that something exists (or that it did exist, was existing, still exists, will exist, and so on) is not (whatever grammar might suggest) to pick out a subject and to provide information about it. Consider the sentence 'John is bald'. If someone uses this sentence and speaks truly of someone we know and call 'John', we would say that he was singling out an individual by means of the proper name 'John', and that he was telling us something about him, viz. that he is bald. Here we can regard 'is bald' as a logical or real predicate as well as a grammatical predicate. The claim of (ii), then, is that forms of the verb 'to exist' do not, whatever grammar suggests, tell us anything about individuals, as, for example, 'is bald' tells us something about John in 'John is bald'.

Yet is that true? Are we not in some sense doing much the same thing when we say, on the one hand, 'John is bald', and when we say, on the other hand, 'John exists'? Or, to change the example, are we not doing much the same thing when we say 'John snores' and 'John exists'? Intuitively, perhaps, the right answer might seem to be 'Yes'. But there are, unfortunately, problems in this area.

Suppose, for example, we assert that something does not exist. And suppose we say that in making this assertion we are talking about the thing and saying something about it as we are when we say, for example, that something is red. Then a statement like 'Intelligent philosophers do not exist' will make an assertion about intelligent philosophers just like the statement 'Intelligent philosophers do not like bad arguments'. But in that case there are some curious consequences. For if 'Intelligent philosophers do not exist' is true, there is nothing for it to be about and it fails to say anything. It purports to be about intelligent philosophers. It presupposes that they exist. But it goes on to deny that they exist. So statements like 'Intelligent philosophers do not exist' end up as somehow contradictory, which seems counter-intuitive to say the least. And not only that. It would seem that statements like 'Intelligent philosophers exist' are true of necessity, which also seems odd.

How can we tidy things up, then? One obvious thing to do would be to suppose that in 'Intelligent philosophers do not exist' we are *not* denying a property to anything. We can also help ourselves if we suppose that we are *not* ascribing a property to anything when we say 'Intelligent philosophers exist'. And this is what many philosophers would now regard as the right move. Yet if that is so, it makes sense to say that 'exists' is not a logical or real predicate, that existence is not a property of objects, or that in saying that something exists we are not conveying information about the thing as we do when we say, for example, that John is bald or that John snores.

But suppose all that is wrong. Can we, perhaps, think of a clear case where 'exist' or 'exists' does *not* give us information about something as 'is bald' or 'snores' seems to give us information about John? Apparently we can. What about 'God exists'? What information could we here be conveying about God parallel to the information yielded in 'John is bald' or 'John snores'? In this case would it not, perhaps, be best to read 'God exists' so as to take 'God' as the logical or real predicate, rather than 'exists'? That, at any rate, seems to make sense. For we could now regard 'God exists' as saying that something or other is God, i.e. that divine attributes belong to something. But in that case it will be false that forms of the verb 'to exist' always function so as to ascribe a logical or real predicate to an object.

Yet someone might now reply that this does not show that if something exists it does not have anything that can be regarded as a perfection. And this, of course, is what is really at issue when it comes to the Ontological Argument as we find it in Anselm, Descartes and Leibniz. Can we not therefore insist that given two things, one of which exists and the other of which does not, one will be better than the other?

The trouble now, however, is that if we do insist on this, we will not be making any sense. For someone who claims to compare two things, one of which exists and the other of which does not, is just not doing what he says he is doing. If we can compare (or contrast) A with B, then both A and B must exist. A non-existent book is not *different* from a real book. Nor is it *similar*. It is just not there to be either different or similar to anything. And this, one might suggest, is more or less what Kant was driving at in his assertion that '*Being*' is 'the positing of a thing' and that 'the real contains no more than the merely possible'. That seems to me to be correct if it means that there is really no difference between non-existing As and existing As. This, too, is what Malcolm is getting at in his remarks about the chancellors. And if Malcolm and I are right here, for a thing to exist is not for it to have a perfection. As Gassendi puts it, whether or not something has any perfections will depend on whether or not it exists in the first place.

One might, indeed, go further than this. For why suppose that when we use 'exist' or 'exists' we are ascribing any kind of property to things, whether the property counts as a perfection or not? The temptation, perhaps, is to say that the answer lies in the fact that we seem so frequently to convey or imply information about things using 'exist' or 'exists'. Yet consider, for example, the following assertions, and imagine that someone is making these assertions before you in all seriousness:

(1) Friendly Americans exist.
(2) Babies do not know that philosophers exist.
(3) Mr Micawber does not exist.
(4) The Eiffel Tower still exists.

We would all, I presume, accept these assertions. But are we obliged to think of their use of 'exists' or 'exist' as ascribing or (in the case of 3) denying any kind of property to anything?

Philosophers will offer different answers to this question, but the right answer is surely 'No'. And one way of seeing this is to note that we can say all that (1)–(4) say without even using the word 'exist' or 'exists'. For what (1)–(4) say is:

(5) Something or other is a friendly American.
(6) Babies do not know that something or other is a philosopher.
(7) Nothing whatsoever matches Dickens's description of the character he calls 'Mr Micawber'.
(8) Something is a structure and is called 'the Eiffel Tower' and stands in Paris, etc.

(1)–(4) could doubtless be analysed differently from this. I am not denying that. But (5)–(8) recognizably repeat what we would normally take (1)–(4) to be saying. And they do so without once implying that information about an object's properties, or lack of them, is being conveyed by means of the words 'exist' or 'exists'. These words may look like terms used to ascribe a property to objects, but we do not have to regard them as such. And, as we saw above (with the examples 'Intelligent philosophers do not exist' and 'Intelligent philosophers exist'), odd consequences follow if we do so regard them. In other words, Kant was basically correct in saying that 'Being is . . . not a real predicate', that 'it is not a concept of something which could be added to the concept of a thing'. In more recent philosophy the point has been stated by Gottlob Frege (1848–1925), according to whom '_ exists' is logically akin to '_ are numerous' (as in 'Puzzled readers are numerous') in that it tells us something about a concept (e.g. puzzled readers), not an object (e.g. Fred Smith). 'Existence', says Frege, 'is analogous to number. Affirmation of existence is in fact nothing but denial of the number nought. Because existence is a property of concepts the ontological argument for the existence of God breaks down' (Frege 1953, §53). In *The Philosophy of Logical Atomism* (1918) Bertrand Russell makes what is much the same point by holding in his terminology that 'Existence is essentially a property of a propositional function'.

A *propositional function* is simply *any expression containing an undetermined constituent, or several undetermined constituents, and becoming a proposition as soon as the undetermined constituents are determined*. If I say 'x is a man' or 'n is a number', that is a propositional function. . . . When you take any propositional function and assert that it is possible, that it is sometimes true, that gives you the fundamental meaning of 'existence'. You may express it by saying that there is at least one value of x for which that propositional function is true. Take 'x is a man', there is at least one value of x for which this is true. That is what one means by saying that 'There are men' or that 'Men exist' (Russell 1956, pp. 230ff.).

On Russell's account to say that God exists is not to ascribe a property to God as to an individual. It is to say that 'x is a God' is sometimes true, that it is true for at least one value of x.

B. *Defining things into existence*

Analyses of existence like those of Kant, Frege, and Russell are matters of philosophical controversy. My suggestion at this point, however, is that they are basically right. Existence is not a property of objects, of individuals, which means, of course, that it is no perfection either and that God's existence does not follow from defining 'God' as something lacking no conceivable perfection or as being supremely perfect. But we can now add to this criticism. For is it not right to suppose that the existence of things cannot be inferred from their definitions? Can we not, in fact, agree with the last of the standard objections noted above to the Ontological Argument?

Some, indeed, would say 'No'. They might allow that there are many definitions which do not entail the existence of what is defined by the definition, but they will say that in the case of the Ontological Argument we have a counter-example which can be accepted as such because of the cogency of the Argument. And this is a reply to take seriously. Good arguments might conceivably give us reason to concede exceptions even to what we have hitherto believed to be unbreakable principles.

In defence of the Ontological Argument one might also add this point: some of those who have rejected the Argument in the light of the principle 'Definitions do not imply existence' have themselves argued badly in doing so. Gaunilo is a case in point. As we have seen, he holds that if Anselm is right then we can prove the existence of an island 'more excellent than all other lands'. But this reply is itself questionable. For one thing, it depends on the assumption that there could be an island than which no greater island can be thought. But, as many have pointed out, one can doubt whether such a thing is possible. As Plantinga puts it:

No matter how great an island is, no matter how many Nubian maidens and dancing girls adorn it, there could always be a greater – one with twice as many, for example. The qualities that make for greatness in islands – number of palm trees, amount and quality of coconuts, for example – most of these qualities have no *intrinsic maximum*. . . . So the idea of a greatest possible island is an inconsistent or incoherent idea; it's not possible that there be such a thing (Plantinga 1975, p. 91).

Then again, Anselm is not arguing for the existence of a God who is more excellent than all other Gods, as someone might argue for the existence of an island more excellent than all other islands. Anselm is arguing for the existence of something than which nothing greater can be thought, i.e. he is arguing for what cannot be conceived to be greater *in any respect*. Now what must such a thing be like? Anselm clearly supposes that it will be such that its non-existence is impossible. But if this supposition is correct, Anselm has a reply to Gaunilo. He can say this: 'We can conceive the non-existence of the most excellent island of all, for that island would be the most excellent *island*, not something which cannot be conceived to be greater *in any respect*. But since what cannot be conceived to be greater in any respect must be such that its non-existence is impossible, we cannot conceive the non-existence of *it*'. (Cf. *Reply to Gaunilo* III.)

But this is not to say that Anselm's argument works, or that the other versions of the Ontological Argument work either. For there is some point in saying that things cannot be defined into existence and that this applies to God as well as to anything else. The reason lies in what Kant seems to be saying in his judgement that one can reject both subject and predicate without contradiction.

Suppose we invent a word, 'W', which is supposed to name a thing of some kind (Ws). Suppose also that existence is built into the definition of these things so that the meaning of 'W' somehow includes that of existence. On these suppositions, we might write a dictionary entry for 'W' which explains that, whatever else is true of Ws, it is also true that Ws exist. Must we now concede that there actually are any Ws?

One's first thought might be that we must since if 'W' means something that exists, then how can there fail to be Ws? And one might compare this reasoning with that of someone who said that one cannot deny that triangles are three-sided since 'triangle' includes in its meaning 'having three sides'.

But the reasoning would be mistaken. Given our definition of 'triangle' we are only committed to holding that if anything is a triangle, then it has three sides. We are not committed to holding that there are any triangles. Nor are we committed to holding that there are any Ws, even though 'W' may have existence built into its meaning as being three-sided is built into the meaning of 'triangle'. In other words, given our definition of 'W', we imply that talk about Ws is talk about existing Ws, and this, in turn, means that statements like 'Some Ws do not exist' are bound to backfire. But we can still ask whether we ought to call anything a W (whether there are any Ws), and we can still say, without contradiction, 'There are no Ws'. 'Non-existing W' may be contradictory, but it is not contradictory to say 'Nothing whatever is a W'. On our definition of Ws, no non-existing thing can be a W. But this does not show that there are any Ws. It only shows that if there are any Ws, then they exist. And, if we concede that existence is not a property of objects, one might even doubt that it shows as much as that. Anyway, even if we say that there is a concept of a being than which nothing greater can be thought and which cannot be thought not to exist, we can still ask whether the concept is realized, whether anything corresponds to it. 'If we say that it is not realized we are not contradicting ourselves. We are not saying that a being which cannot be conceived not to exist can be conceived not to exist; we are not putting "can be conceived not to exist" into the concept, where it would clash with the other part of that concept. We are merely saying that *there is not* a being which cannot be conceived not to exist' (Mackie 1982, p. 54).

Necessary existence

But now one might ask how all this applies to the Ontological Arguments of Malcolm, Hartshorne and Plantinga. If the above arguments are correct, then Anselm, Descartes, and Leibniz are wrong to suppose that they have proved

God's existence, and they are wrong (a) because existence is no perfection, and (b) because from the definition of a thing we need not conclude that anything answers to the definition. Yet though existence is not a perfection, what about *necessary* existence? As we have seen, the notion of necessary existence plays a major part in the arguments of Malcolm, Hartshorne and Plantinga. So could it be that their arguments are successful while those of their predecessors are not?

Here, I think, there is one respect in which they do survive criticism which I have already offered. For it surely does make sense to say that something with necessary existence can be different from and better than something without it. As Malcolm, for example, explains things, something has necessary existence if it does not depend for its existence on anything else, and if its existence cannot be threatened by anything. Now such a thing would clearly differ from things which did depend on other things for their existence. It would also differ from things the existence of which could be threatened by other things. And most people would see some point in saying that a thing of this kind consequently enjoyed a certain privilege or perfection.

But must we now say that if God is understood to have necessary existence, it follows that God actually exists? By no means. For, here again, we can raise the objection that one cannot define things into existence.

Let us concede that 'God' means 'a being which has necessary existence'. What does that mean? It means that if anything is God, it owes its existence to nothing and its existence cannot be threatened by anything. But this is not to say that anything is God. An objector might reply that it is contradictory to say 'Something with necessary existence might not exist'. But it is not contradictory to say this if one means what opponents of belief in God would normally mean when they deny the existence of God. For one would then mean 'Nothing whatever has necessary existence', which is compatible with accepting some absurdity in 'Something with necessary existence might not exist'.

For this reason, therefore, Malcolm's argument fails as an argument for the existence of God. And the same goes for Hartshorne's argument, which resembles it insofar as it holds that if God has necessary existence it follows that God exists. All, in fact, that either argument shows is that if 'God' is defined as the arguments propose, then if there is a God, nothing, as a matter of fact, can bring about his existence and nothing, as a matter of fact, can interfere with it. They show, if you like, that if God exists, he is uncreatable and indestructible. But whether there is a God is another matter. At one level we can assent to the assertion 'God is a necessary being', for we can define God to be a necessary being and we can then recommend the definition. But for all that Malcolm and Hartshorne have shown, we need only assent to the

assertion that God is a necessary being as we can assent to the assertion
'Unicorns are fabulous creatures'. And this no more commits us to the
existence of God than it commits us to the existence of unicorns.

Nor, to move on to Plantinga, does it commit us to accepting the Ontological Argument as he develops it. For why should we suppose that
anything is 'maximally great'? Why should we suppose that there is any
being which exists in all possible worlds and is in all possible worlds
omniscient, omnipotent, and morally perfect? Like Malcolm and
Hartshorne, Plantinga maintains that if God is possible, he is necessary. Yet,
as we have now seen, God can be held to be necessary and we can still consistently say 'Nothing whatever is God'. Like Malcolm and Hartshorne,
Plantinga moves from an 'is' of definition ('God is a necessary being in that
he has maximal greatness') to the use of 'is' where we assert that there is
something of some kind (the 'is' of affirmative predication, as it is sometimes
called). Let us concede that the existence of maximal greatness is possible. Let
us also concede that something with maximal greatness will be omniscient,
omnipotent, and morally perfect in all possible worlds. We have still only
conceded that maximal greatness is possible, not that anything has it.

But suppose that this is all wrong. Suppose it is contradictory to deny the
existence of maximal greatness. There is still a problem with Plantinga's
argument. This has to do with one of its crucial stages – the assumption that
maximal greatness is possible.

As we have seen, Plantinga's terminology leaves him saying that a being
has maximal greatness if it has maximal excellence in all possible worlds. And
Plantinga thinks that there is a possible world in which a being has maximal
greatness (that maximal greatness is possible), from which he concludes that
in all possible worlds there is a being with maximal greatness. But it is surely
also possible that there is no maximal greatness, for it is surely not contradictory to say that there is no being having maximal greatness. If there is a
being who exists in one world and has maximal greatness, then it has
maximal excellence in all possible worlds and God really exists. But if it is
possible that there is no maximal greatness, then in no possible world is there
a being with maximal greatness and we have no means of knowing whether
in this world there is anything which is omniscient, omnipotent, and morally
perfect. In that case, however, we are not obliged to accept that maximal
greatness is possible. It might equally well be impossible and it would be
impossible if possibly nothing has maximal greatness. (For a development of
this point, see Mackie 1982, pp. 55ff., and O'Hear 1984, pp. 180ff.)

CONCLUSION

So the upshot would seem to be that, in spite of its antiquity and longevity, the Ontological Argument does not give us grounds for belief in God. The Argument has intrigued and bemused people for centuries, and will doubtless continue to cast its spell (cf. Gaskin 1984, p. 47). One can also admit that there are objections to forms of it which can be answered when taken individually. But our final verdict must be negative. We cannot show that there is a God simply by reflecting on the concept of God.

But, as I have also tried to argue, we do have reason to believe in the existence of God. To be more precise, we have reason to believe in the existence of a Creator, since we can ask what accounts for the existence of the universe and since we can suppose that our question has an answer. By considering the Argument from Design, we can also rationally conclude that the order in the universe is brought about by whatever it is that accounts for the existence of the universe. The question to consider now is whether we can develop these conclusions any further.

QUESTIONS FOR DISCUSSION

1 It has been said that Anselm's *Proslogion* does not, in fact, offer an Ontological Argument for the existence of God. How would you respond to this suggestion?
2 How would you decide whether something said to exist could possibly exist?
3 Does any version of the Ontological Argument have any relevance to religious belief?
4 Can you attach sense to the expressions 'Something than which a greater cannot be thought' or 'A supremely perfect being'?
5 Is there a genuine distinction between existence and necessary existence?
6 If someone asks 'What exists?', and if someone else replies 'Everything', what would you say?
7 Is existence a perfection? Is it a property of objects?
8 If God is a being who cannot fail to exist, does it make sense to say 'There is no God'?
9 Are there any possible worlds?
10 Could God exist in one possible world, but not in another?

FURTHER READING

A very good translation of Anselm's *Proslogion*, together with the text of Gaunilo's reply and Anselm's response to Gaunilo, is *St Anselm's Proslogion*, trans. and intro. M. J. Charlesworth (Oxford, 1965/Notre Dame, 1979). This volume also contains the Latin texts. Another translation that can be recommended (though it reproduces no Latin) is *St Anselm: Basic Writings*, trans. Sidney N. Deane (La Salle, Ill., 1962). Another translation of the *Proslogion* that can be recommended is in *The Prayers and Meditations of Saint Anselm*, trans. Sister Benedicta Ward, SLG (Harmondsworth, Middx, 1973). I have quoted from Charlesworth's edition in my discussion.

For Descartes's *Meditations*, see *Descartes: Philosophical Writings*, trans. and ed. Elizabeth Anscombe and Peter Thomas Geach (Open University, 1970). I have quoted from this edition.

For Leibniz's *New Essays*, see G. W. Leibniz, *New Essays on Human Understanding*, trans. and ed. Peter Remnant and Jonathan Bennett (Cambridge, 1981). I have quoted from this edition. There is an abridged version of it which was published in 1982.

Malcolm's revival of the Ontological Argument takes the form of an article: 'Anselm's Ontological Arguments', *Philosophical Review* 69 (1960). The article has been much reprinted.

For the Ontological Argument in the work of Charles Hartshorne, see:

Man's Vision of God (New York, 1941).
The Logic of Perfection (La Salle, Ill., 1962).
Anselm's Discovery (La Salle, Ill., 1965).

As mentioned above, Plantinga's version of the Ontological Argument can be found in *The Nature of Necessity* (Oxford, 1974), ch. X, and *God, Freedom, and Evil* (London, 1975). For those with little interest in details of philosophical logic, the second book is the one to go for. It also contains some discussion of other arguments for God's existence (though they are not discussions that I would recommend).

There are two excellent readers on the Ontological Argument. These are Alvin Plantinga (ed.), *The Ontological Argument* (New York, 1965), and John Hick and Arthur McGill (eds), *The Many Faced Argument* (London, 1967). The Hick–McGill volume has a very comprehensive bibliography.

As a background to the Ontological Argument in Anselm, see G. R. Evans, *Anselm and Talking About God* (Oxford, 1978). Also much to be recommended is R. W. Southern, *St Anselm and his Biographer* (Cambridge, 1963).

Beginners will find an admirably clear and concise account of the Ontological Argument's history, together with a discussion of its merits (a good discussion) in chs 5 and 6 of John Hick's *Arguments for the Existence of God* (London, 1970). For a short, somewhat technical, but clever discussion of the Argument see also Jonathan Barnes, *The Ontological Argument* (London, 1972). This volume also contains helpful bibliographical information. So does the volume by Hick.

The mention of possible worlds is much found in the work of those dealing with the discipline known as modal logic. The best introduction to this for readers with no background in logic is G. E. Hughes and M. J. Cresswell, *An Introduction to Modal Logic* (London, 1968). For a shorter introduction to possible worlds, see Robert C. Stalnaker, 'Possible Worlds' in Ted Honderich and Myles Burnyeat (eds), *Philosophy As It Is* (London, 1979).

Far and away the best discussion of existence and predication to emerge in recent years is C. J. F. Williams, *What Is Existence?* (Oxford, 1981). This is a full-scale defence of Frege's account of existence, but it also has a lot to say about authors such as Kant and Russell. Highly recommended for a serious study of the Ontological Argument, to which Williams, in fact, directly refers. The only problem with the book is that it is highly technical and presumes that the reader can cope with advanced discussions in the area of philosophical logic.

Part Two
What is God?

5
Talk about God

Immediately following his attempt in the *Summa Theologiae* to give reasons
for belief in God (Ia, 2, 3), Aquinas observes: 'Having recognized that a
certain thing exists, we have still to investigate the way in which it exists,
that we may come to know what it is that exists'. And that more or less
describes the task now before us. I have argued that we may reasonably
believe in God, considered as the cause of there being a universe, and considered as the cause of there being an orderly universe. We have reason to
believe in the existence of a Creator. But what is the Creator like? And can
philosophical reflection help us to answer this question?

THE NEGATIVE WAY

At this point it is worth drawing attention to something significant about
what is going on when we ask questions. The thing to note here is that there
is a sense in which questions and answers go together since when we ask
questions we can both be ignorant of their answers and yet be sure that
certain answers are impossible.

Consider, for instance, the following questions which one can easily
imagine someone raising:

    (1) Why has my car broken down?
    (2) Why is there cancer?
    (3) Why did Columbus sail to America?

Now imagine someone replying thus:

    (4) Your car has broken down because Paris is the capital of France.
    (5) There is cancer because Wellington won the Battle of
        Waterloo.
    (6) Columbus sailed to America because *Pride and Prejudice* was
        written by Jane Austen.

The obvious thing to say here is that these answers to (1)–(3) just could not be true. And we can know this without having any idea as to what the true answers are.

Suppose, then, we ask 'What accounts for there being a universe?' or 'What must be true of a Creator?'. Might we not possibly proceed by stating what cannot be a correct answer here? This, at any rate, is what one ancient response to our present problems holds. What is the Creator like? What can philosophy tell us about him? The response to which I now refer says that our best move here is to proceed by way of negation. On this view, we should concentrate on what God is not.

And this view clearly has something to recommend it. Indeed, one can see so straight away. For, once one comes to think of it, we can easily realize that at least one thing cannot be true of God, considered as Creator. This is that God cannot be anything bodily. And that is just because at least part of what is at stake when we ask about the existence of the universe is the existence of bodily objects. In other words, if whatever it is that accounts for the universe were something bodily, it would itself be part of the universe and therefore could not account for there being any universe. Only something which is not a body could account for there being any universe of physical objects.

But can we deny more of God than this? And can we not talk of him in anything other than negations?

DIVINE SIMPLICITY

A useful way of approaching the first of these questions is to consider a claim which is nowadays somewhat out of favour among both philosophers and theologians. This is the claim that God is not complex, that he is, in fact entirely *simple*. This doctrine of divine simplicity (as I shall call it) can be found in various classical writers, including, for example, St Anselm and St Augustine (cf. Anselm, *Proslogion* 18; Augustine, *De Civitate Dei* XI, 10 and *De Trinitate* VI, 7, 8). But the most commonly referred-to spokesman for it is Aquinas, so I shall concentrate on the way it is developed by him.

Aquinas on divine simplicity

Suppose we are trying to understand the nature of a cause when we have direct access to nothing but its effect. Suppose, for example, that we are trying to determine what accounted for marks which we find on the sand of a beach. How should we proceed?

We may, for a start, recognize that the marks resemble those which we know can be produced by some particular individual. Suppose the marks are immediately identifiable as human footprints. Then, in the absence of further evidence, we will infer that they were caused by a human being.

But what if the marks resemble nothing we have so far encountered? We might then at least try to rule out the possibility of them having been caused by particular individuals already known to us. If they are nothing like human footprints, for instance, we will suppose that they could not have been caused by anything human.

Now this second procedure is the kind employed by Aquinas in developing his doctrine of divine simplicity. Let us, he says, ask whether God's effects could have been brought about by something with which we are already familiar. If the answer is 'No', then we will at least have learned something about what God cannot be like.

What, then, has God brought about? What are his effects? As I mentioned earlier, Aquinas accepts the reasoning of the First Cause version of the Cosmological Argument. For him, then, God is the cause of there being any universe at all. It will therefore, he says, follow that anything that belongs by nature to things within the universe cannot belong to God as the cause of the fact that these things exist. And so, says Aquinas, we can profitably consider what belongs by nature to things within the universe.

One of their most obvious features is, of course, their materiality. The created order contains what is bodily or physical. So, following the same line of reasoning as I have already given, Aquinas denies that God is a body. If he were a body, then he would merely be part of the universe the existence of which gives us reason to believe in God.

But this, for Aquinas, allows us to deny something else of God. For what is open to bodily individuals? At least two things. They can move around in space and change their appearance. They can also be pushed around by other physical objects which can modify them or extinguish them. But if God is not a body, then these are not possibilities for him. So Aquinas concludes that God cannot be physically modified (either by changing place or physical characteristics), and that he cannot be subject to the action of physical objects working on him either to modify him physically or to extinguish him. I can fly to Barbados and acquire a sun tan. When I get home I can be knocked down by a car and killed. On Aquinas's account, however, nothing like this can happen in the case of God. In Aquinas's terminology (derived from Aristotle), God is not a mixture (*compositio*) of *form* and *matter*. For Aquinas, in other words, to be God is not to be something whose nature allows it to change in any physical sense.

But nor, says Aquinas, is it to be something that we could recognize in the ordinary way as an individual. In God, says Aquinas, there is no mixture (*compositio*) of *suppositum* and *nature*, or *essence*.

Consider two philosophers having a discussion. We will call them 'Bill' and 'Ben'. So far we know nothing about them that would enable us to give a general report on them, but, even so, we can still say this: they are both alike and dissimilar.

How are they alike? Because they are both things of the same sort, for they are people. Whatever distinguishes Bill and Ben, they share a fundamental sameness that could never be shared between, say, a dog and a cat, or a tree and a rock. Aquinas would have put this by saying that they share the same nature or essence. This just means that Bill and Ben are both human beings. They have human nature in common.

But they are not, of course, identical. We are now talking about two different people. So we also have to allow for a distinction between Bill and Ben. We have, in fact, to say that they are two individuals. Aquinas would have said this by observing that in the case of Bill and Ben we are dealing with two *supposita*. A *suppositum*, for Aquinas, is what we might call a 'thing' or 'entity'. From Aquinas's point of view, though Bill and Ben present one nature or essence, they do so as two *supposita*. This just means that they are distinct human beings. They share human nature, but they are two, not one.

Now in the case of God, says Aquinas, things cannot be as we have just seen them to be either with Bill or Ben. In Aquinas's terminology, Bill and Ben are both a mixture (*compositio*) of *suppositum* and nature, or essence. But, so Aquinas thinks, God cannot be like this. And that is because he is not a body. In the case of Bill and Ben, so Aquinas would say, individuality is parasitic on being bodily. For Aquinas, as we might say, being a human individual means being a different bodily creature from some other bodily creature. And, quite generally, it is Aquinas's view that being *anything* that we can recognize as an individual means being bodily. In other words, according to Aquinas, we are able to pick out individuals because they are bodily. In this sense, all that we can understand as individuals are bodily things. So Aquinas concludes that we cannot understand God to be an individual. In God, he says, there is no mixture of *suppositum* and nature, or essence. In other words, whatever God's individuality consists in, it cannot, according to Aquinas, be distinguished from his nature or essence. On this account, Bill and Ben are distinguishable from human nature. They are individual human beings, not human nature itself. God, on the other hand, cannot be distinguished from his nature. In his case, nature (or essence) and individuality are indistinguishable.

And this, in turn, leads Aquinas to deny that God belongs to any genus. We can distinguish between things in the world by classification in terms of genus and species. We can say, for instance, that whales are a species of the genus *mammal*. But this, again, is something we can do because we are dealing with what is bodily. For it is bodily or material difference that distinguishes not only individuals in a species or genus, but also the species and genera themselves. Now God, says Aquinas, is not bodily, not material. So we cannot think of him as belonging to a genus. For Aquinas, in other words, God can be no object of inquiry for biologists or zoologists.

But he can, of course, create such objects. Indeed, says Aquinas, that is what he has done, for he is the cause of there being a universe. With this point in mind, therefore, Aquinas is led to deny one further thing of God. In the case of God, he says, we cannot distinguish between nature, or essence, and existence.

What does this mean? At one time it meant for Aquinas that there is a difference in meaning between the questions 'Is there such a thing? and 'What nature of thing is it?' (cf. *De Ente et Essentia*). But this is not what it means in the context of the *Summa Theologiae* and its discussion of divine simplicity. Here it basically means that God is not created. As we have seen, Aquinas holds that we can come to see that the universe is indeed created and that, therefore, God exists. But God, says Aquinas, is not created. Unlike the universe, he is not made to be *ex nihilo* by anything. And this point, so Aquinas says, can be expressed by saying that, when it comes to God, we cannot distinguish between nature, or essence, and existence. In the case of creatures, he thinks, we can make this distinction. We can, for example, think of Bill and Ben as human beings and as *created* human beings. In other words, we can think of them and then come to recognize that they owe their existence to God for as long as they exist. But we cannot, says Aquinas, think of God as owing his existence to something as Bill and Ben owe their existence to God. In God, therefore, nature, or essence, and existence come together.

Is Aquinas right?

Yet is any of this true? Should we deny of God the things that Aquinas denies of him in his doctrine of divine simplicity? Critics of Aquinas here have offered several counter-arguments to his position, some of which will concern us later (cf. Chapter 7). For the moment, however, we can concentrate on what is probably the most frequently levelled objection to Aquinas on divine simplicity: that the doctrine in Aquinas is a piece of logical nonsense.

Logic and divine simplicity

Why should it be thought that Aquinas on divine simplicity is logically nonsensical? The replies most commonly given are as follows:

(a) If Aquinas is right, then God is identical with his attributes. But nothing can be identical with its attributes.

(b) If Aquinas is right, then God's attributes must be identical with each other. But this is absurd.

(c) If Aquinas is right, then God exists without being an individual. But nothing can exist as God without being an individual.

(d) If Aquinas is right, then God and existence are identical. But this is absurd.

(e) If Aquinas is right, then God can belong to no genus. But God belongs to the genus 'person' or 'God'.

Let us consider each of these objections in order.

(a) It does, indeed, seem nonsense to say that something can be identical with its attributes. Fred may be bald, but his baldness is surely not him. By the same token, then, it would seem nonsense to hold that God and, say, his knowledge are the same (supposing, that is, that we ascribe knowledge to God, and supposing that we say knowledge is an attribute of God).

But is Aquinas asking us to say any such thing? Here it is important to note two things which frequently get overlooked in discussions of Aquinas on God.

First, immediately before he begins his account of divine simplicity in the *Summa Theologiae* (the account occupies Ia, 3) Aquinas explains what he is just about to do. At this point we find him saying this:

> Now we cannot know how God is, but only how he is not; we must therefore consider the ways in which God does not exist, rather than the ways in which he does. . . . The ways in which God does not exist will become apparent if we rule out from him everything inappropriate, such as compositeness. . . . Let us inquire then first about God's simpleness, thus ruling out compositeness.

So Aquinas's doctrine of divine simplicity is an account of what God is *not*. We ought therefore to be immediately suspicious of (a), for that seems to make the doctrine an account of what God is, viz. something with attributes identical with itself. Readers of Aquinas will quickly discover that in talking about God's simplicity he does use language which suggests that he is indeed telling us what God is, that he is offering a positive description of God. And, though he denies that we can say what God is (*quid est?*), he does not mean that we cannot speak truly and positively about God, that 'we cannot make true predications concerning God' (Anscombe and Geach 1961, p. 117). Furthermore, Aquinas can certainly be read as saying that God is identical with his attributes. At one point, for instance, he writes:

> God . . . is identical with his own godhead, with his own life and with whatever else is similarly said of him (Ia, 3, 3).

But remarks like this are part of what is explicitly said by Aquinas to be an account of 'the ways in which God does not exist'. The presumption would therefore seem to be that they are not intended as descriptions of God or as statements about what is positively true of him. They are offered as true statements concerning God. But they are statements intended to say what God is not.

Second (though related to what has just been said), to claim that, for Aquinas, God is identical with his attributes is to draw attention to Aquinas's view that there is in God no mixture (*compositio*) of *suppositum* and nature, or essence. But that is not a view about what is identical with what, as if Aquinas were saying that God's *suppositum* and nature are identical as Mr Smith's house and Mrs Smith's house are identical. As we have seen, it is an attempt to say that while, for example, we can distinguish between Bill and his human nature, we cannot do the same sort of thing when it comes to God. In this respect, so Aquinas is saying, God differs from things like Bill.

In other words, identity is not really an issue in Aquinas's teaching that in God there is a mixture of *suppositum* and nature or essence. Aquinas's language may sometimes suggest the opposite, but his teaching is really an answer to a question. Aquinas is asking whether we can think of God as an individual being having a nature in, for example, the way that we can think of a man as an individual having a nature. His reply is 'No', and in this, I think, he is right. We can distinguish between (a) an individual human being, and (b) his nature as such. And we can sensibly say of some human being (a) that he is an individual human being, and (b) that he is not humanity or 'pure human nature'. But to do all this depends on our being able to single out individual human beings. And how are we to do this except on the assumption that individual human beings differ as bodily creatures? And if God is not a bodily creature, does it not therefore seem best to say that when it comes to God we cannot distinguish between God and his nature? I suggest that the answer is 'Yes'. In Aquinas's way of putting it: 'The individuality of things not composed of matter and form cannot . . . derive from this or that individual matter, and the forms of such things must therefore be intrinsically individual and themselves subsist as things' (Ia, 3, 3). In other words if something is non-material, we have no way of thinking of it as a material individual. Since God is non-material, it follows that we cannot think of him as a material individual.

(b) Again, to begin with, we can admit that there is point to the objection. Think of a British flag. It would be absurd to say that the blueness of the flag is identical with its redness and whiteness. If that were so, then we would have no British flag.

But is Aquinas saying that God's attributes are indistinguishable from each other as if to speak of them were like speaking of the colours of the British flag as if they were indistinguishable?

Some have supposed that he is saying this. But one has to respond that the supposition is not based on a justified reading of what Aquinas actually writes. Here again, the teaching of Aquinas that is at issue is his claim that we cannot distinguish between the *suppositum* of God and the nature of God as we can distinguish between the *suppositum* of Bill and the nature of Bill. For Aquinas this means that whatever God is, he is not an individual to be singled out as we can single out material individuals in the world. And from this he concludes that though we can distinguish between, say, Solomon being wise and Solomon being powerful, we cannot in the same way distinguish between, say, God being wise and God being powerful. But that, too, is surely right. Distinguishing between the properties of a material object depends on picking out the object as a thing of some kind. Before we can distinguish between Solomon being wise and Solomon being powerful, we have to single out Solomon as an individual human being. What, then, happens, if we are not dealing with a material object which we can single out like Solomon the human being? We will not be able to distinguish its properties from each other. And that, so Aquinas is saying, is how we stand with respect to God. Once again, we need to note that what is at issue here is a question of what God is *not*. He is not, says Aquinas, something we can pick out like Solomon, whose wisdom we can think of apart from his power.

(c) The third objection also has merit. Unless we wish to deny God's existence altogether, can we not sensibly say 'God is an individual'? If 'God is an individual' means that there is, indeed, a God, or that 'God' is not the name of some creature of fiction, then, presumably, we can.

But we also need to note that 'God is an individual' is mysterious, to say the least. Does it, for instance, tell us what God is? No, for by the same reasoning as that just given, we can hold, for example, that mountains and elephants are individuals. For there certainly are both mountains and elephants. Yet neither of them, presumably, is God. 'X is an individual' cannot, in fact, serve as an informative answer to the question 'What is X?'. One might therefore wonder just what might be the point of insisting that God is an individual.

Nevertheless, as I have said, those who do insist on this are not talking nonsense. 'God is an individual' can be read as 'There is a God'. But this, of course, is not something that Aquinas would deny. In this sense, at any rate, our third objection fails to engage with his theory of divine simplicity.

Yet those who endorse objection (c) may still feel that this reply does not engage the objection. Why? Because, so it might be argued, Aquinas's teaching on God's simplicity holds that God is a thing of no kind, which is absurd. For how can there be anything which is not a thing of some kind?

Can you, for instance, have an apple that is not an apple?

Clearly not. But, again, this is not something that Aquinas denies. What he denies is that God's individuality is to be encountered or to be spoken about as if it were that of something material. His claim is that being what God is (having the nature of God, being the divine nature) differs from being what anything material is (having the nature of something material, being a material individual). And this, so I have suggested, is something we can accept.

(d) The point behind objection (d) is one that we can now understand in the light of Chapter 4. I argued there that existence is not a property of objects and that one cannot sensibly build 'existence' into the definition of anything so as to conclude that there is something with the property of existence. Now Aquinas holds that we cannot distinguish between God's nature or essence and existence. Suppose we take this to mean that if we ask for a definition of God, 'existence' will be part of the definition. In that case it would seem that Aquinas has misunderstood the nature of existence. And that is the claim of objection (d). As one writer puts it: 'The logical character of the concept of existence is not only enough to render it inadmissible to infer God's existence from his essence, but also renders it inadmissible to infer his essence from his existence – or, again, to identify them' (Penelhum 1960, p. 184).

But again, I think, the objection is confused. As we saw in Chapter 4, Aquinas denies that God can be defined into existence, so we ought not to ascribe to him the doctrine that existence enters into the definition of 'God'. Indeed, we ought not to ascribe to him the doctrine that 'God' can be defined at all. For, as we have also seen, Aquinas maintains that since God is not part of the material world, he cannot be located in terms of genus and species. We can define 'whale' in terms of genus and species. We cannot, in the same sense, define 'God'. Or so Aquinas would have said.

But he does hold that God's nature and existence are indistinguishable. And if that is not a disguised definition, then what is it?

The answer, I think, is the one I have already given in trying to expound Aquinas on divine simplicity. What Aquinas is saying is that God's existence is not created *ex nihilo*. So if we object to his doctrine that God's nature and existence are indistinguishable, what we are objecting to is the assertion that God is not a creature.

Should we, then, object to this assertion? I think we should not, for the following reasons.

(1) Quite apart from any views we might have about Aquinas's thinking, in terms of traditional belief in God it is simply nonsense to say that God is a creature. On the contrary, for traditional theology God is distinct from all

creatures, which is why he is referred to as Creator.

(2) If we say that God is a creature we should also say that there are two Creators. For we have reason to hold that God is a Creator, and if he is also a creature then something other than God must also be a Creator. Yet if something can be described as creating, it cannot be something material. This follows from what has already been said about God as Creator not being material. But to understand that there are two or more things of some kind, and, therefore, that there are two Creators, we need to be able to single out the items whose existence we recognize, and we need to be able to comprehend them as individuals distinct from each other. But how can we do this if we are dealing with what is non-material? It may be true that creation can be the work of more than one individual, but it also seems that our ability to comprehend a distinction between things of some kind is confined to our dealings with material individuals. If there is a dog, there could be many dogs. In virtue of what are they many? Not in virtue of their canine nature, for they share that. Could it be in virtue of the kinds of difference we might try to illustrate by saying, for example, that one is in the garden and another in the house, or that one is black and another is brown? Not so. For to say things like this presupposes that we are dealing with more than one. In the end, so it seems, if we want to know what makes one individual not another of the same kind we have to appeal to the fact that they are as a matter of fact materially distinct. We have to be able to distinguish between them as material individuals. To put it another way, to grasp that some individual is not another of the same kind we have to point to it and to other material individuals. Since Creators cannot be materially distinct, however, since, if you like, they cannot be pointed to, we may reasonably discount the suggestion that there are two Creators.

(3) Someone who rejects this argument might, however, say that consistency demands that if we suppose that the universe is created, we must also suppose that God is created. But this suggestion can also be denied.

In the first place, we have reason to say that the universe is created because we can consider it as a totality and we can then ask what accounts for its existence. But if God is no material individual, then we cannot even begin to consider him as a totality like the universe and his existence cannot be something we need to try to account for as we can try to account for that of the universe. In other words, we have reason to suppose that the universe is created, but we have no reason to suppose that God, as the Creator of the universe, is himself created.

In the second place, however, we can deny that God is created because we can hold that everything that exists apart from God is created by God and that God is created by nothing.

In order to see why this is so we need to return to part of the reasoning offered in Chapter 1. I argued there that we can always ask what accounts for things unless the question is silly. And that principle, so I suggested, allows us to seek to account for the existence of the universe. But can we not do more than ask 'Why is there any universe at all?' or 'Why is there a universe?'? Suppose we banish from our minds any thoughts we may have concerning the existence of God. We look around us and we note that various things exist, that there is, in fact, something rather than nothing. Can we not now ask 'Why is there anything at all?', or 'Why is there something rather than nothing?'?

People respond to this question in different ways. Some, for example, say that there just are things and that is the end of the matter. Others say that there being nothing at all is not a comprehensible possibility and that no question arises as to why there should be something rather than nothing. But there is something rather than nothing. We know this very well. And, though we might not be able to prove that we should ask why this is so, it seems as arbitrary not to ask it as it does to reject the question 'Why is there any universe at all?'. My suggestion, therefore, is that it is perfectly reasonable to ask why there should be something rather than nothing, or why there should be anything at all. And if it is reasonable to ask this question, it is reasonable to suppose that the question has an answer.

What, then, can be said of this answer? One thing should be obvious immediately. This is that whatever answers the question 'Why is there anything at all?' cannot be different from what I have so far referred to in using the word 'God'. 'Why is there anything at all?' evidently includes the question 'Why is there any universe at all?'. Whatever is true of the answer to the second of these questions will therefore be true of the answer to the first. We may therefore say that whatever accounts for there being anything can be referred to as creating the universe. To this we may add that it cannot be thought of as a material individual whose nature can be distinguished from itself. In Aquinas's terminology, it cannot be a mixture (*compositio*) of form and matter, or *suppositum* and nature, or essence.

But now, so we can also add, something else follows. This is that if we can ask what accounts for there being anything at all, there will be no possibility of the answer to our question being something created. Or, to put it another way, whatever accounts for there being something rather than nothing cannot be anything of which we can sensibly ask 'What accounts for its existence?'. Why not? Because if it were like this, it would be part of our initial question. Whatever accounts for there being anything, whatever answers the question 'Why is there something rather than nothing?', cannot be something the existence of which is brought about by anything. If it were, then the question of how it comes to exist would arise again. If it exists at all, therefore, its existence will be underived. Or, to put it another way, whatever accounts for there being anything at all cannot be something created. And in this sense, therefore, we can again agree with Aquinas. We cannot distinguish between God and his existence.

(e) Like the other objections we have just been considering, (e) also seems initially plausible. Surely, so someone might say, everything belongs to a genus, even if there are genera containing only one member. Do we not, then, deny the existence of God if we deny that he belongs to a genus?

If God is something we can understand as belonging to a genus, then the answer is clearly 'Yes'. But can one think of God in this way?

Much, of course, must here depend on how we construe the word 'genus'. But possible meanings of the word need not detain us at this point. For in saying that God belongs to no genus Aquinas basically means that God transcends the material world in which items can be (and are) classified in the light of their physical similarities and differences. For Aquinas, then, 'God belongs to no genus' or 'We cannot distinguish in God genus and difference' (cf. Ia, 3, 5) can be read as repetitions of the claim that God does not belong to the material world. If we accept this claim, therefore, we can reject (e). An objector might reply that if God belongs to no genus, then he is a thing of no kind at all. But that, as we saw above, is not what Aquinas intends us to understand. His major point is that whatever God is, he is not something to be located and defined as an object within his creation.

NOTHING BUT NEGATION?

Returning to our earlier question, then, we can indeed concede that talking of God by means of negation is something it makes sense to do. For we have reason to endorse an account of God's simplicity such as that to be found in Aquinas. God, we can say, is not a material individual. Nor is he something we can think of as distinct from his nature, as having attributes distinct from himself, as dependent for his existence on anything, or as classifiable in terms of genus and species.

But must all talk of God be negative? Can we only say what God is *not*? Some have held that the answer to these questions is 'Yes'. They have also held that by talking about God by means of negation we can somehow come to understand what God is. This, for example, is the view of the Jewish philosopher Moses Maimonides (1135–1204). According to him:

There is no necessity at all for you to use positive attributes of God with a view of magnifying Him in your thoughts . . . I will give you . . . some illustrations, in order that you may better understand the impropriety of ascribing to God any positive attributes. A person may know for certain that a 'ship' is in existence, but he may not know to what object that name is applied, whether to a substance or to an accident; a second person then learns that a ship is not an accident; a third, that it is not a mineral; a fourth, that it is not a plant growing in the earth; a fifth, that it is not a body whose parts are joined together by nature; a sixth, that it is not a flat object like boards or doors; a seventh, that it is not a sphere; an eighth, that it is not pointed; a ninth, that it is not round shaped; nor equilateral; a tenth, that it is not solid. It is clear that this tenth person has almost arrived at the correct notion of a 'ship' by the foregoing negative attributes. . . . In the same manner you will come nearer to the knowledge and comprehension of God by the negative attributes. . . . I do not merely declare that he who affirms attributes of God has not sufficient knowledge concerning the Creator . . . but I say that he unconsciously loses his belief in God (*The Guide for the Perplexed*, pp. 86ff.).

But this clearly will not do. It is, of course, true that by means of negation we can come to make true statements about things. It is, for example, true to say 'London is not a vegetable'. And sometimes we can guess what something is when someone denies only one thing about it. A mother who has just given birth can be told 'It's not a boy', and she will then know at once that the baby is a girl. Yet if we only know what something is not, we do not know what it is. Maimonides may reply that his example proves the contrary. But it really does no such thing. Someone who has all the negations mentioned by Maimonides will not find that he 'has almost arrived at the correct notion of a "ship" '. He could equally well be thinking of a wardrobe or a coffin.

Another problem is this. If we can only say what God is not, can we possibly be talking about God at all? On some views of God, maybe we can; but not if 'God' means what it has traditionally meant within the framework of religions like Judaism and Christianity. These do not just tell us what God is not. They make positive affirmations about God. They say, for example, 'God is the Creator', 'God is powerful', 'God has knowledge', 'God is everywhere', 'God is eternal', and 'God is good'. Sometimes, indeed, what looks like a positive assertion about something may be no such thing. But all the assertions just mentioned not only *look* to be positive ones about God; those who subscribe to them would normally understand them *to be* such. As Aquinas drily puts it: 'When a man speaks of the "living God" he does not simply want to say . . . that he differs from a lifeless body' (Ia, 13, 2). Or, as a modern writer observes:

Religious people have not in fact usually thought of God as wholly Other than themselves or as totally ineffable. They have had many positive and some surprising things to say about him, and they have insisted on saying these things to the unconverted, i.e. to those who supposedly are *not* in the know. To justify their practice we need a theory of religious language which will guarantee positive and generally intelligible meaning to at least some statements about God (Palmer 1973, p. 54).

Presumably, then, we need to ask whether we can offer any such theory.

A first answer: God-talk is meaningless

One influential answer given to this question has been 'No, because all talk of
God is meaningless'. Here I am referring to a line of thinking developed
around the middle of the present century from work done on the theory of
meaning by the so-called 'Logical Positivists', who produced what came to
be referred to as the 'Verification Principle' of meaning, and whose work
came to be applied to topics such as theological discourse.

What was the Verification Principle? The question cannot be quickly
answered since those who have been said to have endorsed it were often really
offering different theories. Roughly speaking, however, and concentrating
on the question of God, what emerged in the wake of Logical Positivism was
an argument that went like this:

(1) Meaningful statements are either (a) mathematical statements,
    tautologies (e.g. 'Cats are cats'), or logically necessary state-
    ments, or (b) statements the truth of which can be confirmed
    (verified) by means of sense experience.
(2) Statements about God belong to none of the above categories.
(3) Therefore, statements about God are meaningless.

Notice that in terms of this view it is not even *probable* that what believers say
about God is true. The idea is that since what they say is meaningless, it is
neither true nor false. Or, as Hume put it (writing long before the rise of
Logical Positivism, but in many ways anticipating it): 'If we take in our hand
any volume; of divinity or school metaphysics, for instance, let us ask, *Does it
contain any abstract reasoning concerning quantity or number?* No. *Does it contain
any experimental reasoning concerning matter of fact and existence?* No. Commit it
then to the flames: for it can contain nothing but sophistry and illusion' (*An
Enquiry concerning Human Understanding*, p. 165).

But, as most philosophers now concede, this form of attack on belief in
God is not really a live option. For this reason I do not propose to discuss it in
detail. Instead, I shall simply summarize some of what many have come to see
as major objections to it.

(1) Suppose we agree that statements about God are not mathematical,
tautological, or logically necessary. Suppose someone then says that such
statements can only be meaningful if their truth can be confirmed by means of
sense experience. On his own admission, his proposal is meaningless. For if
we accept it, we say that a statement is only meaningful if its truth can be
confirmed by means of sense experience, while to say this is not to say something the truth of which can be confirmed by means of sense experience.
Cutting some corners, we can put this by saying that the Verification
Principle does not satisfy its own criterion of meaningfulness.

(2) Whatever Logical Positivists said, it just does seem that people can make sense of assertions about God. Those who believe in God clearly do not regard themselves as talking nonsense. And even those who have no belief in God will frequently observe that they consider their disbelief to be something relating to a genuine issue. They will say, in other words, that though they do not believe in God, they have some notion of what it is in which they do not believe.

(3) Given what 'God' has been taken to mean, it is absurd to suppose that statements about God cannot be meaningful because their truth cannot be confirmed by means of human senses. For statements about God are not usually taken to be statements about a physical object. If 'God exists' were on a level with 'There is a wart on John's nose', then things would be different. Warts and noses are physical, so it would make nonsense to say both that there is a wart on John's nose and that nobody could, even in principle, confirm its presence by any sense experience. But 'God exists' does not report a truth about something physical. One ought therefore not to dismiss it as meaningless because its truth, if it is true, cannot be confirmed by means of human senses. That would be like criticizing a tennis player for not scoring goals.

(4) It is not, in any case, obvious that the truth of statements about God cannot be confirmed by means of human senses. Those who believe in the existence of God have often argued that physical factors (such as the existence of the universe, or the nature of the universe) can rationally be taken as evidence for the truth of belief in God. If such people are even possibly right, then it seems wrong to insist that statements about God are bound to be meaningless.

(5) It is possible to give examples of what are *both prima facie* meaningful statements *and* statements the truth of which cannot in principle be confirmed by means of the senses. To cite an example of Richard Swinburne, consider the following: 'Some of the toys which to all appearances stay in the toy cupboard while people are asleep and no one is watching, actually get up and dance in the middle of the night and then go back to the cupboard leaving no traces of their activity' (Swinburne 1977, p. 27). One may never believe someone uttering such a statement, but it is not meaningless. A critic might say that we could not understand it if it could not be shown to be true or false and that knowing how to show a statement to be true or false means knowing what sense experience makes it probably true or probably false. But one can understand statements without knowing what sense experience would make them probably true or probably false. 'A man can understand the statement "Once upon a time, before there were men or any other rational creatures, the earth was covered by sea", without his having any idea of what geological evidence would count for or against this proposition, or

any idea of how to establish what geological evidence would count for or against the proposition' (Swinburne 1977, p. 28).

A second answer: God and causation

Let us, then, continue to assume that there could be a God. We still need to consider how we might significantly talk of him. This brings us to a second solution that has been proposed: that our talk of God gets its sense in the light of what God has caused.

Suppose we discover a corpse which has clearly been savagely mutilated by somebody. We might describe what we discover as 'horrifying' or 'outrageous', and we might quickly go on to apply both these terms to the person responsible for what we have found. Our justification for doing so lies in the fact that what he or she has brought about can fairly be described as 'horrifying' or 'outrageous'.

In other words, we sometimes ascribe to a cause the same terms we use in talking of what it has brought about. And, in the light of this fact, some have suggested that we can significantly talk about God by noting his effects and by then describing him as we describe them. Thus, for example, it has been argued that we can say that God is good because he is the cause of things that are good. Or we can call God 'wise' because he is the cause of wisdom as we encounter it in people.

But will this really do as a theory about how we can speak positively about God? The answer, it seems to me, is partly 'Yes' and partly 'No'.

In favour of the theory there is, of course, the fact that it often does make sense to describe a cause by the words used to describe its effect, and to do so precisely because of the fact that the cause is the cause of the effect. To add to the example given above: someone who brings about a state of justice might reasonably (though not necessarily) be described as just precisely because of what he has brought about. Then again, confronted by a human baby, we will say that its parents must be human just because the baby is human. Suppose, now, we say that God is the cause of various things. We might then be inclined to describe him as we describe them.

Another point to note is this. Even though we might have little to offer which a philosopher would recognize as a serious theory of causation, we are intuitively inclined to say that if one thing produces another, then what it produces must somehow reflect it. You cannot, as one might say, give what you have not got. A watchmaker is not himself descriptively like a watch, but it makes sense to say that the watches he makes somehow reflect what he is. He 'has watches in him' before he makes them, as one might put it. So, in this sense, one might argue that if A produces B, then what B has is something that is or was somehow in A, even if not in the form that it is in B. And, in the light of this principle, one might argue that if God produces something, then what he produces must somehow be in him, even if he cannot be described in the same way as what he produces, i.e. even if he is not descriptively identical with what he produces.

But even if we agree with all of this (as, indeed, I think we can), we may still deny that it gives us what we are looking for now. And this is so for two reasons.

In the first place, it is not always true that causes resemble their effects. We may sometimes argue from what we take to be an effect to the conclusion that its cause must resemble it. But not always so. Criminals can give birth to saints. Books are written by people. Corpses do not commit murder. (Cf. Kenny 1969, pp. 21f.)

Then again, if we try to build up positive discourse about God on the ground that he has brought things about, we will soon find ourselves committed to absurd conclusions. For if God is the Creator of the universe, then he accounts for the existence of everything in it. And if it makes sense to say that he is, for example, good because he is the cause of good things, and if it makes sense to call him wise because he is the cause of wise things, it also makes sense to refer to him as bodily, since he is the cause of bodily things, or as green because he is the cause of green things. Yet few who believe in God will be happy with that conclusion. Nor should they be if God accounts for the existence of everything in the universe. For if he does that, then, as we have seen, he cannot be corporeal and, therefore, he cannot be a body of any colour (cf. Aquinas, *Summa Theologiae* Ia, 13, 2).

A third answer: Reductionism

Let us therefore try again. What about saying that talk about God is simply intelligible on its own terms so that to believe in God is already to understand what talk about God means, or, at least, to see that it is meaningful? This, at any rate, is what some have said, a good example being D. Z. Phillips, who has tried to explore the topic of meaning and talk about God in a number of publications.

Phillips takes his cue from a distinction made by Wittgenstein between 'surface grammar' and 'depth grammar' (cf. Wittgenstein, *Philosophical Investigations*, para. 664). Roughly speaking, this is a distinction between what utterances or sentences *seem* to mean by virtue of their form, and what they *really* mean. For example: consider the sentence 'The Bishop has bats in the belfry'. In terms of English idiom, that means something like 'The Bishop is rather mad'. But grammatically speaking it resembles sentences like

'The cook has bacon in the pantry', and those unfamiliar with English idiom might easily construe it along those lines. Here, then, we can distinguish between what the first sentence seems to mean and what it really means. It might seem to mean that the Bishop has creatures flying around in his bell-tower. It actually means that he ought to see a psychiatrist.

Now, says Phillips, just as 'The Bishop has bats in the belfry' can be mis-construed, so can talk about God. And this can lead people to ask questions about the meaning of this talk that they ought never to have raised in the first place. And, in Phillips's view, one of these questions is 'How can we talk about God intelligibly?'. In Phillips's view, this question, or ones like it, basically puts the cart before the horse. For, says Phillips, people *do* talk about God, and the proper question to ask in the light of this fact is not 'How can they be talking intelligibly?' but 'What do they mean?'. In other words, according to Phillips, we must start from the fact that there is discourse about God. Then, to a large extent, we will come to see that the question of whether it makes any sense will recede. Phillips, of course, is not suggesting that one can say what one likes about God and still talk sense. But he does seem to be saying that we can start with a presumption that there is sensible talk about God. So his basic answer to the question 'How should we talk about God?' is to say 'Look and see how people actually do talk about God'.

But is this answer acceptable? Here, it seems to me, we can make several points.

(1) Phillips is right to suggest that talk about God should be presumed from the outset to make sense. This is basically because such talk comprises a great deal of human discourse and it seems initially implausible to suppose that it is simply so much nonsense. People, of course, can talk nonsense, and they can do so in large numbers over a long period of time. But talk of God is an ancient phenomenon and it still continues. Furthermore, people who talk about God seem able, in doing so, to communicate with each other and also with those who have no belief in God at all. *A priori*, therefore, we might reasonably suggest that talk of God must make some kind of sense.

(2) Phillips is also right to draw attention to the fact that confusion can arise from not paying attention to what is actually meant by those who talk about God. For such confusion has indeed arisen, and it has accounted for cer-tain criticisms of belief in God which ought to be rejected because they aim at a non-existent target. Here we can refer back to some of the things said about belief in God in the wake of Logical Positivism. As we have seen, some of those influenced by Logical Positivists adopted the conclusion that statements about God are bound to be meaningless since their truth cannot be confirmed by means of sense experience. But why should one suppose that confirmation by sense experience is necessarily relevant when it comes to talk about God?

If I say 'My house is burning', then you have a right to accuse me of talking nonsense if no conceivable sense experience could count in favour of my assertion. But that is because the assertion is, in fact, an assertion about what can be confirmed by means of sense experience. Yet what about the assertion 'There is a God'? Since God is regularly said to be incorporeal, we can immediately deny that this assertion has to be rated as one about something that can be confirmed by sense experience. In other words, someone would be wrong if he said that 'There is a God' cannot be true since God cannot be detected as an object in the physical world. Why? Because 'There is a God' does not have to be taken as asserting the existence of any physical object. It may seem on the surface to do so. At first thought it may be confused with assertions like 'There is a cathedral at Chartres'. But it is not, in fact, an assertion about anything physical, and therefore ought not to be criticized as if it were.

(3)   Yet does it suffice to say that questions about the intelligibility of talk about God can be settled by considering what such talk actually means? Here one surely has to say 'It all depends on what the talk does mean'. Yet as soon as we say that, we are immediately confronted by problems which Phillips, at least, does not seem to have solved.

For one thing, why presume that any general account can be given about the meaning of talk about God? Might not different people mean different things when they talk about God? The amount of disagreement that has existed concerning the nature of God certainly suggests that the answer to this question is 'Yes'.

Then again, can we accept Phillips's own account of the meaning of talk about God? To do justice to this question requires more attention to Phillips's writings than space here allows for. But one might still, I think, say that some of his conclusions about the meaning of talk about God seem highly contestable. We read, for example, that ' "God" is not the name of an individual; it does not refer to anything. . . . To ask whether God exists is not to ask a theoretical question. . . . "There is a God", though it appears to be in the indicative mood, is an expression of faith' (Phillips 1976, pp. 148 and 180f.). Elsewhere Phillips writes: 'The love of God is manifested in the believer's relationship to people and things. In this sense, he can be said to have a love of the world. To see the world as God's world, would, primarily, be to possess this love. To say that God created the world would not be to put forward a theory, hypothesis, or explanation, of the world' (Phillips 1970, p. 56). Yet is all that really so? We may, as I have argued, in one sense deny that God is an individual. And there is an ancient tradition of denying that 'God' is the name of an individual, that it is a proper name. Furthermore, the believer can concede that God is not an explanation of the world, for he might say that explanations are things one understands better than what they explain, while God is decidedly more mysterious than the world. Yet 'There is a God' surely is an indicative statement, at least for most believers. And for most believers the existence of God is indeed a theoretical issue, if that means that one can seriously ask whether or not anything is truly referred to as being divine. 'God', says Phillips, does not refer to anything. But, though it may not do so for some, and though 'God' can be used when no reference is implied at all, for most of those who believe in God the word 'God' does refer, in that 'There is a God' truly asserts the existence of something about which one can go on to make true or false assertions.

In other words, one has the feeling that Phillips has tried to deal with the topic of the significance of talk about God by tacitly denying the existence of God. In this sense, as many have observed, his treatment of God is 'reductionist'. It claims to talk about talk about God, but it frequently seems to be talking about something else. And that, one may suggest, is not going to help us much when it comes to understanding talk about God.

A fourth answer: Metaphor

Let us therefore try yet again. What about saying now that when we talk about God we do so by means of metaphor? This, too, has been suggested, and the argument runs thus.

When we form positive statements about God, we must somehow mean what we say. We must mean that God is what we say he is. But God must clearly be very different from anything in the universe. We need, then, to speak positively about him without denying the difference there is between God and his creation. But we can do this if we think of our talk about God as metaphorical. When you use a metaphor you can speak of two very different things by using the same words in referring to them, or you can refer to something by means of words which you can also use in talking about something very different. One can, for example, speak of the 'ship of State' without implying that the government floats on water. By the same token, then, one can speak about God using words which name or describe things in the universe, but one can do so metaphorically without being committed to absurd consequences concerning the similarity between God and his creatures.

And that may surely be true. For it is indeed a fact that vastly different things can be called by the same name or described in the same way. The companions of Florence Nightingale might have called her a 'rock' without implying that she was a mineral.

The trouble, however, is that we cannot also say that all talk of God is metaphorical. For with metaphorical language one can always raise a question about literal truth. One can ask, for example, whether Florence Nightingale was literally a rock. And if we say that all talk of God is meta-phorical, then we should have to deny that God is really what many would say that he really is.

This may not seem obvious at first. Someone might say 'God is a mighty fortress'. We then ask 'Is that really true? Is God made of stone, for example?'. The answer will be 'Of course not. I am speaking meta-phorically'. Here it would seem that nothing anyone might want to affirm of God is being denied. And we might well see some point in asserting that God is a mighty fortress.

But suppose someone now says 'God is good' or 'God is eternal'. Again, we ask 'Is that really true?'. If the statements are metaphorical, one ought to be able to reply 'No'. But can one do that? Not if one has anything recogniz-able as a traditional belief in God, for that surely accepts that God is literally good and literally eternal.

In short, then, while something may be gained by saying that God can be spoken of by means of metaphor, the suggestion cannot provide a complete account of how one can speak positively of God and still talk intelligibly or meaningfully. One may, in principle, be able to talk sense about God by means of metaphor. But must all talk of God be merely metaphorical? Apparently not.

A fifth answer: Analogy

So we still seem to be left asking how we can talk significantly about God, and now we come to a final answer that has been given to this question. According to this answer, terms can be applied to God and to creatures analogically. As with the doctrine of divine simplicity, it is probably fair to say that the classical spokesman for this view is Aquinas. We can therefore begin to turn to it by seeing how it is developed by him.

Aquinas on analogy

Suppose, then, we say that Macavity and Marmaduke are both cats. And suppose that in this case Macavity and Marmaduke are indeed feline animals, the ones with tails and whiskers. We are therefore saying that in some clear respect both Macavity and Marmaduke have something in common in such a way that the term 'cat' means the same thing when applied to each of them. To say that Macavity is a cat and to say that Marmaduke is a cat is to say exactly the same thing of both Macavity and Marmaduke.

But now consider another example. Suppose we say that something or other is a bat, and that something else is also a bat. Let us call what we are talking about A and B. In that case, A is a bat, and B is a bat. But must 'is a bat' mean the same thing when applied to A and B? A moment's reflection will show that it need not. For A may be the kind of bat that has wings and features in stories about Dracula, while B may be the kind of bat that cricketers use to score a century. The word 'bat' can be applied to two things without meaning the same thing at all.

In more technical language, the difference we have just noted between 'is a cat' and 'is a bat' would be expressed by saying that the word 'cat' is being used *univocally*, while 'bat' is being used *equivocally*. In 'Macavity is a cat' and 'Marmaduke is a cat', the word 'cat' means exactly the same thing. But in 'A is a bat (with wings)' and 'B is a bat (with a handle)' the word 'bat' is being used equivocally. In 'A is a bat' and 'B is a bat' the word 'bat' does not mean the same thing at all. In fact, it means something quite different.

Now if we look at the way people talk about God it soon becomes clear that it often involves applying to God words that normally apply to things in the world around us. So, for example, just as people are sometimes called good and wise, we find that God is called good and wise. Using the above terminology, therefore, we can now ask the following question. Are terms applied to God and to creatures univocally or equivocally? When we say that God is wise and that Solomon is wise, do we mean exactly the same thing? Or do we mean something completely different in the case of God and Solomon?

Aquinas raises this question specifically. And his answer is that terms cannot be applied to God and to creatures univocally. But neither are they only to be applied equivocally.

Why not univocally? Aquinas basically replies to this question by pointing to the vast difference between God and creatures. Suppose we say that Solomon is wise. To say this is to say that Solomon is a wise *man*, something whose wisdom is shown in his behaviour as a material thing of a particular kind. But if Aquinas is right in what we have already seen him to be saying, if his doctrine of divine simplicity is correct, God cannot be wise as Solomon is wise. Or so Aquinas thinks, anyway. On his account, God is not a material thing, while Solomon is. On his account also, God is the reason why Solomon exists at all and he is, therefore, the cause of Solomon's wisdom. In fact, says Aquinas, God must be the cause of all human wisdom, in which case he cannot be another wise individual alongside Solomon and all the other wise people. So, Aquinas concludes, 'Solomon is wise' and 'God is wise' cannot mean exactly the same thing. Or, as Aquinas puts it himself:

The perfection words that we use in speaking of creatures all differ in meaning and each one signifies a perfection as something distinct from all others. Thus when we say that a man is wise, we signify his wisdom as something distinct from the other things about him – his essence, for example, his powers or his existence. But when we use this word about God we do not intend to signify something distinct from his essence, power or existence. When 'wise' is used of a man, it so to speak contains and delimits the aspect of man that it signifies, but this is not so when it is used of God; what it signifies in God goes beyond it. Hence it is clear that the word 'wise' is not used in the same sense of God and man, and the same is true of all other words, so they cannot be used univocally of God and creatures (*Summa Theologiae* Ia, 13, 5).

As a material thing, so Aquinas is saying, Solomon has wisdom as one attribute among many inhering in an individual material subject. For as a material thing, Solomon is a mixture (*compositio*) of form and matter, *suppositum* and nature, or essence. But things are different with God.

Granting all this, one might now say that in that case words must always be used equivocally of God and creatures. One might say that if God is so very different from creatures, then the same term applied to God and a creature cannot mean the same thing at all. But, as Aquinas sees it, this conclusion will not do either. For if words applied to God and to creatures always mean something entirely different, then there is little point in talking of God at all since we will then have absolutely no criteria for applying particular terms to God. In other words, if, for example, there is absolutely no connection between 'Solomon is wise' and 'God is wise', then there is little point in saying that God is wise. Or, as Aquinas puts it:

Although we never use words in exactly the same sense of creatures and God we are not merely equivocating when we use the same word, as some have said, for if this were so we could never argue from statements about creatures to statements about God – any such argument would be invalidated by the Fallacy of Equivocation (*Summa Theologiae* Ia, 13, 5).

What Aquinas is getting at here is this. Suppose we say that God is wise. We cannot mean that God is wise as Solomon is wise, for Solomon and God are different in the ways referred to by Aquinas in talking about divine simplicity. But we learn to use words like 'wise' with reference to things like Solomon. In that case we cannot mean anything by 'God is wise' unless wisdom in God has *some* connection with wisdom in Solomon. In other words, according to Aquinas, anyone who talks of God has the following dilemma to cope with. Either one agrees that terms can be applied to God and creatures univocally, in which case God becomes a creature; or one agrees that terms are always applied to God and creatures equivocally, in which case there seems little point in talking about God at all.

But, as one might expect, Aquinas does not think that there really is a dilemma here. According to him there is another possibility not mentioned in the 'either' or the 'or' or the dilemma. In fact, he says, there is a third way of applying a term to two things. 'We must say therefore', he concludes, 'that words are used of God and creatures in an analogical way, that is in accordance with a certain order between them' (*Summa Theologiae* Ia, 13, 5).

But what does Aquinas mean by this conclusion? One thing he does not mean is that we can only speak of God by means of metaphor. He wants to say that when we speak of God analogically we are speaking in a literal way. If someone asked Aquinas 'Is God really wise?' the answer would have been 'Yes'.

The fact of the matter is that in saying that we can speak of God analogically Aquinas means that in the case of God and creatures it is possible to apply the same terms to both in such a way that it does not have to mean entirely the same in both cases nor something so different that the result is just a metaphor. To take an example of Aquinas, we may say that a man is healthy and that his diet is healthy. In neither case are we speaking metaphorically (if we ask whether both the man and his diet are healthy, the answer can be 'Yes'). But health in human beings and health in diets (or a healthy man and a healthy diet) are different. In the same way, so Aquinas holds, we can apply certain terms both to God and to creatures so as really to mean what we say without saying precisely the same thing in both cases yet without meaning something entirely different. Terms can be used of creatures and God without being used univocally or equivocally.

Is Aquinas right?

So much, then, for Aquinas on talking about God. But the question, of course, is whether what he says is correct. Can we appeal to analogy as allowing us to speak significantly about God?

Clearly Aquinas is right about one thing at least. This is the view that terms cannot be applied to God and to creatures equivocally. For if they were so applied, they would just lack content. As Aquinas himself puts it in a passage I have not yet quoted:

A name is predicated of some being uselessly unless through that name we understand something of the being. But, if names are said of God and creatures in a purely equivocal way, we understand nothing of God through those names; for the meanings of those names are known to us solely to the extent that they are said of creatures. In vain, therefore, would it be said or proved of God that He is a being, good, or the like (*Summa Contra Gentiles* I, 33, 6).

We can apply a term to God which we already apply to creatures, but if the word in no way has even similarity of meaning in both its applications, then in applying it to God we say precisely nothing.

But is it equally obvious that terms cannot be applied to God and to creatures univocally? Some people, at any rate, have felt that here Aquinas is putting things too strongly. They would deny that in statements of the form 'God is X' and Some creature is X' we could never be saying exactly the same thing about God and the creature. On the contrary, so it has been suggested, statements like 'God is good' and 'My mother is good' could be saying exactly the same thing about God and my mother. Or, as one writer puts it: 'When the theist says that God is "good" "good" is . . . being used in a perfectly ordinary sense. The only extraordinary thing being suggested is that it [sc. goodness] exists to a degree in which it does not exist in mundane objects' (Swinburne 1977, p. 71).

Yet this is surely open to question. In one sense, of course, it is hard to dispute. For if we deny that 'good' is applied to God and to creatures equivocally, then we might naturally express ourselves by saying that it means the same thing when applied to God and creatures. In this sense we can concede that terms may be applied to God and to creatures univocally. 'If "univocally" means what it appears to mean, i.e. "in the same sense", then surely a word is being used univocally if it denotes the same property, even if having that property amounts to something very different in different things' (Swinburne 1977, p. 79). But, even allowing for this suggestion, we also need to add some qualifications. For one thing, one might ask whether what we mean on some occasion in calling someone or something good could *ever* be what we *could* mean in calling God good. I shall return to this point in Chapter 8. But, quite apart from this, in 'mundane objects' goodness will exist as what belongs to individuals which can be distinguished from their natures. Good people, for example, are not humanity. Yet if the doctrine of divine simplicity is true, as I have suggested that it is, our statements about God cannot be true because some individual distinguishable from its nature has some property belonging to it. Thus, for example, 'God is wise' cannot be true, if it is true, because God has wisdom as, say, Solomon has wisdom, viz. by being an individual human being of whom we can say 'He is wise'. And this is what Aquinas seems to be driving at. In one sense, therefore, we can deny that terms can be applied to God and creatures univocally. Good people are not humanity, but there is point in saying that if God is, for example, good, then God is goodness. At any rate, we can deny that if God is good, he is good as an individual comprehensible to us as such.

To this extent, therefore, we can agree with Aquinas. Whatever it takes for 'Solomon is wise' to be true cannot be descriptively like whatever it takes for 'God is wise' to be true. But can we also conclude that meaningful, positive statements can be made about God by applying terms to God 'in an analogical way'?

Here, I suggest, the answer is 'Yes'. For, as Aquinas observes, it is possible to apply the same terms in talking of two things without speaking metaphorically, yet without also applying the terms either univocally or equivocally. This point can be illustrated by quoting a useful passage at the beginning of Wittgenstein's *Philosophical Investigations*.

Consider for example the proceedings that we call 'games'. I mean board-games, card-games, ball-games, Olympic games, and so on. What is common to them all? – Don't say: 'There *must* be something common, or they would not be called "games" ' – but *look and see* whether there is anything common to them all. – For if you look at them you will not see something that is common to *all*, but similarities, relationships, and a whole series of them at that. To repeat: don't think, but look! – Look for example at board-games with their multifarious relationships. Now pass to card-games; here you find many correspondences with the first group, but many common features drop out, and others appear. When we pass next to ball-games, much that is common is retained, but much is lost. – Are they all 'amusing'? Compare chess with noughts and crosses. Or is there always winning and losing, or competition between players? Think of patience . . . And we can go through the many, many other groups of games in the same way; can see how similarities crop up and disappear (*Philosophical Investigations*, para. 66).

What Wittgenstein brings out very clearly here is that at least one word can significantly be used in different, related, and yet non-metaphorical senses. And, following the clue offered by his example, we can quickly come to see that many words can significantly be used in this way. Take, for instance, 'good'. You can have good food and good books, not to mention good people, good wine, and a good night's sleep. Or again, there is Aquinas's illustration, the word 'healthy'. As Aquinas says, a man can be healthy, but so can a diet. You can also, of course, have healthy societies, healthy complexions, and healthy climates. In saying that all these things are healthy one is not saying that they are exactly alike in some respect. But nor is one saying that they are different as mammalian bats are from wooden ones.

A further problem

But we are still left with a difficulty. As we have seen, it makes sense to say that we cannot define God as we can define things within the universe. Suppose, then, that we apply a term to God that we also apply to a creature. Suppose, for example, we assert that God is wise. How can we understand what we are saying? We may concede that in, say, 'God is wise' and 'Solomon is wise' the words 'is wise' are not to be understood univocally or equivocally. And we may concede that they are not metaphorical. But if God is not definable as creatures are, will it not be true that wisdom in him will differ so greatly from wisdom in them that 'God is wise' (or any other positive statement about God) will be incomprehensible to us? Does not Aquinas's theory of analogy still leave us asking whether we can understand what we say about God when talking about him by means of positive statements? And are we not left with this question even without reference to Aquinas? For would not most of those who believe in God concede that there is an enormous difference between God and creatures?

At this point it helps to draw a distinction which I shall try to illustrate by means of the word 'faithful'.

Suppose I say that I know of two faithful things. If I say nothing but this, you cannot know what I am talking about, for 'thing' is a kind of dummy word and it does not serve to identify anything. But you can still have some idea about what is meant by calling the things I speak of (whatever they are) faithful. At the same time, since you do not know what things I am talking about, you do not know the exact form taken by their fidelity, i.e. what it is like for each of them to be faithful. For faithfulness, so to speak, has different faces. What is involved in a dog being faithful is different from what is involved in a husband being faithful to his wife. And that, again, is different from, say, a Church being faithful to its traditions.

So one can understand something of what is meant when something is said to be thus and so without understanding what it is like for the thing itself to be thus and so. And that, in fact, is what we now need to note with respect to our present problem. For we can now sensibly say that, though we might not be able to understand what it is like for God to be as he may be said to be, it is still, in principle, possible for us to understand what is meant when he is said to be as he is. In other words, it is, in principle, possible to agree that certain words can signify something that is really in God, that we can understand something of what is signified by these words, and yet that the way in which God is as he is said to be is not something we can understand. And this, in fact, is what Aquinas himself says. He distinguishes between the property signified by a property word (its *res significata*) and the way in which the property is present in the object which has it (its *modus significandi*). And, with this distinction in mind, Aquinas thinks that it is possible to be saying something intelligible in saying that certain words can be applied to God and to creatures. We cannot, he thinks, understand what it is like for God to have the attributes we attribute to him. Aquinas would say that, strictly speaking, God does not *have* any attributes and that in expressing our views about God we are really wholly dependent not on a knowledge of what God is but rather on a knowledge of what creatures are and what God therefore cannot be. But Aquinas still holds that we can mean what we say when we describe God in whatever way we do. So, according to Aquinas, though there is a vast difference between, say, God and Solomon, we can call both of them wise, and speak intelligibly, as long as we add that what is signified by 'wisdom' is present in both Solomon and God in very different ways. God, for Aquinas, can be called wise in a non-metaphorical sense. But Aquinas also holds that what it takes for God to be wise is not something we can understand. We can understand what it is for Solomon to be wise, but that is because Solomon is a creature who is part of the material world. God, on the other hand, is not material, and we cannot understand how wisdom exists in him.

And that, I think, is what we seem forced to say. In other words, there is a sense in which our present difficulty cannot be resolved. If the doctrine of divine simplicity is correct, there is a sense in which we cannot understand the truth of statements like 'God is wise'. Given the doctrine of divine simplicity, we cannot understand what it is like for God to be as we say that he is when we talk about him by means of positive statements. For the doctrine entails that we cannot think of God as a creature with a nature distinct from its individuality while our understanding of positive statements about things generally depends on the fact that we are talking about creatures with natures distinguishable from their individuality.

On the other hand, however, this is not to say that we cannot rationally believe ourselves to be speaking truly when we make positive statements about God. For one can, of course, rationally believe that a statement is true without being able to say what it is like for the statement to be true, without, if you like, understanding what is going on in whatever it is that makes the statement true. One can rationally believe that Fred is ill, and yet one might have no means of understanding what his illness amounts to. One can rationally believe that smoking is dangerous, and yet one might have no biological grasp of the nature of tobacco, and no serious knowledge of human biology. Or, to refer back to the earlier example, when I tell you that I know of two faithful things, you can rationally believe me without being able to say what it is like for my assertion 'There are two faithful things' to be true. In order to get that far, you will need more information. You will, of course, need to know what I am talking about.

THE NEXT QUESTION

So the situation appears to be this:

(1) We cannot apply terms to God and creatures univocally.
(2) We cannot apply terms to God and creatures equivocally.
(3) Terms can be applied to different things analogically.
(4) It seems possible in principle to accept a statement as true without knowing what it is like for the statement to be true.

And, with these points in mind, we can, I think, accept what Aquinas is saying about God and analogy. We can accept, in principle, that talk about God could be literal, and that statements made about God by virtue of analogy might be such that we can reasonably accept them as intelligible, even though we will not understand what it is like for them to be true. We can, in principle, allow for the difference between God and creatures, but we can also, in principle, allow for the possibility of talking positively about God and meaning what we say.

Yet even all this takes us only so far. For it is, as one might put it, nothing but 'talk about talk', and it still leaves us with a question. Suppose we can talk meaningfully about God. Suppose we can mean what we say about him and use words about him with some understanding and in recognition that we are speaking of him in positive terms. *What should we say about him?* The main conclusion of this chapter has been that significant, positive discourse about God is a possibility, that we can, *in principle*, mean what we say when we talk about God positively. But what should be the content of our discourse when we do this? Have we any reason for applying to God one particular term rather than another? Have we any reason for making any positive assertions about God at all? These are matters to turn to next.

QUESTIONS FOR DISCUSSION

1   Do those who say that there is a God need to understand what they are saying?
2   What might God not be?
3   Is the doctrine of divine simplicity a piece of logical nonsense?
4   Does God have a nature?
5   'Now we cannot know what God is, but only what he is not; we must therefore consider the ways in which God does not exist, rather than the ways in which he does' (Aquinas, Introduction to *Summa Theologiae* Ia, 3). Discuss.
6   Can you think of any plausible reason for supposing that talk about God must be meaningless?
7   If God is the cause of what exists in the universe, must he somehow resemble things in the universe? Or must it not be true that things in the universe somehow resemble God?
8   How would you answer the question 'What does it mean to believe in God?'?
9   Can one talk sense about God by means of metaphor? If so, what might one say about him?
10 Can one say both that God is incomprehensible and that we can make true statements about him?

FURTHER READING

There are many good discussions available concerning the general question of whether and/or how we can talk intelligibly about God, though this question is commonly taken up as part of a wider issue: the intelligibility or meaningfulness of 'religious language' (whatever that is). A very useful introduction to this area of debate is Frederick Ferré, *Language, Logic and God* (London/Glasgow, 1970). This deals in a clear way with various theories, including Logical Positivism and analogy. Other books worth noting in this connection are the following:

Stuart C. Brown, *Do Religious Claims Make Sense?* (London, 1969).

Anders Jeffner, *The Study of Religious Language* (London, 1971).

Ian Ramsey, *Religious Language* (London, 1957).

Aquinas's teaching on divine simplicity can be found not only in *Summa Theologiae* Ia, 3 but also in several other places. For a brief statement of it, see the *Compendium Theologiae*.

For more detailed treatments, see *De Potentia* VII and *Summa Contra Gentiles* I, 14–18. For a modern critique of the doctrine of divine simplicity, see Terence Penelhum, *Religion and Rationality* (New York, 1971). A more direct, detailed, and technical critique can be found in Alvin Plantinga, *Does God Have a Nature?* (Marquette, 1980). An article worth consulting on the notion of divine simplicity is Charles J. Kelly, 'The Intelligibility of the Thomistic God', *Religious Studies* 12 (1976). For a good and appreciative exposition of Aquinas's teaching on divine simplicity (one which does justice to its nature as a view of what God is *not*), see David B. Burrell, *Aquinas, God and Action* (London, 1979). The agnostic element in Aquinas's approach to God is also nicely brought out by the following: Josef Pieper, *The Silence of Saint Thomas* (Chicago, 1957); Edward Sillem, *Ways of Thinking About God* (London, 1961); Victor White, *God the Unknown* (London, 1956).

For an introduction to Logical Positivism, see Oswald Hanfling (ed.), *Essential Readings in Logical Positivism* (Oxford, 1981). A good, but rather technical discussion of God and verification is R. S. Heimbeck, *Theology and Meaning* (London, 1969). For a modern, trenchant defence of critiques of belief in God based on notions of verification, see Kai Nielsen's two books *Contemporary Critiques of Religion* (London, 1971) and *An Introduction to the Philosophy of Religion* (New York, 1983). Issues concerning belief in God arising from Logical Positivism can be found discussed in the works by Brown, Jeffner, and Ramsey, mentioned above. For a good, crisp critique of the attack on belief in God derived from ideas of logical positivists, see Alvin Plantinga, *God and Other Minds* (Ithaca, N.Y., 1967), and Richard Swinburne, *The Coherence of Theism* (Oxford, 1977). A famous English critic of religious belief working from principles of logical positivists was A. J. Ayer. See his *Language, Truth and Logic* (1st ed., 1936; 2nd ed., London, 1946). A clever, though technical, critique of Ayer (which is generally reckoned to be pretty decisive) occurs in a review of *Language, Truth and Logic* by Alonso Church in *Journal of Symbolic Logic* (1949).

I have concentrated on D. Z. Phillips as an example of someone dealing with the meaning of talk about God by apparently reducing it to something else. But other writers could have been mentioned as seeming to do the same thing. A famous example is R. B. Braithwaite. See his *An Empiricist's View of the Nature of Religious Belief* (Cambridge, 1955). Works by Phillips include:

The Concept of Prayer (London, 1965).

Faith and Philosophical Enquiry (London, 1970).

Death and Immortality (London, 1970).

Religion Without Explanation (Oxford, 1976).

Phillips is his own best defender. Helpful critiques of his writings can be found in Patrick Sherry, *Religion, Truth and Language-Games* (London, 1977), Kai Nielsen, *Scepticism* (London, 1973), and Roger Trigg, *Reason and Commitment* (Cambridge, 1973). For brief, but very cogent, critiques of Phillips see ch. 6 of the volume by Swinburne, mentioned above, and ch. 12 of John Mackie's *The Miracle of Theism* (Oxford, 1982).

Discussion of analogy can be found in most of the standard philosophy of religion textbooks and in many of the items referred to above (see, especially, the works by Ferré, Penelhum, Sherry, and Swinburne). Those interested in the topic of analogy would do well to consider the work done on it by James Ross. See 'A New Theory of Analogy' in John Donnelly (ed.), *Logical Analysis and Contemporary Theism* (New York, 1972); 'Analogy as a Rule of Meaning for Religious Language' in Anthony Kenny (ed.), *Aquinas: A Collection of Critical Essays* (London, 1970); 'Analogy and the Resolution of some Cognitivity Problems', *Journal of Philosophy* (1970). Two books dealing in detail with analogy are Humphrey Palmer, *Analogy* (London, 1973) and E. L. Mascall, *Existence and Analogy*

(London, 1949). For Aquinas on analogy see *Summa Theologiae* Ia, 13 and *Summa Contra Gentiles* I, 29–36. With respect to Aquinas on analogy there are very good articles at the end of the relevant volume of the Blackfriars edition of the *Summa Theologiae* (Vol. 3, London/New York, 1964).

6
Eternal and Changeless

It is commonly said that God has various attributes or properties. In the light of what we have now seen, however, we can, perhaps, recognize that this common saying needs to be understood with some qualification. Something which *has* attributes or properties can always be distinguished from them. Thus, for example, though I might be strong, I am not my strength, nor am I strength *simpliciter*. Yet with God, so I have argued, things cannot be like this. We cannot distinguish between God and his nature, so we might just as well say that he is his nature and that he is, therefore, his attributes or properties. This is not to suggest that God is nothing but an attribute or property, or that he is simply a cluster of such things. Nor is it to say that, when it comes to God, different attributes or properties can be understood as identical. It is just to say what the doctrine of divine simplicity says: that we cannot understand God as a material individual. Or, to put it another way, our ordinary language for referring to things within the universe and for describing them cannot really do justice to the reality we are trying to talk about when we start talking about God. We have nothing but this language as a tool for talking about God, but we still need to recognize that it is radically inadequate for the job we try to make it perform.

Nevertheless, as we have also seen, we can in principle make true statements about God. So I now want to consider specific things that have been said about him, beginning in this chapter with the assertion that God is eternal. This assertion is very familiar, but have we any reason for supposing that it is true? And what, in any case, could it mean to call God eternal?

THE MEANING OF 'GOD IS ETERNAL'

Let us begin with the second of these questions. What does it mean to call God eternal? Two major answers have been proposed. According to the first, to call God eternal is to say that he is everlasting. According to the second (which I shall call the 'classical' view of eternity), God is eternal since he lacks both beginning and end, and since he is also utterly changeless or immutable.

A. The first view

Little needs to be said to convey the sense of the first view of God's eternity, for its nature should be evident even from the brief description just given of it. The idea, quite simply, is that God is eternal since he is, since he always was, and since he always will be. You and I were born, and we shall soon die. We are not, as it says in the Psalms, 'from everlasting to everlasting'. According to the first view of eternity, however, things are otherwise with God. On this account, there was no time when God did not exist, and there will be no time when he does not exist.

B. The classical view

The classical view of eternity is rather more complex however. For a famous statement of it one can usefully turn to Boethius (c.480–524) whose definition of eternity has been much quoted in discussions of the subject.

According to Boethius, 'Eternity is the total and complete possession of unending life, all at once' (*Aeternitas est interminabilis vitae tota simul et perfecta possessio*) (*The Consolation of Philosophy* 5). The idea here is indeed that God has no beginning or end, no birth and no death, that he differs from us since his life is not one of limited duration. But to this is added the thought of him not having a life marked by successiveness. On this view, therefore, God has nothing that we could recognize as a biography. We have biographies, and these can be recorded because we undergo change. But, on the classical view of eternity, this is not the case with God. In other words, according to the classical view, God does not change in any way that involves a genuine alteration in him or a genuine succession of states through which his life is lived. On the classical view of eternity, therefore, God cannot, for example, grow or learn or move. On the classical view of eternity any suggestion that God undergoes any kind of real change in himself is ruled out. And so, for example, Aquinas defines eternity as follows:

First, anything existing in eternity is *unending*, that is to say, lacks both beginning and end (for both may be regarded as ends). Secondly, eternity itself exists all at once (*tota simul*) lacking successiveness (*Summa Theologiae* Ia, 10, 1).

But defenders of the classical view of eternity have also put their position more strongly than this. For they have often held that if something is totally changeless, and if it is quite distinct from any world of change, then it is also outside time. So defenders of the classical view of eternity have frequently equated eternity with timelessness. On this view, therefore, to call God eternal is to say that he is right outside time. Thus, for example, St Anselm writes:

You were not, therefore, yesterday, nor will You be tomorrow, but yesterday and today and tomorrow You *are*. Indeed You exist neither yesterday nor today nor tomorrow but are absolutely outside all time (*es extra omne tempus*). For yesterday and today and tomorrow are completely in time; however, You, though nothing can be without You, are nevertheless not in place or time but all things are in You. For nothing contains You, but You contain all things (*Proslogion*, 19).

One finds the same sort of thing in the *Confessions* of St Augustine. In Book XI, chapter 13, he considers the question of why God did not create sooner than he did. Augustine's reply is that the question is based on confusion since time and creation go together, since only when something created exists is there any question of there being time. He says:

How could those countless ages have elapsed when you, the Creator, in whom all ages have their origin, had not yet created them? What time could there have been that was not created by you? How could time elapse if it never was? You are the Maker of all time.

And then he goes on to say:

Furthermore, although you are before time, it is not in time that you precede it. If this were so, you would not be before all time. It is in eternity, which is supreme over time because it is a never-ending present, that you are at once before all past time and after all future time. For what is now the future, once it comes, will become the past, whereas *you are unchanging, your years can never fail*. Your years neither go nor come, but our years pass and others come after them, so that they all may come in their turn. Your years are completely present to you all at once. . . . Your today is eternity.

Criticisms of the classical view

In discussions of God's eternity nowadays available, the classical view of God's eternity has come in for a great deal of criticism while the first view of God's eternity is frequently presented as the only tenable option for someone who wants to say that God is, in fact, eternal. So perhaps we can begin to consider what we may rationally believe about the eternity of God by turning to the criticisms commonly levelled against the classical view. Do they refute it, or not?

One reason often advanced by those who think they do hinges on the assertion that God is a person. The germ of the argument here is really quite simple. It runs: 'God is a person. All persons are changeable. Therefore God is changeable'. Thus, for example, in his book *A Treatise on Space and Time* (London, 1973), J. R. Lucas bluntly observes: 'To say that God is outside time, as many theologians do, is to deny, in effect, that God is a person' (p. 200). Lucas evidently supposes that God is a person and that the theologians to whom he refers have somehow got it wrong. And the same conclusion is advanced by Nelson Pike in his book *God and Timelessness* (London, 1970). In chapter 7 of the book (called 'God as a Timeless Person') Pike considers whether or not God can be called a person if he is also said to be timeless. The conclusion offered is that something timeless cannot really count as a person. The implication is that God is not timeless.

The difficulty, however, with this line of thinking is that it seems to presuppose something it ought not to suppose – viz. that someone who believes in God is committed to the formula 'God is a person'. On the contrary, however, we have at least two good reasons for rejecting this supposition.

(1) As I have argued, we have reason to believe in God because we can ask what accounts for there being any universe at all. We can also ask what accounts for there being something rather than nothing. God, we may say, is the reason why there is any universe; he is the reason why there is something rather than nothing. Yet persons, as we understand them, are very much part of the universe. And they are very much part of what we would be puzzled about in asking why anything should exist at all. In that case, therefore, if God is a person like us we are entitled to ask what it is that accounts for his existence. In other words, the formula 'God is a person' naturally invites the question 'What created God?'. Or, to put it another way, to assert that God is a person is to refer to God as the sort of thing the existence of which gives us reason to believe in God in the first place. In terms of the doctrine of creation, persons like us could only be evidence for God, not models to which he must be expected to conform so that we can literally say 'Yes, indeed, God is a person like us'. If persons like us require a Creator, then so does anything else which is said to be a person as we are persons. One might, of course, reply that God is not a person as we are persons. But in that case, however, there seems no obvious reason why his being a person should rule out the possibility of him being eternal in the way supposed by the classical view of God's eternity. In other words, if we reject the classical view of eternity by appealing to the formula 'God is a person' we either make 'person' mean something that God cannot be, in which case 'God is a person' is no argument against the classical view of eternity, or we use 'person' in a new sense, in which case one can ask why it should follow that because God is a person he cannot be eternal as the classical view of eternity supposes him to be.

(2) As we understand them, persons are individual human beings. You and I are persons, and, as such, we are inhabitants of the material world whose individuality and nature can be distinguished and who can be classified in terms of genus and species. Yet, as we have seen, if God is the Creator of the universe, he cannot be thought of as anything material. Nor can his individuality be distinguished from his nature. Nor can he be defined in terms of genus and species.

In reply to objections like this it is sometimes said that the formula 'God is a person' naturally springs from belief in God as that is understood by those

who subscribe to it. To believe in God, so it is said, is to believe that God is a
person. But why should one accept that conclusion? Who are we to take as
examples of people who believe in God? Will orthodox Christians do?
Presumably they will. Yet they are certainly not tied to the formula 'God is a
person'. The formula they are tied to is the Trinitarian formula, 'God is three
persons', which certainly does not mean that God is three persons in one person, and which, in any case, uses the term 'person' in a technical sense, as we
shall later be noting.

I can, of course, well imagine someone saying in response to all this that if
it is true then God must be impersonal. For, so it might be urged, if God is
not a person, what else can he be but impersonal? But to deny that God is a
person as we are persons is no more to say that God is impersonal than
denying that he has a throne is to deny that he can rightly be called a king, or
that denying that he has a body is to deny that he can truly be referred to as a
father. It is to deny that he is a person as we are persons, and it is therefore to
deny that he is created. Why, then, should anyone suppose that there is anything of substance to be gained by insisting that God is a person?

But those who reject this line of reasoning are likely to say that what I have
just suggested simply misses the point. They will observe that, however we
think of God, we must at least concede that he brings things about. And this,
so they will argue, entails that he is changeable. Why? Because, so the
argument commonly runs, things are brought about by virtue of something
changing. Thus, for example, according to Grace Jantzen:

A living God cannot be static: life implies change and hence temporality. This means that
the doctrine of immutability cannot be interpreted as absolute changelessness, which would
preclude divine responsiveness and must rather be taken as steadfastness of character
(Richardson and Bowden 1983, p. 573).

This line of thinking is developed by Nelson Pike and Richard Swinburne,
where the argument is specifically directed against the views that if God is
outside time he can still act and if God is outside time he can create.
According to Swinburne:

If we say that P brings about X, we can always sensibly ask *when* does he bring it about? If
we say that P punishes Q, we can always sensibly ask *when* does he punish Q. . . . If P at t
brings about X, then necessarily X comes into existence (simultaneously with or) subsequently to P's action. . . . And so on (Swinburne 1977, p. 221).

According to Pike, if God creates, then he produces or sustains, but 'the
specialized verbs we use when describing a case of deliberate or intentional
production . . . seem to carry with them identifiable implications regarding
the relative temporal positions of the items produced and the creative activity
involved in their production' (Pike 1970, p. 106). According to Pike,
temporal implications 'seem to be there in every case; they seem to be part of

the "essence" of "produce" ' (p. 107). If we have sustaining activity, therefore, we must have the sustainer doing something that takes time.

Yet this line of argument also seems misguided. With respect to Jantzen
(whom I quote because what she says is said so frequently), she simply
assumes that nothing can be said to have life if it is changeless. But that just
begs the question. What if there is life which is changeless? I suspect that the
crucial word in Jantzen's remarks is the term 'static'. Jantzen evidently
supposes that the classical view of eternity leaves one with a God who is inert.
I shall have more to say about this later.

With respect to Swinburne, though, one can, I think, agree with part of
what he says. If we observe that God brings things about, it would seem
natural to ask 'When does he bring them about?'. But Swinburne is wrong
to suppose that our answer to this question entails that God is himself in time
or that God changes in himself. And Pike, too, is wrong to suppose that
God's creating must involve him in any real change.

Of course it is true that if, for example, you are told that someone
produced, say, a rabbit from a hat, or whatever, you can ask 'When?'. But
we can say when God brought things about without supposing that he
changes in doing so. For something is brought about by an agent, or someone is punished by an agent (to take Swinburne's example) only when the
something in question is brought about or the person in question is punished.
Suppose, then, we say that such and such has been brought about by God.
Then we ask 'When?'. Suppose the answer is 'At 2 o'clock last Friday'.
Does that mean that God must have been undergoing some sort of process at
2 o'clock last Friday? Or does it mean that he must have occupied the time
we call '2 o'clock last Friday'? By no means. It need only mean that at 2
o'clock last Friday such and such came to pass by virtue of God. Whether
God changes in bringing it about is a further question, as is the question of
whether in bringing it about he does so as something existing in time. Or
suppose we say 'The Egyptians have been punished by God'. Then we ask
'When?'. Suppose the answer is 'After they refused to listen to Moses', or
something like that, as it says in the Old Testament. Does that mean that
God must have undergone some process after the Egyptians refused to listen
to Moses'? Does it mean that he must have occupied the time we refer to as
'the period immediately following the Egyptians' rejection of Moses'? By no
means. It need only mean that after they refused to listen to Moses, the
Egyptians were drowned (or whatever). And, again, whether God changed
or occupied time in bringing it about that the Egyptians were drowned (or
whatever) is another question. Swinburne, of course, says that 'If P at t
brings about X, then necessarily X comes into existence (simultaneously
with or) subsequently to P's action'. But that is by no means obviously true
in the sense implied by Swinburne. If 'P' is God, how do we know that his

bringing about can be located in time if that is meant to imply that God is himself in time? We may know that things are brought about at different times, and that God brings them about, that they are there because of God. But this does not show that God cannot bring it about that something can be temporally located without himself being temporally located, without himself being in time. In general, Swinburne confuses 'God brings it about that X is true at t' and 'God, occupying some moment of time, brings it about at that time that X is true'. And this point is relevant to Pike's position. What if we have reason for saying that something has been brought about and yet that there is reason for denying that what accounts for what is brought about – and, therefore, what brings it about – is located in time? Then we have reason for denying that the notion of bringing about always implies that there is something which, by existing at some time, brings things about. Whether or not we could have reason for denying this is not to be decided, as Pike seems to think, by looking at what seems to be true of familiar cases of bringing about. And if the claim is that God brings about without being in time, what is required are not examples of bringing about when it is not God who is said to bring about.

With respect to all of this, an analogy might help. Suppose I ask 'When did John teach his son that scorpions are dangerous?'. The answer here will be 'When John finally got the boy to see that scorpions are dangerous'. You teach not by opening your mouth and handing out information. That is how you *try* to teach, and that is why we can talk of people as being unteachable, even though we have spent hours going over something with them. Teaching itself is something that takes place when learning takes place. John can tell his son that scorpions are dangerous until John is blue in the face. But the teaching occurs when the boy gets the point. In a similar way, so we may say, God's bringing things about need only be understood in terms of things coming about, not in terms of something happening with God, not in terms of God undergoing some process by which he really changes. It is merely a condition and a limitation of my nature that I can only bring about in you the change we call 'learning' by, as a matter of fact, changing myself. There is nothing in the notion of teaching that involves such a change in the teacher. There is thus, I think, no reason why God should not teach you by bringing about a change in you without in any way changing himself. And, more generally, there is, I think, no reason why God should not bring about changes, and, insofar as times depend on changes, times, without himself changing or being in time.

Further criticisms of the classical view

So far, then, we have seen no reason to suppose that the classical view of eternity has to be mistaken. But there are three other major and common objections to it that we have not so far considered and which now need to be introduced and discussed.

According to the first, the classical view of eternity leaves us with a God we cannot admire or respect.

According to the second, it leaves us with a God who cannot choose not to create.

According to the third, it contradicts the Bible.

(1) The first of these objections is enormously popular at the moment, and has been for some time. In theological circles it is associated with the work of the so-called 'process theologians', including, for example, Charles Hartshorne. Other modern writers who have embraced the objection include the German theologian Jürgen Moltmann and the Latin American liberation theologian Jon Sobrino.

According to the classical view of eternity, God is immutable. It therefore follows that he cannot be affected by anything. According to the present objection, however, this just cannot be true. If God is to be really acceptable to us, then he must, so the argument goes, actually be capable of suffering. And this, of course, means changing. So according to Hartshorne, for example, God changes in his relationship with human beings, and his goodness lies in this. When he knows us in our joys, he shares joy with us. When he knows us as suffering, he suffers too. And this means that there can be a personal relationship with God which means something to both parties. God, in short, is a social being.

Much the same theme is put forward by Moltmann and Sobrino, but they state their case by concentrating on Christianity and the notion of the divinity of Christ. According to Moltmann, for example, the great thing about Christianity is that it offers us a suffering God revealed as such in the person of Christ. Traditional Christian teaching holds that Christ is God; but it also denies that this implies that we can say, without qualification, 'God suffers'. A distinction is made between what is true of Christ as man, and what is true of him as God. The conclusion then proposed is that though Christ could suffer as man, he could not suffer as God. But Moltmann will have none of this. For him, the divinity of Christ means that divinity as such is capable of suffering. And in the light of this point we can, says Moltmann, offer some comfort to suffering human beings. People in distress can be driven to say that because of their suffering they cannot believe in God. According to Moltmann, however, God and suffering are not contradictions since God suffers too. And that is what Sobrino also wants to say. As he puts it:

For Saint John, God is love. . . . Is that statement real? . . . We must insist that love has to be credible to human beings in an unredeemed world. That forces us to ask ourselves whether God can really describe himself as love if historical suffering does not affect him. . . . We must say what Moltmann says: 'We find suffering that is not wished, suffering that is accepted, and the suffering of love. If God were incapable of suffering in all those ways, and hence in an absolute sense, then God would be incapable of loving' (Sobrino 1978, p. 197).

Yet is all that really true? Here, it seems to me, a number of points need to be made.

(a) The present objection seems to suppose that Christians are obliged to abandon the classical view of eternity in view of the Incarnation. But this is false. The position of orthodox Christianity is that in the case of the Incarnation we are dealing with a subject who is both God and man, from which it follows that if it is true to say that this subject suffers then it is also true to say that God suffers. According to Christian orthodoxy, however, it is as man that this subject suffers, not as God. In other words, unless one is working with something other than an orthodox understanding of the Incarnation, one is not obliged to abandon the classical view of eternity in the name of Christianity.

(b) Of course we think well of people who are capable in general of sympathetic response. Of course we admire those who are willing to endanger or harm themselves in order to rescue those in adversity. All that can be cheerfully admitted. But, unless we are sadists, we do not, when we suffer, want others to do so as well. We want them to understand what is happening to us, and we want them, if possible, to do something about it. And if they end up suffering themselves, then this is something that we regret. Suffering is a limitation, a restriction on one's freedom. There is therefore no particular reason for thinking better of God if he happens to suffer along with the rest of us as God. We may be in the soup, so to speak; but we can recognize this as a mark of our impotence. Would it, then, be a mark of God's strength if he were in the soup as well? The reverse would actually seem to be the case. In other words, to say without qualification that God undergoes suffering has the opposite effect from that intended by writers such as Moltmann and Sobrino. Their aim is to indicate that God is very admirable. If what they say is true, however, God would seem to be something vulnerable and defective.

(c) Both Moltmann and Sobrino presume that God can only be said to be capable of love if he is also capable of suffering or of somehow being a victim. But this presumption embodies an extremely odd view of the notion of love for it supposes that love and limitation must go together. Yet there is no reason to suppose that this is necessarily so. One may display one's love by limiting oneself. But that is not to say that love and limitation have to go together. Indeed, so one might argue, love is only capable of its fullest development where the lover is not limited by anything.

(d) If writers like Hartshorne, Moltmann, and Sobrino are right, then God is an individual consciousness in addition to all the others that there are, and he must be thought of as something undergoing a succession of physical states or mental states or both. In that case, however, we can surely ask what accounts for his existence, for if we can ask this question of the universe, then we can surely ask it of something so like many of the universe's inhabitants as he appears to be. In other words, what the writers we are now considering refer to as God is something the existence of which raises obvious causal questions. And that ought to leave us asking what right it has to be called divine.

(e) If we are dealing with a suffering individual, then we are dealing with something that can be acted on by something other than itself. We are dealing with something whose freedom is capable of being interfered with. But how can God be interfered with by anything? The answer would surely seem to be 'In no way'. For if God accounts for the existence of everything that is not God (as the doctrine of creation supposes, and as we may, so I have argued, believe), then he cannot be acted on. To be acted on is to be passive. It is to be at the receiving end of the operation of something else. Yet this is what the Creator simply cannot be. With respect to God and his creatures, the causal relationship can only work one way. In other words, the action of everything apart from God must, in a sense, be God's own act. If this were not so, then atheism would be true. That is to say, it would be true that something could exist as it is independently of God.

(f) A likely rejoinder to the points just made is that if we accept them we must therefore conclude that God is indifferent. This is certainly what the classical view of eternity is frequently taken to be saying. The idea is that if you defend it, then you must simply be saying that God is static or lifeless or inert, like an iceberg or a block of wood. But this way of looking at things just misses the point. In the minds of those who have insisted on the classical view of eternity, to call God eternal is to *deny* that certain things are true of him. It is another way of saying what God is *not*. The classical view of eternity is not a description or a definition of God. It is a warning against saying things like 'God really suffers' or 'God really changes'. In other words, the classical view of God's eternity is an attempt to draw our attention to creaturely limitations imposed by being part of a changing world, and the point being emphasized is that, whatever God is, he cannot be subject to these limitations.

(g) Is it really true that if God suffers as he is said to do by writers such as those we are now considering, then we have something worth saying to those who are suffering in the world? People will react to this question in different ways, but one can surely suggest with some reason that it is not very encouraging to suppose that divinity is itself subject to the action of what is not divine. If that were true, then God could be out of control and something could have its way with him and be capable of acting independently of him. Writers such as Moltmann and Sobrino are evidently concerned to provide some sort of consolation in saying that divinity, without qualification, suffers. Their aim is clearly to comfort those oppressed by misery. With some reason, however, one may refuse to be consoled by the notion of God being coerced by the action of what is not himself. Christians, of course, say that the Word made flesh suffered and died, and that this is a source of hope. But those who appeal to this point also need to remember that the biblical writer who stresses it most also presents us with a picture of Christ who can say to his disciples 'I lay down my life that I may take it again. No one takes it from me, but I lay it down of my own accord. I have power to lay it down and I have power to take it again' (Jn 10:17f.). In other words, in the Gospel of St John the passion of Christ is presented as a triumphant move to glory in a drama whose principal figure is always in control by virtue of his divinity. And this is the view taken up in the orthodox doctrine of the Incarnation, according to which Jesus is and was one person with both human and divine natures distinct and unconfused. On this view, we can mean what we say if we say that God suffered and died. But we do not mean that what it is to be divine – that the divine nature – suffered and died. The meaning is that a divine subject suffered and died insofar as the man Jesus suffered and died.

(2) But should we now, perhaps, concede that if God is eternal in the sense proposed by writers like Boethius, he cannot choose not to create? And should we therefore conclude that the classical view of eternity is wrong? The argument that we should runs as follows.

It seems evident that God has created, for there is indeed a world which depends for its existence on God. But if the classical view of eternity is correct, then God is immutable and his will is therefore unchanging and unchangeable. In that case, however, God cannot choose but to create. Creation, it would seem, is necessary since if God is immutable he can only will what he does will, and since he wills to create, then he must will to create. This, however, cannot be true. For God is free and he is therefore not bound to will as he does. In the end, therefore, the classical view of eternity denies the freedom of God.

Yet is that really true? In fact, it is not true at all, for the argument moves too quickly. Up to a point, indeed, the argument is correct. For if God is eternal in the classical sense, he is changelessly the Creator of whatever it is that he creates. In other words, given that God has willed to create, creation is somehow inevitable (assuming, of course, that God's will cannot be thwarted). But given that God is also free, as our present objection explicitly allows, all that now follows is that God has freely willed to create what, by virtue of his changelessness, comes about by virtue of his freely willing to create. Or, as Aquinas succinctly puts it: 'Granted that God wills whatever he does from eternity, the inference is not that he has to except on the supposition that he does' (*Summa Theologiae* Ia, 19, 3 ad 1). In short, God's unchangeable will may ensure from eternity the fact of creation. But if God's unchangeable will is free, whether or not he creates is still up to him. From the fact that God is immutable, it does not follow that creation is necessary in some absolute sense.

(3) So much for that objection, then. But we are still left with the biblical one. The classical view of eternity may be all very well as a philosophical doctrine, some people have said, but it is strictly irrelevant to the God of the Bible. He is not changeless. His life does not lack successiveness. Or, as Richard Swinburne puts it:

> The God of the Old Testament, in which Judaism, Islam, and Christianity have their roots, is a God in continual interaction with men, moved by men as they speak to him. . . . If God did not change at all, he would not think now of this, now of that. . . . The God of the Old Testament is not pictured as such a being. . . . [The] doctrine of divine timelessness is very little in evidence before Augustine. The Old Testament certainly shows no sign of it. . . . The same applies in general for New Testament writers (Swinburne 1977, pp. 214ff.).

But none of this seems to me in the slightest bit decisive against the classical view of eternity. Some, of course, would say that if the biblical notion of God conflicts with the classical view of eternity, then so much the worse for the biblical notion of God. But one does not even have to take that apparently radical line in dealing with the present objection.

It is, of course, true that in the Bible we have what looks like the picture of a changing God. As John L. McKenzie shows, 'The philosophical concept of eternity [sc. the 'classical view'] is not clearly expressed in either OT or NT. The Hb '*ôlam* and the Gk *aiōn* both signify primarily an indefinitely extended period of time, beyond the lifetime of a single person' (McKenzie 1975, pp. 247f.). In the article on *aiōn/aiōnios* in Kittel's *Theological Dictionary of the New Testament* (1965), we read the following summary of the New Testament position:

> The unending eternity of God and the time of the world, which is limited by its creation and conclusion, are contrasted with one another. Eternity is thought of as unending time – for how else can human thought picture it? – and the eternal being of God is represented as pre-existence and post-existence. . . . The NT took over the OT and Jewish view of divine eternity along with the ancient formulae (p. 202).

The biblical case against the classical view of eternity can be stated even more strongly than this. In the Bible, we can assert, God is definitely not changeless. His life does not lack successiveness. In the words of James Barr:

> In the Bible God is presented above all as active and personal: he can change his mind, he can

regret what he has done, he can be argued out of positions he has already taken up, he
operates in a narrative sequence and not out of static perfection (Barr 1977, p. 277).

But what does all this prove? Not, I think, that we are therefore bound to
reject the classical view of eternity in deference to the Bible.

To begin with, if we are in the business of throwing biblical quotations
around, then it ought to be said that though the Bible talks of God as
changing, and though it does so most of the time, it also denies that he
changes. For the Bible does maintain that God stands beyond the world as its
Creator and Lord with whom, as the letter of James puts it, 'there is no
variation or shadow due to change' (Jas 1:17). The Bible certainly refers to
God as if he were part of a changing world, but it also has things to say which
pull in the other direction. As we read in the prophet Malachi: 'I the Lord do
not change' (Mal 3:6).

Yet this is not really the answer to someone who condemns the classical
view of eternity in the light of the language of the Bible. The really telling
considerations are as follows.

(a) If we try to speak of God at all, and if we try to speak of him in a way as
lengthy and picturesque as the Bible does, we are almost bound to find ourselves talking of God as a changing and changeable individual. The mere fact
that our language relies so heavily on tenses is likely to produce this result,
even if nothing else does. But this is not to say that we cannot reflect philosophically on what we find ourselves saying when we talk about God, and it
is not to say that we cannot engage in philosophical reflection about biblical
talk of God so as rationally to conclude that its suggestion that God changes is
something we can deny if offered as literal truth.

(b) Biblical talk of God as changeable does not, by itself, commit someone
who takes the Bible as authoritative to supposing that God is really
changeable. For if it did, then someone who took the Bible to be
authoritative would be committed to thinking of God in an absurd way. For,
as we know perfectly well, the Bible does not only talk of God as if he were
changeable. It says, for example, that he is a rock and a fire (Deut 32:15 and
4:24). Presumably there is no one who wants to suppose that God is literally a
rock or a fire (or many of the numerous other names by which he is called in
Scripture). Why, then, should anyone feel bound by the Bible to the conclusion that God is changeable? Is it just because the Bible speaks of God as if
he were changeable? But the Bible also speaks of God as if he were a rock, a
fire, and all the rest of it. Is it because God is spoken of in the Bible as if he
were a person? But the Bible also speaks of God as if he were not a person. Is
it because the Bible refers to God as bringing things about? Yet, as I have
argued already, God can bring things about without undergoing any real
change in himself.

The truth of the matter is, I think, that from the biblical evidence alone, there is no clear case to be made for rejecting the classical view of eternity. As most biblical commentators have come to realize, in using the Bible one needs to apply a certain amount of sensitivity and common sense. And one will have to pay attention to what one has reason to believe apart from what biblical writers say. We have reason, so one gathers, for denying that the human race began with a pair in the garden of Eden. So we interpret the book of Genesis accordingly. What, then, if we have reason for supposing that God is as the classical view of eternity suggests that he is? Then again, we interpret the Bible accordingly.

IS GOD CHANGELESS?

But this, of course, raises the next obvious question. I have suggested that certain common objections to the classical view of eternity can be answered in favour of the classical view. But do we have positive reason for accepting this view? Take first its assertion that God is changeless. Is there any positive reason for supposing that this is true? At this point I am going to start arguing that there is.

God and physical change

To begin with, we can deny that there is change in God in the sense of 'change' which is, perhaps, most familiar to us. That is to say, God cannot be changed or changeable as a body is changed or changeable. So he cannot move from place to place. Nor can he undergo increases or decreases in size. Nor can he lose or acquire any physical property or characteristic. If we are talking about God, we are talking about the Creator of the universe. It follows, as we have seen, that we are therefore talking about what cannot be material. So change of place, change of quantity, and change of physical property must all be ruled out in his case.

God as the cause of change

But one can, I think, take things further than this. And we can do so simply by reflecting upon questions raised by change itself. For does not change itself call for explanation? Should we not ask why anything in process of change is changing? Should we not ask what it is that brings it about that there is anything changing?

Those questions, of course, will remind many people of the first of Aquinas's Five Ways (*Summa Theologiae* Ia, 2, 3), so let me briefly turn to that. The argument of the First Way is frequently rejected, but it seems to me that we should be rather cautious before declaring ourselves certain that the thing does not work.

The First Way is, in fact, based on the notion of change (*motus*), which included, for Aquinas, what we would count as change of place, change of quantity, and change of quality. And Aquinas asks us to note that change is a fact of life. Things move around. And they alter in other ways. Thin men become fat. Cold milk becomes hot. All this, so Aquinas would say, is evident to the senses, as indeed it is.

But why do things change? Contrary to what some people sometimes suggest, Aquinas seems to have been prepared to say that when something changes in some respect the change might be accounted for with reference to the thing itself. He would have agreed, for example, that if I voluntarily walk from home to work, then I am responsible for my change of place. My freely walking from home to work would, for him, not be determined by the activity of anything else in the world. So he would be happy with the suggestion that things can sometimes change themselves. This is part of his notion of freedom.

Yet what Aquinas does not accept is that something like me walking is totally accountable for in terms of me walking. He would have pressed the question 'Why can there be walking things?'. And he would also have asked 'What, apart from themselves, accounts for the fact that things change in their qualities and quantities?'. One may suppose that if cold milk becomes hot milk then nothing accounts for this apart from the milk itself. Or one may suppose that if a thin man gets fat, then he has made himself fat and that this is the end of the story. But here Aquinas would have been uneasy. For we do not suppose that anything changing is itself the final explanation of the change it undergoes. In other words, we just do try to account for change in things by looking beyond themselves. And we often find that we can account for various changes in an intellectually satisfying manner.

So in Aquinas's view, the changes we discover in the world around us raise causal questions. But now consider, not the fact that certain things change (the position of the hands on the clock, for example); forget about particular instances of change and consider the fact that there is a world of changing things, or that change, *period*, is a pervasive fact.

Why should this be so? Why should there be anything in process of change?

One might say that there just are such things, that there just is change and that it is silly to ask why there is change. But is it silly to raise this question?

One might reply that we can account for what changes now in terms of what has changed in the past, or in terms of what is changing now. And one might add that there can be an infinite number of changers and things being

changed by changing things. In other words, one might say that for any case
of change you care to mention we can account for it in terms of an infinite
series of changing things. But, of course, if change as such is puzzling, then
an infinite series of changing things, whether past or present, is no less
puzzling.

And this is what the First Way seems to be saying. It is suggesting that
change as such is puzzling and that we ought to ask what accounts for it.
And that seems to me a perfectly reasonable thing to say. We ought to ask
why there is any change at all. We ought to ask what accounts for change,
period.

But if we do ask this, then it cannot, of course, be said that the answer lies
in anything changing or changeable. For of any such thing the question
about change would arise all over again.

So, together with Aquinas, I suggest that change as such is puzzling. And
I also suggest that it can only be accounted for in terms of what is not
changing or changeable.

Yet what, one may ask, has all this got to do with God? The answer,
surely, is that it helps us to see why God must be said to be unchangeable.
Why? Because in asking why there is a world of changing things we are, in
effect, back to what I have already suggested to be a reason for believing in
God. This is because we are back to the question 'Why is there any universe
at all?'. In the light of that question we can go on to say that we have reason
to believe in God as Creator of the universe. But the fact that the universe is
changeable and changing, the fact that it contains change, is not something
over and above the fact that it exists. For the universe to exist is for there to
be things changeable and changing. In other words, 'Why is there a
changing universe?' is only another way of asking 'Why is there a
universe?', and our answer to each question will therefore have to be the
same. So we can now maintain that the existence of a changing universe is
due to God, since the existence of the universe is due to God. But in that case,
however, it now follows that God cannot be something changing or
changeable. Why not? For the same reason as he cannot be something
material. If God were something material he would merely be part of the
problem we have in mind in asking what accounts for there being a universe.
By the same token, if God were something changing or changeable, he
would simply be part of what we naturally find puzzling in asking why there
should be a world of change. Or, as Peter Geach puts it: 'Only an
unchanging God can transcend the world as its free cause and sovereign Lord:
a God who was affected by what happened in the world would simply be one
remarkable inhabitant of a changeable world, not the world's Creator'
(Geach 1973, p. 213). In short, if we think of God as Creator of the universe,
we have no option but to think of him as unchanging. Insofar, then, as we

have reason to believe in God as Creator of the universe, we have reason to believe that God is unchanging.

God, change, and limitation

But suppose we waive even this crucial point. And suppose we imagine ourselves to be arguing with someone who believes in God but who also wishes to say that God changes. Can we give him any further reason for denying that there is change in God? I think we can if our opponent at this point is at least prepared to concede that God is somehow *unlimited*. That is certainly what many who believe in God would want to say, and my argument now is that they have some reason for doing so if they also concede that God is changeless. The reason lies in the connection between change and temporality.

In calling something temporal we may be doing many things. But we are at least locating it in a world where various kinds of changes occur. To call something temporal is to say that it is subject to the ravages of time as part of a changing world. And to say that something changes is to say that it is part of a temporal world.

Now one fact about temporal beings is that they are always missing something. Suppose I enjoy a first-class meal on Monday. On Tuesday I have to make do with beans on toast. Now beans on toast may be all very well, but by the time I have them before me, the glorious period of the first-class meal is lost forever. In this sense, change can clearly and intelligibly be seen as a limiting thing.

Suppose, now, we want to say that God is limitless. In that case it would surely be thoroughly appropriate to deny that he changes. In saying this we would not have to mean that God is always enjoying a first-class meal. But we would be saying that the kind of life we have, involving, as it does, the disappearance of what we once enjoyed, cannot be an accurate picture of the life of God himself. Yeats observes that 'The innocent and the beautiful/Have no enemy but time'. If the believer wants to deny that God is similarly vulnerable, an obvious way to do it is in the manner of writers like Boethius and the others who support the classical view of eternity. This, of course, is a purely *ad hominem* argument. It is directed against someone who wants to say that God is unlimited. But the argument seems to me to be quite a powerful one when considered as directed against such a person. The famous Isaac Watts hymn 'O God Our Help in Ages Past' contains the lines:

> Time, like an ever rolling stream,
>   Bears all his sons away;
> They fly forgotten, as a dream
>   Dies at the opening day.

My point is that if you do want to insist that God is not, in this sense, simply a son of time, the classical view of eternity will do the job for you. One might, of course, reply that God can be aloof from the ravages of time without being actually changeless. But this, I think, can only mean that God cannot be killed, or that he cannot grow old and senile. It would still have to mean that he would be constantly losing what once he had. And that, quite intelligibly, suggests limitation.

GOD AND TIME

So we may, indeed, hold that we have positive reason for supposing that God is changeless. Yet, as we have seen, the classical view of eternity is historically bound up with the view that God is also outside time, or that he is timeless. Can we therefore now go on to add to the suggestion that God is changeless by arguing that he is also outside time?

We have already noted that some have said that God cannot be timeless since he brings things about. But that suggestion, so I have argued, is answerable. God can bring things about without himself having temporal location. Yet it has also been held that to suppose that God is timeless is misguided for reasons other than any I have so far mentioned. A notable recent exponent of this suggestion is Anthony Kenny, who aims it directly at Aquinas. As Kenny puts it:

> The whole concept of a timeless eternity seems to be radically incoherent. . . . On St Thomas' view, my typing of this paper is simultaneous with the whole of eternity. Again, on this view, the great fire of Rome is simultaneous with the whole of eternity. Therefore, while I type these very words, Nero fiddles heartlessly on (Kenny 1979, pp. 38f.).

Yet this argument is exceedingly misguided. Kenny, of course, is saying that if *A* is simultaneous with *B*, and if *B* is simultaneous with *C*, then *A* is simultaneous with *C*. And that is undoubtedly true. But what does Kenny mean by 'the whole of eternity'? Since only things occupying times can be simultaneous with anything, 'the whole of eternity' must, as Kenny understands it, mean something like 'something occupying a time'. We can therefore rewrite Kenny's argument as follows:

> On St Thomas' view, my typing of this paper is simultaneous with something occupying a time. Again, on this view the great fire of Rome is simultaneous with something occupying a time. Therefore, while I type these very words, Nero fiddles heartlessly on.

Put like this, however, the argument is clearly not effective. For it assumes that Aquinas sees God's eternity as something occupying a time. Yet what Aquinas says is that God exists outside time. In his own words: 'God is altogether outside the sequence of time, being, as it were, a great citadel of eternity which is altogether at once and beneath which lies the whole course of time in one simple vision' (*In Peri Hermeneias* I, XIV, 195). Kenny's argument against timeless eternity simply does not engage with the position it is supposed to be attacking. All it could be held to refute is the view that God is both timeless and timeful. It has no bite against the view that God is completely outside time.

But this, of course, is not to say that God is outside time. Are we, then, to conclude that he is?

Here, alas, we come to a question that leads into issues of philosophical controversy which I cannot deal with adequately in a book like this. For at this point we clearly need to ask what Time amounts to, and that is a major philosophical problem on which whole books can and have been written. And that is hardly surprising, for the nature of Time is hardly self-evident. At the risk of seeming to jump over-quickly to conclusions, however, I still suggest that the answer to our present question is 'Yes'. We can say that God is outside time, and we can do so because we can say that he is absolutely changeless. For if something is absolutely changeless, does it not follow that the thing is outside time?

Some people, of course, would say 'No'. It was the exception in ancient Greek thought to allow time without change (cf. Sorabji 1983, p. 83). And this situation is reflected in post-Newtonian physics according to which determining simultaneity depends on one's motion or rest. But some have clearly held that there can be time without change, as, for example, did Isaac Newton (1642–1727). According to him:

Absolute, true, and mathematical time, of itself, and from its own nature, flows equably without relation to anything external and by another name is called duration: relative, apparent, and common time, is some sensible and external (whether accurate or unequable) measure of duration by the means of motion, which is commonly used instead of true time; such as an hour, a month, a year (Newton 1953, p. 17).

On this account, it would not follow that if there is no change in God, then God is outside time.

Yet things can be said to be in time since they have a history, since we can speak of them in terms of before and after, since, in this sense, they change. Change, in this sense, and time go together, for it is with reference to change as succession that the passing of time is established. Newton's view of time allows for there being time in the absence of any change. For Newton, there can be time without succession. Yet the absence of succession would involve the absence of anything changing with respect to succession. And in the absence of any such thing there would be no way of cashing, or justifying, or making intelligible the statement that any period of time has passed. One could not even make the statement, for making statements involves succession. And for this reason, it seems hard to see what can be meant by God being in time if it is also allowed that he changes in no respect.

One may, of course, reply that something may change in no respect and still be in time for it might occupy a single moment of time and, in this sense, have location in time. But this is no defence of God's timefulness since nobody would argue that God only occupies a single moment of time. It may be said that God is utterly changeless in himself, but is still in time since he exists for as long as changing things exist. Yet this brings us back to the point that time and change seem to go together. What sense does it make to speak of something existing through time but changing in no respect? One might reply that an object can be changeless since it can retain its character in a changing world. But it would then be part of a changing world, in which case it would not be God. One might reply that God can be unchanging but also in time since he could exist before or after the existence of a world of changing things. Yet how are we to make sense of something existing in time yet before or after the existence of a world of changing things? We could do so if the notion of absolute time were intelligible, as on Newton's supposition. But, so I am suggesting, that supposition is questionable. We might suppose that each period of time with an end must be followed by a period of time, and that every instant must be followed by another. We might then suggest that if material objects ceased to exist, or if all changing things ceased to exist, there would still be time, and that the same holds if we talk of the beginning of material objects or changing things. But there could be no way of noting the passage of time in the absence of change, so the notion of time before and after the existence of changing things seems to be an idle one.

This argument has been contested on logical grounds, for it has been urged that time without changing things is logically conceivable. Thus, for example, in *Space and Time* (2nd ed., London, 1981, p. 172), Richard Swinburne has written:

Time, like space, is of logical necessity unbounded. After any period of time which has at some instant an end, there must be another period of time, and so after every instant. For either there will be swans somewhere subsequent to a period T, or there will not. In either case there must be a period subsequent to T, during which there will or will not be swans.

But how does Swinburne know this? Why may not swans cease to exist *and there be no time which is: the time after which they cease to exist*? If swans exist after T, then there is a time after T at which swans exist. But if there are no swans after T, we do not have to conclude that there is a time after T. There may just be nothing and no time.

In contesting this suggestion Swinburne appeals to an argument derived from some remarks of Sydney Shoemaker. He suggests that 'it seems logically possible that there should be a period of time in which there was nothing existent, preceded and followed by periods of time in which physical objects existed' and that one could have *inductive* evidence for the existence of such periods.

There could be a world, divided into three regions, A, B, C. On A physical objects vanish for a year every three years, after which objects similar to those which disappeared reappear. The objects in B vanish for a year every four years, and those in C for a year every five years, similar objects reappearing in the two regions after the year. These cycles of disappearance will coincide every sixty years. There would then be a period of a year in which there was nothing existent. Observers would have inductive evidence of the existence of such a period (Swinburne 1981b, p. 174).

But this example is of no help to Swinburne either. Suppose objects in A disappear. How do observers know that they have ceased to exist? And if they have ceased to exist, why suppose that there is any way of determining the time of their non-existence apart from the fact that objects in B and C continue to change? If people in B and C know that A has gone for one year, what can this mean but that B and C have enjoyed a year? And what can this mean except that there have been changes which constitute the measure for time passing in B and C? And how would one know that there had come a time when A, B, and C ceased to have any members? I do not see how one could know this at all. Swinburne might say that one could infer at some time that there was a previous period when nothing existed, a period sandwiched between two periods when there were things. But to talk of a period here makes no sense. What can a period be but a duration distinguished by virtue of things in relationship involving change? How can there be a 'period' when there is nothing at all? One may intelligibly talk of a thing 'disappearing' for a while. But one can only do this if one is able to determine the time of the thing's disappearance with reference to the existence of changing things in relation. If we say, for example, that the magician's rabbit 'disappeared' for ten minutes, what else can we mean but that the hands of the clock (and various other things) moved thus and so, and that we saw no rabbit?

ETERNITY AND TALKING ABOUT GOD

My suggestion, then, is that we also endorse the classical view of eternity insofar as that maintains that God is timeless as well as changeless. For this reason, therefore, we can reject the first view of eternity noted at the beginning of this chapter. We can deny that God is eternal simply because he is everlasting. God, so we can say, is eternal since he is timeless and totally changeless. That, of course, entails that with God there is no beginning or end.

But if this, now, is true, then do we not face yet another problem? For are we not, in fact, bound to talk of God as if he were something changeable or timeful?

Suppose, for example, that somebody starts thinking of God on Sunday. On Saturday, the person in question has no thought of God at all. But on Sunday he starts thinking of God. Then, so it would seem, it makes sense to say 'God came to be thought of by this person on Sunday'. And that seems to be saying that change can somehow be ascribed to God.

Then again, suppose you believe with the Old Testament writers that God smote the Philistines at some time past. Suppose that you also believe with the New Testament that God will judge the quick and the dead at some time future. In that case, you will talk about God by means of tenses, and you will seem to be saying that he *did* something and that he *will do* something.

Yet, for all that, we can still retain the classical view of eternity. The reasons are as follows:

(1) Of course it is true that if God exists and if he comes to be thought of by somebody, then it is true to say so and our way of talking will then seem to ascribe change to God. But it need not be thought of as ascribing real change to God. Consider the case of a father being outgrown by his son. When the son is taller than the father it will be true to say 'The father has become shorter than the son'. But that, of course, does not imply that any real change has taken place in the father. The real change here occurs in the size of the son. By the same token, though God may come to be thought of by somebody, we need not conclude that he has in himself undergone some process of real change. What we mean is that someone has changed in that he has come to have thoughts which he previously lacked. In other words, the statement 'God has come to be thought of by someone' need not imply any change except on the part of some creature. And the same goes for other comparable statements such as 'God has become our Saviour', 'God has been rejected by his people', 'God will come to be worshipped by his saints', and so on.

(2) In talking about what God brings about (or has brought about, or will bring about) we naturally use tenses. We might therefore indeed say things like 'God smote the Philistines' and 'God will judge the quick and the dead'. But, as I argued earlier, the notion of God bringing things about need not be thought to imply that when things occur which are brought about by God (i.e. when things occur which are created by God) then God must be doing something as an agent whose existence and action need to be dated as simultaneous with what is brought about by him. And if God is eternal as the classical view of eternity maintains, this cannot, in fact, be true. Nevertheless, the tenses we use in talking about God and creation will still be

appropriate. For they will serve to locate the effects of God's creative activity insofar as these are part of the world of change and time. If God, then, *smote* the Philistines, that will be because at some time past something happened to the Philistines by virtue of God. If God *will judge* the quick and the dead, that will be because the time will come when something will happen to the quick and the dead. But in neither case do we have to imply that God himself is a creature of time and change. What we imply is that what happens to such creatures does so by virtue of God and can be dated. And, given the classical view of God's eternity, we also imply that what happens to such creatures happens by virtue of a changeless act of a God beyond the confines of time and change. Here it becomes appropriate to say that in a single act of creation God brings about effects which are timeful and changing. It also becomes appropriate to deny that the existence of these effects itself implies that God is timeful and changing. Or as E. L. Mascall has put it, God's act is

at its subjective pole (at God's end, if we may use that phrase), timeless, even though at its objective pole (at the creature's end) it is temporal. God timelessly exerts a creative activity towards and upon the whole spatio-temporal fabric of the created universe. This will be experienced as temporal by each creature who observes it and describes it from his own spatio-temporal standpoint; but it no more implies that God is in time . . . than the fact that I describe God in English means that God is English (Mascall 1971, p. 166).

Some people will feel that this view of God still makes him far too remote and aloof for comfort. They will say that a God outside time is a God who cannot be present to his creatures in the way that he is said to be in the context of traditional belief in God. But here one might well ask whether things are not really the other way around. For those who have insisted on the timelessness of God have also insisted that in his timelessness God has knowledge, and that this extends to the whole of his creation. On this view, therefore, the time-less Creator never fails to be present to the whole of his creation, including its parts whatever their time and place. Or, as Mascall again expresses it:

Difficult, and indeed impossible, as it is for us to imagine and feel what timeless existence is like, we can, I think, understand that a God to whom every instant is present at once has a vastly greater scope for his compassion and his power than one would have who could attend to only one moment at a time. Thus, in emphasising the timelessness of God, we are not conceiving him as remote but quite the opposite (Mascall 1971, pp. 171f.).

It is also worth noting that once one accepts the timelessness of God then one thereby finds oneself able to respond to an ancient difficulty concerning God and his creation which springs from the notion that there is knowledge in God. But more of that in the next chapter.

QUESTIONS FOR DISCUSSION

1 What would you mean by calling God 'eternal'?
2 In what sense, if any, can God be called a 'person'? Why might one want to call God a person?
3 If you are a person, and if God is a person, what must be true of you and God?
4 Must it take time for God to create?
5 Can causes account for their effects without themselves changing?
6 What must God be like if he is worthy of respect and admiration?
7 Can a changeless God freely create?
8 To what extent must one's view of God be determined by what is said about God in the Bible?
9 If God is changeless, must he be aloof and remote?
10 Can there be time without change?

FURTHER READING

For a somewhat dated, but still very informative, survey of the history of the notion of eternity, see F. H. Brabant, *Time and Eternity in Christian Thought* (London, 1937). Classical and contemporary views about God, change, and time can be found in H. P. Owen, *Concepts of Deity* (London, 1971). For a quite excellent introduction to and discussion of classical views of God, change and time, see Richard Sorabji, *Time, Creation and the Continuum* (London, 1983), especially chs 6, 8, 9 and 16.

The most comprehensive and recent philosophical treatment of God and time is Nelson Pike, *God and Timelessness* (London, 1970). Two other notable recent works which have defended the changeability of God are Richard Swinburne, *The Coherence of Theism* (Oxford, 1977) and Keith Ward, *Rational Theology and the Creativity of God* (Oxford, 1982).

The view that God changes is especially associated with the work of the so-called process theologians. For a clear, sympathetic and informative introduction to Process Theology the best text to go for is John B. Cobb and David Ray Griffen, *Process Theology: An Introductory Exposition* (Belfast, 1976). This book also contains a great deal of bibliographical information.

The topic of God, change, and time has been much discussed in various articles among which the following should prove especially helpful:

William Kneale, 'Time and Eternity in Theology', *Proceedings of the Aristotelian Society* 61 (1960–61).

Eleonore Stump and Norman Kretzmann, 'Eternity', *Journal of Philosophy* 78 (1981).

R. L. Sturch, 'The Problem of Divine Eternity', *Religious Studies* 10 (1974).

Stewart R. Sutherland, 'God, Time and Eternity', *Proceedings of the Aristotelian Society* 79 (1978–79).

J. L. Tompkinson, 'Divine Simplicity and Atemporality', *Religious Studies* 18 (1982).

Illtyd Trethowan, 'The Significance of Process Theology', *Religious Studies* 19 (1983).

Nicholas Wolterstoff, 'God Everlasting' in Clifton Orlebeke and Lewis Smedes (eds), *God and the Good* (Grand Rapids, 1975).

The authors of the above-mentioned articles differ widely in their conclusions. Perhaps I should mention that those most in favour of supposing that God is changeless, or timeless, or both are Stump and Kretzmann, Tomkinson, and Trethowan.

There are many recent philosophical treatments of time, though I know of no book which deals with things in a terribly elementary way, except, perhaps, Michael Shallis, *On Time* (Harmondsworth, Middx, 1983). Two volumes worth mentioning, however, are J. R. Lucas, *A Treatise on Time and Space* (London, 1973) and W. H. Newton Smith, *The Structure of Time* (London, 1980).

7

Omnipotent, Omniscient, and Omnipresent

I have so far argued that we can reasonably believe in the existence of God as Creator of the universe, as the cause of the fact that the universe displays a high degree of temporal order, as the reason why there is anything at all, and as the reason why there is change in the universe considered as something changing and changeable. I have also suggested that, though God is simple, as the doctrine of divine simplicity holds, we can also make positive assertions about him, and, in particular, that we can refer to God as eternal, meaning that he is changeless and timeless. In this chapter I now want to turn to three other assertions about God, ones which those who believe in God have usually been particularly anxious to insist upon. These are:

(1) God is omnipotent.
(2) God is omniscient.
(3) God is omnipresent.

Are these statements true? Have we any reason to believe that they are true? That is what we are now asking.

GOD IS OMNIPOTENT

What does it mean to call God 'omnipotent'? The word, by virtue of its Latin derivation (it comes from *omnipotens*), can evidently be taken to mean 'all-powerful'. But what does it mean to say that God is all-powerful? Three main answers have been given.

(1) God can do anything.
(2) God can do anything, including what is logically impossible.
(3) God can bring about the existence of any conceivable thing.

Let us consider each of these possibilities in turn.

(1)   God can do anything

I can think of no particular writer who has, without some qualification or other, defined God's omnipotence so as to mean that God can do anything. But 'God can do anything' is often what people will say if asked to explain what God's omnipotence amounts to. There are, however, at least three objections to this way of talking.

(a) To begin with, it is not very informative. The problem here lies, of course, in the word 'anything', for that is an excessively vague term. In other words, 'God can do anything', taken by itself, does not really seem to specify the range or extent of God's power.

(b) Secondly, given the nature of God, it seems false that God can do anything. Can God get married, for example? One might think that if God can do anything, then he can. But he surely cannot, for getting married seems only open to human beings in a material context, while God, as we have seen, can be no such thing. And from this it follows that there are many things God cannot do. He cannot go running or swimming, for example. And, as we saw in the last chapter, he cannot change.

(c) Third, if we say that God can do anything, it looks as though we could truly assert 'God can __', where the blank is filled in with a reference to any logically possible feat. Yet there must be some logically possible feats that are beyond God's power. As Peter Geach puts it:

One good example suffices: making a thing which its maker cannot afterwards destroy. This is certainly a possible feat, a feat that some human beings have performed. Can God perform the feat or not? If he cannot there is already some logically possible feat which God cannot perform. If God can perform the feat, then let us suppose that he does. . . . Then we are supposing God to have brought about a situation in which he *has* made something he cannot destroy; and in that situation destroying this thing is a *logically* possible feat that God cannot accomplish, for we surely cannot admit the idea of a creature whose destruction is logically *im*possible (Geach 1977b, pp. 15f.).

(2)   God can do anything, including what is logically impossible

Suppose, then, we say that God can do anything, including what is logically impossible. Could that be true?

Here we can indeed refer to at least one famous author whose answer to this question appears to be 'Yes'. For the view that God can do even what is logically impossible seems to have been entertained by Descartes. In some of his writings Descartes alludes to 'eternal truths', by which he seems to mean truths of logic (e.g. 'Either P or not P') and mathematics (e.g. 'The three angles of a triangle are equal to two right angles'). Many would hold that such things are logically necessary, that they are logical truths, meaning that to deny them somehow involves one in contradiction. And yet, so Descartes appears to be saying, God could overturn them. Why? Because, in Descartes's view, they owe their existence to God just like anything else which God has created.

Mathematical truths . . . were established by God, and depend on him entirely, like all other created beings. . . . In general we may affirm that God can do everything we can comprehend, but not that He cannot do what we cannot comprehend. . . . Not even the so-called eternal truths, like *a whole is greater than its part*, would be truths, if God had not established things so (cf. Anscombe and Geach 1970, pp. 259ff.).

On this view, then, 'God is omnipotent' can be taken to mean that God could, for example, bring it about that circles are square, or both that I have existed and that I have never existed. Or, to take the example given by Descartes, it could be taken to mean that God could bring it about that a whole is not greater than its parts.

But could this possibly be true? In one sense, of course, what Descartes says is irrefutable. For to refute any theory at all one has to begin by supposing the truth of at least some basic logical laws. The refutation of theories involves the use of arguments, and arguments can only be engaged in if one supposes the truth of premises and certain rules for determining validity or invalidity. If one's opponent in an argument supposes that such rules could be overturned, then it becomes impossible to argue with him and, in this sense, impossible to refute him. As J. L. Mackie puts it, Descartes

need never be disturbed by any reasoning or any evidence, for if his omnipotent being could do what is logically impossible, he could certainly exist, and have any desired attributes, in defiance of every sort of contrary consideration. The view that there is an absolutely omnipotent being in this sense stands, therefore, right outside the realm of rational enquiry and discussion (Mackie 1962, p. 16).

In other words, a defender of Descartes on omnipotence need not, on his own premises, accept any counter-argument to Descartes's theory. He can say that any such argument inevitably depends on presuming the absolute impossibility of what Descartes is asserting to be possible.

Yet Descartes's position, once we are allowed to discuss it rationally, is still highly questionable. One ought, perhaps, to concede that it is often hard to determine whether or not we are dealing with what is really logically impossible. As any logician will tell you, logic is not a discipline with a finite set of agreed results which we can consult like a timetable on any occasion so as quickly to determine whether or not what is said to be so could be so. Yet expressions like 'square circle' are clearly contradictory. And strings of words which use them, though maybe in order grammatically, cannot be used to describe anything. In that case, however, we may rationally deny that God can make it to be that a contradiction is true. For 'a logical contradiction is not a state of affairs which it is supremely difficult to produce, but only a form of words which fails to describe any state of affairs' (Mackie 1962, p. 16). Or, as Aquinas puts it:

It is incompatible with the meaning of the absolutely possible that anything involving the contradiction of simultaneously being and not being should fall under divine omnipotence. Such a contradiction is not subject to it, not from any impotence in God, but because it simply does not have the nature of being feasible or possible.... Anything that implies a contradiction does not fall under God's omnipotence. For the past not to have been implies a contradiction; thus to say that Socrates is and is not seated is contradictory, and so also to say that he had and had not been seated. To affirm that he had been seated is to affirm a past fact, to affirm that he had not been is to affirm what was not the case. Hence for the past not to have been does not lie under divine power (Summa Theologiae Ia, 25, 3 and 4).

An objector might retort that to argue in this way is to put a restriction on God's power. And many people do argue just this. But that would really be to miss the point. To say that something has power is to say that it can do something that can be done. Yet what is logically impossible cannot be done. 'A logically impossible action is not an action. It is what is described by a form of words which purport to describe an action, but do not describe anything which it is coherent to suppose could be done' (Swinburne 1977, p. 149). Some would reply that to argue with reference to such points is to detract from God's honour. But if one does hold that God can defy contradiction, if one insists that he can abolish what is true of logical necessity, then it seems hard to see how one can have any positive doctrine of God at all. As Geach has put it: 'As we cannot say how a non-logical world would look, we cannot say how a supra-logical God would act or how he could communicate anything to us by way of revelation' (Geach 1977b, p. 11).

(3)   God can bring about the existence of any conceivable thing

This, then, leaves us with the suggestion that God is omnipotent in that he can bring about the existence of any conceivable thing. This is a fairly standard view, endorsed, for example, by Aquinas. In his words:

God's power, considered in itself, extends to all such objects as do not imply a contradiction.... And as regards things that imply a contradiction, they are impossible to God as being impossible in themselves. Consequently, God's power extends to things that are possible in themselves: and such are the things that do not involve a contradiction (De Potentia I, 1, 7).

At first glance it might seem that what Aquinas is saying here is just that God can do whatever is logically possible. And that is how some have interpreted Aquinas on omnipotence (cf. Kenny 1979, p. 92). But Aquinas, in fact, agrees that not all that is logically possible can be done by God. He agrees, for example, that God cannot be moved and 'therefore that he cannot walk nor perform any other bodily actions, since these are inseparable from movement' (*De Potentia* I, 1, 6). So, presumably, Aquinas is not saying that God can do whatever is logically possible. What, then, is he saying? The answer, I think, is that according to Aquinas God can make whatever one can describe without contradiction. In other words, on Aquinas's account God's omnipotence is defined in terms of God's ability to create. If something is able to exist, absolutely speaking, then, so Aquinas thinks, God can bring it about that the thing exists. Or, as the formulation of 'God is omnipotent' that we are now considering puts it: God can bring about the existence of any conceivable thing.

But is this true? Those who object to the theory usually do so because they think that there can be something created, or that there can be something conceivable, which cannot be created by God. A common example given here is the one noted earlier: 'Something its maker cannot destroy'. It seems possible that there should be such a thing. But how could God create it? If he created it, would he not be its maker? And if God is its Creator, would he not always be able to destroy it?

Then again, what about the existence of something which can be thought to exist, but which God has promised not to create? Many would say that God cannot break his promises. Suppose, then, that he has promised never to create, say, another species of butterfly. If God cannot break his promises, then he cannot create the new species. Yet a new species of butterfly is surely something that can, absolutely speaking, be thought to be created.

Yet these, I think, are not really counter-examples to Aquinas's understanding of omnipotence, and, thus, to the thesis that God can bring about the existence of any conceivable thing. Take, to begin with, the first of them. What that actually says is that it is contradictory to assert that God can create something he cannot destroy *and* that he can destroy anything he creates. Yet, as we have seen, Aquinas does not suppose that omnipotence involves the possibility of what is contradictory. Then again, suppose that God cannot break his promises and that he has promised not to create a new species of butterfly. It follows that 'God can create a new species of butterfly' is false. But what would one be saying if one said that in the light of the suppositions just mentioned? One would be saying 'God cannot create what he cannot create', which is, again, something that Aquinas can accept because its negation is contradictory.

But can God create whatever absolutely speaking can be thought to be created? Can he bring about the existence of any conceivable thing? There is a problem here since if we say that he can, there is a sense in which we do not know what we are supposing that God can create. For we cannot compile a complete list of things which can, absolutely speaking, be thought to be created. Nor can we compile a complete list of conceivable things. But we can, however, say this (which is what I take our third account of omnipotence basically to be saying): Anything the existence of which is logically possible can be created by God if to say that it is created by God does not involve one in contradiction. And we can say this (a) because if the universe did contain something logically possible, then the thing would be created by God, and (b) because nothing can be said to be created by God if to say that it is created by God would be to say something contradictory. (a) here is true since, as I have already maintained, we can suppose that the universe exists because it is created by God, in which case anything that exists in the universe will be created by him. (b) is true in view of the nature of contradiction.

In other words, if God stands to the universe as Creator, then anything which could be part of the universe will owe its existence to God if it exists at all, and if one can say that it exists as created by God without contradicting oneself. Thus, to return to the examples mentioned above: there could be something in the universe which its maker cannot destroy, and there could be a new species of butterfly. If there were such things, they would be created by God and his power could be said to extend to creating them or anything possible as they are. But this could not be said by someone who adds that, for example, nothing can be such that God cannot destroy it, or by someone who asserts both that God has promised never to create a new species of butterfly and that God cannot break his promises. In short, as long as we can put a reference to something describable in the blank after 'God can make it to be that _', and as long as the resulting assertion does not contradict what we also wish to assert, then we get a true statement. In this sense God can be called omnipotent.

Can God sin?

My suggestion, then, is that we have reason to agree that God is omnipotent. But before passing on to other matters it is worth saying something about a question frequently raised in discussions of omnipotence. This is the question 'Can God sin?'. Those who believe in God would normally say that he cannot. But some have thought that if this is true, then God, after all, is not omnipotent. Should we, then, say that God can sin? And if we suppose that he cannot, do we not place some constraint upon his power?

In dealing with these questions, some have felt obliged to accept that God can indeed sin (cf. Pike 1969). To some extent this issue will concern us in

Chapter 8, where our topic will be the assertion that God is good. But here, I think, it is at least worth making the following points.

(1) The concept of sin is a theological one. Leaving aside the question of Original Sin, to sin, for theology, is not just to do something wrong; it is to go against the will of God and to do so deliberately. Let us, then, suppose, that God does something. If what he does is to commit sin, then he deliberately goes against the will of God. But if God does something deliberately, he must be acting in accordance with his will. For this reason, if for no other, the notion of God committing sin seems to contain a paradox. One might reply by saying that God can deliberately will to do what at some level goes against his will. But that possibility only seems to make sense on the assumption that God is to be thought of as a human individual struggling to do what he believes to be right, and failing. Given the notion of divine simplicity, however, such a picture of God is bound to be grossly askew. Furthermore, it implies that God can somehow be constrained to act against his will as people can when they want to do one thing but find themselves doing something else. As we have seen, however, we should deny that anything can be thought to act on God. We should deny that God can be passive to the action of anything. So the notion of God being constrained, like people, to act against his will should be rejected.

(2) The notion of sin is bound up with the notion of doing something as a being capable of change. Nobody supposes that sinners (even if they are angels) can be totally changeless. Yet, as we have seen, the life of God cannot be marked by successiveness. God cannot be something changing or changeable. It follows that we can get no purchase on the notion of God sinning.

(3) There is no reason to suppose that the ability to sin is a mark of power in the individual who possesses it. In fact, quite the contrary. For, in the theological sence of the verb, 'to sin' is to fall short in some way. In other words, the notion of sin is bound up with the notion of deficiency. In that case, however, the sinner is somehow deficient, and we can intelligibly deny that being in some way deficient is a mark of power in anything. In other words, one can argue that far from God's omnipotence entailing that he can sin, it entails that he cannot. As Aquinas neatly puts it: 'To sin is to fall short of full activity. Hence to be able to sin is to be able to fail in doing, which cannot be reconciled with omnipotence. It is because God is omnipotent that he cannot sin' (*Summa Theologiae* Ia, 25, 3 ad 2). The same point is made by St Anselm. In his words:

How are You omnipotent if You cannot do all things? But, how can You do all things if You cannot be corrupted, or tell lies, or make the true into the false . . . and many similar things? Or is the ability to do these things not power but impotence? For he who can do these things can do what is not good for himself and what he ought not to do. And the more he can do these things, the more power adversity and perversity have over him and the less he has against them. He, therefore, who can do these things can do them not by power but by impotence (*Proslogion* 7).

GOD IS OMNISCIENT

In the Bible God is portrayed as supremely knowledgeable. Nothing that happens in the world seems to escape his notice. This conclusion has subsequently been expressed by the assertion that God is omniscient. Yet this assertion has been differently understood by different exponents of it. One may therefore say that there is no single view of what it means to call God omniscient. Instead we have a variety of interpretations of the assertion that he is.

The main ones can be stated as follows:

(1) God knows all that is true, i.e. he knows all true propositions.
(2) God knows all that has happened, all that is happening, and all that will happen.
(3) God knows all that has happened, all that is happening, and all that will happen in the future insofar as that is now already necessitated in its causes.
(4) God always knows all that can be known.
(5) God timelessly knows all that has happened, is happening, and will happen.
(6) God knows all that has happened, is happening, and will happen. He also knows all that could have happened, all that could be happening, and all that could happen in the future.

But should we concede that God is omniscient in any of these senses, or in some of them combined? Perhaps I can begin to turn to this question by first trying to give some account of what many have believed to be objections to them.

Objections

(1) It might seem obvious that if God is omniscient, then he must know all true propositions. But some have thought that if God's omniscience only amounts to this, then his knowledge is restricted. Consider, for example, the proposition (an example of what philosophers have called 'future contingent propositions'): 'America will go to war with Russia in 1990'. According to some philosophers, this proposition, because it is a future contingent

proposition, is *neither* true *nor* false. Why? Various reasons have been given, including, for instance, the suggestion that if the proposition is true then war in 1990 is inevitable (which, so it is held, is false), while if it is false, then there being no war in 1990 is also inevitable (which, again, so it is held, is false). Suppose, then, that it is neither true nor false that America and Russia will fight in 1990. If God only knows all true propositions, it would seem that he does not know whether or not America and Russia will fight in 1990. But that, so it has been said, must be false. If God is omniscient, so the argument runs, he must know the future, in which case if God only knows all true propositions, and if future contingent propositions are neither true nor false, it would seem that he is not omniscient.

(2) But could God know what will happen? Some have denied that he can since the future does not exist and cannot be an object of knowledge to anyone. Others have argued that God cannot know everything that will happen since this must include the free actions of human beings which cannot be known by God in advance. Why not? Because, so it is said, if God knows in advance (if he foreknows) that someone will do something, then the person will do it, nothing can prevent the person from doing it, and the person's action cannot be free. Thus, for example, according to Richard Swinburne, if P knows X, then (a) X is true, (b) P believes X, and (c) P is justified in believing X. It follows from this that if God foreknows a future free action he must believe that it will occur and be justified in doing so. Yet, says Swinburne, nothing can justify God's belief that someone will freely do something in the future. For free actions are 'not necessitated by other agents or prior states of the world' (Swinburne 1977, p. 170). So if someone, A, is free, then 'nothing in the past in any way influences what A does' (p. 172). Swinburne therefore concludes that God cannot know future free actions, and this leads him to offer what he calls a modified account of omniscience. According to this:

A person P is omniscient at a time t if and only if he knows of every true proposition about t or an earlier time that it is true *and* also he knows of every true proposition about a time later than t, such that what it reports is physically necessitated by some cause at t or earlier, that it is true (p. 175).

So Swinburne's suggestion is that God cannot know the future free choices of people. Nor can he know what his own choices will be because they are the choices of a perfectly free agent (pp. 171ff.). On the other hand, Swinburne adds, God may be said to know now all that is future and causally determined by the present.

(3) Yet according to others it *does* make sense to say that God knows everything that will happen, including the free choices of people. It has, for example, been argued that God knows the future timelessly and that he can

therefore have knowledge of future free choices since God's timeless knowledge of the future cannot impose any necessity on it. Others have urged that, even if God has foreknowledge of future free choices, the choices can still be free. Why? One answer given is that, though it is true that if God foreknows that someone will do such and such then the person will do such and such, it is false that the person must therefore do such and such of necessity. According to this view, God can foreknow that I will freely go walking tomorrow, but this does not entail that my walking tomorrow is in any way necessitated. I can, so it has been said, freely go walking tomorrow even if God knows today that I will do so.

(4) Can God, however, always know all that can be known? This brings us to the fourth view of omniscience, but this, too, has been challenged, notably by Norman Kretzmann, whose argument can be introduced like this (cf. Kretzmann 1966).

When you get to the end of the next sentence, ask yourself what time it is. Actually stop reading and give an answer.

If you were right in your answer, then you knew what time it was then ('then' being the time at which you answered). But that means that when you gave your answer you could truly say 'I know what time it is now'. So it seems that among the things that can be known is what time it is now.

But can God know this? A few moments ago you could say 'I know what time it is now'. But the time referred to here is past and nobody can know that it is now that time. Does it not therefore follow that God cannot know all that can be known? Kretzmann suggests that the answer is 'Yes'. And he therefore concludes that the notion of omniscience is incoherent.

(5) What, then, of the view that God timelessly knows all that has happened, is happening, and will happen? This view (which is often held by those who also think that God knows all true propositions) has been recommended for at least two reasons. First, so it is said, we have grounds for supposing that God is outside time and that if he has knowledge he therefore has it as one outside time. Second, so it has been argued, if God knows things timelessly, his omniscience cannot be called into question on the supposition that he cannot know future free choices. Why not? Because if God knows things timelessly, he does not, strictly speaking, have any foreknowledge. He just knows. And one can know that someone acts freely without posing a threat to the person's freedom.

Yet in reply to arguments like these it has been retorted that the notion of God having knowledge as one outside time is something to be rejected. Why? For reasons which I noted in the last chapter and which, therefore, need not be repeated here. In brief, however, the idea is that God cannot have knowledge as one outside time since God is changeable or timeful or both.

(6) The last view of omniscience has been advanced chiefly in order to

accommodate two views that its exponents have felt it necessary to preserve in any account of omniscience.

The first is the view that if God is omniscient he cannot know only what has happened, is happening, or will happen. For there is more to be known than that. What about what could have happened, what could be happening, and what could happen in the future? These, so the argument runs, are things that can be known, and if God is omniscient then he must know them.

The second is the view that God must know what will happen, but his knowledge of this cannot interfere with human freedom. The argument then states:

(1) God must know future free actions.
(2) He can only know these if he first has knowledge of them as uncreated possibilities.

The suggestion then made is that God does know uncreated possibilities since he has something called 'middle knowledge' (*scientia media*). According to advocates of this proposal (e.g. Luis de Molina [1535–1600]) God knows what free agents would do if they were created, and he therefore knows what they will do as created. But since, in knowing what they will do as created, he knows what they freely do as individuals who, if created, will freely do whatever they freely do, this, so the argument, means that God's knowledge of their future free (created) actions is no threat to their freedom. As one commentator explains:

By this middle knowledge, according to Molina, God knows, previous to any pre-determining decree, how a free will would act if placed in certain circumstances, and how, in certain other cases it would decide otherwise. After that God decides, according to his benevolent designs, to render this free will effective by placing it in those circumstances more or less favourable or unfavourable to it (Garrigou-Lagrange 1936, vol. 2, p. 82).

Yet all of this has seemed highly dubious or even unintelligible to many of its critics. Why should we believe that there are any such actions as actions which would have been performed if their agents had been created? And if God knows that someone would have done such and such if created, and if he knows that the person will be created, will he not still know in advance what the person will do as created? And will that not mean that the person's action will not, then, be free after all? These are some of the questions typically raised in objection to the sixth view of omniscience.

Comments on the above objections

Are we, then, to conclude that God cannot be omniscient on any of the standard readings of 'God is omniscient'? Here I shall need to say something about each of these readings and about some of the objections to them noted above.

(1) Whether or not future contingent propositions are true or false is a difficult philosophical question which can hardly be adequately discussed here. But if they are neither true nor false, God's omniscience cannot be called into question if he does not know whether they are true or false. For one can only know what is knowable, and if the truth or falsity of future contingent propositions is not knowable, then it is no objection to 'God is omniscient' that God cannot know it.

(2) Whether or not future contingent propositions are true or false, it seems extremely odd to say both that God is omniscient *and* that he does not know all true propositions. For 'omniscient' and 'all-knowing' are synonymous, and how can anything be omniscient if some true proposition is unknown to it? In other words, if God is omniscient, it would seem that he must know all true propositions.

(3) If God is omniscient, then he must know what has happened and what is happening. For it is surely using the word 'omniscient' in the oddest way to hold both that something is omniscient and that it is ignorant of past and present.

But could anything be said to know all that is future? If we conceive of the future as a set of events which are somehow there although they have not yet happened, then the answer must be 'No'. For how could it be that there are events which have not yet happened? But someone who holds that God is omniscient can still hold that he knows the future in at least one sense. For if God is omniscient, then he presumably knows himself. And, since the universe depends for its existence on him for as long as it exists, whatever exists or comes to pass in its future history will do so by virtue of him as Creator. Whatever exists or comes to pass in the future history of the universe, therefore, can, presumably, be known by God insofar as he knows himself as Creator. One may therefore suggest that God can know the future by knowing himself as Creator of whatever goes to make up the universe as time goes on.

An objector might reply that God cannot know the future in this sense because this would mean knowing what he will freely do in the future and nobody can know in advance what anyone will freely do. The objector might also add that God cannot know the future since the future will contain free choices by people and since God cannot know in advance what these will be. But neither of these objections will work if God has no foreknowledge, for the objections depend on the view that foreknowledge of an action renders the action inevitable. Yet, as we have seen, we have reason to suppose that God is outside time. So we can indeed hold that God lacks foreknowledge, and we can say that he simply knows all things as they are, whether free or otherwise. As Boethius puts it:

Since, therefore, all judgement comprehends those things that are subject to it according to its own nature, and since the state of God is ever that of eternal presence, His knowledge, too, transcends all temporal change and abides in the immediacy of His presence. It embraces all the infinite recesses of past and future and views them in the immediacy of its knowing as though they are happening in the present. If you wish to consider, then, the foreknowledge or prevision by which He discovers all things, it will be more correct to think of it not as a kind of foreknowledge, but as the knowledge of a never ending presence. . . . Men see things but this certainly does not make them necessary . . . And if human and divine present may be compared, just as you see certain things in this your present time, so God sees all things in his eternal present. So that this divine foreknowledge does not change the nature and property of things; it simply sees things present to it exactly as they will happen at some time as future events. . . . The divine gaze looks down on all things without disturbing their nature; to Him they are present things, but under the condition of time they are future things (*The Consolation of Philosophy* 5, 6).

In terms of this view, God can know the future by knowing himself and thereby knowing what in the universe will come to pass by virtue of him. And that, I think, is true. The obvious reply to this suggestion is that it seems to imply that future free actions of people will come to pass by virtue of God. This is a point to which I shall return in Chapter 8. To anticipate matters briefly, however: we must surely say that if there are actions of people at any time, then, whether they are free or not, they come to pass by virtue of God. For the actions of people are very much part of the universe, and we have reason to suppose that the universe is caused to exist by God for as long as it exists.

(4) As I have said, it has been urged that God can have foreknowledge of free actions. But in one sense, at least, this can be denied. For suppose it is said that God's foreknowledge is like that of people. Then one might argue that he cannot have foreknowledge of free actions. This is not because his knowledge would impose necessity on the actions. It is just that the only way he could have knowledge of future events would be if they were in any case necessitated. My claim to know what will happen tomorrow could only be justified by my knowledge of something happening today which necessitates what is to happen tomorrow.

So if God is said to have foreknowledge of free actions as people might be said to have knowledge of what is going to happen, it would seem that he cannot really have foreknowledge of free actions. His claims to such knowledge would have to be based on what would guarantee their falsity.

But this does not show that God cannot know what people will do freely. For we can now suppose not that God knows things as we do, but that he timelessly knows himself. For, as I have argued, we can suppose that God is not in time. In that case, however, he timelessly knows his creation. Here it will be misleading to speak of God having foreknowledge of what people will freely do, and there will be no question of him knowing what will come to pass as we might know this. But it will also be true to say that he knows what people will freely do. On the assumption, then, that God is timeless, it makes sense to say that God can know what people will freely do.

(5) An objector might at this point contest what has just been said by proposing instead something like Swinburne's 'modified account of omniscience'. For what it is worth, therefore, one might as well point out that what Swinburne, at any rate, says about omniscience will not, by itself, stand. For his account of omniscience is internally inconsistent, as one can see by putting to it the question 'How can God know what is future and determined by physical laws of causes?'. Swinburne supposes that one can attribute knowledge of such things to God, but he also denies that God can know what the perfectly free choices of an agent will be and he accepts that one can only be said to know that-p if it is true that-p (Swinburne 1977, p. 169). From this last admission it follows that God can only know what is future and physically necessitated by present and past causes if he can know that in the future there will be the continued operation of physical laws. Yet, according to Swinburne, God is perfectly free and it is his free choice to create or sustain that ultimately acounts for any state of the universe at a given time. 'That the particular laws of nature operate', says Swinburne, 'is presumably the result of a basic action of God' (p. 141). Yet in terms of Swinburne's own account of God's knowledge God cannot know his future free choices, from which it would seem to follow that he cannot know whether causal laws which depend on them will continue to operate. In fact, Swinburne's account of God's knowledge seems to entail that God can be constantly taken by surprise, that he can know nothing about the future at all, or, at least, that he can know nothing about the future of any material being. In short, the account ascribes to God knowledge which, on Swinburne's own admission, God cannot have.

(6) The argument that God cannot always know all that can be known has been rejected on the ground that, though we may agree that at time 2 God may not be able to say 'I know that it is now time 1' (since at time 2 it is not time 1), it is still true that at time 2 God could know what somebody knew at time 1 if he knew at time 1 that it was then time 1. Thus, for example, Richard Swinburne argues:

A knows on 2 October the proposition 'it is now 2 October'. Surely B on 3 October can know that A knew what he did on 2 October. How can B report his knowledge? By words such as 'I know that A knew yesterday that it was then 2 October'. How can we report B's knowledge? As follows: B knew on 3 October that on the previous day A knew that it was then 2 October. Hence . . . B knows on 3 October what A knew on 2 October, although B will use different words to express the latter knowledge. In reporting B's knowledge of this item, we need a different referring expression to pick out the day of which being 2 October is predicated; but what is known is the same. . . . What A knows on 2 October and B knows on 3 October is that a certain day which can be picked out in many and various ways, according to our location in time, as 'today' or 'yesterday' or 'the day on which A thought that it was 2 October' (or even '2 October') is 2 October (Swinburne 1977, p. 165).

Yet this argument is unsatisfactory. It is, of course, true that two people can know the same thing even though they express themselves differently. Suppose we both know that Jones committed the crime, and suppose we both know that Jones is the husband of Margaret. I might say 'Jones did it', and you might say 'The crime was committed by Margaret's husband'. And here we might reasonably be taken to be in possession of the same item of knowledge. Yet 'It is now 2 October' can only be known to be true on 2 October, for, as uttered by a speaker, the assertion, if true, is an assertion about what is the case as the speaker speaks. And if it is not the case as the speaker speaks, then the assertion is just false. Swinburne says that B on 3 October can know what A knew when A knew on 2 October that it was then 2 October. But all B can know on 3 October is that A *knew* on 2 October that it was *then* 2 October, which is not the same as knowing what A knew, for he knew that 'It is now 2 October' was true. What A knew on 2 October was that, as he spoke, it was 2 October. On 3 October B may know that A had knowledge on 2 October, but he cannot know what A knew, for A knew something which by 3 October could not be known by anyone.

Another difficulty with Swinburne's argument is that it erroneously supposes that the way something is 'picked out' is not part of the content of knowledge. Swinburne says that A and B can know the same thing even though they express the fact of their knowing by expressions which pick something out but which can yet be different. But the way one picks something out may determine what one knows, and it may be false that two people, picking something out in different ways, can be said to know the same thing. Suppose that the man upstairs committed the crime, and suppose that he is the father of Michael. Suppose also that while I know that the crime was committed by the man upstairs you are completely ignorant of this fact. But you say 'The father of Michael committed the crime', and you know that what you say is true. Do you, then, know what I know? No. You know that the father of Michael committed the crime, which is not the same as knowing that the man upstairs committed the crime even though 'the man upstairs' and 'the father of Michael' might each serve to pick out the same man. By the same token, then, though I may know that 'Today is 2 October' and though you may know that 'Yesterday was 2 October', it does not follow that we know the same thing, though 'Today' and 'Yesterday' may serve to pick out a single day.

In short, it seems to me that Kretzmann may be right. There are difficulties in supposing that something can be omniscient in that it can always know all that can be known.

(7) If we concede that God has no foreknowledge because he is outside time, then it does seem true that he can know what people will freely do without compromising their freedom. My knowledge of today that you will do something tomorrow may only be possible if your action of tomorrow is unpreventable; yet if God has no foreknowledge, then future free actions are, presumably, simply actions which he just knows. And knowing that someone acts freely certainly seems possible. Indeed, one cannot know that someone acts freely if the person's action is not free.

But should it be agreed that if God has knowledge then he has it as one outside time? I have already argued that we can reasonably maintain that God is in fact outside time, so here I therefore simply suggest that God does have knowledge as one outside time and that he can, therefore, know even future free actions. It is, I suggest, as Boethius explains in the passage already quoted from him. The same idea is expressed as follows by Aquinas:

God is altogether outside the sequence of time, being, as it were, a great citadel of eternity which is altogether at once and beneath which lies the whole course of time in one simple vision; hence in one vision he sees everything that will happen in the course of time, and each thing in itself, not as though future to him and his vision, as though he simply saw them in their causes (though he does also see that order of causes) but he sees eternally each thing that happens at whatever time – just as with our eyes we see Socrates sitting and not in his causes (*In Peri Hermeneias*, I, XIV, 195).

That might seem to imply that God somehow sees the future as present, and that God therefore misperceives. Or it might be taken to suggest that, for Aquinas, past, present, and future are all simultaneous. But none of this seems to be what Aquinas is saying. His point seems to be that God timelessly knows past, present, and future for what they are. His reference to God seeing Socrates as we see Socrates with our eyes might be held to pull in the other direction. But the reference is clearly metaphorical, as is the reference to God being a citadel. Aquinas's point is that just as we can see Socrates sitting without it being true that Socrates does not sit freely, so God's timeless knowledge allows him to know what will happen without it being true that the future cannot contain things that do not come to pass of necessity.

(8) What, then, of God knowing what could have happened, what could be happening, and what could happen in the future? And what of *scientia media*? One thing, at any rate, seems clear. It does make sense to speak of knowing what could have happened, what could be happening, and what could happen in the future. So if knowledge is ascribed to God at all, it would seem that God must have at least some knowledge of possibilities. I might never have been born. I know this, and so do lots of other people. Is it not,

therefore, natural to say that if God knows anything, then he knows this too?

But it is one thing to say that God knows possibles, and another to say that he could know what people would freely do if they were created and that he can therefore have knowledge of future free actions. Here, it seems to me, at least two points can be made.

(a) As I noted above, the notion of there being such things as actions which would have been performed if their agents had been created has been held to be a dubious one. And surely it is indeed that. The whole point about such actions is that they are to be thought of as not having come to pass. They are pure possibilities. But what kind of action is one which has not come to pass? Surely it is no action at all, and therefore cannot be known as an action.

(b) According to defenders of *scientia media*, God can know what someone would do if created, and he can know this without knowing the person as created and therefore as doing particular things. But this is false. God could only know what someone would do if he also knew him as created and as doing what he does as created. As Anthony Kenny puts it: 'If it is to be possible for God to know which world he is actualizing, then his middle knowledge must be logically prior to his decision to actualize; whereas if middle knowledge is to have an object, the actualization must already have taken place' (Kenny 1979, p. 71). In other words, it seems that the whole notion of *scientia media* rests on a misguided premise, viz. that there can be knowledge of what people would do if created, and that this knowledge can be had without knowledge of what people do as created.

Is God omniscient?

So I suggest that if God is omniscient he timelessly knows all true propositions, and he knows all that has happened, all that is happening, and all that will happen. If God is omniscient he also knows all that could have happened, all that could be happening, and all that could happen in the future. But do we have any reason to suppose that God is really omniscient?

Those who have defended belief in God's omniscience have offered several reasons of which the following are the most common:

(1) Knowledge must be ascribed to God because one must think of God as personal. God knows himself. He therefore knows all that proceeds from him as Creator. God is therefore omniscient.
(2) God is perfect. Nothing can be perfect if it is not omniscient. God is therefore omniscient.

(3) Knowledge must be ascribed to God. But nothing can restrict the knowledge God has. So God must be omniscient.

(1) Omniscience and God's knowledge of himself

As I suggested in Chapter 2, we have reason to believe in God since we have reason to account for the existence of the orderly universe in terms of something analogous to human intention or intelligent agency. In that case, however, it seems reasonable to think of God as personal. And if it is reasonable to do that, then it would also seem that knowledge can be ascribed to God. For, as we normally understand it, to act intentionally and with intelligence as people do presupposes knowledge in the agent who acts intentionally and with intelligence. In this sense, therefore, we can agree with the first premise of (1). Knowledge can be ascribed to God.

But does it therefore follow that God knows himself? I suggest that it does for at least three reasons:

(a) Knowledge implies self-awareness, which is a matter of self-knowledge. It is, of course, true that people can know things without understanding themselves. Other people may, in various ways, know us better than we do ourselves. But it is hard to see what could be meant by saying that there can be knowledge without self-awareness of some kind.

(b) If God is the Creator, then his act of creating is free in the sense that nothing apart from himself can make him create. In that case, however, it would seem that, absolutely speaking, God need never have created. But if God has knowledge, and if God is changeless, then God could never fail to have knowledge. Yet knowledge implies an object (something known). Suppose, then, that God never created. He would still, it would seem, have knowledge. But what could be the object of his knowledge? In the absence of anything apart from God, it could only be God himself. So we may suggest that knowledge of himself belongs to God. If God creates, there would be something other than God for God to know. But we may also suppose that God changelessly knows and that this is true whether or not it is true that he creates. In this sense, therefore, we may suppose that God knows himself.

(c) If God has knowledge, then something stands to him as knowable, and it is true that God knows it. But he cannot know it by being acted on by anything knowable outside himself in such a way that the thing acts on him so as to bring it about that he knows it. For God, as we have seen, cannot be acted on by anything. The knowledge God has must therefore begin and end in himself. It cannot, that is to say, be produced in him by something other than himself. For this reason, therefore, we may also conclude that God knows himself.

We may suppose, then, that God knows himself. In that case, however, something further would seem to follow. For if the doctrine of divine simplicity is correct, we cannot distinguish between the individuality of God and the nature of God, and we can therefore get no purchase on the idea of God having knowledge of himself which is only knowledge of part of what he is. Or, to put it another way, given the doctrine of divine simplicity, God either knows himself for what he is, or he does not know himself at all. If I have any knowledge, then I have knowledge of myself. But I may well fail to know myself completely. Yet this can only be because I can know myself without knowing what, in fact, I am. Suppose, however, that what I am cannot be distinguished from myself. Then it would seem that knowing myself cannot be distinguished from knowing what I am. And that, as we may argue, is how it must be with God. Given that God and his nature are not to be distinguished, it would seem that in knowing himself at all, God knows himself for what he is.

What, then, is God? I have already argued that we can at least think of God as Creator of the universe. I have also suggested that we can think of him as accounting for the existence of everything apart from himself. In that case, however, it would seem that if God knows himself for what he is, then he knows himself as Creator of all that has existed, all that does exist, and all that will exist. It would also seem that he knows himself as Creator of what could have existed, what could now exist, and what could exist in the future. And from this it would seem to follow that he knows all that has existed, all that does exist, and all that will exist. It would also seem to follow that he knows all that could have existed, all that could exist now, and all that could exist in the future. In this sense, therefore, we can agree with the conclusion of (1).

Yet does this mean that God knows all true propositions? From what I have so far argued it would seem that God does know many true propositions. For he knows that he exists, and, by virtue of knowing himself, he knows what has existed, what does exist, and what will exist. He also knows what could have existed, what could now exist, and what could exist in future. These facts can be expressed by saying:

(a) God knows the proposition 'There is a God'.

(b) God knows all true propositions about what has existed, does exist, and will exist.

(c) God knows all true propositions about what could have existed, what could exist now, and what could exist in the future.

We can say these things because we can say that God knows himself and that, in doing so, he knows himself as Creator and he therefore knows his creation.

Yet could there be true propositions other than 'There is a God' and other than those which God can be said to know by virtue of knowing himself as Creator? And, if so, does God know them?

The answer to the first question is surely 'Yes'. For what about propositions that are true of logical necessity? If we disagree on omnipotence with writers like Descartes, we can hardly maintain that the truth of such propositions is something created by God. It must rather be that his act of creating is somehow determined by their truth. But does he then know them?

I suggest that he must, and the reason for saying so is that since God knows his creation he knows what cannot possibly be true and therefore what is true of logical necessity.

At this point we need to note something about logical necessity (though the whole subject here is a difficult one and philosophers currently disagree about it considerably). This is that propositions which are true of logical necessity are true only if their negations involve some kind of contradiction. Thus, for example, 'No proposition can be simultaneously true and false' is true of logical necessity because it is contradictory to say 'It is not the case that no proposition can be simultaneously true and false'.

But contradiction is parasitic on the fact that there are words or symbols which are bearers of meaning. And, if anything can be thought to be created, then these can. For they are as much a part of the universe as tables and chairs. As such, therefore, God knows them. And if he knows them, then, presumably, he knows them as the bearers of meaning that they are, in which case he knows their meaning.

Let us therefore say that God knows the meaning of the (created) words or symbols which can be used in saying what is contradictory. In that case he will know that any particular contradictory assertion is contradictory. That is to say, if a contradictory assertion is made, God will know it to be contradictory. But he can only know this if he knows what must be true of logical necessity. For one can only know that an assertion is contradictory by knowing that it conflicts with a proposition that is true of logical necessity.

So for any assertion you care to mention, if it is contradictory, then God knows that it is contradictory. And in knowing this he knows some proposition that is true of logical necessity. In that case, however, all propositions that are true of logical necessity are known to be such by God. God cannot know the full possible range of assertions which are logically contradictory without also knowing the full range of propositions that are actually true of logical necessity. This is not to say that logical truth is created by God. Nor is it to say that logical truth is determined only by the way we happen to use words or symbols. The point is just that one will know that a proposition is true of logical necessity if one knows that its negation is contradictory, and one will know this if one knows the meanings of the words or symbols by means of which the negation is propounded. Since words and symbols can be held to be created by God, and since God can know what he creates, it follows that he will know all possible assertions which are contradictory and therefore that he will know all propositions that are true of logical necessity. He will know them by knowing the meaning of the words or symbols by which their negations might be expressed, and he will know this by knowing the words or symbols because he is their Creator.

(2) Omniscience and God's perfection

Although I have so far said nothing of the view that God is perfect, the view, I think, can be defended. Here we need to note the following points.

(a) To call something perfect is to say that it could not be improved upon considered as the kind of thing that it is. A perfect X is simply an X which lacks nothing that could improve it considered as an X. And, by the same token, an imperfect X is simply an X which does lack something that could improve it considered as an X.

(b) Yet something can only be improved upon if it first exists and then if it exists with a further property or reality of some kind. For something to improve, its existence, so to speak, has to expand. This is not to say that things improve only by getting bigger. The point is that they improve by being added to with respect to their existence. A perfect diamond, for instance, contains more than an imperfect one; it contains what it would lack if imperfect. In this sense, a perfect X contains more reality, or amounts to more reality, than an imperfect X.

(c) As we have seen, there can be no change in God, and it is false to say that God exists in time. It follows, therefore, that there can be no room for improvement in God. And from this in turn it follows (together with [a] above) that God cannot be improved upon and that he is therefore perfect.

In other words, if God exists at all, he can lack nothing as God. In this sense, God is perfect. But does it follow from this that God is omniscient?

One might say 'No' because one might think that God can be perfect and yet fail to be omniscient. For may it not be that something can lack a perfection and yet be called perfect? And may God not therefore be perfect without being omniscient?

But this argument can be challenged. Certainly we can say that something is perfect and that it lacks some perfection. It is a perfection in dogs to be able to see, but something can be perfect without being able to see. A diamond, for instance, can be perfect without any sight. Indeed, there can be no perfect diamond with sight. But we still need to ask whether it would be a mark of imperfection in God if it were true that he is not omniscient. And I think we can see that it would be.

The reason has to do with the fact that we can ascribe knowledge to God. By thinking of God as Creator, we are licensed to think of him as knowing or intelligent. Or, to put it another way, one may ascribe intellect to God or one may refer to him as intellect. In that case, however, it would surely be better for God to be omniscient than for him to be less than omniscient. It is no imperfection in a diamond that it fails to know something knowable. But it is an imperfection in a knower that it fails to know something knowable. If God, then, is perfect, and if there is knowledge in God (or if God is a knower), it would seem to follow that if there is something to be known, then God knows it. From the perfection of God, therefore, we can infer his omniscience.

(3) Omniscience and the lack of restriction

But can we now add that God must be omniscient since his knowledge cannot be restricted? Here, once again, a number of points need to be made.

(a) If God has knowledge, then in one obvious sense his knowledge cannot be restricted. For the knowledge something has can be restricted as the knower's range of knowledge decreases. Yet a knower's range of knowledge can only decrease if the knower is capable of change. We can, however, deny that God is changeable. We can therefore deny that his range of knowledge can in any way decrease. The content of God's knowledge, like God himself, must be unchanging and, in this sense, non-restrictable.

(b) There are certainly knowers whose knowledge can be restricted. For people know, and yet their knowledge can be restricted. But by what can it be restricted? The following seem to be the possibilities:

  (i)   Physical location: people cannot be everywhere at once and their vision can be obstructed by bodily things.
  (ii) Temporal location: people cannot know all that has existed, does exist, or will exist.
  (iii) Changeability: people's knowledge can be limited by changes which they undergo. People also have to grow into knowledge by being changing beings undergoing change. Thus, they need to learn or engage in reflection.
  (iv) Interference: people's knowledge can be restricted by the action on them of other things.
  (v)   Physical and/or psychological constraint: people's knowledge can be restricted by damage to their bodies (e.g. brain damage) or by natural lack of intelligence and the like.

Yet it seems reasonable to say that God's knowledge cannot be restricted by any of these factors. Since God is not material, his knowledge cannot be affected by bodily matters such as physical location. And, as I shall suggest in the section below, we can say that God is indeed everywhere. As we have seen, it also appears that God could know all that has existed, all that does exist, and all that will exist. Then again, since God is unchangeable, his knowledge cannot be restricted by limitations imposed on him as a changeable individual. Nor can we think that his knowledge could be restricted by something able to interfere with him. As I have suggested, we can say that God accounts for the existence of everything apart from himself. In that case, however, anything other than God is what it is by virtue of God, and how can any such thing be thought of as literally able to interfere with him? It seems more plausible to say that if there is anything other than God, then it will do what it does only by virtue of God.

(c) So we can deny that God's knowledge can be restricted in the ways that we can conceive of people's knowledge being restricted. On the other hand, however, might it not be true that God is less than omniscient and that his knowledge is not restricted in these ways? For may it not be that God's knowledge is somehow limited and yet, *so far as it goes*, unrestricted in any conceivable way? In other words, can we infer 'God is omniscient' from 'God's knowledge is unrestricted in any conceivable way'? Would it not be more proper only to conclude 'The knowledge God has is unrestricted in any conceivable way'? If someone were to raise these questions as a criticism of the present argument for God's omniscience, they would, I think, have a point.

(d) Yet, having admitted that, it also seems to me odd to hold both that God has knowledge as one whose knowledge cannot be conceived to be restricted and that God is not omniscient. For if a knower has knowledge, and if one cannot conceive of the knower being restricted as a knower, one is surely entitled to say that the knower has unrestricted knowledge. Since that can quite plausibly be expressed by saying that the knower is all-knowing, it therefore seems to me that if God's knowledge is unrestricted, we may say that he is all-knowing and therefore omniscient.

The knowledge of God

So my conclusion is that we are rationally entitled to say that God is indeed omniscient. Before turning to our next topic, however, it is worth adding that if we concede that God is omniscient, we must also note that his knowledge must differ from knowledge as we can have it or come to have it. And it must do so in the following ways:

(1) God's knowledge cannot be something acquired. This follows from the fact that God is changeless and timeless.

(2) God's knowledge cannot be distinguished from himself. This follows from the doctrine of divine simplicity. So it makes as much sense to say 'God is his knowledge' as it does to say 'God has knowledge'. In fact, the former assertion would be more accurate.

(3) God's knowledge cannot be something arrived at by rational reflection such as that involved in coming to a conclusion on the basis of premises. One might put this by saying, as theologians have traditionally said, that God's knowledge cannot be discursive. This follows from the fact that God is changeless and timeless, for arriving at knowledge by rational reflection is something that takes time and involves change in the knower.

(4) God's knowledge cannot be added to. This again follows from the fact that God is changeless and timeless.

GOD IS OMNIPRESENT

We come, then, to the last assertion to be considered in this chapter: that God is omnipresent. Would it be true to say that?

In one sense, obviously not. For to say that something is present anywhere is normally to say that it has some physical location. Since God is not material, however, he cannot, as God, occupy any physical location.

Some, of course, have rejected this view on the ground that God *is* all physical locations because everything material is divine. On this view (often referred to as Pantheism), God is everywhere since he is identical with the universe. Others (supporters of what is sometimes called Panentheism) have said that though God is more than the universe, his being includes that of the universe so that he is everywhere by including in himself the reality of all physical objects (cf. Owen 1971, pp. 65ff.).

Yet neither of these solutions can be accepted if it is true, as I have argued, that God creates the universe *ex nihilo*. The doctrine of creation explicitly distinguishes between God and the universe, and, given the doctrine, one is bound to deny that God can be physically located as can material objects.

Does it therefore follow, however, that God cannot be said to be present anywhere? The answer is surely 'No'. For God, in fact, can be said to exist in everything. Why? Because if he is the Creator of everything, then he must be present to everything as making it to be. In other words, as the cause of the existence of everything, God must be present to everything, and, in this sense, can be said to exist in everything. As Aquinas puts it:

God exists in everything... as an agent is present to that in which its action is taking place... [God] causes existence in creatures.... And God is causing this effect in things not just when they begin to exist, but all the time they are maintained in existence. . . . During the whole period of a thing's existence, therefore, God must be present to it. . . . Now existence is more intimately and profoundly interior to things than anything else. . . . So God must exist and exist intimately in everything (*Summa Theologiae* Ia, 8, 1).

That seems to me exactly right. God, we may say, is in everything since everything exists by virtue of God's presence to it as Creator.

And if this is true, then something else follows. For we can add that God is also everywhere. For if God can be in everything as creating everything, he can be everywhere as creating everywhere. Or, again, as Aquinas puts it:

First, he is in every place giving it existence and the power to be a place, just as he is in all things giving them existence. . . . Secondly, just as anything occupying a place fills that place, so God fills all places. But not as bodies do (for bodies fill places by not suffering other bodies to be there with them, whilst God's presence in a place does not exclude the presence there of other things); rather God fills all places by giving existence to everything occupying those places (*Summa Theologiae* Ia, 8, 2).

We cannot say that God is everywhere by virtue of being physically anywhere. But since places are part of creation, and since God is present to everything created as its Creator, then God can be said to be everywhere by being present to all places as their Creator. This is not to say that places are independent entities created by God as such. But it is to say that they are constituted by what is created by God and that, in this sense, they are occupied by him.

So we can, I think, conclude that God is omnipresent. Yet if that is so, must he not also be present in us? More specifically, must he not also be present in what we do? These questions bring us to the topic of the relationship between God and human action. In the next chapter we shall turn to this topic in the context of asking whether or not we can say that God is good.

QUESTIONS FOR DISCUSSION

1 What do you understand by the assertion 'God is omnipotent'? Why do you adopt the understanding that you do?

2 Comment on the following:
   'With men this is impossible, but with God all things are possible' (Mt 19:26);
   'What is impossible with men is possible with God' (Lk 18:27).

3 What would you say to someone who argued that God can do even what is logically impossible?

4 Can one relate the power of God to the fact that God is the Creator? If so, how? If not, why not?

5 How would you understand the assertion 'God is omniscient'? Why do you adopt the understanding that you do?

6 Must there be things that God cannot know?

7 'God knows what I shall do, so I shall not do it freely'. Discuss.

8 Why suppose that God is omniscient? Could God be God if he were not?

9 Consider the merits and demerits of Pantheism and Panentheism.
10 Where is God?

FURTHER READING

For an introductory discussion of omnipotence and omniscience, together with an account of recent work on these concepts, see Ronald H. Nash, *The Concept of God* (Grand Rapids, 1983), chs 3–5. Nash's book also provides a very good bibliography of books and articles relevant to the concepts. For a general account of views of God's power and knowledge, see also H. P. Owen, *Concepts of Deity* (London, 1971).

Two recent and philosophically sophisticated books dealing at some length with the topics of God's power and God's knowledge are: Anthony Kenny, *The God of the Philosophers* (Oxford, 1979), and Richard Swinburne, *The Coherence of Theism* (Oxford, 1977). Kenny's book is a sustained defence of the view that no coherent account can be given of God's attributes and that there is, therefore, no God. Swinburne's book argues for the opposite thesis. I have discussed Kenny's views in some detail in 'Kenny on God', *Philosophy* 57 (1982).

For Descartes on the eternal truths, see Harry G. Frankfurt, 'The Logic of Omnipotence', *Philosophical Review* 73 (1964), and Émile Bréhier, 'The Creation of the Eternal Truths in Descartes's System' in Willis Doney (ed.), *Descartes: A Collection of Critical Essays* (New York, 1967).

There are several interesting and lively essays available on the topics of omnipotence and omniscience. Especially worth noting are the following:

Hector-Neri Castañeda, 'Omniscience and Indexical Reference', *Journal of Philosophy* 64 (1967).

Paul Helm, 'Timelessness and Foreknowledge', *Mind* 84 (1975).

Anthony Kenny, 'Divine Foreknowledge and Human Freedom' in Anthony Kenny (ed.), *Aquinas: A Collection of Critical Essays* (London/Melbourne, 1969).

Norman Kretzmann, 'Omniscience and Immutability', *Journal of Philosophy* 63 (1966).

John Mackie, 'Omnipotence', *Sophia* I (1962).

George Mavrodes, 'Defining Omnipotence', *Philosophical Studies* 32 (1977).

Nelson Pike, 'Divine Foreknowledge, Human Freedom and Possible Worlds', *Philosophical Review* 86 (1977).

A. N. Prior, 'The Formalities of Omniscience', *Philosophy* 37 (1962).

Philip Quinn, 'Divine Foreknowledge and Divine Freedom', *International Journal for Philosophy of Religion* 9 (1978).

C. Wade Savage, 'The Paradox of the Stone', *Philosophical Review* 76 (1967).

Roland J. Teske, 'Omniscience, Omnipotence and Divine Transcendence', *The New Scholasticism* 53 (1979).

Readers of these essays will find a variety of views expressed as well as some discussion in some of the essays of other essays in the list.

For a clear, forthright, and philosophically stimulating discussion of omnipotence and omniscience, see also P. T. Geach, *Providence and Evil* (Cambridge, 1977). Geach rejects the term 'omnipotent', preferring to call God 'almighty', and he argues that God knows the future by controlling it.

On God's ability to sin see, in particular, the following:

Steven T. Davis, *Logic and the Nature of God* (London, 1983).

Thomas P. Flint and Alfred J. Freddoso, 'Maximal Power' in Alfred J. Freddoso (ed.), *The Existence and Nature of God* (Notre Dame/London, 1983).

Nelson Pike, 'Omnipotence and God's Ability to Sin', *American Philosophical Quarterly* 6 (1969).

The volume by Davis also has detailed discussions of omniscience and omnipotence.

Those interested in reading accounts and discussions of Pantheism and Panentheism can profitably begin with Owen's *Concepts of Deity* and with the bibliography provided there. For a recent view that God's presence can be spoken of by somehow identifying him with the universe, see Grace Jantzen, *God's World, God's Body* (London, 1984). According to Jantzen, the universe is to God as my body is to me. As she puts it: 'Just as human persons are embodied but yet transcendent, so also the universe can be the body of a transcendent God' (p. 127). This, of course, is a very different conclusion from that of writers like Aquinas. For Aquinas on God's presence see, for example, *Summa Theologiae* Ia, 8.

8

God and Goodness

One of the most common assertions made about God by those who believe in him is that God is good. For many people, indeed, it is God's goodness that makes him really significant for human beings. But is God good? And if we say that he is, what should we understand ourselves to be saying?

THE PROBLEM OF EVIL

In discussions of these questions over the centuries (and the questions certainly have a long history) the issue that has probably loomed largest is what is normally referred to as the 'problem of evil'. Whatever our beliefs about God, few of us would deny that there is a great deal of evil in the world. People behave in ways that are morally despicable. And there is a great deal of suffering and pain. In that case, however, how can we affirm that God is good? This is the essence of the problem of evil, and, since it directly concerns the question of God's goodness, perhaps we can approach the topic of God's goodness by turning to it at the outset.

God, evil, and contradiction

One influential line of thinking on the problem of evil is that the fact of evil proves that there is no God. Why? The argument here usually runs somewhat as follows.

As well as being good, God is also said to be omnipotent. But this means that he has the ability to prevent or obliterate all evil. If he is good, therefore, he will do so. But, since he clearly does not, he is not omnipotent or not good. Or he is neither of these things. Whichever way we have it, there is no omnipotent, good God.

Notice that the charge here is not just that evil casts some doubt on the truth of belief in God. Nor is it simply being said that evil suggests that belief in God is probably false. The claim is that to accept that there is both God and evil is somehow to contradict oneself. Thus, for example, as H. J. McCloskey puts it: 'Evil is a problem for the theist in that a contradiction is involved in the fact of evil, on the one hand, and the belief in the omnipotence of God on the other' (McCloskey 1960, p. 97). Then again, in the words of John Mackie:

It can be shown, not that religious beliefs lack rational support, but that they are positively irrational, that the several parts of the essential theological doctrine are inconsistent with one another. . . . In its simplest form the problem is this: God is omnipotent; God is wholly good; and yet evil exists. There seems to be some contradiction between these three propositions so that if any two of them were true the third would be false. But at the same time all three are essential parts of most theological positions: the theologian, it seems, at once *must* adhere and *cannot consistently* adhere to all three (Mackie 1955, p. 200).

But does this argument work? Here, I think, the following points can be made.

(1) To assert 'There is a God and evil exists' is not like asserting 'There is a God and it is false that there is a God'. To offer the second assertion is to contradict oneself in the most obvious way. But one does not do that by offering the first assertion. We can recognize at a glance that the second assertion is contradictory, but it seems implausible to say the same of the first assertion. We can express this point by saying that 'There is a God and evil exists' is not *explicitly* contradictory (cf. Plantinga 1974, pp. 12ff.).

(2) Nor does it seem that 'There is a God and evil exists' is, as one might put it, *formally* contradictory. Suppose I offer an argument the conclusion of which contradicts one of the argument's premises. Then the premises of the argument, together with the conclusion, make up a set of propositions which, taken as a whole, involves a contradiction. We can put this by saying that the set, taken as a whole, is formally contradictory. But 'There is a God and evil exists' is clearly not contradictory in this sense. Here, so it seems, we have no conclusion contradicting any stated premise and asserted together with it.

(3) Nevertheless, one might argue that once we understand the full import of 'There is a God and evil exists' we can still see that the assertion is somehow contradictory. But how might we come to see this? Presumably by showing that accepting the assertion somehow involves us in contradiction. Yet that, of course, only raises another question. How are we to show that accepting the assertion somehow involves us in contradiction? The answer would seem to be: by showing that the assertion conflicts with what we know to be true of necessity. Suppose I say 'John is a good husband, but he sometimes commits adultery'. That seems to be neither explicitly nor formally contradictory, but many would say that it is somehow contradictory. How are they to prove their case? They will clearly have to

prove that the assertion conflicts with what simply has to be true. So they might, for example, say 'No man can be a good husband if he commits adultery', and, if they are right, then they have a case for holding that there is some contradiction in holding to the truth of 'John is a good husband but he sometimes commits adultery'.

But can we now appeal to any proposition known by us as simply having to be true (as true of necessity), and can we then say that, in the light of this, we somehow contradict ourselves in saying 'There is a God and evil exists'?

Some have argued that we can, and here they have appealed to various propositions. It has, for example, been said that an omnipotent and good God will prevent any evil and that this shows that we contradict ourselves in accepting both that there is a God and that evil exists. Others have argued that in this connection we need to take account of the fact that God is said to be omniscient. They have then maintained that an omniscient, omnipotent and good God will prevent any evil and that this shows that we contradict ourselves in accepting both that there is a God and that evil exists.

The trouble, however, is that neither of these suggestions seems to state what simply has to be true. Taking them together we might ask how anyone can know that if God is omniscient, omnipotent and good, he will prevent any evil. After all, people who can prevent certain evils which they know about are not obviously not good if they do not. So how can we be sure that an omniscient, omnipotent and good God will prevent any evil? And how, in general, can we be sure about what an omniscient, omnipotent and good God will do? An objector might reply that since God is omniscient and omnipotent, then there is no possible evil known to him which he will not prevent if he is good. But, again, how do we know that this has to be true? Is it absolutely impossible that an omniscient, omnipotent, good God should fail to prevent some evils? Can we be certain in advance that, for example, his goodness might not lead him to create what cannot possibly be created without some concomitant evil?

In other words, it is by no means easy to see what we can appeal to as having to be true such that we can go on to prove that there is a contradiction in saying 'There is a God and evil exists'. For this reason, therefore, one might well be suspicious of the claim that this assertion involves a contradiction. That, of course, may seem a somewhat dogmatic conclusion, as indeed, to some extent, it is. But the reader may begin to see what I am driving at if he turns to something like chapter 5 of Alvin Plantinga's *God and Other Minds* (Ithaca, N.Y., 1967). Here Plantinga mentions a host of premises which might be used to show that contradiction is involved if they are added to 'There is a God and evil exists', and he effectively indicates just how hard it is to prove that these premises have to be true. And at this point I must say that I agree with Plantinga's discussion of this matter and that, in the light of this, I doubt that the charge of contradiction in this area is going to be established.

(4) Suppose you have good reason for believing that Jones is at home watching television. Someone then tells you that Jones is walking in the park. Your grounds for believing that Jones is actually at home could be reasonably taken by you as evidence against the truth of the claim that he is in the park. So good reason for believing that something is the case is good reason for believing that the same thing is not the case.

But now consider someone who thinks that he has good reason for believing both that there is a God and that there is evil. If he is right, then he has reason for rejecting the claim that he cannot be right. So in trying to decide whether evil disproves God's existence it may just not be enough to consider some argument to the effect that 'There is a God and evil exists' is contradictory. One may have to consider whether there are grounds for believing both in the reality of God and in the reality of evil.

In other words, if one has reason to believe both that God exists and that there is evil, one may reasonably deny that evil disproves the existence of God because 'There is a God and evil exists' is contradictory. I have already argued that we have reason to believe in the existence of God. I shall shortly argue that we can rationally accept both that there is evil and that God is good. So I therefore suggest that we reject the response to the problem of evil which we have so far noted. It is possible to suppose both that there is a God and that there is evil.

Evil as illusion

Could it, however, be that this is just false for a reason not so far mentioned? Another response to the problem of evil argues that it is simply because there is no reason to concede the reality of evil. Why not? Because, so the argument goes, evil is an illusion, an 'error of the mortal mind'. This is the view of Christian Science, according to which, in the words of its founder,

Sin, disease, whatever seems real to material sense, is unreal in divine Science.... All inharmony of mortal mind or body is illusion, possessing neither reality nor identity though seeming to be real and identical (Mary Baker Eddy 1971, p. 257).

Yet this view, if anything, seems even less plausible than the view that one can prove a contradiction between 'There is a God' and 'Evil exists'. It is, of course, true that many have been attracted to the suggestion that evil is an illusion. And they have, as a consequence, often been clearly helped. But the suggestion is surely grossly counter-intuitive. Can any rational person hold that, say, the hunger of a starving child is simply an illusion? And even if one could rationally defend this odd conclusion, there is another difficulty. As

Peter Geach nicely puts it: 'If my "mortal mind" thinks that I am miserable, then I am miserable, and it is not an illusion that I am miserable' (Geach 1972, p. 305). And, as others have pointed out, even if evil is an illusion, it is a painful one and it is therefore false that evil is nothing but illusion.

Justifying evils

But might we not argue that although evil is no illusion it is something which God is justified in permitting and, therefore, that it is something which can exist without casting doubt on the goodness of God? This question brings us to what is, perhaps, the most popular response to the problem of evil, though we need to note that it is one that has taken a number of different forms.

(1) Evil and punishment

One of them focuses on the notion of evil as punishment. The idea here is that evil can simply be seen as punishment which is justly inflicted by God. There are elements of this view in St Augustine, connected with his theory of the Fall of Adam and Eve. In Albert Camus's novel *The Plague* it is dramatically expressed by the character of Fr Panneloux, who preaches a sermon which begins with the startling words: 'Calamity has come upon you my brethren, and, my brethren, you deserved it' (ch. 3).

But once again, it seems that we are dealing with an unconvincing solution. For it seems hard to believe that we can regard all evil as something deserved. Take, for example, the case of Down's syndrome. Are we to say that newly born babies with this condition have done anything for which this can be regarded as justly inflicted punishment? Questions like this have been pressed very hard, and with good reason. The eighteenth-century Lisbon earthquake killed about 4,000 people, and some tried to make sense of it by calling it divine retribution. Voltaire (1694–1778) replied: 'Did God in this earthquake select the 4,000 least virtuous of the Portuguese?'. The question, of course, is to the point. Disease and other misfortunes do not seem to be obviously distributed in accordance with what is deserved. It is said in the Bible that suffering can be seen as justly inflicted punishment. As the book of Proverbs has it: 'The Lord's curse is on the house of the wicked, but he blesses the abode of the righteous' (Prov 3:33). Yet, as the book of Job protests, not only the wicked suffer. 'It is all one: therefore I say, he destroys both the blameless and the wicked. When disaster brings sudden death, he mocks at the calamity of the innocent' (Job 9:22–23). And Jeremiah can ask, 'Why does the way of the wicked prosper? Why do all who are treacherous thrive?' (Jer 12:1). In the New Testament there is an explicit denial of a

necessary connection between suffering and guilt. 'Do you think that these
Galileans were worse sinners than all the other Galileans, because they
suffered thus? I tell you, No' (Lk 13:2–3). In John's gospel, Jesus meets a
man born blind. His disciples ask him whether the man is blind because he
sinned or because his parents sinned. The answer given rejects the assumption
of the question. 'It was not that this man sinned, or his parents, but that the
works of God might be manifest in him' (Jn 9:3).

(2) The Free Will Defence

But if evil cannot be squared with the goodness of God on the ground that it
is justified punishment, might it not be said that it is compatible with God's
goodness since he permits it in order that there should be something which
we can easily recognize as good? According to many thinkers the answer is
'Yes', and one of their reasons for saying so (a very popular one) lies in what
is commonly referred to as the 'Free Will Defence'. This takes two forms
with a common thread running between them.

The first form is intended as a way of dealing with one kind of evil, namely
bad human beings or bad human behaviour. The argument here runs as
follows.

Much evil in the world is due to the actions of people. And this is indeed a
bad thing. But a lot of it is brought about by people's free decisions. Now
God could, perhaps, have done something to prevent this evil. Or he could,
maybe, step in to stop it now. But this would mean him not creating a world
where human beings have free will to do good or evil. And it is better that
the world contains human beings with free will than that it should not
contain such beings. And it is better that human beings should be allowed to
exercise their freedom than that they should not. So human freedom is a sign
of God's goodness. It does, however, mean that there will be the possibility
of evil (maybe great evil) brought about as a result of (by virtue of) human
freedom. But this is not God's fault. It is the fault of people who freely
choose to do wrong. And God's role with respect to their choices is only that
of one who permits them to occur.

The second form of the Free Will Defence (not always accepted by those
who support the first form) is merely a projection of the first into what you
might call the cosmic stage. Some evil results from what people do. That is
clear enough. But people are not responsible for all that we can call evil. Take,
for example, plagues and earthquakes which kill people. These might
conceivably come about by virtue of human decision, but they are usually
things with which people are simply confronted. Yet could they possibly be
attributed to free will? And might one not therefore regard them as evils
arising from a good of some kind? The second form of the Free Will Defence

replies in the affirmative. Let us say that evil which cannot be ascribed to free human choices is 'natural evil' (this is terminology frequently used). According to some writers this might be accounted for as the result of free choices made by *non*-human creatures. It has been argued, for instance, that we may account for it as the work of fallen angels who are able, through their free decisions, to wreak havoc on the material universe. St Augustine, for example, speaks of the angelic darkness which follows the separation of good and evil angels after the fall of Satan, who, says Augustine, was created good but who fell into rebellion (cf. *The City of God*, Book II). Devils or demons, says Augustine, are fallen angels and the originators of various natural evils. They are evil spirits come down from the higher heaven and anxious to harm us. You can find a similar view in C. S. Lewis's *The Problem of Pain* (London, 1940), and in Alvin Plantinga's *God, Freedom and Evil* (London, 1975). Lewis says that it seems to him

a reasonable supposition that some mighty created power had already been at work for ill on the material universe . . . before ever man came on the scene. . . . This hypothesis is not introduced as a general 'explanation of evil'; it only gives a wider application to the principle that evil comes from the abuse of free-will (pp. 122f.).

According to Plantinga, it is possible that

natural evil is due to the free actions of nonhuman persons; there is a balance of good over evils with respect to the actions of these nonhuman persons; and it was not within the power of God to create a world that contains a more favourable balance of good over evil with respect to the actions of the nonhuman persons it contains (p. 58).

So according to the Free Will Defence, free, human wrongdoing and natural evil are compatible with the goodness of God since freedom is a good thing which is justifiably tolerated by God in the course of his bringing it about that there are creatures with freedom. But is that really true?

Some have argued that we cannot think of evil in this way because God could have created a world in which people (and, by implication, other free creatures) always freely do what is right. Thus, for example, John Mackie writes:

If there is no logical impossibility in a man's freely choosing the good on one, or on several, occasions, there cannot be a logical impossibility in his freely doing the good on every occasion. God was not, then, faced with a choice between making innocent automata and making beings who, in acting freely, would sometimes go wrong: there was open to him the obviously better possibility of making beings who would act freely but always go right. Clearly, his failure to avail himself of this possibility is inconsistent with his being both omnipotent and wholly good (Mackie 1955, p. 209).

But others have rejected this line of thinking, a notable example being Alvin Plantinga, who responds to it by drawing on the notion of possible worlds (cf. above, Chapter 4).

According to those who think it useful to talk about possible worlds, one can say things like 'There are many possible worlds', 'There is a possible world in which . . . ', and 'God knows all possible worlds and can choose to create one'. Plantinga accepts this way of talking and, on this basis, he takes issue with arguments like that of Mackie. That argument holds that it is logically possible that all free agents always freely choose to do what is good. One can put this by saying that, according to Mackie, there is a possible world in which all free agents always freely choose to do what is good. One might therefore ask why God has failed to make actual (to actualize) that world rather than our world, the actual world. But how do we know that there are possible free agents who, if actualized, always freely choose to do what is good? We might accept that there are plenty of possible worlds where people are free to do wrong but always do right. But could God have actualized any of them? Plantinga thinks that the answer to this last question may be 'No'.

Let us suppose that we have a possible world in which everyone freely does what is right. We want to know whether God could have made it actual. Mackie seems to be saying that God could have made it actual and that, since he has clearly failed to do so, then he is not good.

Now let us take one person in our possible world. We will call this person 'Egbert' and we call our possible world 'Gamma'. So, in Gamma, Egbert always freely does what is right. But could God have actualized Gamma?

Suppose that Egbert exists both in Gamma and in the actual world. And suppose that in the actual world he freely does what is wrong on at least one occasion. In Gamma he does not go wrong; but if he does go wrong in the actual world then this, so Plantinga thinks, has implications for what is true of him in Gamma. It will, in fact, be true of him in Gamma that if he had been actual he would have freely gone wrong at least once, namely on the occasion on which he did wrong in the actual world.

Now let us consider Egbert in Gamma at some particular moment when he is going right, when he is doing something good rather than something bad. Suppose if Egbert had been actual he would not have done right at exactly the same moment. Then, in Plantinga's view, in Gamma at the moment in question, it is true of Egbert that if he had been actual, then he would have gone wrong.

Could God have made Egbert actual without it being true that Egbert goes wrong on the occasion now in question? Not according to Plantinga. Why? Because it is true of Egbert that if he had been actual then he would have freely gone wrong. In Gamma he does not go wrong on the occasion in question. But it is true of him that he would have gone wrong on that occasion in the actual world and that he would have done so freely.

So according to Plantinga there is at least one possible world that God cannot actualize. He cannot actualize Gamma, which contains Egbert who, in Gamma, always goes right but who, if actual, would freely go wrong at least once.

But now, what if all the worlds that are not actual but which do contain free agents are like Gamma? Suppose they all contain someone who would, if actual, freely go wrong at least once? Then, according to Plantinga, God cannot actualize any of these worlds either. Yet it is, says Plantinga, possible that all possible worlds containing free agents are like Gamma in that they all contain some free agent who would, if actual, have gone wrong at least some time. And in that case, Plantinga thinks, it is perhaps not possible for God to actualize any world in which no free agents freely go wrong. In other words, the notion of an agent freely choosing to do something in the actual world cannot be separated from the fact of his actually choosing. And, while it is possible that an agent should do right on every occasion, it is outside God's control whether or not he actually does so when actualized. God might cause an actual agent to behave well on all occasions, Plantinga concedes. But, he adds, that agent will not then be free. Or, as Plantinga says himself in summing up his position on God and freedom:

The creation of a world containing moral good is a co-operative venture; it requires the un-coerced concurrence of significantly free creatures. But then the actualization of a world W containing moral good is not up to God alone; it also depends on what the significantly free creatures of W would do if God created them and placed them in the situations W contains. Of course it is up to God whether to create free creatures at all; but if he aims to produce moral good, then he must create significantly free creatures upon whose co-operation he must depend. Thus is the power of an omnipotent God limited by the freedom he confers upon his creatures (Plantinga 1974, p. 190).

Yet this line of reasoning, which is very typical of those who accept the Free Will Defence (even if they do not indulge in talk about possible worlds), is surely open to question. And this is so for at least two reasons.

In the first place we can ask why we should suppose that if we believe in possible worlds we should believe that God could not have made actual a possible world in which everyone freely does nothing but what is good. According to Plantinga, every possible person might be such that, if actualized, he will freely go wrong. Yet it is surely not logically impossible that every created person should always act rightly. And that must mean that it is not logically impossible that every created person should always act rightly. In that case, however, there is no reason to suppose that God cannot create a world where people always act rightly (cf. Mackie 1982, p. 174).

Secondly, and perhaps more importantly, the Free Will Defence supposes that the free actions of creatures cannot be caused by God, and this supposition is wrong. For the free actions of creatures are part of creation, and, if creation (i.e. what is created) is caused to be by God, then the same is surely true of the free actions of creatures.

This point can, perhaps, be made clearer if I draw attention to some remarks of Antony Flew. In his book *The Presumption of Atheism* (London, 1976) he attacks the Free Will Defence since, as he puts it, the Defence ignores 'the essential theist doctrine of Divine creation'. 'That doctrine', Flew observes, 'apparently requires that, whether or not the creation had a beginning, all created beings – all creatures, that is – are always utterly dependent upon God as their sustaining cause. God is here the First Cause in a procession which is not temporally sequential' (p. 88).

Now that, I think, is correct. The doctrine of creation does hold that creatures are always utterly dependent on God as their sustaining cause. According to the doctrine of creation, nothing created can exist for so much as a second unless God causes it to exist. Yet the free choices of creatures (whether human or not) are just as much part of creation as anything else. They are also created. So they cannot be thought of as coming to be independently of God but must, instead, be thought of as being caused to be by God. If God exists, then they are there because God makes them to be there, not just in the sense that he lays down the conditions in which they can arise, but also in the sense that he makes them to be for as long as they are there. In other words, if one accepts that there is a God who is the Creator, then one seems obliged to accept that the free actions of creatures cannot be independent of God's causality, that God, in fact, must be intimately involved in them existing since he makes them to be. Or, as Aquinas puts it:

Just as God not only gave being to things when they first began, but is also – as the conserving cause of being – the cause of their being as long as they last . . . so he not only gave things their operative powers when they were first created, but is also always the cause of these in things. Hence if this divine influence stopped, every operation would stop. Every operation, therefore, of anything is traced back to him as its cause (*Summa Contra Gentiles* III, 67).

In short, if we believe in the view that God is the Creator, then we cannot hold that free actions of creatures are not caused by God and we must therefore reject the Free Will Defence. I have already argued that we can accept that God is the Creator. So now I suggest that we reject the Free Will Defence. All free actions of creatures must be caused to exist by God.

(3) Particular evils as necessary for certain goods

But might one not still maintain that there are various good things which depend on the existence of some evils? And might one not try to deal with the problem of evil by appealing to these? Here we come to another line of thinking that has seemed attractive to many. The Free Will Defence holds that the possibility of some evil is bound up with the good of human (or non-human) freedom. But it has also been said that there are other good things which depend somehow on evil and that discussions of the problem of evil should take account of these.

Two philosophers who have recently argued in this way are John Hick and Richard Swinburne. According to Hick, the adverse conditions which we find in the world allow us to develop and to become more mature in our relationship with God. As Hick puts it, echoing what he takes to be the views of St Irenaeus (c.140–c.202):

> My general conclusion is that this world with all its unjust and apparently wasted suffering, may nevertheless be . . . a divinely created sphere of soul-making. . . . A world without problems, difficulties, perils, and hardships would be morally static. For moral and spiritual growth comes through response to challenges; and in a paradise there would be no challenges. Accordingly, a person-making environment cannot be plastic to human wishes but must have its own structure in terms of which men have to learn to love and which they ignore at their peril (Hick 1977, pp. 226ff.).

Swinburne's view is rather similar. Like Hick, he thinks that numerous evils in the world provide various opportunities which would be impossible in the absence of the evils. For example, says Swinburne, natural disasters provide opportunities for the development of human knowledge of the universe and its operations, a development which, in the conditions in which it occurs, is both desirable and such that it could not come about without the evils on which it depends.

> If men are to have knowledge of the evils which will result from their actions or negligence, laws of nature must operate regularly; and that means that there will be what I may call 'victims of the system'. . . . If men are to have the opportunity to bring about serious evils for themselves or others by actions or negligence, or to prevent their occurrence . . . then there must be serious natural evils occurring to man or animals (Swinburne 1979, pp. 210f.).

In Swinburne's view, natural evil allows us to develop in our knowledge of the way the world works and, as a result of the knowledge we acquire, we have the opportunity to do good or harm and to do so freely and in the realization of what we are about. He also thinks that it is a good thing that we have the opportunity to bring about evils on a large scale, for he thinks that this opportunity gives us a desirable measure of responsibility. Better that we should have the opportunity to start a nuclear war, say, than that we should live in a 'toy world, a world where things matter, but not very much' (p. 219).

But is this line of reasoning acceptable? Does it help us to see how we might relate belief in the reality of evil to belief in the goodness of God?

Some would immediately reply that it does no such thing because it invites us to reconcile the reality of certain evils with the goodness of God by accepting that God is justified in bringing about evils which he cannot be justified in bringing about. Suppose we accept that there are evils which do seem to be necessary conditions of certain goods. Suppose then we say that these can be squared with God's goodness because the goods to which they are related are worth the price paid for them in terms of evil. In that case we would seem to be agreeing with writers like Hick and Swinburne. But is the price referred to here worth paying? And can we conceive of God as good if he asks for it to be paid? These questions are very much to the foreground in a famous speech in Dostoyevsky's novel *The Brothers Karamazov*. Here Ivan talks to Alyosha about the suffering of children. Nothing, he says, can compensate for some of the forms this takes and one must dissociate oneself from God for allowing them even if one acknowledges his existence and even if one can see that they are necessary for certain goods. Hick and Swinburne appeal to what we might call a 'higher harmony' in the light of which we can regard certain evils as justified. But Ivan's approach is very different:

I renounce the higher harmony altogether.... Too high a price has been placed on harmony.... It's not God that I do not accept, Alyosha. I merely most respectfully return him the ticket (*The Brothers Karamazov*, Part II, Book 5, ch. 4).

A similar sentiment has recently been forcefully expressed by D. Z. Phillips in commenting specifically on the approach to God offered by writers such as Hick and Swinburne. 'What then are we to say of the child dying from cancer?', he asks (Phillips 1965, p. 93). The reply is: 'If this has been *done* to anyone, it is bad enough, but to be done for a purpose, to be planned from eternity – that is the deepest evil. If God is this kind of agent, He cannot justify His actions, and His evil nature is revealed' (*ibid.*).

This seems to be a powerful point. But, even if we waive it, there are still various problems raised by what Hick and Swinburne say, taking their accounts individually.

It is, of course, true that there is much that we can admire which springs from situations that from one point of view are clearly undesirable. People may sail through life without difficulty, but it is often in the face of difficulty that people are able to exhibit great goodness. There would be no works of mercy if no one were in need. There would be no heroism if no one were in danger. And so on. But is it true, as Swinburne says, that there is particular value in the fact that we can inflict great damage on each other? Swinburne clearly thinks that God is morally justified in creating a world in which we can do this. But a moralist might reasonably reply that a morally good God could have arranged for plenty of moral goodness in the absence of the conditions under which people as a matter of fact have the opportunity to exercise it in this world. Then again, is it true, as Hick says, that a paradise would be morally static? Why should we suppose that it would be? Some would reply by saying that moral goodness demands effort. The idea here is that if being morally good is an easy thing, if it comes naturally, so to speak, then there is something suspicious afoot. Better to grit your teeth (if they have not decayed) and do good than to do good effortlessly. But here we surely ought to ask (as, for example, philosophers such as Aristotle would have asked) whether there really is a necessary connection between virtue and struggle. And this, in turn, might lead one to ask whether there could not, in fact, be a world of great moral value and no hardship in which moral goodness comes to light. Hardship and adversity may prove the occasion for people to display virtue or moral goodness. But is it really clear that moral goodness would be impossible if there were no hardship?

The morality of God

So one may, in fact, doubt that the existence of various goods depends on there being some of the evils with which we are familiar. And we may therefore doubt that the problem of evil is adequately dealt with by appealing to them. At this point, however, another question arises of which I have so far said nothing. It is, as one might put it, a question of strategy, and it concerns what people ought to think of themselves as doing in turning to the whole issue of the problem of evil. More specifically, it concerns the way in which such people should understand the assertion that God is good.

In discussions of the problem of evil there is frequently a premise shared both by those who believe in God and by those who do not and who think of evil as constituting some kind of argument against God's existence or goodness. This is the premise that God's goodness consists in him doing what he is morally bound or obliged to do. Critics of belief in God say that evil shows that if there is a God, then he has slipped up on his moral obligations and is therefore not good. Believers frequently reply that this is not true and that God, in fact, always does what he ought to do even if it does not look that way at first glance.

But should we suppose that there is any question of God having moral obligations? Should we suppose that there is any question of God being bound by any kind of duty? And should we suppose that in talking about the problem of evil we should be concerned to show either that God does what is morally obligatory or that he does not?

Questions like this frequently strike people as very odd, and many (if not most) discussions of the problem of evil ignore them altogether. If there is a God, so it is regularly supposed, then he is bound by moral obligations, and this fact must be taken as part of the context for discussions of the problem of evil. Thus, for example, according to Hick: 'It is part of the meaning of

Christian monotheism that there is an ultimately responsible moral being ... whom we may trust' (Hick 1977, p. 69). In the light of this principle, Hick seeks to show that God is indeed good in spite of the evil we encounter. Then again, according to Swinburne:

If moral judgements have truth values, an omniscient person will know them. His judgements about which actions are morally bad and which actions are morally obligatory, will be true judgements. Hence a perfectly free and omniscient being can never do actions which are morally bad and will always do actions which are morally obligatory, and so he will be perfectly good. ... God will always do any action for doing which there is over-riding reason, never do any action from refraining from doing which there is over-riding reason; and only do an action if there is a reason for doing it. We may call this aspect of God's nature his complete rationality. It includes his perfect goodness, and gives us some expectations about the sort of world he will be expected to create (Swinburne 1979, p. 101).

With reference to all this, Swinburne, like Hick, approaches the problem of evil as if it were a problem about God's moral integrity. For both these writers, as for many others, the problem of evil boils down to this: In the face of evil, can we defend God's status as an individual with moral duties and obligations?

But ought we to think of God as an individual with moral duties and obligations? And ought we to believe in the existence of a problem of evil which derives from the fact that God is such a thing?

One point worth noting is that if we say 'Yes', to these questions, then our reply can be challenged on biblical grounds. Writers like Hick and Swinburne claim to be speaking out of what we might loosely call the 'Judeo-Christian tradition', and their remarks about God and evil are offered as a defence of this tradition. But is it really part of this tradition that God is, in Hick's expression, 'an ultimately responsible moral being'? Is it part of this tradition that God, as Swinburne puts it, 'will always do actions which are morally obligatory'? From the biblical viewpoint, at any rate, the answer is surely 'No'. The impression given by the Old Testament is that duties and obligations come from God, not that they are binding on him. As the Old Testament presents it, God provides creation, puts people into it, and gives them rules for the direction of their actions. There is no suggestion that God is himself bound by rules for action. Nor is there any suggestion that he acts in what we might nowadays regard as a particularly moral way. He shows chronic partiality for Israel and is a menace to kingdoms around it. His behaviour in this respect would earn him little applause at the United Nations. In the book of Job he is described as inflicting on an innocent man a whole range of misfortunes. And in both the Old and the New Testaments he is described as being above reproach. According to St Paul, for example, 'God has mercy upon whomever he wills, and he hardens the heart of whomever he wills' (Rom 9:18). Are we in a position to object to this? Not

according to St Paul. 'But who are you, a man, to answer back to
God? . . . Has the potter no right over the clay, to make out of the same lump
one vessel for beauty and another for menial use?' (Rom 9:20–21). And,
according to the prophet Isaiah, God is explicitly responsible for misfortune
as well as fortune. 'I am the Lord and there is no other. . . . I form light and
create darkness, I make weal and create woe, I am the Lord, who do all these
things' (Is 45:5–7). All of that seems a pretty far cry from the notion of God
as someone who does his duty.

Apart from all this, however, there are three other reasons for denying that
God can be subject to moral duties and obligations.

(1) The first has to do with God's changelessness. As we have seen
(Chapter 6), since God is the Creator we can deny that he is capable of real
change. But, as we understand them, those who are subject to moral duties
and obligations are essentially changeable. To be subject to moral duties and
obligations is to have the chance to become something one is not – i.e. either
morally good or morally bad. Yet to become something one is not is only
possible if one is able to undergo real change. If God is changeless, however,
it follows that he cannot become something he is not. And from this it
follows that he cannot be subject to moral duties and obligations.

(2) The second follows from the fact that, normally speaking, to have
moral duties and obligations depends on being a human being with a capacity
to choose between alternative courses of action. That, of course, is why we
do not refer to the moral duties and obligations of turnips or parrots. But
God is not a human being. We may therefore deny that he is subject to moral
duties and obligations as human beings are. An objector might reject this
point by saying that though God is not a human being, he is still something
personal. As we have also seen, however (Chapter 5), though we can apply
one and the same term to God and to creatures, we cannot understand what it
is like for God to be as we say that he is when talking about him by means of
terms which we also apply to creatures. We may therefore deny that in
calling God personal we understand what it is like for him to be personal. In
that case, however, we are in no position to insist that God is subject to moral
obligations and duties simply because he is personal. In order to do that we
will need to be clear that anything truly called 'personal' is subject to moral
duties and obligations. But how can we be sure that this is so? The natural
reply is that nothing can be called personal if it is not subject to moral duties
and obligations. But that can be denied. We can, for example, speak of
something as personal if we can ascribe to it something analogous to human
intention or intelligent agency (see above, Chapter 7), while something can
surely be personal in this sense without also being subject to moral duties and
obligations. From 'God is personal', therefore, we cannot simply conclude

that God is subject to moral duties and obligations. From 'God is not a human being', however, we can conclude that he is not subject to moral duties and obligations in the way that human beings are.

(3) The third lies in the implications of saying that God is the Creator *ex nihilo*. If that is true, then three things follow:

(i) God is not a member of the world: he is distinct from his creation.
(ii) There is nothing presupposed to God's action: he does not create out of anything.
(iii) There is no context or background against which God's act of creating can be evaluated.

Yet with individuals having duties and obligations things, of course, are different. One has duties and obligations as part of a definite, describable context. A nurse, for example, has certain duties in the light of such things as hospitals, drugs, sickness, doctors, and patients. A parent has obligations against a background of families, children, and society. And so on, for other examples. In that case, however, it makes sense to deny that God has duties and obligations. In the light of what context can he be said to have them? There would seem to be no context at all, and the notion of him having duties and obligations is therefore an idle one. If anything, it should be said that God must be the cause of duties and obligations, for, if God is the Creator, he must be the cause of there being situations in which people have such things.

An objector might reply that God does have obligations in that he has obligations to his creatures as a parent has obligations to his or her children. Before you produce a child, someone might argue, it is indeed true that you have no obligations to it. But having produced the child you do have obligations. And, so the argument might conclude, this is how it must be with God.

But this reply would simply miss the point. Let us suppose that God has obligations to his creatures. How is he to fulfil them? He could only do so by *creating*, by bringing it about that certain events come to pass. But how can God be obliged to create? Against what background can there be an obligation to create *ex nihilo*? If we think of God as a human craftsman fashioning something out of already existing materials, then it might make sense to say that his creating has a context and that, in the light of this, he has some kind of duty or obligation. But, as we have seen (Chapter 1), the model of a human craftsman is misleading when it comes to talking about creation *ex nihilo*. As St Augustine says, any human craftsman must himself be created, and so must the materials out of which he makes his product.

So one may reasonably suggest that something has gone wrong at the outset if one turns to the problem of evil and treats it as a problem about whether or not God is doing his duty or meeting his obligations. This is not to say that God is immoral, or that he cannot be called good. The point being made is that God is not to be thought of as an agent subject to moral duties and obligations as people are; his goodness, if you like, ought not to be conceived in such creaturely terms. We are in no position to say that God ought or ought not to have done something and that he is morally at fault or morally excusable for not doing it or for doing it. In this sense, so one might argue, there is no problem of evil.

IS GOD BAD?

Yet there is indeed much evil in the world. And if God is the Creator, then he is somehow responsible for it. And some would say that, in that case, God wills evil directly and for its own sake and that this is proof of his badness. So now, perhaps, we should ask whether or not this is true. And we can begin by considering things which are victims of evil. What is true of them? It is, of course, true that they are in a bad way, that there is badness which happens to them. But what does it mean to say this?

Here, I think, it is important to note three related facts about badness in general. The first is that it is in one sense relative. The second is that it is negative. The third is that it is parasitic on goodness.

Badness is not a characteristic that all bad things share, as, for example, redness is a characteristic that all red things share. Furthermore, what counts as badness for things or in things will vary from case to case depending on the things in question. What is bad, for example, for people need not be what is bad for fish. Or again, a bad pint of milk will not be bad for the same reason that a bad tooth is bad. In order to understand what is bad for something, and in order to understand that something is bad, we need to know what the thing is. In this sense badness is relative (which is not, of course, to say that it is subjective, that it merely reflects our tastes or whims).

But it is also negative. The point here (an ancient one, usually referred to as the theory that badness is a matter of *privation*) is that to say that something is affected by what is bad for it, or to say that something is bad, is always to say that in some way or other it does not come up to expectations. To say, for example, that someone is sick, is to say that the person is lacking what we expect to find in a healthy human being. Or again, to say that a pint of milk is bad is to say that it fails to meet the requirements, that it is lacking in perfections, appropriate to milk. In short, to say that badness is happening to something or to say that something is bad is to draw attention to something missing.

Please notice that in saying this I am not denying the reality of evil. I am not, for example, supporting the view of Christian Science. I am not saying without qualification that badness (or evil) is not there. And the falling short which leads us to talk of badness (or evil) can be and is recognized as something of which one has to take account. As Herbert McCabe has put it:

The hole in my sock is simply an absence of wool, but it is just as real as the stone in my shoe. It would be absurd to say that holes in socks are unreal and illusory just because the hole is not made of anything. Nothing in the wrong place can be just as real and just as important as something in the wrong place. If you inadvertently drive your car over a cliff, you will have nothing to worry about; and it is precisely the nothing that you will have to worry about (McCabe 1981, p. 8).

But since that, too, is true, to draw attention to badness is to draw attention to something negative. This is not, of course, to say that badness is only present because something tangible is not there, because something tangible is literally missing. Badness may strike something, or something may be bad, because something which it needs is *not* there. But the problem may also lie in the fact that something which it does *not* need *is* there. 'A washing machine may be bad not only because it has too little – as when there is no driving belt on the spin drier, but also because it has too much, as when someone has filled the interior with glue' (McCabe 1981, p. 8). But it still remains that badness is negative in that success is somehow lacking when badness is present. Badness involves defectiveness, and, in this sense, something missing.

But it is not simply a matter of nothing but what is missing. This is the third point which, so I think, needs to be noted about badness: that it depends on goodness or that it is parasitic on goodness. By this I mean that in order for something to be defective it must at least be what it is. A sick child must at least be a human being. A bad pint of beer cannot be called a bad pint of milk. In this sense, for badness to be present there must still be some degree of success. The sick child must succeed in being human, otherwise it will not be a sick human. A bad pint of milk must succeed in being milk, otherwise it will not be bad milk. In other words, it makes no sense to speak of a thing so bad that there is nothing good about it. Something that was sheerly bad would simply not exist.

In the light of these points, then, let us turn to badness which affects things. What does this consist of?

To begin with, it consists of things which are in some way failing to be what they need to be. This is what it means for them to be affected by badness. It is because of this that they can be called victims of evil.

But it also consists of things which somehow succeed in being what they are. For otherwise they could not be said to be affected by badness or to be bad.

Are we, then to say that in creating a world of such things God is directly willing evil? As we have seen, if God is the Creator, he must be responsible for what is there. So we can say that God is somehow responsible for there being something like a sick person or a bad pint of milk. But we can also deny that God wills evil directly and for its own sake so that we can also conclude that he is actually bad. For God cannot will evil as something positive and brought about by him as individuals or positive characteristics are brought about by him. He cannot, that is to say, *create* evil. For things are bad, or they are affected by badness, in virtue of what they fail to be. Yet a failure, as such, has no independent reality. In that case, however, God cannot bring about the badness in things or the badness of things as he can bring about the things themselves or the positive characteristics they exhibit. In this sense badness cannot be caused by God simply because there is nothing to cause. But what is there can and must be caused by God. And what is really there when something is bad or defective is at least enough of a success to be whatever it is that it is. Indeed, as far as what is there goes, when a thing is bad or defective there is literally nothing but success. The trouble lies in the fact that there is not more of this, or that there is too much of it in the wrong place.

The point I am making then (and it is one which can be found in authors like Augustine and Aquinas) is that when badness is present, there is success, which must be caused by God, and failure, which cannot be thought of as something caused to be and which cannot, therefore, be thought of as something caused to be by God or directly willed by him. As one modern spokesman for this view puts it:

The creator causes states of affairs which involve evil, but does not cause evil, since evil does not require a creative cause. Evil is the nonobtaining of what might have obtained and ought to have obtained but does not obtain. What does not obtain does not require a cause of its nonobtaining as such (Grisez 1975, p. 294).

And that is to say that with respect to victims of evil God's causal role is that of one who only produces goodness. Hence we can deny that God directly wills evil for its own sake. It would be more accurate to say that everything directly brought about by God, everything created as a positive reality, is nothing but good. This is not to say that it is as good as it might be or as it needs to be. It is just to say that, insofar as it is created, it is good.

And to this point we can add another. For in the case of the victims of evil there is always more good involved than is present in the victim itself. This is because when badness affects things, or when they become bad or defective, they do so because other things are, as we might put it, positively flourishing. In the case of badness that happens to things we do not presume that we are dealing with a defect which has no cause. We presume that it has an explanation, and we also presume that this will be in terms of something able to account for the defect because of its nature and because it is not itself being thwarted. As McCabe, again, puts it:

There can never be a defect inflicted on one thing except by another thing that is, in doing so, perfecting itself. When I suffer from a disease it is because the bacteria or whatever are fulfilling themselves and behaving exactly as good bacteria should behave. If we found a bacterium which was not engaged in inflicting disease on me we should have to judge that, like a washing machine that did not wash clothes, it was a defective or sick bacterium. The things that inflict evil on me, therefore, are not themselves evil; on the contrary, it is by being good in their way that they make me bad in my way. . . . Always there is a natural explanation and always the explanation is in terms of some things, cells or germs or whatever, doing what comes naturally, being good. Sometimes, of course, and rather more often than he admits, the doctor is baffled. But he puts this down to his own ignorance; he says: 'Well eventually we may hope to find out what is causing this, what things are bringing it about simply by being their good selves, but for the moment we don't know'. What he does *not* say is this: there is no explanation in nature for this, it is an anti-miracle worked by a malignant God (McCabe 1981, pp. 10f.).

In other words, in the case of badness that happens to things, the badness in question is a necessary concomitant of certain kinds of good, and it is only by willing these goods that God can be said to will evil in the case of badness that happens to things. And this, of course, is not to will evil directly and for its own sake.

But that, on the other hand, can hardly be the end of the story. For there is evil or badness not just because things are the victims of evil and therefore in a bad way. There are evil people who are evil or bad of their own accord. Some evil or badness is freely willed moral evil – or so most people who believe in the reality of freedom would agree. One therefore needs to ask whether this shows that God is bad.

In view of what I have already argued in this chapter, one might now suggest that it does. For, so I have argued, the free actions of creatures are caused by God. One might therefore want to say that, in the case of free actions which are bad, God directly wills evil for its own sake and is therefore bad. For, to cast the matter in more theological language, does it not now follow that God causes sin?

In one sense, it does. Since God is the Creator, he must bring about those processes in the world which we have in mind when we speak of people sinning (acting badly of their own accord). Take, for example, an act of adultery. This is perfectly real. It is a genuine process in the created world. So God must be involved in its coming to be. It must be created by him.

But in another sense it is wrong to say that God causes sin. For that might be taken to mean that when sin occurs it is God who sins. Or it might be taken to mean that sinners are forced to sin by God. And neither of these viewpoints is tenable.

The first must be false for a fairly obvious reason. This is that in talking about sins we are talking about what people do, not what God does. Consider, again, the case of adultery. An act of adultery must be created, otherwise it would not be there. But it is people who commit adultery, not God. It would be absurd to say that when people are committing adultery then God is doing the same. That would be like saying that when sleeping pills send you to sleep they are themselves going to sleep. You sleep by virtue of the pills, maybe. But the pills do not go to sleep. You do. By the same token, you commit adultery by virtue of God, but it is not God who commits adultery. You do.

One might, however, say that when you take sleeping pills then the pills force sleep upon you. And, with this analogy in mind, one might now press the second of the above views. One might, that is, say that God forces people into sin. One might ask 'How can my sin be created without it being true that I am forced to sin?'.

At this point some would say that there is only one possible reply. If the actions of creatures are caused by God, then they cannot be free and God determines all that people do, in which case he forces them to sin if they do, in fact, sin. On this view, free human actions cannot be caused by God. Thus, for example, according to John Hick:

If all our thoughts and actions are divinely predestined, then however free and responsible we may seem to ourselves to be, we are not free and responsible in the light of God but must instead be God's puppets (Hick 1983, p. 42).

The same point is made by many other writers including, to take a second example, Keith Ward. According to him, if 'all that happens is determined solely by God himself', then 'any real doctrine of personal responsibility is in danger of being undermined' (Ward 1982, p. 79).

But this conclusion is, I think, false. Here we need to note the following points.

(1) If the doctrine of creation is true, then there must be a sense in which 'all our thoughts and actions are divinely predestined' or 'all that happens' is 'determined' by God. As the Creator of his creatures, God must be ultimately responsible for the reality which comprises his creation. That, as we have seen, is why the Free Will Defence can be challenged.

(2) But what if God's creation includes the free actions of creatures? In that case there can still be free, creaturely action which is also created. In other words, if we have reason to say that an action is free and if we have reason to believe in the doctrine of creation, we have reason to believe that the doctrine of creation does not entail that there cannot be free actions. Or, to put it in Ward's terms, if we have reason to believe that there is personal responsibility and if we have reason to believe in the doctrine of creation, then

we have reason to believe that the doctrine of creation does not rule out the possibility of personal responsibility.

(3) Philosophers have given many different accounts of what it means to be free, but there is certainly a general consensus to the effect that an agent's action is free if it is not determined in its causes by anything in creation apart from the agent himself. And this, in fact, is how we normally do think of freedom. Thus, for example, most people would agree that if it could be proved that, for example, all human behaviour follows of necessity from the operation of material causes, then no human behaviour could be counted as genuinely free. Or, to be more specific, if, for example, Jones shoots Smith because he is under the influence of a drug, or because someone moves his finger to pull the trigger, then we would normally concede that Jones does not shoot Smith freely. By the same token, if we can discover nothing other than Jones which results in the shooting of Smith, we entertain the idea that Jones shoots Smith freely.

In that case, however, it makes sense to say that an agent's action can be free and caused by God. For in saying that it is free one need only mean that nothing in creation determines that the agent acts as he does, while God is not anything in creation. In other words, one may reasonably argue that knowing that God is causally involved in an agent's action (knowing that the action is created) is not to know that it is not free. An objector might reply that if an agent's action is created, then it cannot be free. But we do not have to suppose that this is so. We may, instead, suppose that an agent's action is free if it is not determined in its causes by anything in creation apart from the agent itself.

(4) If there are free actions of creatures, then that is because they are created by God. For the free actions of creatures must be as much a part of creation as anything else. In that case, however, if there are any free actions of creatures, the fact that God creates them will be a necessary condition of them occurring in the first place. But a necessary condition for something occurring cannot interfere with the occurrence being what it is. On the contrary. The occurrence being what it is will depend on the necessary condition. In other words, in terms of the doctrine of creation there would be no creaturely freedom without God, who cannot, therefore, be a threat to it. As Herbert McCabe puts it:

It is the creative causal power of God that makes me *me*. . . . I am free in fact, not because God withdraws from me and leaves me my independence . . . but just the other way round. . . . So God is not an alternative to freedom, he is the direct cause of freedom. We are not free in spite of God, but because of God (McCabe 1980, p. 460).

The same point has been recently made as follows by James Ross:

Nothing can be or come about unless caused to be by the creator. So the fact that God's

causing is necessary for whatever happens cannot impede liberty; it is a condition of it. . . .
Nothing possible can be impeded by its necessary conditions (Ross 1983, p. 131).

So it does not seem inconsistent to hold that an agent's action is caused by
God (since it is created by him) and that the action is free. In that case, however, we need not conclude that if God causes free human actions, then God
forces people to sin. Sinful actions can be both created and free, and, in this
sense, it does not follow that God causes sin.

And to this point one can add another which is related to what was said
above concerning badness or evil and failure. This is that God can be said not
to cause sin because there is a real sense in which sin is not something that
God can be said to cause. Why? Because, as with all that is bad or evil, sin is a
matter of failure. More precisely, it is a matter of failure in an act. The man
who shoots his wife is, of course, acting. And if he went through the action
of shooting something other than his wife, we might well see nothing
wrong in it. I mean that if, for example, he shot a lion to save his wife's life,
we would probably congratulate him. But in shooting his wife he sins
because he fails to achieve the good which we look for in a husband, which
we look for, indeed, in any human being. It is our knowledge of what he is
not doing that makes us speak of the evil in his action. And what he is not
doing is no more being done by God than it is by him. In this sense, also, we
can therefore deny that God causes sin. What people do may be sinful, and it
can therefore be said that sin is real enough. But its reality is that of failure and
it is therefore a matter of something not being actually there. In that case,
therefore, we can deny that it is caused by God. As Creator, God can only
account for what is there, for that is all there is to account for creatively. Since
sin consists essentially in something not being there, it cannot be directly
accounted for by God as Creator. We may say, if you like, that it is permitted
by God; but we cannot say that it is created by him and we can therefore deny
that he causes it. God, that is to say, can make actions; but he cannot, in the
same sense, make the evil involved in sin.

Nor, by the way, can he be faulted in view of the fact that people actually
sin. Suppose one concedes that sin lies in failure and that it is therefore not
something directly willed by God. It still remains that people sin and that we
blame them for this. Should we not therefore blame God for creating a world
in which people sin? Some would reply that we should, but it seems to me
that the reply would spring from what can justly be called a misguided view
of God. One can blame, say, a husband who shoots his wife. But one cannot
in the same sense blame God. The husband is blamed because it is his business
to seek goals other than murder. We can blame the sinner for his sin because
it is his job to avoid sin. But it is not God's job to avoid sin. Indeed, as I
suggested in Chapter 7, it does not even make sense to think of God as
sinning. One might reply that God can be blamed for sin as sinners can be

blamed for it since God has created a world in which people sin and since it therefore seems that God sins if they do. It might also be said that God sins with the sinner since if the free actions of people are caused by God, he should have seen to it that nobody ever sins. But these objections bring us back to points noted earlier. As part of God's creation, you might commit adultery. But it is wrong to say that God therefore commits adultery. And if we hold that God should have seen to it that nobody sins, we presume that he is guilty by neglect since there is something which he ought to be doing and is not, while it is false to suppose that God has obligations. In other words, God cannot be guilty by neglect.

THE GOODNESS OF GOD

So we can deny that God wills evil directly and for its own sake and we can deny that he is bad because he does so. God, we may say, does not create evil. But this is not to show that God is good. Can we therefore suppose that he is?

Reasons for believing that God is good

Is there any philosophical reason for supposing that God is good? Those who think that there is have generally done so because they accept one or more of the following suggestions:

(1) God is good because he gives evidence of acting as a good person acts.
(2) God is good because he is perfect.
(3) God is good because he causes what is good.
(4) God is good because he is desirable or attractive.

(1) God as a good person

The idea involved in (1) is relatively straightforward. We have some idea of what we would take as evidence that some person is good, and, so it has been said, there is similar evidence which allows us to conclude that God is good.

But this view is open to at least three objections.

(i) If we say that God is good as persons are good, we seem strongly committed to the formula 'God is a person'. Yet, as I have argued, that is a formula we can challenge. Persons, as we understand them, are human beings. But God is no such thing. He is the changeless, timeless, omnipotent and omniscient Creator who can be said to be simple as the doctrine of divine simplicity asserts.

(ii) If we have evidence for supposing that God is good as a person can be good, then it would seem that our evidence tells us that God, like good people, is virtuous as people are virtuous, or (if one thinks of human goodness in terms of meeting duties and obligations) that he does his duty or does what he is morally obliged to do. Yet one may reasonably doubt that either of these possibilities is open to God. Some virtues ascribable to people (e.g. courage, temperance) clearly cannot be ascribed to God except, perhaps, in a metaphorical sense (for God can hardly be thought of as being in danger or as being moderate with respect to bodily needs and desires), and, as I have argued, we have reason to deny that God is bound by duties or obligations. One might reply that there are virtues which people can share with God since to have them is compatible with being God. Thus, for example, one might argue that God can be just. But it still remains that God cannot be virtuous as people are virtuous since people acquire virtues as perfections for which they strive and as perfections which they might not have had, while the changeless God cannot be thought of as striving or as lacking what might have been his.

(iii) One may rationally doubt that there is any clear evidence that God is good as people are good. Good people would not, for example, normally allow others to die if they could prevent it. Yet God clearly does this kind of thing on a grand scale. He also, apparently, permits a great deal of suffering which could, in principle, have been avoided. Hence the problem of evil considered as a problem concerning God's moral integrity. One may, of course, reply that it is always possible to explain what happens in the world so as to indicate that one is not forced into the conclusion that God is morally wicked, or that God is bad. But that is beside the point at the moment. I am not now arguing that God is bad, nor am I saying that we can prove that he is not good as people are good. My point is that God seems to permit what good people would not permit and that this, to say the least, puts an enormous question mark over the view that we have evidence for him being good as people are good.

(2) Goodness and perfection

But could it be argued that God is good because he is perfect? Those who say that it can naturally assume that God *is* perfect, and they take this to entail that God is therefore good. Yet does the inference work?

Here I must say that I think it does and that the argument from God's perfection to his goodness is, in fact, acceptable. For, as I have already suggested, we can rationally hold that God is perfect (Chapter 7), and this, I think, means that he is good.

Some, of course, would deny this immediately. They will say, for example, that if God is good at all then he is good as people are good and that we have no reason to suppose that he is this. But this reply supposes that all goodness is human goodness, which is false. Many things can be called good without it being implied that they are good as people are good. The reply to this may be: 'But we can only judge God by human standards'. Yet why should we accept that? Here I agree with Peter Geach. He notes the objection that, being human, we 'can only judge God by human standards'. Then he adds:

The last phrase is merely equivocal. If what is meant is that we men can only judge God by standards that we men judge by, then we have an uninteresting tautology. If what is meant is that our standards for deciding whether God is lovable and admirable must be the same as our standards for deciding whether men are lovable and admirable, then I simply deny this: they need not be and they should not be the same (Geach 1977b, pp. 80f.).

On the other hand, however, there is a natural connection between goodness and perfection. To say that something is good is to say that it has what is appropriate to it considered as what it is. And to say that something is perfect is to say that it lacks nothing appropriate to it considered as what it is. In Aquinas's terminology: 'Things are called perfect when they have achieved actuality, the perfect thing being that in which nothing required by the thing's particular mode of perfection fails to exist' (*Summa Theologiae* Ia, 4, 1; cf. Ia, 6, 3). In this sense, perfection includes goodness. Given, therefore, that God can be called perfect, it follows that he can also be called good. This is not to say that we can understand what God's goodness amounts to. But it is to say that we have reason for calling him good.

(3) Goodness and causation

The third main argument that has been given for ascribing goodness to God holds that something is good if it causes what is good and that since God causes what is good, it follows that he is good. Taken just like that, however, the argument is surely very dubious. For one thing, something defective might produce what is admirable, as, for example, a couple of rogues might give birth to a saint. Then again, if God is good simply because he causes what is good, it would seem that God is many things which he cannot be. God, as Creator, causes peanuts and dandelions, for he makes them to be. But we presumably cannot suppose that God is therefore a peanut or a dandelion, or that he literally resembles them.

On the other hand, however, if God is the Creator he does bring about what is good for people and for other things (whatever else he brings about). And someone who brings about what is good for people and other things would naturally be thought of as good unless, for example, the person concerned does this by doing what is morally wicked. Might one not therefore argue that God can be called good since he brings about what is good for people and other things?

The obvious rejoinder is that God also brings about what is bad for things, people included. Yet if God is the Creator he must bring about the existence of all that we recognize as good in the universe. And we can deny that God creates badness as such. We can also deny that his moral integrity can be impugned as can that of human beings. It therefore seems to me that there is force in the view that God can be called good because he brings about what is good. This is not to say that we have clear evidence that God is good as people are good. But it is to say that a reason for calling someone good can be cited as a reason for calling God good.

(4) Goodness and desirability

And to this point we can, I think, add another. For I now suggest that there is cogency in the fourth of the main reasons given for calling God good. We can call God good since we can say that he is desirable or attractive.

I have already denied that goodness is definable in terms of any particular quality. A good X is not an X with a particular property shared by all good things, as, say, an orange X is an X with a particular property shared by all orange things. Yet, though goodness is not definable in terms of any particular quality, we can, I think, still make one general comment about it. In the *Nicomachean Ethics* Aristotle suggests that 'the good' is 'that at which all things aim' (cf. I, 1, 1094a3), and it seems to me that Aristotle is right here. To be a good X is what all Xs aim at, for to be a good X is simply to be what an X is by nature, to be an unimpeded X. And what a thing is by nature, what it is when unimpeded, is what, as Aristotle would say, it aims to be. In other words, one can say of anything that it aims at being itself, that it aims at being whatever it is that it is – not in any conscious way, necessarily; but by nature, by virtue of what John Stuart Mill (1806–73) calls its 'tendencies' and Aquinas calls its 'inclinations' or 'appetites'. A thing is what it is by virtue of being by nature a thing of some sort. And it will tend to be, or it will incline to be, whatever it needs to be. This is what Aristotle seems to mean by saying that the good is 'that at which all things aim'. He means that things are good insofar as they have succeeded in being what they naturally tend to be. And he also means that success in being what something tends to be, that in which the goodness of something consists, is that to which it is drawn. Here there is a firm connection made between goodness and desirability or attractiveness. Goodness in general is that which is desirable or attractive; it is that to which things are drawn – though what it amounts to in terms of qualities or properties will vary.

Now, as I say, I agree with Aristotle on this point. One can, I think, equate being good with being what is desired or attractive. The good is what all things desire. But what is the relevance of this to the goodness of God? My reply can be stated thus:

(1) What all things desire or are attracted to is good.
(2) All things desire or are attracted to God.
(3) Therefore, God is good.

But this argument needs some elaboration.

I have already suggested why to be good is to be desirable or attractive. A thing naturally desires or is attracted to its good. The good for an X is what an X is attracted to or desires *qua* X. But how can things be said to desire or be attracted to God? Does a rabbit desire God? Are all people attracted to God? If 'desire' means 'consciously desire' and if 'is attracted to' means 'is consciously attracted to', then the answer is clearly 'No'. But with this qualification made, I think the answer is 'Yes'. All rabbits desire God. All people are attracted to God. Why? Because they are all aiming at (tending to) what God intends for them, and because God's intentions for them are no different from God himself.

An analogy is useful at this stage. Let us suppose that a baker makes bread. And let us suppose that he makes good bread, and that he does so deliberately. Insofar as it is good bread that the baker produces, what he makes achieves a degree of perfection, and its good lies in this. This is what it aims at *qua* bread. But what is it aiming at here? Not just being good bread, we may say. For the bread has a maker and it is therefore aiming at what its maker intends for it. I mean by this that what the bread tends to in being good bread is just what the baker intends it to be. And in this sense the perfection, the goal, of the bread lies first in the baker and only secondly in the bread. The baker is not a good loaf of bread. He is not to be described as, say, 'crusty' and 'tasty'. But the loaf he makes is there by virtue of him, and in being good bread it aims to reproduce the goal conceived by the baker. In this sense, so we can say, the baker has in him the perfection that his bread seeks, the perfection by which it succeeds (if it succeeds) in being good bread.

Now the point I want to make is that the analogy I have just introduced is one way of indicating what it can mean to say that God is good. God is not a baker, and he can be said to make things by creating them, which is different from making in the ordinary sense because it is *ex nihilo*. Yet to talk about God is to talk about a maker. It is, in fact, to talk about the Maker of everything apart from himself, the first cause, the reason why there is anything at all. It is also to talk about what has knowledge and power and what can be conceived of as acting in terms of intelligence or purpose. And included in what God makes are things which are good, things which aim at or tend to or desire their perfection. And from this it can be argued that insofar as things are good they exist in accordance with the intention of God. For he is their Maker and something that is made acts in accordance with the intention of its maker when its maker is acting intentionally. In other words, since God is the Maker of all good things, he has in himself all that things are aiming at or tending to insofar as they are aiming at or tending to what is good for them. Just as the bread, in tending to its perfection *qua* bread, is tending to what the baker has intentionally in him, just as it is, in this sense, seeking to reflect him, so all created things can be said to be tending to what God has in him as their maker. And this cannot be thought of as different from God himself. Why? Because in the case of God we cannot distinguish between individuality and nature. Having the perfection of bread in him is something that can be distinguished from the nature of the baker, and the baker's intention in making bread is not to be identified with the baker himself. But with God, so we may argue, things are different. And for this reason, fumbling in the dark though we are in doing so, we seem forced to deny that God's intending the natures of what he creates is something distinguishable from him. This, of course, is the doctrine of divine simplicity again. God is, you might say, what God intends.

One obvious reply to this line of reasoning is that if it is true then we cannot understand what God's goodness amounts to. But that, I think, is true. To understand what God's goodness amounts to would depend on understanding what God is, and I have already tried to explain why I think we cannot do this (Chapter 5). Yet, as I have argued, we can say why we need to talk about God, and we can now, I suggest, say why we can hold that God is good. We can call God good because he is perfect and because he brings about what is good. And we can talk of God as the Maker who has in him the perfections to which his creatures tend. We can talk of God as having in himself that to which things are seeking to conform in seeking their perfection, which, in turn, is something they do because they are made to be by God. As Aquinas puts it:

Goodness should be associated above all with God. For goodness is consequent upon desirability. Now things desire their perfection . . . [and] . . . since God is the primary operative cause of everything, goodness and desirability fittingly belong to him. . . . In desiring its own perfection, everything is desiring God himself, for the perfection of all things somehow resembles divine existence (*Summa Theologiae* Ia, 6, 1).

That is what I have just been trying to say. And, in this sense, I think, we may rationally conclude that God is good. He is good, so one might put it, as the beginning and end of all things which reflect what he is as their Maker insofar as they tend to the perfection which they aim at by virtue of the intention of God himself.

CONCLUSION

So we can deny that belief in God's goodness is something we need rationally abandon in view of the problem of evil. We can also deny that it needs to be abandoned in deference to the claim that God wills evil for its own sake. Belief in the existence of God is compatible with the recognition that evil is more than an illusion. And we can give reasons for denying that God is bad and for asserting that he is good. God wills no evil directly, and he is good because he is perfect, because he is the Creator of various good things, and because, as its Maker, he is the source of everything that is good apart from himself. God is the cause who has in him what his creatures have insofar as they tend to what is good.

Yet all of this may sound too abstract for words. For what about Christianity? What about the fact that God has become man? What about the fact that through the promises of God we can believe that we are offered the prospect of becoming 'partakers of the divine nature' (2 Pet 1:4)? Can we not talk of God's goodness with reference to things like this? And can we not in general hold that there is more to be said about God than anything we might affirm apart from Christian revelation? I have argued that we have reason to make certain assertions about God, but I have so far said little about any specifically Christian teachings about God. One may therefore ask whether we can still continue to think about God in the light of these. And that is what I now propose to consider.

QUESTIONS FOR DISCUSSION

1 'If there is evil, there cannot be a God. But there is evil. Therefore God does not exist.' Discuss.
2 'There is nothing either good or bad but thinking makes it so.' Could this sentiment be usefully employed with reference to the problem of evil?
3 Can any evil be regarded as justly inflicted punishment? If so, why? Can all evil be regarded in this way? If not, why not?
4 What sort of world might God have made? What sort of world might one expect God to have made?
5 Is the Free Will Defence compatible with the doctrine of creation? Even if it is, can one regard it as an adequate answer to the problem of evil? If it is not, then what are the implications?
6 Could God have created a world as good as ours without the evil which we encounter in it? Should he have created a world as good as ours?
7 'The real world is the best of all possible worlds.' Discuss.
8 In what sense, if any, is there a problem of evil?
9 Does God cause evil? If so, how? If not, why not?
10 Why call God good?

FURTHER READING

The topic of God's goodness is most commonly dealt with in works on the problem of evil. All of the standard textbooks on philosophy of religion deal with this problem, so one might profitably begin to consider it by turning to some of them. I list some examples in the Further Reading appended to Chapter 1 of this book.

There are several helpful readers available on God and evil. Two in particular worth noting are: Nelson Pike (ed.), *God and Evil* (London, 1971), and Stephen T. Davis (ed.), *Encountering Evil* (Edinburgh, 1981). See also the following, which contain selections of writings on the topic of God, evil and goodness: William L. Rowe and William J. Wainwright (eds), *Philosophy of Religion: Selected Readings* (New York, 1973); James Churchill and David V. Jones (eds), *An Introductory Reader in the Philosophy of Religion* (London, 1979); Peter Angeles (ed.), *Critiques of God* (New York, 1976); Steven M. Cahn and David Shatz (eds), *Contemporary Philosophy of Religion* (Oxford, 1982); Baruch A. Brody (ed.), *Readings in the Philosophy of Religion* (Englewood Cliffs, N.J., 1974). The articles by McCloskey and Mackie to which I have referred are both reprinted in the volumes edited by Pike and Brody.

For a survey of religious responses to suffering one can warmly recommend John Bowker, *Problems of Suffering in Religions of the World* (Cambridge, 1970). This is packed with information and is clearly written. The same goes for what is probably the standard modern treatment of God and goodness, viz. John Hick, *Evil and the God of Love* (2nd ed., London, 1977). In this book Hick provides a survey of Christian and non-Christian responses to the problem of evil, together with a defence of his own position to which I have referred.

Apart from the volume by Hick, there are several good books devoted to the question of God's goodness. A short book well worth consulting is M. B. Ahern, *The Problem of Evil* (London, 1971). Two well-known and popular studies are: C. S. Lewis, *The Problem of Pain* (London, 1940), and A. Farrer, *Love Almighty and Ills Unlimited* (London, 1961). Also to be recommended is P. T. Geach, *Providence and Evil* (Cambridge, 1977).

Among recent discussions of God and evil by analytical philosophers, especially worth noting are Richard Swinburne, *The Existence of God* (Oxford, 1979), ch. 11, and John Mackie, *The Miracle of Theism* (Oxford, 1982), ch. 9. Swinburne offers a defence of God's moral integrity in terms of means and ends. Mackie argues that, unless belief in God is drastically modified in a non-traditional direction, evil shows that God's existence is unlikely. In several of his writings D. Z. Phillips has challenged the view that believers need to defend God's moral integrity and there is a lively debate between him and Swinburne to be found in Stuart C. Brown (ed.), *Reason and Religion* (Cornell, 1977).

For an excellent exposition of St Augustine on evil, see G. R. Evans, *Augustine on Evil* (Cambridge, 1983). For Aquinas on evil see *Summa Theologiae* Ia, 19–26, 44–49, and 103–109. For Aquinas on God's goodness see also *Summa Theologiae* Ia, 5 and 6. An updated version of Aquinas's position (to which I am much indebted) can be found in Herbert McCabe, 'God: III – Evil', *New Blackfriars* 62 (January 1981).

For a recent defence of the views that evil is privation and that God is not the cause of evil though he is the cause of freedom, see Germain Grisez, *Beyond the New Theism* (Notre Dame/London, 1975), chs 18 and 19. For a good, straightforward defence of the claim that God's creation of freedom is no threat to it, see Herbert McCabe, 'God: II – Freedom', *New Blackfriars* 61 (November 1980). See also two essays by James Ross: 'Creation', *Journal of Philosophy* 77 (1980), and 'Creation II' in Alfred J. Freddoso (ed.), *The Existence and Nature of God* (Notre Dame/London, 1983). Grisez, McCabe and Ross all more or less agree on God and freedom. For a different approach the reader might consult Antony Flew, 'Divine Omnipotence and Human Freedom' in Antony Flew and Alasdaire MacIntyre (eds), *New Essays in Philosophical Theology* (London, 1955), and *The Presumption of Atheism* (London, 1976). For arguments to the effect that God is the author of sin, see Anthony Kenny, *The God of the Philosophers* (Oxford, 1979).

Alvin Plantinga's work on God and evil can be found in several publications including: *God and Other Minds* (Ithaca, N.Y., 1967); *The Nature of Necessity* (Oxford, 1974); *God, Freedom and Evil* (London, 1975). Plantinga devotes a great deal of his time to defending the Free Will Defence and to trying to indicate why one can deny that 'There is a God and evil exists' is contradictory. For a useful discussion of this last question, see also Keith E. Yandell, *Christianity and Philosophy* (Grand Rapids, 1984).

Part Three
God and Christianity

9

Belief in God and Christianity

A distinction has often been made between 'theism', on the one hand, and 'Christian theism', on the other. The idea is that one can believe in the existence of God without believing what Christians uniquely believe about God. One can be a theist without being a Christian theist.

This distinction has been challenged, but it does make sense. Few Christians may *first* believe in the existence of God and *then* believe in the truth of Christianity. And 'God', for the Christian, means 'the Christian God'. Yet what are we to say about people like the authors of the Old Testament? What are we to say about Muslims? They can surely be said to believe in God. But they are not Christians. The Christian understanding of God has been dominated by distinctive doctrines about God, but cannot people be intelligibly said to believe in God even though they do not subscribe to these doctrines?

Once we allow for this point, however, new questions arise. I have so far argued that there is reason to believe in God and that there is reason for speaking about him in certain ways. In other words, I have argued that we have reason to believe in the truth of theism. But what about Christian theism? Is it reasonable or unreasonable? Are we entitled to accept it? Are we obliged to reject it?

ANSWERS GIVEN TO THE QUESTIONS

One common response to such questions is that Christian theism is irrational, and therefore untenable, because it is contradictory. We shall return to this suggestion in the next chapter. For the moment, however, we can here note that at least six other main answers have been given to our questions. All of them have had different exponents some of whom accept more than one of the answers, some of whom disagree on details, and most of whom develop their cases in distinctive and complex ways which cannot be followed out here. One can, however, indicate their nature in bold strokes.

A.   Christian theism should be rejected because theism should be rejected

A fairly common (and perhaps obvious) solution advanced is that Christian theism is simply a write-off since the same is true of theism as such. This view has been held by those who think that there is insufficient reason for belief in God and by those who think that belief in God is somehow impossible because it is meaningless or contradictory. It is, of course, the natural conclusion about Christian theism for an atheist to draw, and many of them have drawn it.

B.   The truth of Christian theism can be proved

Others, however, have taken what is basically the opposite line. On their account Christianity represents the best available outlook from what we might call a strictly rational or philosophical point of view since its truth can be somehow proved. How? Different answers have been given. Some have held that historical evidence can be thought of as clinching the case in favour of Christianity. Others have appealed to premises concerning God or human nature. All, however, are agreed that the truth of Christian theism can somehow be shown to be compelling. On this account (which was particularly prevalent among Catholic apologists in the first half of the twentieth century) the case for Christianity is an objectively decisive one and no impartial and intelligent person can fairly reject it.

C.   Christian theism can be based on experience

A third view, one which has proved especially popular in recent years, is that the truth of Christian theism can be recognized on the basis of experience. The main idea here is that Christians can be said to have a faculty of perception which allows them to discover the presence of God as he is proclaimed to be by the major doctrines of Christianity, or at least by some of them. On this view, therefore, one is, for example, somehow able to recognize by experience that God is Trinity or that Christ was God. Defenders of this solution frequently deny that the truth of Christian theism can be rationally established by argument or inference. But they do generally hold that the acceptance of Christianity is a rational business. Many people would say that there are truths of experience which can be known without us being able to argue for them in the abstract. By the same token, so it has been suggested, there are truths about God which can be known by experience even though we cannot produce them at the end of a chain of reasoning. These truths, so it is said, include the essentials of Christianity.

D.   Christian theism is based on faith

Others, however, have placed the emphasis differently again. According to them Christian theism is based on faith. On this account the Christian does not appeal in his defence to reason or argument considered as something which can establish the truth of Christianity by its own resources. D therefore rejects B. Nor does it stress the idea of experiential knowledge of the Christian God such as that to which defenders of C appeal. But it does emphasize that Christianity is a matter of revelation which can be embraced without question on its own terms. An objector might reply that one must have compelling reason for supposing that Christianity *is* best construed as a matter of revelation. But supporters of D would in general reject this response. Faith, so they say, need not be based on reasons which force one to conclude that it is true. In this sense, so the argument runs, faith is above reason.

E.   Christian theism is a matter of both faith and reason

But might it not be true that Christian theism is also reasonable? People sometimes make a sharp contrast between faith and reason so as to suggest that the two of them are virtually opposed to each other. But might not a Christian think of the Christian position as involving a mixture of both faith and reason? This question brings us to E, which is also often accepted by advocates of D. E also holds that there are Christian beliefs which cannot be 'proved'. In this sense it preserves a distinction between faith and reason. Some would put it by saying that it preserves a distinction between 'faith' and 'philosophy'. But E also stresses that faith is not opposed to reason. Why not? Two main answers have been given. According to the first, though the truth of Christian theism cannot be proved there are rational arguments or grounds which render it *probable*. The second answer is more modest in its claims. It simply states that Christian theism is *not unreasonable*.

F.   Christian theism can be rationally defended if it is reinterpreted

Could it be said, though, that Christian theism is both unreasonable and reasonable? This brings us to our last answer, which I introduce by means of this odd-sounding question because there is a sense in which supporters of F do hold that Christian theism is both unreasonable and reasonable. But they are not to be thought of as intending to express a contradiction. Their point is that we can reject one understanding of Christian theism on rational grounds while at the same time accepting beliefs which are reasonable and which can be regarded as expressing a Christian point of view. The issue here usually turns on doctrines such as the doctrine of the Incarnation as taught by those who formulated the text of documents such as the creed of Nicaea (325) and the definition of Chalcedon (451). According to supporters of F we can no longer rationally assent to such doctrines, but we can assent to restatements or reinterpretations of them. In this sense, so it is held, Christian theism can be rationally defended if it is reinterpreted. Thus, for example, as Maurice Wiles puts it, with respect to the doctrine of the Incarnation there are considerations which 'make it more reasonable for us to see the doctrine as an interpretation of Jesus appropriate to the age in which it arose than to treat it as an unalterable truth binding upon all subsequent generations' (Hick [ed.] 1977, p. 4). According to Wiles, it makes sense to reject what defenders of Nicaea and Chalcedon taught about Christ, but this does not mean that the game is up with Christianity. We can express the significance of Christ in non-traditional terms because we can 'see Jesus not only as one who embodies a full response of man to God but also as one who expresses and embodies the way of God towards men' (Hick [ed.] 1977, p. 8).

COMMENTS ON THE ANSWERS

But are any of these answers acceptable? Do they represent useful or cogent ways of dealing with the questions noted above?

A.   Theism and Christianity

One might suppose that if one accepts A then one is automatically committed to abandoning Christianity or to saying that in some serious sense it is a position which is finally untenable. And that, as I shall argue, is a justified reaction. But it is worth noting that not everyone would agree with this. Some would say that there are reasons for denying that theism and Christianity are bound up with each other so that rejection of the first implies rejection of the second.

Why should it be thought that this is so? Two lines of thinking have been particularly popular.

(i) The first draws a distinction between theism, considered as something assertive, and Christianity, considered as something practical or having to do with behaviour or conduct as opposed to the acceptance of assertions.

According to this distinction, theism is to be primarily understood as belief that there are certain truths about God. Christianity, on the other hand, is not this. Or so the argument runs. The conclusion then advanced is that one can abandon theism without giving up Christianity. One might, of course, ask what is left of Christianity if theism is abandoned, and many would regard this as an important and damaging query for the position now in question. But its exponents have not lacked replies. They have said, for example, that Christianity is a distinctive expression of something like an ethical response to life. On this account one can, apparently, subscribe to Christianity without actually subscribing to the truth of statements which are actually thought of as telling us something about God. Such statements, so it is said, can be rejected or disbelieved without it following that the one who rejects or disbelieves them has rejected Christianity.

(ii) The second answer concentrates on the distinctiveness of Christianity. As I suggested above, it makes sense to say that one can believe in God without believing in Christian theism. But does Christian theism involve belief in God? Or, to put the question another way, is it best construed as a development of theism? Some have said 'No' and in doing so can be thought of as challenging the view that Christian theism stands or falls with theism as such. They would say that theism and Christian theism (or 'theism' and 'Christianity') must be distinguished from each other. On this view, Christianity is not just theism with complications (so to speak). It is something new, something that goes beyond mere theism, especially if that is considered as something the truth of which a philosopher might be said to establish by means of arguments such as those we have considered in Part One. The conclusion then drawn is that the acceptance of Christianity need not be affected by one's rejection of theism. If Christianity is really something new, if it is not just theism with complications, then it is false that the rejection of theism entails the rejection of Christianity. By the same token, it is false that the acceptance of Christianity entails the acceptance of theism. Or so the argument goes.

But these conclusions, though one can doubtless make sense of them and agree with them up to a point, are also surely questionable in the extreme. In their favour one can make several points. One can stress, for example, that Christianity frequently does present itself as a guide for conduct rather than a body of propositions concerning some non-human reality. And it is also, perhaps, true that while many Christians will be reluctant or tongue-tied if asked for a doctrine of God, the majority will have strong views about what they ought or ought not to be doing. Then again, it is easy to see why one might wish to distinguish between Christianity and theism. Many of those who have called themselves 'theists' have believed none of the doctrines one

so naturally associates with Christianity. Often, for example, they have had
no belief in the Incarnation and nothing to correspond to the doctrine of the
Trinity. And, as many have pointed out, they have often laid stress on the
notion of God considered as something aloof or remote, which seems a far cry
from Christianity and, for example, its proclamation that 'God so loved the
world that he gave his only Son, that whoever believes in him should not
perish but have eternal life' (Jn 3:16). On the other hand, however, it is
implausible to suppose that Christianity can be characterized without
qualification as being about action or conduct and not about God. For,
whether one believes them or not, assertions about God are very much part of
the Christian tradition and one will hardly depict that tradition fairly if one
ignores them altogether. And even though Christianity can be readily distinguished from much that is called 'theism', it has also traditionally included
much of this. The Nicene creed begins with a profession of belief in God as
the Creator. Those who hammered out the Chalcedonian definition and the
Athanasian creed (fifth century) did so in the precise recognition that, though
what they were saying was somehow new, it was also consistent and
continuous with what had been believed before. In other words, Christian
theology has regularly been written on the assumption that Christian
teaching incorporates beliefs about God which stand whether or not one
believes in the truth of Christianity. And for this reason one is entitled to
agree that if theism is false or misguided, then so is Christianity. Suppose we
say that a theist typically believes in the doctrine of creation. That seems true.
But it is also true that a Christian theist typically believes in the doctrine of
creation. Insofar as a theist is confused, therefore, so is the Christian.

But this is not to say that the theist is confused. In previous chapters I have
considered some objections to belief in God and I have tried to indicate why
they can be rejected and why one can hold that there is reason to believe that
there is in fact a God. The upshot would therefore seem to be that A is not a
compelling line of thinking. Its strength lies in the recognition that theism
and Christianity can be viewed as bound up with each other. But we do not
have to conclude that this entails the falsity or meaninglessness of Christianity.

B. Proof and Christianity

Can we go further than this, however? Is the truth of Christianity provable?
Is there a case to be made for the truth of Christian theism such that no
impartial person can fairly reject it?

(1) Religious belief and proof

Some have held that the right answer to these questions is definitely negative since no religious assertion could ever be proved to be true. Why not? The following replies are the most common.

(a) Religious belief is meaningless or unintelligible and it therefore follows that there could be no proof of any religious belief.
(b) Though religious belief is not meaningless or unintelligible, its nature indicates that what is believed by those who have it cannot be open to proof. Religious belief is not the sort of thing with respect to which it is relevant to talk about proof.
(c) Proof of religious belief is impossible because human reasoning is corrupted by sin.

Yet these arguments are open to the following objections.

(a) We have reason to suppose that there is indeed a God. Since belief in the existence of God would seem to qualify as a religious belief, it follows that not all religious belief is meaningless or unintelligible. Even waiving this point, how can we be sure in advance that proof of one or more religious beliefs is impossible since such beliefs are meaningless or unintelligible? To repeat what I have already said, proof that such and such is true is proof that what is said to be true is not meaningless or unintelligible. So it is simply begging the question to say that proof of religious belief is impossible because all such belief must be meaningless or unintelligible.

(b) Why should one suppose that religious belief *is* something with respect to which it is irrelevant to talk about proof? It does seem clear that there are many religious believers who have no concept of proof and who have not arrived at their religious positions by means of anything that can be regarded as a proof. For this reason one can sympathize with comments such as the following by Rush Rhees. He observes:

Those who hold to rational theology seem to argue that a man might be brought to a belief in God, and also to a belief in the immortality of the soul, by formal argument alone, even though he had never known anything like an attitude of 'trust in God'. Here I cannot follow them, and I wonder if I understand at all what they are saying.

I feel like repeating what I have said more than once: I do not know any of the great religious teachers who has ever awakened men to religious belief in this way. (When the author of Isaiah, or the author of the book of Job, or the authors of certain of the psalms were trying to keep the faith of the Jews alive during the Exile – did they do anything of the sort? Do you find anything of the sort in the New Testament?)

Suppose you had to explain to someone who had no idea at all of religion or of what belief in God was. Could you do it in this way? – By proving to him that there must be a first cause – a Something – and that this Something is more powerful (whatever this means) than anything else: so that you would not have been conceived or born at all but for the operation of Something, and Something might wipe out the existence of everything at any time? (Rhees 1969, p. 112).

But this does not show that there could be no proof of religious beliefs. Nor does it show that proof of a religious belief must always be regarded as irrelevant. And it is surely hard to see how such conclusions could be shown to be true independently of a consideration of purported proofs of beliefs that can be recognized as religious. Is it not true here, as so often, that we need to proceed with particulars – in this case with particular proofs to be examined on their merits? Some would reply that in debate on religious topics people tend only to accept purported proofs when they are already convinced of the beliefs for which the proofs are supposed to be proofs. But that may be doubted. And, even if it were not, it would still not follow that proof is irrelevant with respect to all religious beliefs. The fact that people only accept proofs of what they already believe does not mean to say that the proofs are not really proofs. Nor does it follow that there could be no proofs of religious conclusions since there may always be people who reject all proofs for such conclusions. Such people may be bad at following proofs. Or they may be unable to recognize the truth of the premises out of which the proofs they reject are constructed. In any case, it is not hard to indicate conditions under which it would be true for someone to say that he has a proof of a religious conclusion. 'If a person is quite convinced that only if there is a God ought he to go to Church, *and* that he ought to go to Church, he is perfectly entitled to infer from these two premises that God exists' (Prior 1976, p. 58). One may reply that nobody is likely to be convinced of the premises here without already being convinced of the conclusion. Yet states of mind like this are conceivable and maybe not even unusual.

A man may be absolutely convinced that only if God exists would he be obliged to live in a certain way – for example, to respect certain freedoms in other people even when violation of these freedoms seems the only way to avoid some grave social disaster – and may also be absolutely convinced that he *is* obliged to live in this way; and a man in this state of mind would surely be not only rational in drawing the conclusion that God exists, but positively *ir*rational in not drawing it (Prior 1976, pp. 58f.).

In response to examples like this some would simply insist that there can only be a proof of some conclusion where there is both a valid argument leading to the conclusion and a set of true premises out of which that argument is constructed. Others would go even further and maintain that the premises must be known to be true by the person offering the proof, by those to whom the proof is offered, by both, by someone else, by several other people, by all of the possibilities here mentioned, or by a certain number of them. Yet even if we accept such qualifications, it still does not follow that there can be no proof of a religious belief. For how can we determine in advance that a given belief may not be provable in the sense or senses now stipulated? Does it not appear that here again we need to proceed piecemeal and by examples? Some would say 'No' since religious belief is not subject to proof precisely because it is belief. The idea here is that if anything is a belief it cannot be subject to proof. Yet something may be believed by one person and known to another by virtue of proof. And, in any case, though we often use the word 'belief' in referring to what is somehow open to question (and therefore, perhaps, not provable), we also use it to refer to what we think of ourselves as able to prove. Thus, for example, we speak of ordinary, everyday beliefs, not things which we think of as doubtful or uncertain, but things for which we can give solid and (to our minds) conclusive grounds. 'Belief' often suggests the presence of doubt; but not always. Sometimes we know what we believe. 'I should mislead people if I described my wife as the woman I live with, and I might say, "No, she's my wife," if asked whether she is the woman I live with. Nevertheless, my wife is the woman I live with. What is true is that I do not *merely* live with her. Likewise, if I know that p, I do not merely believe it, but I do believe it all the same' (Edwards 1967, vol. IV, p. 346). And even if we waive this point, there is another to note. This is that one can first believe something which may later be proved to one. Let us accept for the sake of argument that nobody can have a proof for what he only believes. Does it follow that what he believes is in principle unprovable? By no means. On Monday a man might merely believe that his wife is unfaithful to him. On Tuesday, however, he might have cast-iron evidence for the conclusion that she is unfaithful.

(c) The view that human reasoning is clouded by sin has been considerably stressed in the writing and preaching of many Christians. And one can readily concede that it may contain much truth. Though there is a clear sense in which our beliefs are not subject to our choices or our will (cf. Swinburne 1981a, ch. 1), our reasoning or thinking can evidently be determined by our choices and it is conceivable that by virtue of sinful choices one might be led to embrace conclusions which are false and explicable in terms of sin. But this does not mean that all human reasoning is corrupted by sin so that proof of religious beliefs is impossible. And it is, in fact, hard to see what could show this in a way that could justify us in always rejecting purported proofs of religious beliefs. For whether or not a purported proof is a real proof will depend on the nature of the purported proof, and that cannot be known before it is considered. One might reply that people's sinful nature often leads them to accept what we can know to be false and that this must lead us to doubt the cogency of any purported proof of a religious belief. But the fact that people are sometimes wrong does not mean that they are always wrong, and if one can know that a purported proof is misguided one must already concede that the human mind is capable of getting things right. Most of us would, in fact, readily concede that people can get things right. And, given the existence of disciplines such as logic and mathematics, it seems highly implausible to suggest that proof as such is impossible. So how can we be sure that it is impossible to have proof of religious beliefs? The right answer, surely, is that we cannot be sure of this. Particular purported proofs may indeed be no proofs at all. But it is wrong to suppose that the same must be true of all particular purported proofs.

(2) Christianity and proof

So we can challenge the suggestion that no religious assertion could ever be proved to be true. But what about the truth of Christian theism? Is that provable?

One influential view is that the answer is clearly 'No' since proof must proceed from self-evident principles and there are no self-evident principles which entail the truth of Christian theism. But this view is debatable for at least two reasons. For one thing, its proponents often suppose that certain principles are 'evident in themselves', and this is a difficult supposition to accept since it is hard to see how one can distinguish between what is evident in itself and what is evident to this or that person (cf. Prior 1976, pp. 57f.). Then again, it is by no means obvious that all proof must proceed from self-evident principles. Those who speak of self-evident principles in the context of discussions about proof usually equate them with propositions which are true of logical necessity. But there can be proofs which do not appeal to anything that can at all plausibly be regarded as true of logical necessity.

Having made these points, however, we also need to note that there are others which pull in a different direction. Take, for example, the way in which Christians have spoken on the topic of faith. They have often maintained that some religious assertions are open to proof, or that some religious assertions can be known to be true. But there is also an ancient Christian emphasis on the unprovability of central Christian claims or on the need for Christians to have recourse to faith where 'faith' is contrasted with knowledge or vision and where what is believed 'in faith' is therefore not regarded as provable or knowable as conclusions are knowable when they are proved to one. According, for example, to St Paul, 'We walk by faith, not by sight' (2 Cor 5:7). According to the letter to the Hebrews, 'Faith is the assurance of things hoped for, the conviction of things not seen' (Heb 11:1). In Catholic thinking one can find a particularly sharp distinction made between faith, on the one hand, and matters knowable or provable, on the other. Here I have in mind the work of writers like Aquinas, and texts like the First Vatican Council's *Dogmatic Constitution on the Catholic Faith*. According to Aquinas, some religious beliefs are indeed knowable or provable. They are, in Aquinas's terminology, 'objects of science'. And yet, so Aquinas adds: 'Matters set before the whole human community for belief . . . are in no instance the object of any science, and these are the object of faith pure and simple' (*Summa Theologiae* IIa IIae, 1, 5). Elsewhere we read:

There is a twofold mode of truth in what we profess about God. Some truths about God exceed all the ability of the human reason. Such is the truth that God is triune. But there are some truths which the natural reason also is able to reach. Such are that God exists, that He is one, and the like. In fact, such truths about God have been proved demonstratively by the philosophers, guided by the light of the natural reason (*Summa Contra Gentiles* I,3).

On this account there are major items of Christian belief which just cannot be proved. Similarly, according to Vatican I, faith is 'above reason' though 'there can never be any real discrepancy between faith and reason' (ch. IV). On this view, some truths about God can be known 'by reason', but others must be accepted in faith which is to be thought of as different from reason not because it is unreasonable or irrational but because what it proclaims is not, as such, provable or knowable 'by reason'. According to Vatican I 'we are bound to yield to God, by faith in His Revelation, the full obedience of our intelligence and will' (ch. III). And this faith, says the Council, 'is a supernatural virtue, whereby, inspired and assisted by the grace of God, we believe that the things which He has revealed are true; not because the intrinsic truth of the things is plainly perceived by the natural light of reason, but because of the authority of God himself, who reveals them, and who can neither be deceived nor deceive' (ch. III). The conclusion, then, is that 'besides those things to which natural reason can attain, there are proposed to our belief mysteries hidden in God, which, unless divinely revealed, cannot be known' (ch. IV).

A second point worth noting is that, regardless of the respect which we accord to writers like Aquinas or to texts like those of Vatican I, there are difficulties raised by the claim that proof is available for certain central items of Christian belief. Take, for example, the doctrine of the Incarnation. In its orthodox form (by which I mean the form promulgated by Nicaea and Chalcedon) this asserts that Christ was both divine and human and that divinity and humanity in Christ are inextricably united though unmixed, that the divine and human natures of Christ co-existed 'without confusion' and 'without separation'. But what could prove the truth of this? The problem here is not that one cannot construct a valid argument with the doctrine of the Incarnation as its conclusion. One might, for instance, argue as follows:

(1) London is in England and the doctrine of the Incarnation is true.
(2) Therefore, the doctrine of the Incarnation is true.

But it seems odd to describe this as a proof of the doctrine of the Incarnation. Those who say that Christian theism is provable usually mean that one can appeal to an argument the premises of which entail the conclusion that Christian theism (or one of its key elements) is true. They are therefore concerned with what we can call 'proof from premises'. But if anything is a successful proof of this kind, it seems reasonable to say that, though the premises must imply the conclusion, one must not be stating the conclusion in stating the premises (cf. Penelhum 1971, p. 26). Yet in the argument above the conclusion is, in fact, stated in the first premise. A proof of the Incarnation (one which could be stated in the form of a valid argument, at any rate) would seem to depend on someone being able to know the truth of premises which entail the doctrine but which do not state it. And it is here that the problem lies. For can anyone know the truth of premises which entail the doctrine of the Incarnation but do not state it?

Some have argued that the answer here lies in truths which we can know about both God and man. An example of this line of reasoning has been thought (rightly or wrongly; the matter is disputed) to occur in the work of St Anselm. In his *Cur Deus Homo?* he offers what many have read as a proof of the Incarnation based on the nature of God and the fact that people are sinners. R. W. Southern restates the argument as follows:

A.1. Man was created by God for eternal blessedness.
   2. This blessedness requires the perfect and voluntary submission of Man's will to God.
   3. But the whole human race is guilty of disobedience.
   4. Any deviation of Man's will must either be punished by deprivation of blessedness or rectified by an offering greater than the act of disobedience: there can be no free remission.
   5. No member of the human race can offer anything to God beyond his due obedience: there is no human capital with which to redeem the past, not to speak of the present and future.
   6. Therefore the whole human race must forfeit the blessedness for which it was created.

B.1. On this argument, God's purpose in the creation of man has become frustrated.
   2. But this is impossible.
   3. Therefore a means of redemption must exist.
   4. But the offering necessary for redemption ought to be made by Man.
   5. And since Man has nothing to offer, it cannot be made by Man.
   6. The offering required is greater than the whole existing Creation.
   7. Nothing is greater than the whole Creation except God.
   8. Therefore only God can make this offering.
   9. Since only God can, and only Man ought to make this offering, it must be made by a God-Man.
  10. Therefore a God-Man is necessary.
  11. Therefore the Incarnation is necessary (Southern 1963, pp. 92f.).

But if this argument is read as a proof of the Incarnation it must surely be judged a failure. The argument seems to say that only man ought to make the offering for sin, but he cannot, and only God can make the offering, but he ought not. The conclusion then drawn is that only a God-Man can and ought to make the offering. Yet as Southern himself observes:

It is clearly impossible to join together 'ought (but cannot)' and 'can (but ought not)' to get 'ought and can', in the same way that two partners can join together to combine their assets. If one of the partners *ought not* to pay, that is the end of the matter. No amount of argument can bring him into a combination in which he both can and *ought*. The reason for this is that 'ought not' does not express a mere absence of the quality of obligation but an absolute moral disability which can in no circumstances be overcome. And this is what Anselm requires, or at least seems to require. For if he is not asserting on God's side an absolute moral disability to pay Man's debt, then the whole force of his dilemma is lost and the Incarnation is not necessary or not necessary in the way that he tries to show that it is (Southern 1963, p. 115).

Then again, how can we know that God could not simply waive the need for an 'offering necessary for redemption'? What can show that God is bound to demand for man's disobedience either 'punishment by deprivation of blessed-ness' or 'an offering greater than the act of disobedience'? Can we be certain that God is unable simply to forgive the disobedient? One may, of course, argue (as many Christians have done) that the Incarnation is a fitting way for God to deal with sin. But does this make it necessary? Here, perhaps, we can agree with some remarks of Aquinas. At one point he asks whether the Incarnation of the Word of God was necessary for the restoration of the human race. The reply given is that it was not.

We refer to something as necessary for an end in two senses. First, when the goal is simply unattainable without it, e.g. food for sustaining human life. Second, when it is required for a better and more expeditious attainment of the goal, e.g. a horse for a journey. In the first sense the Incarnation was not necessary for the restoration of human nature, since by his infinite power God had many other ways to accomplish this end. In the second sense, how-ever, it was needed for the restoration of human nature (*Summa Theologiae* IIIa, 1, 2).

Arguments like that of Anselm have not, however, been all that prevalent among those who think that one can know the truth of premises which entail the doctrine of the Incarnation but do not state it. Much more popular has been the claim that one can appeal to historical considerations. Consider the Gospels in the New Testament. These contain a whole series of narratives in which Christ features prominently and in which he is described as saying and doing various things. According to the view now in question we can regard these narratives as historically accurate reports and we are forced to conclude that they entail the divinity of Christ somehow. According, for example, to some, the divinity of Christ is proved by the fact that he performed miracles. Others have appealed both to what they take to be miraculous and to what they take to have been the teaching of Christ. In the words of one author:

We have proved, therefore, through the testimony of friends and enemies, that Christ died and was buried; we have proved through the testimony of witnesses who were honest and, at the same time incredulous, and through the success which attended the preaching of the Apostles, that Christ rose from the dead. Christ claimed to be God. In proof of His claim Christ said he would rise from the dead. He rose from the dead. Therefore His claim is true (Sheehan 1962, p. 119).

But can we be as sure about the historicity of the Gospels as arguments like this presume? And even if we can, would it be right to claim that historical data oblige us to acknowledge the divinity of Christ? Neither of these questions admits of quick or easy answers, but one can, at least, note problems in supposing that the Gospels are to be treated as historically reliable records or that the appeal to historical data can form part of a proof of the doctrine of the Incarnation.

With respect to the first supposition there is the fact that most New Testament critics would now agree that we actually do the Gospels violence by treating them as straightforward historical narratives written with the interests and methods of modern historians. Several recent writers (authors such as Günther Bornkamm, C. H. Dodd, J. Jeremias, Ernst Käsemann, Norman Perrin, J. M. Robinson, and Eduard Schweitzer) have suggested ways in which we may try to use the Gospels to find out what 'really' happened and what was 'really' said. And there are, apparently, grounds for denying that the evangelists were totally unconcerned with historical accuracy as we understand it. But the general scholarly verdict still seems to be that the Gospels were never intended as straightforward descriptions of past events. Nor is it clear that we can treat them as such given what they actually say. For there are well-known problems of discrepancy and the like which have to be recognized. Take, for example, the Gospel accounts of the Resurrection. As one critic puts it:

When we compare the narratives of the four evangelists we see that their accounts differ considerably. It is not merely a question of differences in details though these are not insignificant. So there are variations in the names and numbers of the women who went to the tomb and also in their motives for going. More important, what (or rather whom) they encounter there is described very differently. In Mark they see a young man: in Matthew they behold an angel of the Lord descending from heaven whose 'appearance was like lightning and his raiment white as snow'. In Luke they encounter two men 'in dazzling apparel': in John Mary Magdalene, who goes first to the tomb, and the disciples who run there, see no one at all in the tomb and it is only later that Mary beholds 'two angels in white, sitting where the body of Jesus had lain' (Franklin 1982, pp. 59f.).

One might say that differences such as these are small. Yet, as the author just quoted goes on to observe (echoing many others), the Gospel accounts of the Resurrection contain yet other discrepancies 'of such a kind as to make it impossible to bring the four narratives together to display a single chronological order of events without doing considerable violence to at least one of the gospel accounts' (Franklin, p. 61). Not surprisingly, therefore, yet another critic can summarize his conclusions about the resurrection narratives in this way:

It is not simply difficult to harmonize these traditions, but quite impossible. Attempts to combine them by means of inspired guesses and hypotheses, of which F. F. Morrison's *Who*

Moved the Stone? has been for so long known as an outstanding and brilliant example, are really defeated from the start. For what have to be combined are not a number of scattered pieces from an originally single matrix, but separate expressions of the Easter faith. Each of these is complete in itself; each has developed along its own line so as to serve in the end as a proper conclusion for an evangelist of his own particular version of the gospel. Behind and within all the traditions, of course, is the conviction that Jesus of Nazareth continues to be and to operate, and that in him past, present and future are somehow related; but the mode of this continuation is differently conceived in the four gospels, and in each case is closely related to the theology of the particular gospel concerned. Each evangelist gives his own version as a total version, which was not intended to stand up only if it stood alongside another, or was supplemented by another (Evans 1970, p. 128).

As for the second supposition, there is this problem. Let us suppose that the historicity of the Gospels could be conclusively established. Would that prove the truth of the doctrine of the Incarnation? Arguably not. For while it may be shown that certain events happened in the past, or that certain words were uttered, an interpretation going beyond the evidence would still be required if the events of words are to be taken as establishing the truth of the claim that Christ was God. This is because of what we can say about God independently of any consideration of specifically Christian teaching. God, we may say, is the non-material and eternal Creator *ex nihilo*. In that case, however, how can anything historically observable be taken as compelling evidence that some historical subject can be truly referred to as God? Given the non-creaturely nature of divinity, there is a clear sense in which it seems possible to deny that we are confronted by God no matter what historical data we have before us. Let us, for example, suppose that we could be absolutely certain that a text like the 20th chapter of St John's gospel is straightforward historical reporting of the kind which we expect from a good modern historian, or perhaps a reporter. Would we thereby be forced to conclude that Christ was divine? Surely not. For what would force us? Some would reply that nothing but God could be as Christ is described as being in the chapter now in question. But how can we know that? Why may it not be false that Christ was God and true that he was all that St John describes him as being in chapter 20 of his gospel? Here I am reminded of some remarks of Aquinas. He cites an argument which appeals to that part of John 20 which tells us of Thomas and his acknowledgement that Christ is God. The argument maintains that 'the object of faith is something seen' since Jesus tells Thomas that he (Thomas) believes because he has seen. Yet Aquinas rejects the argument. 'Thomas,' he observes, 'saw one thing and believed something else. He saw a man; he believed him to be God' (*Summa Theologiae* IIa IIae, 1, 4 ad 1). Aquinas is not denying that what Thomas saw gives him reason for believing that Christ was divine. But he does deny that one can see the divinity of Christ as one can see what is open to historical investigation. And that is surely true. In this sense, so one can argue,

historical data cannot by themselves prove the truth of a doctrine like that of
the Incarnation. The doctrine itself is not just a report of historical facts and
its truth (what constitutes its truth) cannot be simply identified with such
facts (cf. Sutherland 1984, p. 133).

And to points like this we can add yet another – one which to many minds
puts a very big question mark over the assertion that one can prove the truth
of Christian theism. The issue here turns on the nature of God and the limits
of the human mind. For consider the claim that God is the Creator. If that is
true then, as I argued in Chapter 5, it follows that we do not really understand the reality to which we refer in using the term 'God'. In that case,
however, how can we construct a proof to the effect that God is what he is
said to be in the teachings of Christian theism? One might reply that there
are logically necessary truths which entail doctrines like those of the
Incarnation and the Trinity. But what truths are these? I do not know of anybody who even supposes that there are any. One might say that what is
created contains, or has contained, objects or situations which could not have
existed unless doctrines like those of the Incarnation and the Trinity were
true. But how are we to show that this is so? What created reality would be
impossible if God were not Incarnate or Triune?

Are we to conclude, therefore, that nobody can know the truth of
premises which entail the truth of doctrines such as that of the Incarnation
without stating them? Are we to conclude that nobody can know the truth
of premises which entail the truth of Christian theism without stating it?
Maybe not from anything I have said so far. Perhaps there are people who
know the truth of premises which entail the truth of Christian theism without stating it. But I do not know what these premises could be or how one
could be said to know them. Readers who know differently here have the
advantage over me at this point.

C. Experience and Christian theism

Yet someone might object that proof need not be confined to what can be
stated by means of argument. And this brings us to the view that the truth of
Christian theism can somehow be grasped by experience, for can we not
appeal to experience as providing a sort of proof? And even if not, can we not
appeal to experience as a way of coming to see that what Christians uniquely
believe about God is true?

Here one must surely allow that there is a way of talking that would seem
to concede that proof by experience can be genuine proof. Suppose that John
claims to be very strong. I say 'Prove it'. He flexes his muscles and lifts me
from the ground with one hand. Describing this scenario many would say

that I have proof of John's strength. But it is not proof by argument. Here one can say that I have 'direct' proof or proof 'from experience'.

Then again, consider the fact that we can know that something is there, and that it is thus and so, because we have come across it for ourselves. Discovering in this way that something is there and that it is thus and so might be described as having a proof that the thing is there and that it is thus and so. Alternatively, it might be described as knowing the presence and nature of the thing by experience.

But we can appeal to anything like this as an analogy for understanding what might be going on with respect to Christians and the content of Christian teaching? One may not deny that we can have reason for believing certain things without having followed any particular argument. One might allow that we can know things by coming across them. But can we conclude that the truth of Christian theism can be grasped by 'experience' as such, or by 'experience' as opposed to 'argument'?

Those who think that we can often defend themselves by arguing that their conclusion at least does justice to the fact that the Christian life should be thought of as a relationship of encounter with the living God rather than as subscription to a body of doctrines. Many theologians have said that to be a Christian is to assent to a number of propositions (e.g. 'Jesus is God', 'God is Trinity') and to act on the belief that these propositions are true. But according to the view to which I am now referring this suggestion is at best inadequate and at worst misleading. As, for example, John Coventry writes:

Faith is primarily in Christ, and not in doctrines; in God presenting himself for recognition as a person, and not in any series of doctrinal statements or propositions, which we are asked to believe. . . . Faith is the correlative of revelation. Those who believed when confronted with Christ's life, death and resurrection, were those who recognized that it was God who confronted them. This is faith . . . not a process of argument resulting in a conclusion; not the acceptance of a proposition; but a religious experience, sometimes sudden and overwhelming, that you are confronted with God, to which you may well respond by saying 'depart from me for I am a sinful man, O Lord' (Coventry 1968, pp. 9ff.).

Yet this way of putting things is surely very puzzling, to say the least. For is it not true that all belief ultimately rests on the acceptance of propositions? This is not to say that when we believe things we are consciously assenting to propositions considered as things to which our attention is drawn. It makes sense, for example, to say that people have beliefs even when they are asleep. But to believe something is always to believe *that* something is the case, and, in this sense, it is irreducibly propositional. One might reply that there is a difference between accepting a proposition and believing God, and, on this basis, one might urge that Christianity can be a matter of non-propositional belief. But one cannot believe God without believing something about God, e.g. that he is there, that he is rightly called 'God', that what he tells one is true, etc. And since to believe something about God is to believe that certain things are true, we are again brought back to the propositional nature of belief. This is not to say that the object of a Christian's belief must be propositions and *not* God. One might believe a proposition and still believe God, just as one might believe that Jones is hungry and believe Jones since one believes him when he says that he is hungry. But one is still left with a propositional element even when what is in question is the case of believing God or believing Jones. To believe God must include believing something about God (e.g. that what he tells one is true), and the same applies to believing Jones. In this sense one can only render intelligible the statement that someone believes if one is told what he believes. In this sense belief is propositional. Coventry says that 'those who recognized that it was God who confronted them' were not displaying 'the acceptance of a proposition'. But how can one recognize *that* one is confronted by God without believing something about God? According to Coventry, faith is not in propositions though 'those who believed when confronted with Christ's life, death and resurrection were those who recognized that it was God who confronted them'. Yet 'It was God who confronted them' *is* a proposition.

But this does not mean that the truth of Christian theism cannot be recognized on the basis of experience. It only indicates why a believing Christian can be said to accept that certain propositions are true. Yet there are several problems with the suggestion that the truth of Christian theism can be recognized on the basis of experience.

The first concerns the meaning of the suggestion. The problem here lies with the word 'experience', for the word is used in so many different ways. What, then, are we supposed to be accepting if we accept that the truth of Christian theism can be recognized on the basis of experience? What is it that is here supposed to provide the basis for recognizing the truth of Christian theism?

In reply to such questions people have distinguished between 'experience' and 'inference'. They have also said that in this context 'experience' means something like 'being aware' or 'seeing' or 'perceiving' as these terms might be used in statements like 'I was aware of something beside me', 'I saw Fred on Tuesday', and 'He perceived the dog running on the lawn'. But, though we can distinguish between knowing something 'by experience' and knowing something 'by inference', the distinction is not a clear one if only because it makes sense to say that making an inference can be part of one's experience. An experienced logician will normally be one who has made many inferences. Then again, there is this difficulty. Why should one suppose that the truth of Christian theism can be based on 'being aware', 'seeing', or 'perceiving' as those words are used in sentences like the ones cited above? One can certainly be aware that something is beside one. But can one be aware of the truth of Christian theism in the same way? Does it occupy a spatial position? Does the Christian God do this? And what about seeing and perceiving? Is the truth of Christian theism like a human being that one can meet? Is the Christian God simply like this? Can one perceive the truth of Christian theism with one's eyes? Can one perceive the Christian God in this way? Given what Christians have traditionally believed about God, the answer to all these questions (which some, I should warn, would characterize as silly or irrelevant) must surely be 'No'. In that case, however, just how much light is shed by elucidating 'The truth of Christian theism can be recognized on the basis of experience' with reference to being aware, seeing, and perceiving as in the sentences noted above? Here one faces the same sort of problems as those noted above in the section of Chapter 3 headed 'What is an experience of God?'. One may say that the truth of Christianity can be recognized on the basis of experience, and one may add that this is so because there is experience of the Christian God. But these assertions seem (to me, at any rate) baffling if 'experience' here means what it does when we say that we see, perceive, or are aware of things within the world.

Could it be said, however, that recognizing the truth of Christianity by experience *is* like something with which we are perfectly familiar? Some would certainly say that it is. The truth of Christianity, so it has been urged, can be recognized by experience since there is experience of the Christian God which is experience of a person considered as an object of one's experience. Unfortunately, however, this suggestion brings us to a second major difficulty with the assertion that the truth of Christian theism can be recognized on the basis of experience. For why should we suppose that there is an experience of the Christian God which is like the experience of anything else and which can therefore be understood by analogy with the experience of anything else? The reply might be that just as there are various experiences of things so there is an experience of the Christian God, and just as there are experiences of persons so there is an experience of the Christian God considered as a person. But how can this be so if 'the Christian God' means 'God as proclaimed by orthodox Christianity'? To say that there are experiences of things presumably means that there are objects in the world which one can somehow come across or make contact with and which one can recognize for what they are by coming across them or by making contact with them. Yet from the viewpoint of orthodox Christianity God is not something which one can come across as an object in the world: he is the Creator of such objects. Nor is he a person, at least if our notion of 'person' is taken from its use as applicable to human beings. Persons, as we understand them, are creatures of God who occupy space and time. Are we supposed to say that God is like this?

Some would here reply that persons like us are not, in fact, material. They would then add that since we can come across them or encounter them in spite of this, there can be no objection to the idea that there is an encounter with God or a coming across him considered as a non-material person. As, for example, Dermot A. Lane puts it: 'It is only in and through our experience of the bodily activity of another human being that we can begin to discover the existence of that dynamic transcendent reality we call a person. Equally, it is only in and through our experiences of the rhythm of life in the world that we can discover God as that transcendent reality who is immanently present to the world' (Lane 1981, p. 19). But this way of putting things raises yet more problems. Why should we say that persons are not bodily? Where 'person' means what you and I are, does it even make sense to speak of 'non-bodily persons'? And does anyone come across or encounter persons like you and me without coming across or encountering things whose nature and origin depend on bodily factors? The answer is surely 'No'. In that case, however, why compare coming across or encountering God with coming across or encountering persons? Or is God supposed to be something whose origin and nature depends on bodily factors? One might say that such questions are irrelevant since God can be experienced even though he is distinct from the world and very different from the persons of our acquaintance. According once again to Lane:

Experience involves first and foremost a human subject and reality. . . . Following on this there must be some form of encounter between the subject and reality if there is to be any genuine experience. . . . Moving from encounter we go on to posit a process of interaction between subject and reality. . . . Experience, therefore, is the product that arises out of the interaction that takes place between the subject and reality. . . . It is the critical assessment of reality by the subject through the movements of response, refraction and critical reflection. . . . God is co-experienced and co-known through the different experiences and knowledge of the human subject (Lane, pp. 8ff.).

But this seems to say little more than that people can have knowledge and beliefs about God, and one therefore wonders what is gained by the use of the word 'experience' in this context. Why not just say that there is knowledge of God or that people have many beliefs about God? Does the appeal to 'experience' add anything of significance here? Maybe it does, but one might well wonder what that is. The point may simply be that believing Christians are not people who have or who have followed some complex argument and who somehow have proof of their position which no one can reasonably reject. And if that is what is meant, then, as I have said, one can agree with it. Alternatively, the idea may just be that one's convictions, beliefs, and assumptions are able to show one some truth about God. And that is a con-clusion which I have already accepted and which I shall again be defending later. But this conclusion can be questioned if it is taken to mean that one's convictions, beliefs and assumptions are infallible guides to what is really true about God. Convictions, beliefs and assumptions can simply be wrong and consulting them may lead one nowhere near the truth. As we saw in Chapter 3, some would say that one's certainty can distinguish between error and truth. But that is wrong. The most vivid certainty may turn out to be mistaken, and if we are inclined to suppose that one can feel a difference (or perceive a difference) between certainty which is never deceptive and that which might be mistaken we should consider some of the things which people have said they knew because they were certain of them. Some instances are cited by P. T. Geach in reporting some certainties of the Oxford philosopher H. A. Prichard (1871–1947):

Prichard was certain, and therefore 'knew', that waves cannot be said, as physicists suppose, to have a velocity, since a wave is not a body and only bodies have velocities. He records, with no sense that the story might be against himself, the fact that when he said this sort of thing to physicists they thought he was 'just mad': they ought to have 'thought a bit more', but 'you cannot make a man think any more than you can make a horse drink' (*Knowledge and Perception*, O.U.P. 1950, p. 99). Furthermore, he 'knew' that his ego was a substance, and that no substance can be generated or destroyed – so that he was in the world in the days of Julius Caesar (Geach 1976, pp. 13f.).

As Geach goes on to say, 'these claims he (Prichard) no doubt made *bona fide* and with a feeling of certainty; but for others they may throw some doubt on Prichard's claim that he could always tell when he had the kind of certainty that cannot be wrong' (p. 14).

So where does all that leave us? To return to the question with which we began: Can we safely conclude that the truth of Christian theism can be grasped by 'experience'? The reader may feel that I have said nothing which shows that we can *know* that the answer is 'No'. But what I have said does seem to me to raise serious questions for the opposite answer and for some of the ways this answer has been defended. At this point, therefore, I turn to another line of thinking: the view that Christian theism can be believed to be true by faith.

D.   Christian theism and faith

In the critical and scientific atmosphere of the twentieth century people have become used to expecting evidence and proof for assertions propounded for one's acceptance. Indeed, the demand for evidence with respect to belief is something that goes back a long way beyond the twentieth century. Hume, for example, speaks of the consideration of evidence as if it were a hallmark of rationality. 'A wise man', he writes, 'proportions his belief to the evidence' (*An Enquiry Concerning Human Understanding*, p. 110). To take another famous example, there is the English mathematician and philosopher W. K.

Clifford (1845–1879). According to him, no belief is rationally acceptable unless there is sufficient evidence for it, and 'it is wrong always, everywhere, and for anyone to believe anything upon insufficient evidence' (cf. Clifford 1879, pp. 345f.).

If this line of thinking is right it would seem that we ought to deny that the truth of Christian theism can be accepted on faith. On the contrary, so one might argue, if Christian theism is true the evidence must show that it is true. Alternatively, so one might suggest, its truth must be somehow provable. And that is what many have said. Since they have also frequently concluded that the demand cannot be met, they have often gone on to suggest that it must be wrong to believe in the truth of Christian theism, that one is not rationally entitled to do so.

But can anything be said on the other side? Suppose I hold that the truth of Christian theism cannot, as it were, be shown to be true from outside. Suppose I say that it is to be accepted by faith on its own terms as something revealed. Can I make no defence of myself?

Exponents of D have here given several replies of which three in particular are especially common.

(1)   *The nature of God implies the necessity of faith.* The idea here is that given the nature of God there are bound to be truths about him which must be accepted in faith rather than on the basis of any rational inquiry or investigation of the kind that human beings can conduct. Why? Because, so it is said, God is something which human nature cannot comprehend and it therefore follows that we either take his word for what he is or we remain in a state of ignorance concerning him.

(2)   *Human reasoning is clouded by sin and cannot arrive at the truth about God by its own efforts.* This is a suggestion we have met already. Basically, the idea is that the thinking of human beings is somehow infected by a culpable disposition or a series of culpable choices so that the result is always a failure on the part of human reason to see what God actually is. The conclusion then offered is that this situation can only be overcome if human beings accept what God reveals about himself without supposing that this can be grasped or shown to be true by human reasoning apart from revelation.

(3)   *Christian theism teaches a new and unprovable concept of God.* Defenders of this suggestion are not necessarily committed to either of the above lines of thinking, for they can (and often do) hold that people can reach truths about God by the use of reason and without reference to any particular revelation. But they then add that what Christians uniquely believe about God goes beyond what human reason can discover or prove on its own. On this view

the teachings of Christian theism add to what reason can know of God (in this sense they are new) and what they add can only be accepted by faith. In other words, there is a point at which reason gives out and one either continues in faith or one does not continue at all.

Let us consider each of these positions in order.

(1) On some views of God it would seem that the first of them is by no means compelling. Suppose we agree that although there is a sense in which God must be mysterious to us, he is also very like things which we already know quite well. Suppose, for example, we say, as many do, that God is very like the persons of our acquaintance. In that case we might argue that what he is can be guessed or inferred by means of analogy and that it will suffice for us to confine our beliefs about God to what we can guess or infer in this way.

On the other hand, however, there is surely a strong case to be made for denying that God is very like things we already know quite well. As we have seen (Chapters 5 to 8) we may rationally suppose that God is not material, that he is not distinct from his nature or attributes, that he is not dependent for his existence on anything, and that he is not classifiable in terms of genus and species. We may also say that God is eternal (*qua* timeless and changeless), omniscient, omnipotent, and omnipresent. And all of that surely suggests that God is indeed seriously beyond our understanding. This is not to say that we cannot with good reason make true statements about God. But, as I suggested in Chapter 5, in making such statements there is a sense in which we will not understand the significance of what we are saying. And that allows one to add that God is indeed incomprehensible to us. And if that is accepted, why should one not concede as a consequence that there might well be truths about God which we are confined to accepting on the authority of God? That, at any rate, has been the conclusion of many Christians down the ages. In the words of Vatican I:

Reason never becomes capable of apprehending mysteries as it does truths which constitute its proper object. For the divine mysteries by their own nature so far transcend the created intelligence that, even when delivered by revelation and received by faith, they remain covered with a veil of faith itself, and shrouded in a certain degree of darkness, so long as we are pilgrims in this mortal life, not yet with God (*Dei Filius*, ch. IV).

(2) But this view already supposes that there can be some knowledge of God apart from revelation, which brings us to (2). So is that a position we need to accept?

In its defence we might mention several points. For one thing, if God is the Creator then everything apart from himself depends for its existence on him, from which one might conclude that there is a sense in which human reasoning cannot do anything by its own efforts. The point here would be that since human reasoning is created, it is therefore dependent on God. Then again, it is true that our reasoning in general can often be influenced by less than rational considerations, and these may often lie in facts about ourselves for which we are culpable. In this connection one may instance such possibilities as wishful thinking and self-deception. One might also argue that it is not implausible to suppose that people have actually reasoned about God without reaching truth and this can be explained in terms of human culpability. Can we, for instance, be sure that all chains of reasoning about God have been unaffected by what can justly be regarded as base motives or desires?

Yet even if we acknowledge the force of questions like this, we are not obliged to agree that human reasoning cannot reach true conclusions about God. And if what I have argued in Parts One and Two is correct, we would, in fact, be wrong to do so. In any case, if reason is so clouded that it cannot make a true statement about God by its own powers, then it cannot even say that God is 'beyond' reason. For there is only human reason to make such a claim. A Christian might reply that human reason does not make the claim. He might say that it is made by revelation. But why should the Christian say this? Is there any teaching to which a Christian as such is bound and which explicitly teaches that human reason is too clouded to make a true statement about God by its own powers? Does the Bible teach this? If it does, then the fact is not obvious (cf. Bouillard 1969, ch. 1). There are elements of such teaching in the writings of John Calvin (1509–64), but it has certainly not been universal and in the Catholic tradition it has been pretty generally denied.

(3) But this still leaves us with a problem. I may have reason to believe that someone is in the room next door but I may have no reason for believing that this person matches any particular description. I may have no reason for saying what the person is like. So might it not be that though we can know truths about God by reason, we cannot by reason know *the* truth (i.e. all the truth) about him? Here, so it seems to me, the third of our theses may be right. For, as I have already suggested, there are difficulties in the view that all Christian doctrines can be proved to be true or that one can know the truth of premises which entail them without stating them. In other words, insofar as we are unhappy with B, we have reason to support (3).

Yet at this point it may seem that we have now come full circle. For many would now say that if one cannot prove that a given belief is true, or if the belief cannot be based on evidence, then one has no right to hold it. And what can one make of the appeal to faith in the light of this criticism? Is the appeal vulnerable to the position advanced by people such as Clifford?

Here, I think, we need to note several things.

(a) Not all our beliefs are provable or based on further beliefs. As Geach puts it, 'Much of our rational belief about the world is an inference from premises; but if we are to believe anything at all, there must be uninferred beliefs to start with' (Geach 1976, p. 23). This is not to say that all uninferred beliefs are true. Nor is it to say that one is entitled to believe what one likes. It is just to say that there is no objection in principle to someone believing without doing so on the basis of yet further beliefs. In fact we are all bound to do this sooner or later, and, whether we like it or not, belief is often quite fundamental. This point is well brought out by Wittgenstein in his last notes *On Certainty* (Oxford, 1969). 'Language', Wittgenstein observes, 'did not emerge from reasoning' (para. 475). Nor does much that we take for granted, such as the fact that material things do not cease to exist without a physical explanation.

The child learns by believing the adult. Doubt comes *after* belief. . . . In general I take as true what is found in text-books, of geography for example. Why? I say: All these facts have been confirmed a hundred times over. But how do I know that? What is my evidence for it? I have a world picture. Is it true or false? Above all it is the substratum of all my enquiring and asserting . . . Does anyone test whether this table remains in existence when no one is paying attention to it? . . . Doesn't testing come to an end? . . . The difficulty is to realize the groundlessness of our believing. . . . At the foundation of well-founded belief lies belief that is not founded (Wittgenstein 1969, paras 160–166, 253).

(b) We are often entitled to believe things even though, for one reason or another, we cannot prove the truth of what we believe. A clear example of this is provided by our reliance on experts. If we fall ill and go to see a medical specialist we may find him assuring us that we have such and such an illness. And unless there are special circumstances, we will believe that this is so. Nor would it be thought odd or wrong for us to do this. Yet, not being doctors ourselves, we may have no means of proving that we are ill in the way we are told that we are.

(c) Belief is sometimes a matter of simply accepting what we are told, and it need not be subject to criticism just because of that. Consider, for example, the fact that we frequently believe people and that we regard ourselves as entitled to do this. Some, of course, would say that we should only believe people when we have independent evidence that they are speaking truly. But this objection misses the point. For we normally accept that we can be entitled to believe people, and accepting what someone says while already believing it or already believing that there is evidence for it is not *believing the person*. As Elizabeth Anscombe put it:

You can't call it believing Jones just if Jones says something or other and you do believe that very thing that he says. For you might believe it anyway. And even if it's someone's saying something that *causes* you to believe it, that doesn't have to be believing *him*. He might just be making you realize it, calling it to your attention – but you judge the matter for yourself. Nor is it even sufficient that his saying it is your *evidence* that it is true. For suppose that you are convinced that he will both lie to you, i.e. say the opposite of what he really believes, and be mistaken? That is, the opposite of what he thinks will be true; and he will say the opposite of what he thinks. So what he says will be true and you believe it because he says it. But you won't be believing him! (Anscombe 1981, Vol. III, p. 116).

An objector might reply that believing people plays a relatively small role in our lives and that there is little of significance to be gained by noting that we believe people. But a very great part of our knowledge rests on beliefs that we put in things we have been taught or told. As Anscombe elsewhere observes:

You have received letters; how did you ever learn what a letter was and how it came to you? You will take up a book and look in a certain place and see 'New York, Dodd Mead and Company, 1910.' So do you know from personal observation that that book was published by that company, and then, and in New York? Well, hardly. But you do know it *purports* to have been so. How? Well, you know that is where the publisher's name is always put, and the name of the place where his office belongs. How do you know that? You were taught it. What you were taught was your tool in acquiring the new knowledge. 'There was an American edition', you will say, 'I've seen it'. Think how much reliance on believing what you have been told lies behind being able to say that. It is irrelevant at this level to raise a question about possible forgery; without what we know by testimony, there is no such thing as what a forgery is *pretending* to be.

You may think you know that New York is in North America. What is New York, what is North America? You may say you have been in these places. But how much does that fact contribute to your knowledge? Nothing, in comparison with testimony. How did you know you were there? Even if you inhabit New York and you have simply learned its name as the name of the place you inhabit, there is the question: How extensive a region is this place you are calling 'New York'? And what has New York got to do with this bit of a map? Here is a complicated network of received information (Delaney 1979, p. 144).

(d) Thinkers who have reasoned broadly in the tradition of Clifford have sometimes held that those who appeal to faith can be ruled out of court since they believe propositions which are not evident to the senses, not self-evident, or not derived from such propositions by a process of reasoning. Yet this conclusion depends on the assumption that the beliefs of a rational person should consist only of such propositions, and this conclusion can be challenged. As Anthony Kenny observes:

Such a theory appears to be self-refuting, in that this criterion for rational belief seems to be itself neither self-evident or evident to the senses, nor is it easy to see by what process of reasoning it could be derived from such premises (Kenny 1983, p. 25).

And, as Kenny adds, one can instance 'propositions which are rationally believed without evidence, while being neither self-evident nor evident to the senses' (*ibid.*). An example is 'Human beings sleep'. What evidence for the falsity of this would be any less questionable than the proposition itself? (cf. Kenny 1983, pp. 21ff.).

In the light of these points I suggest that one may well be entitled to stick by beliefs held by 'faith' as opposed to 'by proof' or 'with reference to evidence'. In this sense it seems to me that a Christian may be perfectly entitled to account for his belief by appealing to faith. A likely objection to this conclusion would hold that, in that case, there is nothing to stop anyone believing anything, no matter how fantastic. But this objection would rest on a misunderstanding. The conclusion does not state that one is entitled to believe absolutely anything at all. It merely rejects the view that one is only entitled to believe on the basis of proof or evidence. You might put the point by saying that the conclusion rejects a criterion for legitimate belief, not that it says what one might legitimately believe. This difference is an important one, as we can see by considering an analogy. In Chapter 5 I referred to logical positivists and the verification principle. According to the positivists it was possible to state a criterion for distinguishing sense from nonsense. Now suppose we reject that criterion, and suppose we have no alternative one to offer. Are we thereby committed to accepting that no utterance whatsoever can be cited as a piece of nonsense? Of course not. We can, for example, deny straight off that ' 'Twas brillig; and the slithy toves did gyre and gimble in the wabe' makes sense (cf. Plantinga and Wolterstorff 1983, pp. 74f.).

So again I suggest that with reference to the truth of Christian theism the appeal to faith could be perfectly legitimate. But, having said that, I should add a few additional points.

For one thing, some uniquely Christian beliefs are arguably subject to empirical falsification. Consider, yet again, the belief that Christ was God. In view of what I have said, I do not see that in some absolute sense this is a belief the truth of which has to be proved, provable, or based on evidence. It could be held on faith. But it also surely makes sense to say that it could be disproved or that evidence could tell decisively against it. Suppose, for example, that historians of the future were able by rigorous investigation to give us as much reason to believe that Christ never existed as they can now give us to believe that Victoria was Queen of England in the nineteenth century. What then? It would surely be true that those who believe in the divinity of Christ in any orthodox sense (implying that Christ did exist) would not have a leg to stand on. In such circumstances one might justifiably deny that the truth of Christian theism can be held by faith alone.

In the second place, and related to the above point, if it can be proved that what one believes is somehow contradictory, then what one believes cannot be true no matter how legitimate it may be in principle to hold a belief on the basis of faith. So the Christian who appeals to faith ought, presumably, to add a caveat. He ought to allow that what he says would not be true if it can be proved to be contradictory. This is not to say that it can be proved to be contradictory. Nor is it to say that one is obliged to accept any purported proof that it is contradictory. With respect to what Christians believe it may be that 'in any given proof that an adversary sets up against it there is some fallacy to be found if one is sharp enough: *manifestum est probationes quae contra fidem inducuntur non esse demonstrationes sed solubilia argumenta*' (Geach 1972,

p. 293). But if what a Christian believes is contradictory, then it cannot be true. Some would here reply in the manner of Descartes. They would say that God can bring about what is logically impossible. But, as we saw in Chapter 7, this view is untenable.

In the third place, believing something by faith is often contrasted with believing something in the light of reason, yet this is not obviously a hard and fast distinction. Suppose I say that I believe nature behaves in a regular way. I do, in fact, believe this, and so does anybody who assumes that when he jumps out of bed the floor will support him unless conditions prevail the nature of which (if understood) will explain why the unexpected has now occurred. But do I believe this by faith or by reason? One might say 'by faith' since belief that nature behaves in a regular way is something I presuppose, not something which I believe on the basis of premises or evidence. But it is also, surely, a rational belief. If it is not, then what is? Why not, then, say that it is one which I hold by reason? My own view is that I could well be said to hold it by reason, even though I do not hold it on the basis of premises or evidence. If, therefore, one can believe by faith since one believes without premises or evidence, it would also seem that in believing by faith one can also believe by reason.

And to all of this we may add one final point. This is that though one might hold that one believes such and such by faith, one is not committed to holding that the truth of one's belief is not something which can be supported by reason or argument. Consider, for example, the belief that Germany exists. As it happens, I do believe this. It would also seem odd to say that my belief here is based on premises or evidence. For the reasons I could cite in defence of the existence of Germany seem no better founded than that very belief. Yet this does not mean that I cannot cite reasons or arguments for believing in Germany if someone should suddenly doubt that there is such a place. I could, for example, appeal to books, newspapers, films, atlases, friends who have been to Germany, and so on. In this sense my belief in Germany may well be open to rational support, and, in this sense, it seems *a priori* open to someone who believes by faith in the truth of Christian theism to say that this too is open to rational support. Which brings us to E.

E.   Christian theism, faith, and reason

In the light of the preceding discussions we can, perhaps, already suggest at the outset that E is at least partly defensible. For it overlaps with D. It denies that the truth of Christian theism is open to proof, which is plausible. And it supposes that one may legitimately believe on the basis of faith, which is also acceptable. But E, of course, does more than this. It also holds that what Christians uniquely believe is not opposed to reason. So the main question would seem to be whether or not this is true. And since, as I noted above, defenders of E have explained 'not opposed to reason' in at least two ways, this question in turn can be divided into two. (1) Are there rational arguments or grounds which render what Christians uniquely believe probable? (2) Is what they believe just not unreasonable? Since there are a number of things which Christians can be said uniquely to believe, let us consider these questions with reference to just one major Christian belief – the one I have already considered: the belief that Christ was God.

Reason and the divinity of Christ

(1) Is the divinity of Christ probable?

It is as well to note immediately that in saying that something is probable people do not always mean the same thing. According, for example, to J. L. Mackie, 'there are at least five clearly distinguishable probability concepts, with subdivisions within several of them, as well as links between them' (Mackie 1973, p. 154). This point, however, need not detain us, for it is fairly clear what people have in mind in saying that the divinity of Christ is probable. They mean that there are very strong reasons indeed for supposing that Christ was divine. They do not want to say that the divinity of Christ is provable in a sense which should command the assent of anyone. But they do want to say that the rational balance can be clearly seen to tilt in the direction of Christ's divinity. And those who have urged that this is so have favoured one or both of two lines of argument.

(a) Christ and history

The general idea behind the first is that historical facts strongly support the conclusion that Christ was God. But what facts? According to some, there are the teachings of Jesus. These, so it has been suggested, contain moral truths which can only have been delivered by one who was God. Others have held that they amount to a claim that Christ was divine and that they strongly suggest the truth of that claim. Another common suggestion is that the answer lies in the deeds of Jesus or in things that happened to him. In this connection reference is often made to the miracles of Christ and to the Resurrection. Yet another line of argument invites us to consider the way in which the doctrine of Christ's divinity has had effects in the world. In the words of St Athanasius (c.296–373):

For if, now that the cross has been set up, all idolatry has been overthrown, and by this sign all demonic activity is put to flight, and only Christ is worshipped, and through him the Father is known, and opponents are put to shame while he every day invisibly converts their souls – how then, one might reasonably ask them, is this still to be considered in human terms, and should one not rather confess that he who ascended the cross is the Word of God and the Saviour of the universe? (*Contra Gentes* I, 25ff.).

(b)   Christ and God

The second line of argument is best understood by considering an analogy. Suppose I receive a letter which purports to be from John. I am then asked why I should believe that it is from John. I might reply that its contents are to be expected given what I already know about John. In the same way, so it has been suggested, belief in the truth of Christ's divinity is confirmed or shown to be highly plausible given what we can already know about God.

But in what way? Here again we meet different answers. Some have held that since we can know that God is good we have strong confirmation that Christ was divine since a good God would be likely to express his goodness by means of incarnation. Another suggestion offered is that since God is essentially mysterious he could only inform us of certain truths about himself by himself becoming human and by telling them to us. Or again, to take another argument, it has been said that since God is perfect it follows that he is no deceiver and it is therefore unlikely that he has allowed those who have believed in the divinity of Christ to be in error.

Comments

Should we, then, accept these lines of thinking?

(a) We can dismiss from the outset the view that the moral teaching of Christ could only have been delivered by God. This view generally supposes that the teaching in question is a matter of knowledge, but anyone who asserts that this is so already implies that he knows what Christ knew and he cannot claim that this can only have been delivered by God unless he claims that he is God himself. We must therefore consider other elements of (a).

One of the chief problems raised by them brings us back to the topic of the historical reliability of the New Testament. There is general consensus among scholars now that the New Testament documents cannot be read as reliable historical texts in the modern sense. So can we appeal to events and sayings which they report as making probable the truth of belief in Christ's divinity? That will depend on the events and sayings reported, but some would conclude that we cannot take them as historical evidence for anything beyond the theology of the reporters.

Yet this is an extreme view and it is only fair to observe that a very different account has been given even by those who are thoroughly conversant with modern developments in biblical research. A notable recent example can be found in the work of C. F. D. Moule, who presents his case in a much acclaimed book called *The Origin of Christology* (Cambridge, 1977). According to Moule we are entitled to suppose that Jesus's self-understanding, evidenced in his claim to be 'Son of God' and 'Son of Man', allows us to call him divine. Moule also argues that belief in Christ's divinity was a notable guiding force in the development of the New Testament, which simply draws out what was implicit in Christ's own claims. One may, says Moule, advocate the tendency 'to explain all the various estimates of Jesus reflected in the New Testament as, in essence, only attempts to describe what was already there from the beginning. They are not successive additions of something new, but only the drawing out and articulating of what is there' (pp. 2f.). 'The evidence', Moule adds, 'suggests that Jesus was, *from the beginning*, such a one as appropriately to be described in the ways in which, sooner or later, he did come to be described in the New Testament period – for instance, as "Lord" and even, in some sense, as "God" ' (p. 4).

But is that right? An adequate answer will partly depend on an assessment of issues in the field of New Testament scholarship, and I am not qualified to offer that. But we surely need to be very cautious before agreeing that the right answer is 'Yes', if that answer, in turn, is taken to imply that the divinity of Christ is probable. This is so for at least three reasons.

(i) Historical conclusions such as those of Moule are not universally accepted even by scholars who share Moule's belief in our ability to indicate in some detail the actual contents of Jesus's teaching. If one turns, for example, to an author like E. P. Sanders, one will find rather a different picture from that offered by Moule (cf. Sanders 1985). As Maurice Wiles observes, scholarly work on the historical Jesus 'is inevitably tentative in character, and the "historical Jesus" of one scholar may be very different from the "historical Jesus" of another' (Wiles 1982, p. 55).

(ii) Even if it could be established that Jesus explicitly taught that he was divine, or even if it could be established that his teaching implied this conclusion, one can doubt that there would then be a strong reason for supposing that Christ was divine. For what would count as a strong reason for supposing that anyone is divine? Could it, for example, be that the person claims to be divine? But why should the claim to divinity be seen as strong evidence of divinity? Unless we have evidence to the contrary, we do generally suppose that things are as people tell us (cf. Swinburne 1979, pp. 271ff.). So one might argue that if someone claims divinity then he is divine unless we have evidence to the contrary. But we do have evidence that people are not divine, for (1) as I have argued, we can reasonably believe that God is the non-material, eternal, omniscient, omnipotent and omnipresent Creator of the universe, and (2) we have evidence to believe that people are not this. For people are part of the universe and they are, for example, temporal, fallible and frequently powerless.

(iii) To say that Christ is divine is to say that he is God. But, as we saw in Chapter 5, we have reason for denying that we can understand what we are talking about when we talk of God. This is not to say that we cannot make true statements about God. Nor is it to say that we cannot explain why we should make them. But it is to say that we may reasonably doubt the assertion that someone understands what it is to be God. In that case, however, it follows that we may doubt whether anyone understands what it is for a man to be God. And from this we may argue that one can always doubt that anyone has strong reason (apart from simply believing it) which points in favour of the conclusion that someone was God. If we cannot understand what it is to be God, how are we supposed to have strong reason to believe that someone actually was God?

This last point also suggests an answer to the conclusion that the divinity of Christ is probable apart from anything we might consider to be historical information concerning Christ. And even if one denies this, there are other difficulties. Even if the miracles associated with Christ occurred, and even if we could know that Christ rose from the dead, why should we go on to claim that belief in his divinity is therefore probable? How are we to determine what is and is not probable with respect to divinity? Why should we suppose that events in history make it more likely than not that someone is divine? Can they not all have been brought about by God considered simply as Creator? And as for the history of those who have believed in Christ, why should that be taken as tilting the balance in favour of the truth of the divinity of Christ? Why not try to account for it in terms of human psychology or human belief? Why not account for it in terms of the mysterious designs of God the Creator? Unless we begin with the presumption that Christ is indeed divine, I know of no answers to these questions which ought to leave us supposing that the divinity of Christ is probable. Some would reply that there are stacks of historical data of which sense can be made if we grant that Christ was God. But that is not now the issue. The question is whether the data by themselves make it probable that Christ was God.

(b) Some of the arguments offered in support of (b) again bring us to matters already discussed. Thus, for example, the view that Christ taught what can only be revealed by God depends on the belief that we can have a good idea of what Christ taught. The cogency of the view will therefore depend on what we have reason to believe about Christ historically speaking. Even if we can satisfactorily deal with this issue, however, there is a general problem with (b). The difficulty concerns being able to say on the basis of reason what God is or is not likely to bring about in history (a difficulty hinted at above). Defenders of (b) generally seem to be arguing like this:

(i) Reason tells us that God is/is not likely to bring about such and such in history (e.g. the existence of a man who is God; someone who teaches what, if true, could only be revealed; people who believe things about God and who are right in their beliefs).

(ii) Therefore, the coming about of such and such in history is/is not probable or likely.

But on the basis of what reason are we to say what God is or is not likely to bring about? Some would say that the answer lies in God's character. Others have appealed to what they know of God by virtue of revelation, e.g. that God has promised that something or other will or will not happen. But neither of these replies seems of very much value as far as (b) goes. (b) suggests that we might conclude that something is probably true on the basis of reason, not revelation. And our assessments of what is probable or likely given a character are normally made with reference to people, while one may, as I have argued, challenge any easy comparison between God and people.

(2) Is belief in the divinity of Christ 'not unreasonable'?

So there are difficulties with the assertion that the divinity of Christ is probable. But what about the weaker claim? Might one not hold that it is just not unreasonable to believe in the divinity of Christ? Here, I think, one can be a bit more positive.

At first thought this might not seem so. For how are we to decide whether any belief is 'not unreasonable'? The difficulty lies in the fact that 'reasonable' is clearly a word which means different things to different people as well as different things to the same people. So we might say that 'reasonable' is not readily definable and that the same therefore goes for 'unreasonable'. 'What men consider reasonable or unreasonable alters. At certain periods men find reasonable what at other periods they found unreasonable. And vice versa' (Wittgenstein 1969, para. 336).

But even if we cannot define a word we might still use it intelligibly. And we might well use it to make assertions which we are perfectly entitled to make (cf. Geach 1976, p. 39). So let us consider when it would make sense to agree that someone's belief is not unreasonable.

To begin with we can mention a negative condition. We can reject what someone says if the person utters a contradiction and if he thereby fails to say anything. So a belief cannot be 'not unreasonable' if one has to contradict oneself in order to state it.

But when might a belief be not unreasonable? Here we can make four points.

(i) If a belief coheres with what we know to be true, or if it coheres with what we have reason to think is true, then we might allow that it is 'not unreasonable' if at the same time we do not know that the belief is false. If the bus does not arrive, if we know that many workers in the area are supporting a general strike, and if we do not know that the bus men are not on strike, we might concede that it is not unreasonable to suppose that the bus men are on strike.

(ii) If we know or strongly believe that something is the case, we might well concede that a purported explanation of the thing being the case is not unreasonable if we do not also know that the purported explanation is false and if we can give no better explanation or if we can cast doubt on another explanation. It might not be unreasonable for us to believe that the bus men are on strike if the bus does not arrive, if we do not know that the bus men are not on strike, if we can give no better explanation of the bus's non-arrival, or if we can cast doubt on other explanations of this.

(iii) We might accept that someone's belief that-P might not be unreasonable if we do not know that not-P and if the truth of P could be thought to account for something or other. If the teacher finds a coat in the classroom, he might suppose straight off that a pupil has forgotten it. We might accept that it is not unreasonable for him to do so if we do not know that the coat has not been forgotten by a pupil.

(iv) We might accept that someone's belief that-P might not be unreasonable if we do not know that not-P and if it is not impossible that-P. Thus, if it is not impossible for people to fly to Venus in space ships, we might concede that it is not unreasonable for scientists to believe that people will one day fly there.

Now in the light of these points might it make sense to assent to belief in the divinity of Christ? Not if we can know that this belief is contradictory or false. But on the assumption that it is neither I think that the answer is 'Yes' and that those who agree with me can defend themselves by making all or some of the following observations, which are echoes of points made by defenders of E.

(i) The fact that things are as people believe that they are can often be cited as accounting for the fact that people believe as they do. The Christian religion has developed over time to become a major determining influence on the lives of countless people. Given that Christianity is bound up with belief in the divinity of Christ, this would cohere with belief in the divinity of Christ and the truth of this belief could, in turn, help to account for the spread of Christianity. One might, of course, reply that one can account for this spread in completely non-religious terms. But that is not to say that one has to do this or that only such an account is possible. Nor is this true. For we have reason to believe that whatever comes to pass in creation does so by virtue of God.

(ii) Whatever our views about the historical Jesus, it seems very evident that Jesus did have an enormous impact on those who knew him. The result was that within a relatively short time people were ascribing to him a crucial role in God's plan for humanity. Some were also ascribing to him language traditionally used to refer to God. Here one naturally thinks of John's gospel; but there are other texts to which one can refer.

The New Testament exhibits numerous instances of the transfer to Christ of passages in the Scriptures originally relating to God – and that, at an early stage in New Testament thinking. Phil.2: 10f. is one of the most remarkable. At latest, it represents Paul himself, or, at earliest, a pre-Pauline formula; and it boldly transfers to Jesus a great monotheistic passage from Isa.45: 23, in which God is represented as declaring that he must have no rivals: it is now to *Kurios Iesous Christos* that every knee shall bow, and it is he whom every tongue shall confess (Moule 1977, pp. 41f.).

These facts would be explicable if it were indeed true that Christ was God. They also cohere with the belief that he was God.

(iii) If 'Christ was God' is possibly true, and if it can be not unreasonable to believe that-P if P is possible and if we do not know that not-P then it can be not unreasonable to believe that Christ was God if we do not know that he was not God. But it is far from clear that we can know that Christ was not God, as I shall argue in Chapter 10. It might therefore be not unreasonable to believe that he was God.

(iv) As I argued in Chapter 2, certain events, if they occurred, could be described as miraculous. If the New Testament is taken at its face value, its authors do seem to be saying that such events have occurred. They seem, for example, to be saying this with reference to the Resurrection. Now we may take leave to doubt that we can have conclusive historical grounds for affirming the Resurrection of Christ. But arguments can also be given for supposing that New Testament accounts of the Resurrection are not simply fabrications (cf. Burns and Cumming 1981, pp. 152–166 and O'Collins 1973). If they are not so (which may be supposed even if it cannot be conclusively established), this would cohere with the belief that Christ was God. And the truth of that belief could be held to account for the fact that they are not so. For if Christ was God, one might expect him to be rescued from the grip of bodily death since death is arguably a tragedy for its human victims and one can reasonably deny that God need be subject to tragedy since, as we understand it, the victim of tragedy is subject to the action of other things while God, so I have argued, cannot be so subject if he is the Creator. Some such idea as this presumably lies behind the biblical proof-text cited in Acts 2:27: 'For thou wilt not abandon my soul to Hades, nor let thy Holy One see corruption'. The point has been recently re-stated by H. P. Owen. In his words: 'It is reasonable to suppose that one effect of Christ's divine nature on his human nature would have been to prevent his body from disintegrating and to transform it into a new body of the kind that the evangelists describe. Moreover a bodily resurrection would uniquely signify, in a manner especially compelling for Jewish Christians, the fact that Jesus embodied within "this age" the eternal life of "the age to come" ' (Owen 1984, p. 47).

(v) Given the occurrence of sanctity in Christians one might hold that belief in the divinity of Christ is not unreasonable. According to Newman: 'As "the heavens declare the glory of God" as Creator, so are the saints the proper and true evidence of the God of Christianity' (Blehl 1963, p. 334). This line of thinking has been recently revived by Patrick Sherry. He notes that Christian saints have seemed to some people morally abhorrent or in other ways not especially admirable. But suppose, as many do with respect to the saints (the view is hardly eccentric) that we have a set of virtues which we can agree to be wholly admirable. 'Let us assume, too, that we find a set of people who embody these virtues to a high degree, who have not always done so, and who have been helped to do so through the practice of a religion' (Sherry 1984, p. 39). Might we draw any conclusions from this? We can ask what caused the change, and, in answering our question we might appeal to causes within the world which we can understand. But we might also ask whether there is an 'external cause'. One might reject this move as Kant rejected explanations in terms of divine grace. Kant 'admits that certain inexplicable movements leading to a great moral improvement do occur in people, but he insists that we cannot distinguish between the effects of nature and grace, because we cannot recognise a supra-sensible object within our experience; hence he labels "grace" a "transcendent" idea' (Sherry, p. 45; cf. Kant, *Religion within the Limits of Reason Alone*, Bk. IV, Pt. ii, pp. 162, 179f.). Yet 'a man may feel the "givenness" of grace without necessarily wishing to claim acquaintance with the giver', and one needs to allow for 'the feeling which some people have that they are being changed by a power outside them, against their own natures and even against their wills' (Sherry, p. 45). One might therefore not unreasonably conclude that the occurrence of sanctity is some evidence for the truth of theism.

For if the occurrence requires explanation, the activity of God is one possible explanation; moreover, looking at it another way, the occurrence is something to be expected, given belief in the Judeo-Christian God, and therefore it confirms this belief (assuming that we have other grounds for it). This relationship is a weaker one than logical entailment, for it allows that there could be other explanations of the occurrence to be explained (Sherry, p. 47).

Sherry speaks here only with reference to belief in 'the Judeo-Christian God'. But the argument could be re-cast with reference to a belief in Christianity. And in the light of this it could be employed to suggest that there is some evidence for the truth of belief in Christ's divinity. An objector might ask, as I did earlier, what right one has to say what God will or will not bring about. But the present suggestion is not that independent rational considerations make it probable that God will or will not do such and such. The point is that the occurrence of sanctity can be readily accommodated into a specifically Christian view of things which, on this account, can be rationally linked with the judgement that sanctity has occurred.

So one can, I think, argue (as, for example, Aquinas does) that though one may deny that the divinity of Christ is probable, one could accept that to believe in it is not unreasonable. This is not to say that reason compels one to believe in it (I have already said why I think it is not provable). Nor is it to say that in some purely neutral sense it is implied or strongly suggested by the evidence (I have already said why one may doubt that it is probable). It is just to say that belief in it need not be regarded as unreasonable. And in this sense we may suggest that E is a position of some merit. One might indeed hold that Christian theism is a matter both of faith and of reason.

F.   The reinterpretation of Christian theism

Turning, then, to our final theory: can we conclude that Christian theism is something one can reasonably accept on condition that it is reinterpreted? Here, I think, one can usefully make the following points.

(1) If traditional understandings of key Christian doctrines can be shown to be certainly contradictory, then some reinterpretation of these doctrines will be essential if any case for the reasonableness of Christianity is to be made at all. Consider yet again the doctrine of the Incarnation. Is it even possibly true in the terms taught by Nicaea and Chalcedon? Not, for example, according to John Hick, whom one can cite as a modern exponent of F. According to him: 'To say, without explanation, that the historical Jesus was also God is as devoid of meaning as to say that this circle drawn with a pencil on paper is also a square' (Hick [ed.] 1977, p. 178). If we can know that this is true, then we must either reinterpret the doctrine of the Incarnation along non-traditional lines or we must ditch it altogether.

(2) On the other hand, there are grounds for denying that at least some key Christian doctrines are contradictory if understood in a traditional sense. I shall return to this point in the next chapter. If the point is correct, however, consistency need not obviously oblige us to abandon traditional expressions of Christian teaching.

(3) Those who argue that Christian theism can be reasonably accepted on condition that it is reinterpreted generally mean that one is not entitled to accept it if it is not reinterpreted. This, in turn, frequently means that one is not entitled to believe that Christian theism is true unless its truth is provable or based on evidence. Yet, as I have argued, we do not have to accept that one is only entitled to believe what is provable or based on evidence. And I take this to mean that one may indeed be entitled to accept that Christian theism is true even though its truth is not provable or based on evidence. In this sense, therefore, one is not obliged to believe that Christian theism can be reasonably accepted on condition that it is reinterpreted.

(4) Those who have urged a reinterpretation of key Christian doctrines frequently depend on historical judgements which can be questioned. Some, for example, have held that we can believe in the divinity of Christ since the historical Jesus taught or expressed in his deeds truths about God which we have independent reason to accept. According, for example, to Hick:

> (Jesus) was so powerfully God conscious that his life vibrated, as it were, to the divine life; and as a result his hands could heal the sick, and the 'poor in spirit' were kindled to new life in his presence. We would have felt the absolute claim of God confronting us, summoning us to give ourselves wholly to him and to be born again as his children and as agents of his purposes on earth . . . In Jesus' presence, we should have felt that we are in the presence of God – not in the sense that the man Jesus literally *is* God, but in the sense that he was so totally conscious of God that we could catch something of that consciousness by spiritual contagion (Hick [ed.] 1977, p. 172).

But can we be historically justified in believing all this? How does Hick know how we should respond to Christ if we met him as he was in the time of his earthly life? And can Hick be confident of what Christ was like then? The problem of reading the New Testament as history raises problems here. And there are questions of a different kind posed by other assertions which have been made about Christ as part of an attempt to reinterpret key Christian doctrines. Some, for example, have said that though Christ was not divine (not literally divine) he was unique since the historical evidence shows that he pointed to permanent truths about God in a way that no one else has done. But what historical evidence could establish this? Can we really be confident that historical evidence alone points clearly to the view that Jesus taught truths about God that no one had recognized before? Some have held that Christ was unique because the historical evidence shows that he was morally perfect or sinless. But, again, what historical evidence could establish this? As Denis Nineham writes:

> To prove an historical negative, such as the sinlessness of Jesus, is notoriously difficult to the point of impossibility. How, for example, could even the most constant companion of Jesus have been sure that he remained unbrokenly true to his own principles and never, for example, 'looked on a woman to lust after her' in the sense of Matthew 5.28? Such a

question is not for a moment asked with any intention of casting doubt on the sexual purity of Jesus; it is meant simply as an example designed to show that the sort of claims for Jesus we are discussing could not be justified to the hilt by *any* historical records, however full or intimate or contemporary they might be, and even if their primary concern was with the quality and development of Jesus' inner life and character (Hick [ed.] 1977, p. 188).

(4) Those who offer reinterpretations of Christian teaching such as those envisaged by defenders of F typically hold that these are sufficiently continuous with traditional understandings of Christianity as to justify those who accept them in calling them Christian teaching. Christians used generally to believe that the doctrine of creation as taught in the book of Genesis committed them to believing in the historical existence of a first couple called Adam and Eve. This is no longer widely supposed, though the fact is not commonly taken to entail that those who subscribe to the currently fashionable view cannot believe in the doctrine of creation or in the truth of the book of Genesis. And, so it has been said, something similar applies with reference to the reinterpretation of Christian theism intended by supporters of F. But this can be contested. Hick, for example, clearly thinks it false that Christ was literally God. Yet this means that he holds that what Nicaea and Chalcedon say is false, for Nicaea and Chalcedon say that Christ was literally God ('God from God . . . true God from true God' etc.) Can one, however, hold that what Nicaea and Chalcedon say is false and still call one's teaching 'Christian'? The issue, perhaps, cannot be decided in terms that will appeal to everyone. Yet one might justly feel (as I do, for example) that to assert the falsity of what Nicaea and Chalcedon say is to assert the falsity of Christian teaching. For the teachings of such councils have shaped our understanding of Christianity, as writers like Hick are well aware. One might reply that though this is so, it does not really matter. One might say, with Don Cupitt, that 'The classical doctrine of the incarnation belongs, not to the essence of Christianity, but only to a certain period of church history now ended' (Hick [ed.] 1977, p. 134). But why should we feel obliged to say this? Some would say that Cupitt is right since the classical doctrine of the Incarnation is an aberration in the history of Christian thinking. But some people can be very stupid. The doctrine asserts that Christ was God. Are we seriously to believe that this assertion is an aberration in the history of Christian thinking? It has surely fashioned such thinking. Some would reply that the assertion is an aberration when looked at from the perspective of the New Testament. But that, too, is surely open to question. Its contradictory, at any rate, has certainly been affirmed by many biblical scholars. And some have put things more strongly than this. According, for example, to Gerald O'Collins: 'Modern attempts to deny that *first-century Christians* acknowledged the risen Jesus' divine status will go the way earlier such attempts have already gone. The New Testament evidence all too clearly tells against the reductionist case'

(O'Collins 1983, p. 171). A standard reply to comments like this is that one can acknowledge the divinity of Christ and deny that Jesus was divine as Nicaea and Chalcedon supposed him to be (and deny, that is, that 'Christ is God' is true). But it is hard to see how one can make 'Jesus was divine' not mean 'It is false that Jesus was not God', and it is the teaching of Nicaea and Chalcedon that it is false that Jesus was not God.

What does all this mean, then? It does not, I think, mean that one cannot offer a reasonable reinterpretation of Christian theism. Perhaps there are many possible statements of belief which can be called both 'Christian' and 'reasonable' even though they differ from what Christians have traditionally accepted. This is presumably why theologians are constantly seeking to find new ways of expressing the faith of the Christian Church. But one can deny that Christians are obliged to accept such statements as ones which they are more entitled to make than traditional ones. One may also deny that all such statements as have been offered are either compelling on historical grounds or legitimately described as Christian. And this, I think, means that F is an option which might be rationally tenable but which no one is obliged to accept and which a Christian can reject on the grounds that it can lead to what is not Christian.

CONCLUSION

I began this chapter by asking whether Christian theism is reasonable or unreasonable, whether we are entitled to accept it, and whether we are obliged to reject it. Since raising these questions I have not discussed all that might be held to be part of Christian theism, but if my arguments are sound one may, I think, hold that though one may deny that the truth of Christian theism is provable or probable, one may indeed say that what Christians uniquely believe (i.e. the truth of Christian theism) can be held as a matter of faith, and one may subsequently indicate how it might be argued that it is not unreasonable. So, though I have tried to write this chapter in a way that will help the reader to think critically about its subject matter, and therefore to disagree with me, I suggest that one can profitably pursue the conclusions enshrined in what I have referred to as D and E.

But these, of course, would be untenable if it could be shown that the Christian is committed to a position which is fundamentally contradictory. For that would involve him in believing what cannot be true. In the next chapter, therefore, I shall consider whether or not we are obliged to suppose that this is indeed his fate.

QUESTIONS FOR DISCUSSION

1 Is there a difference between theism and Christian theism? If so, at what point can one safely conclude that someone is a Christian theist and not just a theist?

2 Under what conditions might I be said to have a proof that something is the case? If these conditions are met, does it follow that you have a proof as well?

3 How much can we know about the historical Jesus? Are there any general criteria which we can use to test theories about the historical Jesus?

4 How much of what the New Testament says about Christ can one doubt and still be said to believe in Christ?

5 Can someone be called a Christian if he has no belief in the possibility of discovering truths about Christ on the basis of experience?

6 'I do not know why I believe in Christianity; but I do and that is enough.' Is this comment irrational?

7 Must Christianity make the best sense of the available evidence?

8 What is the difference between a reasonable belief and an unreasonable one? Or is there no answer to this question?

9 Would it be unreasonable to doubt the truth of Christianity?

10 Can there be a purely rational Christian theology?

FURTHER READING

Many of the questions referred to in the preceding chapter are related in one way or another to the topic of revelation. A very helpful survey of theories about revelation is Avery Dulles, *Revelation Theology: A History* (London, 1970). Dulles has also provided further surveys and a discussion of revelation in *Models of Revelation* (Dublin, 1983). Both books provide many useful references to assist in further reading. Other general works on revelation worth noting are: John Baillie, *The Idea of Revelation in Recent Thought* (Oxford, 1956); Paul Helm, *The Divine Revelation* (London, 1982); R. Latourelle, *The Theology of Revelation* (New York, 1966); Aylward Shorter, *Revelation and its Interpretation* (London, 1983). For conciliar statements on revelation see Vatican I, *Dei Filius: Dogmatic Constitution on the Catholic Faith*, and Vatican II, *Dei Verbum: Dogmatic Constitution on Divine Revelation*. A major reference work for *Dei Filius* is Jean-Michel-Alfred Vacant, *La Constitution Dei Filius* (2 vols, Paris/Lyon, 1895). For an informative and well-written introduction to Vatican II, the text to go for is Christopher Butler, *The Theology of Vatican II* (2nd ed., London, 1981).

A well-known philosophical account of the nature of proof is G. E. Moore, 'Proof of an External World' in *Philosophical Papers* (London, 1959). A helpful account and discussion of Moore can be found in Terence Penelhum, *Problems of Religious Knowledge* (London, 1971), ch. 2.

With respect to Christianity and experience, most of the further reading appended to the discussion in Chapter 3 above is relevant. A short, recent attempt to state the importance of experience for Christian theology is Dermot Lane, *The Experience of God* (Dublin, 1981). For a good survey of theological positions written from the perspective of support for an experiential approach to Christianity, see Illtyd Trethowan, *The Absolute and the Atonement* (London, 1971).

For general discussions of the topic of faith, the reader can consult some of the currently available single-volume studies on the content and nature of Christian theology. Examples of these which can be recommended include Gerald O'Collins, *Fundamental Theology*

(London, 1981) and Karl Rahner, *Foundations of Christian Faith* (London, 1978). For one classical philosopher's discussion of reason and Christianity, see John Locke, *An Essay Concerning Human Understanding*, Bk. IV, chs 17–19, and *The Reasonableness of Christianity* (ed. I. T. Ramsey, London, 1958). Recent philosophical treatments of faith include the following (all of which contain much to recommend them though their authors are in disagreement): G. E. M. Anscombe, 'Faith' in *Collected Philosophical Papers*, vol. III (Oxford, 1981); Peter Geach, *The Virtues* (Cambridge, 1977), ch. 2; John Hick, *Faith and Knowledge* (2nd ed., Cornell, 1966); Anthony Kenny, *Faith and Reason* (New York, 1983); Richard Swinburne, *Faith and Reason* (Oxford, 1981). For a short introduction to Christian thinking on faith, see John Coventry, *The Theology of Faith* (Cork, 1968). A major survey of theologies of faith is Roger Aubert, *Le Problème de l'Acte de Foi* (Louvain, 1945). For some very neat philosophical discussion of the relationship between belief and evidence see Alvin Plantinga and Nicholas Wolterstroff (eds), *Faith and Rationality* (London/Notre Dame, 1983). For an exposition of the view that the truth of Christianity is provable, see Michael Sheehan, *Apologetics and Catholic Doctrine* (Dublin, 1962). For a clear rejection of the view that Christianity needs any support from without, a writer of major importance is Karl Barth. A simple introduction to his thinking is John Bowden, *Karl Barth* (London, 1971). A good survey of Barth's writing, together with good surveys of several writers who have concerned themselves with issues raised in the preceding chapter, is Alasdair I. C. Heron, *A Century of Protestant Theology* (Guildford/London, 1980). For more advanced discussion see S. W. Sykes (ed.), *Karl Barth – Studies of his Theological Method* (Oxford, 1979). Excellent discussions of Anselm on the Incarnation can be found in G. R. Evans, *Anselm and Talking About God* (Oxford, 1978), J. McIntyre, *St Anselm and his Critics: a Reinterpretation of the Cur Deus Homo* (Edinburgh, 1954), and R. W. Southern, *St Anselm and his Biographer* (Cambridge, 1963). A classical and influential account of faith can be found in the work of Aquinas. See, for example, *Summa Theologiae* IIa IIae, 1–7 and *Summa Contra Gentiles* I, 1–9. A recent philosophical discussion of Aquinas on faith is Terence Penelhum, 'The Analysis of Faith in St Thomas Aquinas', *Religious Studies* 13 (1977).

For an introduction to problems involved in attempting to discover the historical nature of the Gospels, readers might start with a general work on biblical interpretation. An example is Paul Burns and John Cumming (eds), *The Bible Now* (Dublin, 1981). Scholarly discussions of the historical Jesus are legion. The following are examples of studies by leading writers: G. Bornkamm, *Jesus of Nazareth* (London, 1960); C. H. Dodd, *The Founder of Christianity* (London, 1971); I. Howard Marshall, *I Believe in the Historical Jesus* (London, 1977); Ernst Käsemann, *Essays on New Testament Themes* (London, 1964); C. F. D. Moule, *The Origin of Christology* (Cambridge, 1977); Norman Perrin, *Rediscovering the Teaching of Jesus* (London, 1959); E. P. Sanders, *Jesus and Judaism* (London, 1985); Eduard Schweitzer, *Jesus* (London, 1971). For two very contrasting philosophical discussions of our ability to ground major Christian beliefs on the witness of the New Testament, see David Brown, *The Divine Trinity* (London, 1985), chs 3 and 4, and Stewart R. Sutherland, *God, Jesus and Belief* (Oxford, 1984), chs 8–11.

For a concise set of suggestions favouring the view that Christianity is not unreasonable, see Hugo Meynell, 'On Believing in the Incarnation', *The Clergy Review* LXIV (1979). For a more detailed but similar approach, see Huw Parri Owen, *Christian Theism* (Edinburgh, 1984), chs 2 and 3. Owen states his position in further detail in *The Christian Knowledge of God* (London, 1969). He also has a helpful account and discussion of some modern views about Christ in 'The Person of Christ in Recent Theology', *Religious Studies* 13 (1977).

For a lucid statement of reasons favouring a reinterpretation of Christian doctrines, and for an indication of possible results, the reader can profit from recent work by Maurice Wiles. In particular, see the following: *The Remaking of Christian Doctrine* (London, 1974); *Working Papers in Doctrine* (London, 1976); *Faith and the Mystery of God* (London, 1982).

10
Sense, Nonsense and Christianity

I argued in the last chapter that belief in Christianity can be a matter of faith and reason. But since what is contradictory cannot be true, an objector might reject this suggestion on the ground that the Christian is committed to what is contradictory. And that is what many believe. Some would express themselves by saying that Christianity does not make sense, or that Christianity is nonsense.

But is the Christian committed to contradiction? One's answer, of course, will depend on what one presumes to be the content of Christian belief. Yet it would hardly be controversial to speak of Christians as those who uniquely subscribe to the doctrines of the Incarnation and the Trinity, and these, in fact, are the Christian doctrines which have most commonly provoked the charge of contradiction. Let us therefore concentrate on them. Are they really contradictory?

THE DOCTRINES IN QUESTION

A.   The Incarnation

It is not to be supposed that those who profess belief in the doctrine of the Incarnation are all in agreement about what they are professing. Traditionally speaking, however, the content of the doctrine can be identified with the teaching concerning Christ of the councils of Nicaea and Chalcedon. According to Nicaea, Christ is

the only begotten generated from the Father, that is from the being (ousia) of the Father, God from God, Light from Light, true God from true God, begotten not made, one in being (homoousios) with the Father, through whom all things were made, those in heaven and those on earth (Neuner and Dupuis 1983, p. 6).

Chalcedon puts things at greater length. Its position is stated as follows.

Following therefore the Holy Fathers, we unanimously teach to confess one and the same Son, our Lord Jesus Christ, the same perfect in divinity and perfect in humanity, the same truly God and truly man composed of rational soul and body, the same one in being (homoousios) with the Father as to the divinity and one in being with us as to the humanity, like unto us in all things but sin. The same was begotten from the Father before the ages as to the divinity and in the latter days for us and our salvation was born as to His humanity from Mary the Virgin Mother of God. We confess that one and the same Lord Jesus Christ, the only-begotten Son, must be acknowledged in two natures, without confusion or change, without division or separation. The distinction between the natures was never abolished by their union but rather the character proper to each of the two natures was preserved as they came together in one person (prosopon) and one hypostasis. He is not split or divided into two persons, but He is one and the same only-begotten, God the Word, the Lord Jesus Christ, as formerly the prophets and later Jesus Christ Himself have taught us about Him and as has been handed down to us by the Symbol of the Fathers (Neuner and Dupuis, pp. 154f.).

But what does all this mean? To some extent the answer should be clear from the quotations. But it might help to note the following points.

(1) One of the main concerns of Nicaea was to deny that Christ is a creature. In this respect the council was reacting to the followers of Arius (c.250–c.336), a priest of Alexandria who taught that Christ was a finite being who depended for his existence on God just like everything else. As the famous Arian slogan had it: 'There was when he (Christ, the Word) was not' (cf. Kelly 1972, pp. 231ff.). So in affirming its profession of faith the council of Nicaea was certainly teaching that Christ enjoys equal status with God and that, like God, he is uncreated.

(2) At the same time, however, Nicaea also teaches that Christ is fully human. And this teaching is emphasized by Chalcedon. We may put the point by saying that according to both councils Christ had a human nature as well as a divine one. By this we can mean that according to both councils it is true to say 'Christ was human' and 'Christ was divine'.

(3) Nicaea also says that Christ is homoousios with the Father. The precise meaning of homoousios in the context of the teaching of Nicaea is a matter of debate (cf. Kelly 1972 and Stead 1977). According to some it signifies that Christ is identical with God as, for example, Charles Dickens was identical with the author of Oliver Twist. Others have held that it is only used to indicate that Christ is like the Father as I am like you – that Christ and the Father are things of the same kind. As Nicaea came to be interpreted, however, the meaning of homoousios is not in doubt. More precisely, in the minds of those who produced the teaching of Chalcedon to say that Christ is homoousios with the Father is to say that Christ and the Father, though distinct, are one God. On this account, sentences with 'Christ' as subject can

be rewritten with 'God' as subject. As it is sometimes put, Christ is *homoousios* with the Father in that Christ and the Father, insofar as they are divine, are numerically identical. They are not two Gods, but one God. Or, to put it another way, Christ and the Father do not add up to two Gods.

(4) According to Nicaea and Chalcedon, Christ and the Father are the same since they are both God. But the councils assert a distinction between Christ and the Father, and Chalcedon does so by saying that they are two *personae* or *hupostaseis*. Though this is not commonly realized, the meaning here is not that they are two centres of consciousness as you and I are. The point being made is that the Father and the Son are somehow distinct subjects even though they are also identical since they are God. On this account, to say that the Father and the Son are *personae* or *hupostaseis* is to say that in some sense they are two as well as one, that the Father is not the Son and the Son is not the Father even though both are God and even though this does not mean that there are two Gods.

(5) Chalcedon says that Christ has a human nature as well as a divine nature and that these natures are united but distinct. But the council does not state how Christ's natures are united to form one individual. The implication, however, is that they are united since they both belong to Christ who is therefore a divine and human individual. It is also implied that this individual existed from eternity with God since he is God. This, of course, raises the question 'Where was the human nature of Christ before the birth of Jesus?'. The answer implied by Chalcedon is that it was nowhere. The idea here is that the subject we refer to as 'Christ' existed apart from the man Jesus, but with the presence of Jesus was united to someone human since this human person was a divine subject who was also human.

Summing all this up, then, we can represent the doctrine of the Incarnation by means of the following propositions:

(1) There is one God, not two.
(2) The Father is God (i.e. his nature is divine).
(3) The Son (Christ) is God (i.e. his nature is divine).
(4) The Son is fully human (i.e. his nature is human).
(5) The Father and the Son are distinct individuals (i.e. the Father is not the Son nor the Son the Father).

B. The Trinity

For a classical statement of the doctrine of the Trinity we could refer to the creed promulgated by the First General Council of Constantinople (381), which reaffirms the teaching of Nicaea and which adds that the Holy Spirit is 'the Lord and Giver of life who proceeds from the Father, who together with the Father and the Son is worshipped and glorified' (Neuner and Dupuis, p. 9). But for a more systematic statement we can cite the so-called Creed of Athanasius, a document produced some time after the middle of the fifth century and commonly taken as a touchstone of Trinitarian orthodoxy. The relevant part of the text runs thus:

We worship one God in the Trinity and the Trinity in unity, without either confusing the persons or dividing the substance; for the person of the Father is one, the Son's is another, the Holy Spirit's another; but the Godhead of Father, Son and Holy Spirit is one, their glory equal, their majesty equally eternal. Such as the Father is, such is the Son, such also the Holy Spirit; uncreated is the Father, uncreated the Son, uncreated the Holy Spirit; infinite (immensus) is the Father, infinite the Son, infinite the Holy Spirit; eternal is the Father, eternal the Son, eternal the Holy Spirit; yet, they are not three eternal beings but one eternal, just as they are not three uncreated beings or three infinite beings but one uncreated and one infinite. In the same way, almighty is the Father, almighty the Son, almighty the Holy Spirit; yet, they are not three almighty beings but one almighty. Thus, the Father is God, the Son is God, the Holy Spirit is God; yet, they are not three gods but one God. Thus, the Father is Lord, the Son is Lord, the Holy Spirit is Lord; yet, they are not three lords but one Lord. For, as the Christian truth compels us to acknowledge each person distinctly as God and Lord, so too the Catholic religion forbids us to speak of three gods or lords. The Father has neither been made by anyone, nor is He created or begotten; the Son is from the Father alone, not made nor created but begotten; the Holy Spirit is from the Father and the Son, not made nor created nor begotten, but proceeding. So there is one Father, not three Fathers; one Son, not three Sons; one Holy Spirit, not three Holy Spirits. And in this Trinity there is no before or after, no greater or lesser, but all three persons are equally eternal with each other and fully equal (Neuner and Dupuis, pp. 11f.).

Here, so it seems, we are once again asked to accept that Christ is God and that the Father is God, though this does not mean that there are two Gods. In addition, however, the point is made that the Holy Spirit is God as are the Father and the Son. The conclusion then drawn is that what is true of God is true of Father, Son and Spirit. On the other hand, so it is said, the Father, Son and Spirit are distinct in that what is true of each is not true of all. The Father is not created or begotten. The Son is begotten. The Spirit proceeds from the Father and the Son. In other words:

(1) The Father is God.
(2) The Son is God.
(3) The Spirit is God.
(4) The Father is not the Son or Spirit.
(5) The Son is not the Father or Spirit.
(6) The Spirit is not the Father or Son.
(7) There is one God, not three.

THE CHARGE OF CONTRADICTION

So are these doctrines contradictory? Here it seems to me worth making the following points immediately.

(a) An assertion may seem contradictory when in fact it is not. Someone may ask if I am happy. I may reply 'Well, yes and no'. On the surface this seems contradictory, but we all know that it need not be. It may mean that I am happy in some respects and unhappy in others. So the appearance of an assertion is not a sure guide to the presence or absence of contradiction. We may have to dig below appearances. Some have spoken as if contradiction can always be detected at a glance. But this is false. Some contradictions can, of course, be quickly spotted. This is the case with, for example, 'John is a married bachelor' if that is taken to mean both that John is married and that he is a bachelor. But contradiction can be present in a set of assertions which cannot be held together before the mind in one act of vision. It may also be implied by such a set and this will mean that the set is contradictory.

(b) People sometimes insist that one should be able to prove that what one says is not contradictory independently of proving that what one says is true. But this demand needs to be set beside the fact that proving contradiction apart from truth is no easy matter. This is apparent in mathematics where the work of Kurt Gödel (1906–78) has seemed to establish that 'a mathematical theory cannot ordinarily be proved to be free of internal contradiction except by resorting to another theory that rests on stronger assumptions, and hence is less reliable, than the theory whose consistency is being proved' (Quine 1981, p. 144). In the words of two other writers, Gödel

proved that it is impossible to establish the internal logical consistency of a very large class of deductive systems – elementary arithmetic, for example – unless one adopts principles of reasoning so complex that their internal consistency is as open to doubt as that of the systems themselves. In the light of these conclusions, no final systematization of many important areas of mathematics is attainable, and no absolutely impeccable guarantee can be given that many significant branches of mathematical thought are entirely free from internal contradiction (Nagel and Newman 1959, p. 6.).

(c) Apart from the general difficulty of proving contradiction in all contexts, a case can be made for denying that it is reasonable to demand proof that the doctrine of the Trinity, at least, is not contradictory. For let us suppose that the truth of the doctrine cannot be proved. In that case it would seem that it cannot be proved that it is not contradictory. The doctrine claims to tell us about the inner life of God, about what is true of God in himself and apart from creatures. Since what God is in himself is what God is eternally and changelessly, this in turn means that what the doctrine expresses is no contingent matter. If God is Trinity, it is an eternal truth that he is Trinity. In that case, however, proof that God could be Trinity (proof that the doctrine of the Trinity is not contradictory) would be proof that something which cannot fail to be true is true, and it would therefore be true that it is true. If it cannot be proved that God is Trinity, therefore, it follows that it also cannot be proved that it is not contradictory to assert that he is Trinity (cf. Geach 1972, p. 293). Some would reject this argument on the ground that the doctrine of the Trinity does not tell us about the inner life of God apart from creatures. Theologians have distinguished between the 'immanent Trinity' (what God is in himself from eternity) and the 'economic Trinity' (what God is known to be through the emergence of Christianity in the light and wake of the Incarnation). Invoking this distinction, some have held that God is only the economic Trinity and that the doctrine of the Trinity depends for its truth on facts about what has been created. But this could only be so in the sense that since God is changeless we can infer that his creation is changelessly willed by him and that he is, in fact, the changeless Creator. And this is not to say that God is bound to create. If God is Trinity, therefore, this is not something that depends on what is created. So the doctrine of the Trinity can indeed be seen as teaching about the inner life of God apart from creatures.

It seems, therefore, that we will need to be cautious about supposing that contradiction is either something obvious or something whose absence can be demonstrated in all cases. We can also add that at least with respect to the doctrine of the Trinity there is a case for denying that it is reasonable to demand a proof of non-contradiction. And that, I think, means that one can reasonably maintain that there is an onus of proof on someone who thinks that he detects a contradiction in the doctrines of the Incarnation and the Trinity. They may *look* contradictory, but this does not mean that they are. One may suppose that their non-contradictory nature must be proved, but others may reasonably reject this supposition. If someone still holds that they are contradictory, therefore, one can fairly ask him to show where the contradiction lies. So let us now put our question this way: Has it been shown that the doctrines are contradictory?

ARGUMENTS AGAINST THE DOCTRINES

At this point we encounter a problem which is, perhaps, somewhat surprising. For though it is certainly true that many people have sided and do side with the conclusion that the doctrines are contradictory, this has not resulted in a solid batch of arguments to which one can easily refer. What we seem to have is more like a general and weakly articulated hunch that something must be wrong in saying that a man can be God or that God can be one in three. Yet some have at least given voice to their hunches, and, with respect to the doctrine of the Incarnation, we can cite two notable modern examples. These are John Hick and Maurice Wiles.

John Hick

According to Hick it seems clear immediately that the doctrine of the Incarnation is contradictory. He writes:

Orthodoxy insisted upon the two natures human and divine. But orthodoxy has never been able to give this idea any content. It remains a form of words without assignable meaning. For to say, without explanation, that the historical Jesus of Nazareth was also God is as devoid of meaning as to say that this circle drawn with a pencil on paper is also a square (Hick [ed.] 1977, p. 178).

But is this right? One may well take leave to doubt so.

One reason for saying so concerns Hick's use of the word 'meaningless'. According to Hick, the Chalcedonian teaching about Christ is meaningless as is the assertion 'This circle drawn with a pencil on paper is also a square'. Since this assertion is contradictory (see below) one presumes that according to Hick the Chalcedonian teaching about Christ is meaningless because it is contradictory. But that cannot be right since being contradictory does not entail being meaningless. Some, to be sure, have seemed to equate the contradictory and the meaningless. According, for example, to Peter Strawson, 'Contradicting oneself is like writing something down and then erasing it, or putting a line through it. A contradiction cancels itself and leaves nothing' (Strawson 1952, p. 3). But if a self-cancelling utterance is meaningless, then contradiction is not meaningless. A proposition of the form 'P and not-P' is contradictory, and so is any proposition or set of propositions from which such a contradiction follows. But the very fact that we can speak here of 'following' shows that the contradictory is not meaningless. The meaningless neither entails nor is entailed.

Then again, what is wrong with 'This circle drawn with a pencil on paper is also a square'? The answer, presumably, is that it is contradictory. But why? Because being a square excludes being a circle: the two figures have mutually exclusive characteristics.

Would it be coherent to claim that there exists a thing that is (imitating the language of Chalcedon) 'truly a square' and 'truly a circle'? . . . Let us say that a thing is a square if it is a geometrical figure with four equal sides and four equal angles. And let us say that a thing is a circle if it is a closed geometrical figure all of whose points are equidistant from the centre. Now we can see what a thing would have to be if it were 'truly a square' and 'truly a circle'. It would have to be a closed geometrical figure with four equal sides, four equal angles, and all its points equidistant from the centre. And this clearly is incoherent. It is logically impossible for a thing to have four equal sides, four equal angles, and all its points equidistant from the centre (Davis 1983, p. 121).

In that case, however, if we are to agree with Hick we require a proof that the Chalcedonian teaching about Christ ascribes mutually exclusive characteristics to one and the same thing. The trouble, however, is that Hick does not give us any such proof. In reply it might be said that just as our understanding of circles and squares forces us to conclude that no circle can be square so our understanding of God and man forces us to conclude that no man can be God. But we understand both circles and squares as definable figures while we can deny that God is definable if that means that he is something whose nature is clear to us. So why should we say that our understanding of God and man forces us to conclude that no man can be God? Some would say that the answer lies in the fact that to call a man God is to ascribe mutually exclusive characteristics to one and the same thing. But why should we believe that? Is it because if something is a man it cannot be God since anything that is a man will have characteristics which God cannot have? Is it because if something is God it cannot be a man since if something is God it will have characteristics which cannot be had by what is a man? But how do we know that all this is true? Why may a subject not have all the characteristics appropriate both to God and to men? We may not understand what such a subject would be like. But that is not to say that we contradict ourselves by asserting that there is such a subject. A likely rejoinder is that one can refer to characteristics appropriate to God and to men and that one can see a contradiction in ascribing them to one and the same subject. Thus, for example, some will say that since God is changeless and men change it follows that nothing can be both God and man since it would then be both changeless and changing, which is impossible. But that does not follow. It does follow that nothing can be changing as God and changeless as man. But that leaves open the possibility of something being as God changeless and as man changing, which in turn is compatible with something being both changeless and unchanging. Consider the case of Abbot X. He is abbot of Abbey Y and brother of Mary. As abbot of Y he has jurisdiction over his monks. As brother of Mary he has the right, shall we say, to inherit her fortune. But he does not have the right to inherit the fortune as abbot of Y. Being abbot does not guarantee him this right. Nor does being the brother of Mary entitle him to jurisdiction over the monks of Y. In the same way, so we may say (and so many Christian theologians have said), Christ can be a subject of whom different things are true depending on whether we think of him as man or as God. In that case, however, why cannot it be true of him that he is as God changeless and as man changing? It might be thought that this would mean that 'Christ is changeless' and 'Christ is changing' are both true and this is impossible since the first statement contradicts the second. But are the statements contradictory? If X as abbot can have what he does not have as brother of Mary, and *vice versa*, why may not Christ as God be what he is not as man, and *vice versa*? We may not be able to see how he can be this. But where is the contradiction in asserting that he is? If there is one, then Hick, at any rate, has not exposed it.

Maurice Wiles

What, then, of Wiles? Like Hick, he is worried about the doctrine of the Incarnation. But, unlike Hick, he does not suppose that the doctrine can be dismissed since it resembles 'This circle is also a square'. To think that it can, says Wiles, is 'too simple'. 'The self-contradiction there (sc. in 'This circle is also a square') is far clearer and more precise than in the case of God and man, because squares and circles are far clearer and more precise concepts' (Wiles 1977, p. 543). Yet Wiles does sense a contradiction in the doctrine of the Incarnation. Why? Because he thinks that the meaning of 'man' seems to exclude the possibility of a man being God.

It seems to me not unreasonable to regard 'being created' as part of the *meaning* of man . . . and 'not being created' as part of the meaning of God. Now if there is an analogical relationship between God and man, if indeed there is any real relation . . . then they inhabit a common logical world, though not of course a common logical world of shapes. *Prima facie* at least there is a case of self-contradiction involved (Wiles 1977, p. 543).

But is there even a *prima facie* contradiction involved in saying that a man is God? Wiles's worry clearly springs from his belief that 'being created' is part of the meaning of man and 'not being created' is part of the meaning of God. But this belief can be rejected. If it is part of the meaning of man that he is created, then 'This man was not created' would be contradictory, like 'This triangle has not got three angles'. And that would mean that we could prove the existence of God merely by reflecting on the meaning of the word 'man'. In any case, how can 'being created' be part of the meaning of anything? Here I agree with some remarks of Herbert McCabe.

Being created could not possibly be part of the meaning of man or of anything else (except of course 'a creature'); being created could not possibly make any *difference* to anything. If it did, creation would be impossible. God might set out cheerfully to create, let us say, a Nicaraguan okapi but he would never be able to do so; all he would be able to create would be a *created* Nicaraguan okapi, which would, on this hypothesis be different. But maybe all he ever proposes to create is a created Nicaraguan okapi? Alas for the vanity of divine wishes; he would have to end up with a *created* created Nicaraguan okapi, and that would be different again (McCabe 1977, p. 550).

Here we may again apply a point which I noted earlier. In referring to the doctrine of creation *ex nihilo* I observed that it rules out thinking of creation as some kind of change. To say that something is created is not to say that it has been modified. In that case, however, being created can make no more difference to what a thing is than can the existence of a thing (see above, Chapter 4). As McCabe goes on to observe, 'Being created . . . could not enter into the description of anything. We could not ever say "If this is created then it must be like this and not like that" ' (McCabe, p. 550).

FURTHER DIFFICULTIES

And yet, so some have said, the doctrine of the Incarnation is indeed contradictory. And the same goes for the doctrine of the Trinity. Why? Four lines of argument are common.

(1) According to the doctrine of the Incarnation, Christ and the Father are God. But this means that they are identical. According to the doctrine of the Incarnation, however, Christ and the Father are distinct. So if Christ and the Father are God they are both identical and distinct. But this is impossible.

(2) According to the doctrine of the Trinity, Father, Son and Spirit are God. But this means that they are identical. According to the doctrine of the Trinity, however, Father, Son and Spirit are distinct. So if Father, Son and Spirit are God they are both identical and distinct. But this is impossible.

(3) According to the doctrine of the Incarnation, there is only one God. But the doctrine of the Incarnation says that two persons are God. It therefore follows that according to the doctrine of the Incarnation there are two Gods. In that case, however, the doctrine is contradictory.

(4) According to the doctrine of the Trinity, there is only one God. But the doctrine of the Trinity says that three persons are God. It therefore follows that according to the doctrine of the Trinity there are three Gods. In that case, however, the doctrine is contradictory.

But these arguments are also unsuccessful as proofs of contradiction. The reasons are as follows.

(a) To say that Father, Son and Spirit are God is to say that they are divine and that the result is not more than one God. And it is true that we can deny that there is more than one God, for divinity is not something subject to multiplication. This follows from the doctrine of divine simplicity (Chapter 5). As Aquinas observes:

Socrates can share what makes him man with many others, but what makes him this man can belong to one alone. So if Socrates were this man just by being a man, there could no more be many men that there can be many Socrates. Now in God this is the case, for . . . God is himself his own nature. . . . And thus it is impossible for there to be many Gods (*Summa Theologiae* Ia, 11, 3).

Yet though divinity is not subject to multiplication it does not follow that only one thing can be divine. All that follows is that if more than one is divine the result will not be more than one God. The reply might be that if divinity is not subject to multiplication, then only one thing can be divine. But how do we know that? The reply might be that if A, B and C are divine, then A, B and C are identical and therefore only one thing. But if A, B and C are divine, it only follows that they are identical by virtue of being God. It does not follow that they are not also somehow distinct. Some would say that if A, B and C are divine, then, if there is only one God, A, B and C are the same God and therefore identical. But why can it not be true that A, B and C are distinct, that A is God, B is God and C is God, and that nothing is as God subject to multiplication? Could it be that if A, B and C are divine persons and if each is God then A, B and C are the same God as each other and therefore the same person as each other? But why could it not be true that A, B and C are God even though they are distinct? If A, B and C are the same God that will be because each is divine and this will mean that each is what is not subject to multiplication. But that does not entail that what is divine cannot be subject to multiplication. It does not entail that more than one cannot be truly divine.

(b) The doctrines of the Incarnation and the Trinity do hold that more than one person is God. But this does not entail that there are two Gods. For why may not several things be indivisible insofar as they are divine? The reply might be that just as if A and B are cats there is more than one cat so if A and B are God there is more than one God. But why so? There can be many cats, but there cannot be more than one God if divinity is not subject to multiplication. For this reason, therefore, we can deny that if two are God it follows that there are two Gods. In other words, so we may argue, whether divinity is subject to multiplication is not to be decided on the basis of knowing how many are divine. Even if we know that a hundred are divine, that by itself will not settle the question 'How many Gods are there?'.

God and Christ

So it still does not seem that the doctrine of the Incarnation and the doctrine of the Trinity are contradictory. But some might now say that there is yet a problem in view of the assertion that Christ was God. For if Christ was God, then it presumably makes sense to say of Christ what believers have wished to say of God. It would also seem to make sense to say of God what believers have wished to say of Christ. But would this not involve us in contradiction? God has traditionally been said to be omniscient, changeless and omnipresent. But how can we say that Christ was omniscient, changeless and omnipresent? How can a man be any of these things? Then again, Christ was bodily, changing, and spatially located. Yet how can we say that God was like this?

Here, perhaps, it helps to reflect a bit on terms used in stating the doctrine of the Incarnation as expounded by Nicaea and Chalcedon. The doctrine taught is that Christ was one person with a human nature and a divine nature. But how are we to read that teaching?

Let us begin with 'Christ is one person'. As we have seen, for the purposes of the Nicaean and Chalcedonian doctrine of the Incarnation 'person' does not mean 'centre of consciousness', not, at any rate, if that is thought to conjure up a picture of a human being or, perhaps, a shadowy human being. This is not to say that 'person' in theology is unrelated to the word as used in nontheological contexts. Indeed, it seems generally agreed that its modern nontheological use derives from its use in expositions of doctrines like that of the Incarnation. But the doctrine does not hold that there is, so to speak, a kind of invisible man tied to the man whom we refer to as Jesus. For the doctrine of the Incarnation, to call Christ a person (*persona, hupostasis*) is to say that he is a distinct subject. 'Just as the divine Son and the human Jesus constitute one individual reality, so the Son, by whom the hypostatic union is effected, is as much an individual reality as the Father and the Spirit' (Owen 1984, p. 60). And this, I think, means that we can usefully read 'Christ is one person' as what some would call a 'remark of logical grammar'. For the statement is not so much describing Christ as indicating the function of the word 'Christ'. It is telling us that what 'Christ' stands for is a distinct subject. As C. J. F. Williams helpfully puts it:

To say that Christ is a person is to say that the word 'Christ' is a proper name. To say that Christ is one person, or, more misleadingly, that there is one person in Christ, is to say that in all singular statements which we make with 'Christ' as subject he to whom we refer is the same. What may be said of him may vary: the subject of whom these things are said is one. There is more than one predicate, but there is only one subject (Williams 1968, p. 522).

Take, for example, 'Christ went walking and Christ went running'. If Christ is one person, we can read this as saying that a subject went walking and a subject went running and it was the same subject who walked and ran. This subject we call 'Christ'.

What now of 'Christ had two natures, divine and human'? Here we will clearly need to consider what is involved in saying that something has a particular nature. Suppose, therefore, that something is said to have a nature. Suppose, for example, it is said to have a human nature. What will be meant by that?

One's first thought might be that the thing is being defined. But that cannot be true. For to say that something has a human nature is to say what it is, and one can say what something is without defining the thing. 'It's a human being' is no more a definition than 'It's raining'.

It is, however, a remark which will set up certain expectations in our minds even if we are not altogether conscious of them. The point can be brought out if we consider the following imaginary dialogue.

A. 'There's something buried under all this rubble.'

B. 'What is it?'

A. 'I think it's a human being.'

B. 'I do hope its petals aren't damaged.'

A. 'I said I think it's a human being.'

B. 'I know what you said. But it's surprising to find one out so early in the year. They don't usually flower until March.'

A. 'I said I think it's a human being.'

B. 'Then I'd better go and get a vase of water to put it in. We don't want it to go limp.'

Here, I presume, we would be inclined to say that A and B are talking at cross purposes. We would, in fact, say that while A is talking about one kind of thing, B is talking about another. And we would say this because of the way in which we expect (or do not expect) people to talk about human beings. We may not be able to define 'human being', but if asked what something is we can say that it is human. And in recognizing that something is human we recognize the appropriateness of some ways of talking about it and the inappropriateness of others. We recognize, for example, that it is not appropriate to speak of a human being as having petals, as blooming around March, and as benefiting from a spell in a vase of water. That sort of language is appropriate with reference to something like a snowdrop. And if someone persists in using it to speak of a human being, we would have to conclude either that he is joking or that he does not know what a human being is.

So there seems to be a clear connection between knowing what something is and knowing what it is appropriate to say about it. Or, as some have put it, to know what something is means knowing what it makes sense to say about it. And this fact can help us in trying to understand what we are doing in saying that something has a particular nature. To ascribe a nature to something is to say what the thing is, and this, in turn, is to locate the thing linguistically. Recognizing that something is a such and such (a human being or a snowdrop) is having some grasp of how the thing can intelligibly be talked about. As when we say that something is a person, when we say that something has such and such a nature we are not so much describing as indicating how we should speak.

And this, I think, means that to say that Christ has a particular nature is to say that certain ways of talking about him are appropriate. To say, for example, that Christ has a human nature is to say that what can appropriately be said about human beings can appropriately be said about Christ. As Williams once again puts it:

What is meant by saying that Christ has a human nature is that where a statement of the form 'All men have flesh and blood' is true there is a corresponding true statement of the form 'Christ has flesh and blood'. Generalizations about men have implications for

Christ. . . . To talk about 'nature' in connection with Christ is to talk about a particular type of common noun which can enter into true statements of which Christ is the subject (Williams 1968, p. 522).

So what, then, of 'Christ had two natures, divine and human'? What does that mean? Given that we can say 'Christ is a person', at least part of the answer is surely obvious. To say that Christ had a human nature and a divine nature is to say that Christ was a subject of whom we can talk in two different ways. It is to say that with Christ it is true to say of him what it is appropriate to say both of what is human and of what is divine. Of what is human we can say 'It breathes', 'It can get tired', 'It needs food'. So of Christ it was true that he breathed, that he could get tired, and that he needed food. Of what is divine we can say 'It is uncreated', 'It is omnipotent', 'It is omnipresent'. So of Christ it was true that he was uncreated, omnipotent, and omnipresent. And since it makes sense to say certain things about some human beings though these things are not true of all, we can also add that it makes sense to say certain things about Christ which are not true of all. It will be possible, for example, to say things like 'Christ slept in that room on such and such a night', or 'Christ scratched his nose at exactly such and such a time'.

So the main point is that if we say that Christ is one person with a human nature and a divine nature, we are licensing statements like 'Christ was tired' and 'Christ was omnipotent'. And this means that what I imagined as a consequence in the first paragraph of this section is correct. If Christ was God, then it makes sense to say of Christ what believers have wished to say of God. But are we now to add that the result must be contradiction?

Why should we? A common answer would be 'Because we would therefore be saying that being human involves being, for example, omniscient, and that being divine involves, for example, being capable of fatigue'. But in view of what I have been saying it ought to be clear that we need not accept this at all. According to Chalcedon, the divine nature of Christ and the human nature of Christ are not to be confused, so in saying that Christ is one person with a human nature and a divine nature we are not saying that being human and being divine are one and the same thing. We are saying that one and the same thing can be spoken of in ways in which it makes sense to speak of human beings and in ways in which it makes sense to speak of God. And that, I think, is not to say what we can know to be contradictory. The obvious rejoinder would be that it is contradictory since (a) what is true of a human subject could never be true of God, and (b) what is true of a divine subject could never be true of a subject which is human. But how do we know that this is so? If a subject is only human, then it is not divine. And if a subject is only divine, then it is not human. But what makes it impossible for a subject to be human and divine? And what makes it impossible for a subject to be divine and human? It is easy to see that, for example, something's being square excludes it being triangular. But what excludes something's being human and divine?

Circles and squares and triangles and such occupy their mutually exclusive territories in the common logical world of shapes. It is part of the *meaning* of a circle that it is not a square or any other shape; hence to say that something is both a circle and a square is to say both that it is and is not a circle. . . . Similarly being human and being, say, a sheep occupy mutually exclusive territories in the common logical world of animals. It is part of the meaning of being human that one is not a sheep. And so on. But just what or where is the common logical world that is occupied in mutual exclusion by God and man? A circle and a square make two shapes; a man and a sheep make two animals: God and man make two what? (McCabe 1977, p. 353).

The reply might be that being God is being a thing of a kind which prevents God being a thing of the kind to which human beings belong. But since we can affirm that God is simple (that he is not comprehensible to us as a subject with a nature distinct from himself or as a subject with attributes distinct from himself and from each other) we have no reason to say that being God is being a thing of any kind. If I am a thing of some kind, then God cannot in the same sense be understood as being like me. Another reply might be that a subject which is human could not, for example, be omniscient. And to this it might be added that a subject which is divine could not, for example, be tired. But while it can be true that a subject which is human cannot be omniscient insofar as he is human (though one might well wish to contest this as many generations of Christians have done by ascribing great knowledge to the human Jesus), what is to stop him being omniscient insofar as he is God? And while it seems true that a subject which is divine cannot be tired insofar as he is divine, what is to stop him being tired insofar as he is human? To take up the earlier example, as abbot of Y, X has jurisdiction over his monks, but not the right to inherit Mary's fortune. As Mary's brother, however, he may be entitled to what she leaves behind. Here something can be true of a subject under one description and false under another. So why cannot something be true of Christ under one description (Christ *qua* man) and false under another (Christ *qua* God)? The reply might be that Christ *qua* man and Christ *qua* God are identical so that what is true of Christ *qua* man must be true of Christ *qua* God. Yet why so? X *qua* abbot and X *qua* brother of Mary may be identical. But what is true of X *qua* abbot is not true of X *qua* brother of Mary, and *vice versa*. We can see how someone can be an abbot without being entitled to inherit someone's fortune. We cannot, perhaps, see how something can be a human subject without being what excludes that subject being divine. But this is no proof that a subject cannot be both human and divine.

God and the Trinity

But suppose it were now suggested that even if it is not contradictory to say 'Christ is one person with a human nature and a divine nature' we still have a *prima facie* contradiction in the assertion that God is Trinity. Can we say anything which might help us to see that this need not be so? One might reply that if this would mean proving that the doctrine of the Trinity is free from contradiction, then the answer is 'Why should we have to?' or simply 'No'. Yet even if proof of non-contradiction is not attempted, might one not still try to indicate how the doctrine of the Trinity is not contradictory? For might one not suggest that, far from the doctrine having a *prima facie* appearance of contradiction, it appears *prima facie* to be non-contradictory?

Possibly not. But not, I think, certainly not. Take, for example, a crucial section of the doctrine as stated by the so-called Athanasian creed. According to this, the following propositions are all true:

(1) The Father is uncreated.
(2) The Son is uncreated.
(3) The Holy Spirit is uncreated.
(4) There are not three uncreated things, but only one.

Now that may seem a manifestly contradictory way of speaking, but (and without suggesting that we now have a model for the Trinity) it is at least worth noting that we are led into it in other than theological contexts. An example is given by G. E. Hughes.

I listen to a symphony, and I find the orchestration admirable, the form admirable, the harmonic texture admirable. The orchestration is not the same thing as the form, nor is either of these the same thing as the harmonic texture. Now let us ask: how many admirable things have we here? I want to say that this question is ambiguous in an important way.

There is an obvious sense in which the answer is: at least three – the orchestration, the form and the harmonic texture. The sense in question might be explained in this way: There are at least three distinct, non-identical, values of x which make 'x is admirable' true.

But there is a sense in which the answer 'At least three' is distinctly misleading. Finding the orchestration, the form and the harmonic texture of a symphony all admirable is not like finding three distinct symphonies all admirable; and the answer 'At least three' makes it sound *too* like this. Orchestration, form and harmonic texture are not separable items as the three symphonies are. When we look at it this way, we are inclined to answer 'Only one' to the question 'How many admirable things are there here?' – for there is only one thing here to be admirable (or not admirable), the symphony itself.

So we can quite consistently answer (taking the question in one way) 'At least three', and (taking the question in another way) 'Only one'. One answer, however, which we cannot sensibly give is 'At least four – the orchestration, the form, the harmonic texture and the symphony'. This would be to mix the logical types. We might be inclined to say that the symphony has a different ontological status from its orchestration, its form or its harmonic texture; at all events, we can say that the expression 'the symphony' belongs to a different logical type from 'the orchestration' etc. The symphony is not something additional to, on the same level as the orchestration, the form, the harmonic texture (and the other relevant things of this kind). We might even say that these things, each of which (let us say) we find admirable, just *are* the one single thing – the symphony – which we find admirable (Hughes 1963, p. 5).

Applying all this to the case of the Trinity, we can now say this. It can be *prima facie* non-contradictory to say that something is thus and so, that it is constituted by distinct elements each of which is thus and so, and that the result is not three thus and sos but one. Following Hughes's example we can say:

(1) The orchestration is admirable.
(2) The form is admirable.
(3) The harmonic texture is admirable.
(4) There are not three admirable beings, but one.

Yet this way of talking is employed in stating the doctrine of the Trinity. So stating the doctrine is to say what is *prima facie* not contradictory. One might reply that the opposite is true since what the doctrine says is that the Father is God, the Son is God, and the Spirit is God, while this contradicts what the doctrine also states, viz. that the Father, the Son and the Spirit are not identical. Another argument might be that the doctrine of the Trinity is a manifest contradiction since it speaks of Father, Son and Spirit as one, but also insists that they are distinct. But neither of these objections is conclusive and they may be replied to as follows.

(a) If the Father is identical with God, if the Son is identical with God, and if the Spirit is identical with God, then the Father is identical with the Son and the Son with the Spirit. According to the doctrine of the Trinity, however, 'the person of the Father is one, the Son's another, the Holy Spirit's another'. On this basis, therefore, one might conclude that the doctrine is contradictory. But in order to do so one would have to take 'The Father is God', 'The Son is God' and 'The Spirit is God' as using what we might call the 'is' of identity as we find it in statements like 'Cesario is Viola', 'Ganymede is Rosalind', 'Aliena is Celia', and so on. And this in turn means taking 'God' as a name (like 'Viola'). But we do not have to take 'The Father is God' and so on as logically on a level with statements like 'Cesario is Viola'. We can take them as ascribing a nature to a subject and as predicating something of a subject as, for example, 'is tired' predicates something of a subject in 'John is tired'. And that would seem to follow the logic of the Athanasian creed, for that does not use 'God' in the way that it uses the expressions 'the Father', 'the Son' and 'the Spirit'. These expressions signify subjects said to be thus and so (uncreated, infinite, eternal, almighty). But

'God' is not used in this way at all. And, so we might add, there is no reason why it should be.

(b) There is truth in the assertion that according to the doctrine of the Trinity, Father, Son and Spirit are both one and distinct. According to the Athanasian creed, there are statements predicating the same thing of Father, Son and Spirit. Thus we can, for example, say

(a) The Father ⎫
     The Son   ⎬ is uncreated.
     The Spirit ⎭

(b) The Father ⎫
     The Son   ⎬ is infinite.
     The Spirit ⎭

(c) The Father ⎫
     The Son   ⎬ is eternal.
     The Spirit ⎭

(d) The Father ⎫
     The Son   ⎬ is almighty.
     The Spirit ⎭

(e) The Father ⎫
     The Son   ⎬ is Lord.
     The Spirit ⎭

(f) The Father ⎫
     The Son   ⎬ is God.
     The Spirit ⎭

In view of these statements we might therefore conclude that Father, Son and Spirit are one and not distinct, that they are identical without qualification (not three, but one). But the creed has more to say than (a)–(f). For it also adds

(g) The Father has not been made by anything and is not created or begotten by anything.

(h) The Son is begotten by the Father but is not made or created by anything.

(i) The Spirit proceeds from the Father and the Son but is not made or created by anything.

And these statements mean that the creed is not identifying the persons without qualification. For in terms of these statements it is false that all that can be said of one person can be said of all. The Son is begotten by the Father, but it is false that the Father is begotten or that the Spirit is begotten. The Spirit proceeds from the Father and the Son, but the Father and the Son do not. The Father begets the Son, but the Son and the Spirit do not. In other words, though some of the statements licensed by the creed do not allow us to distinguish between the persons, others do. We may therefore deny that the doctrine of the Trinity says both that the persons are identical and that they are not. They are distinguished by their relations. To this one might reply that one does not understand what it would be like to be something distinguished relationally. But that is not now the issue. We are asking whether the doctrine of the Trinity is contradictory since it says that the persons of the Trinity are distinct things and not distinct things. I am saying that the doctrine is not saying this. Although it asserts that all the persons are God, it also asserts a distinction between them.

So again it seems to me that we are not obliged to refer to the doctrine of the Trinity as *prima facie* contradictory. One can just as well say that it is *prima facie* not contradictory. And this, I think, applies even when we are considering what, for many people, is the most glaringly contradictory aspect of the doctrine: its insistence that though there is distinction within God there is also unity. Is that insistence *prima facie* contradictory? It could just as well be said that it is inevitable if we are to hold that there is distinction in God at all. For talk of God is talk of the Creator, which, as we have seen, is not talk of something capable of undergoing real change. But this in turn must mean that God cannot acquire aspects or features or characteristics which at some time are lacking to him. Whatever God is he is changelessly and from eternity. And whatever aspects or features or characteristics he has he has by nature, by being God. As Scholastic writers would have said, there can be no 'accidents' in God. Whatever God is belongs to his nature; it cannot be something he may or may not be as, for example, people may or may not be bald. There cannot be an aspect or feature or characteristic of God which is anything other than the divine nature itself, which is anything other than what God is. Yet that, as I have also argued, is not something we can distinguish from God himself. What God is and who God is are not for us separable. In that case, however, whatever is *in* God *is* God. And if there is distinction in God, then what is distinct in God is God. In this sense there being distinction within God is not conceivable without there also being unity. This is not, of course, to say that we can imagine or understand what distinction and unity amount to in God. But it is to say that if there is the first there is also the second. Whatever is in God is God.

MAKING SENSE OF CHRISTIAN THEISM

In such ways as this, then, it seems to me that one may respond to the suggestion that the doctrines of the Incarnation and Trinity are contradictory. That is not to say that one can definitively prove that they are not contradictory. But it is to say that certain objections to them favouring the charge of contradiction can be met.

At this point, however, someone might ask for more. Suppose we concede that the doctrine of the Incarnation and the doctrine of the Trinity are not contradictory. Are they intelligible? Can we understand the nature of the truths which they are attempting to proclaim?

One view is that the answer is 'No' and that this is what makes Christian theism unique. The idea here, which is very common, can be represented by the following argument:

(1) Belief in the existence of God is fairly straightforward. We have a fairly good understanding of what it means to say that God exists.

(2) Christian theism, however, introduces the notion of mystery. That a man is God is a mystery. That God is three and one is a mystery. Here our understanding is defeated in a way that it is not by the simple truth that God exists.

(3) So Christian theism takes us into mystery as theism does not. In this sense its truths are not intelligible or understandable.

Yet in view of what I have already said, we can, perhaps, see that this line of reasoning is not quite right. For we can fairly deny that what makes theism true is something we can readily understand. God, we may say, is the Creator *ex nihilo*. As such, he is the eternal source of all that we can comprehend as individual subjects. In himself, he defies our attempts to classify in terms of genus and species. In a real sense, therefore, we do not know what we are talking about when we talk about God. We may even add that to believe in God is actually to be a kind of agnostic – not in the modern sense, but in the sense that to believe in God is to see that behind the universe lies something we cannot single out as a comprehensible object. The modern agnostic says 'We do not know, and the universe is a mysterious riddle'. One who believes in God does not say this. Yet he can say 'We do not know what the answer is, but we do know that there is a mystery behind it all which we do not know, and if there were not, there would not even be a riddle. This unknown we call *God*. If there were no God, there would be no universe, and nobody to be mystified' (White 1956, pp. 18f.). In that case, however, we can readily deny that our reason breaks down only with reference to the truths of Christianity. It has already broken down with God as such. In this sense, therefore, we can deny that Christianity is unique because it presents us with mystery. If we say that it is not intelligible, if we deny that we can understand what makes it true, we ought not to mean that it is not intelligible or not understandable by contrast with theism. It cannot be that Christianity is mysterious while God is not.

Yet even though many people accept that this is so they sometimes try to make things clearer by means of analogies. If someone is trying to teach us about something which is new to us, he will often proceed by trying to compare it with what is already familiar. And this is what has been done by those who have taught the distinctive truths of Christianity. In trying to expound them they have striven to find models for them in things with which we are at home to begin with. The following question therefore arises: Can we make sense of Christian theism in the light of available analogies?

A famous example of someone who goes at least some way in suggesting that we can is St Augustine. He holds that there are traces (*vestigia*) of the Trinity in creation and he offers two much-discussed analogies for thinking about it (*De Trinitate* IX and X). The first of these is *mens, notitia,* and *amor* (mind, knowledge, and love). The second is *memoria, intelligentia, voluntas* (memory, intelligence, will). According to Augustine, we can think of the divine persons as something like various faculties of the human mind. The persons, like the faculties, are distinct. But they also constitute a unity.

Yet is that right? Some (such as the twentieth-century theologian Karl Barth [1886–1968]) have been nervous of the suggestion since it could be taken to mean that the truth of the doctrine of the Trinity is something that people can discover independently of divine revelation (cf. Barth, *Church Dogmatics* I/1, pp. 332ff.). Others have noted that Augustine's analogies badly limp. The second, for example, supposes that memory, intelligence (or understanding) and will are distinct faculties while the truth, so it has been argued, is that they are no such thing. As one writer puts it: 'There are no entities corresponding to the so-called faculties; they are merely a convenient form of speech which might easily be replaced by an alternative way of dividing up the mind' (Brown 1985, p. 273).

On the other hand, however, one can accept that something must be revealed without supposing that the truth revealed cannot be reflected in what we are familiar with apart from revelation. Then again, though one might be wary of saying that, for example, memory, intelligence and will are distinct entities, one can also consider them as somehow distinct. One can, for example, write about the concept of memory without producing a treatise on knowledge or voluntary behaviour. And it is surely true that I am as much present in my remembering as I am in my willing and understanding. The Augustinian analogies may be challenged, and anyone who has read some philosophy of mind will doubtless find plenty of holes to pick in them. Some would add that if they are pressed they lead to something other than the doctrine of the Trinity (cf. Owen 1984, p. 61). But that is not to say that the analogies are bound to mislead or that they cannot be positively helpful in trying to indicate something of what the doctrine of the Trinity is teaching. Even when we know that a model or analogy is defective, it can still help us to understand things. In his early work *Tractatus Logico-Philosophicus* (1921), Wittgenstein stresses the idea that propositions stand to the world as a picture stands to that of which it is a picture. Here we have Wittgenstein's famous 'picture theory of meaning'. In later writings he brings out the difficulties with this, and philosophers have applauded him for doing so. But few would reject absolutely everything that Wittgenstein says in the *Tractatus* about pictures and propositions. Mistaken as one might find the *Tractatus*, it does bring something out. One might say the same of theological assertions such as those which speak of God as 'Maker' and 'cause'. One can see why we might start saying that God exists, and one can see why we might refer to him as if he were like makers and causes with which we are familiar. But it still remains that the comparison between them falls down in the end. No non-divine makers produce their products *ex nihilo*. Neither does any non-divine cause.

But it is one thing to say that an analogy can be cited for something, and another to say that by appealing to the analogy we can understand that to which the analogy stands as an analogy. Nor should we in fact suppose this. A child may be told that the American President is rather like the headmaster. And that might be as good a way of putting things as is possible in the circumstances. But the child will get things badly wrong if he continues within the framework of the analogy as he grows older. And when it comes to analogies for doctrines like that of the Trinity there is an added problem. For the use of any such analogy will inevitably involve thinking of God as a creature, as an identifiable member of the universe distinguishable from other created things as another item in the universe beside them and as able to be understood by us as such. And for reasons which I have tried to indicate, that cannot be an adequate way of thinking. So for this reason, if for no other, one would be justified in answering our present question with 'No' rather than 'Yes'. We cannot make sense of Christian theism by means of analogies. We do not have a blueprint for the Christian God.

THE SIGNIFICANCE OF THE TRUTH OF CHRISTIANITY

Does this, however, mean that the central doctrines of Christianity form nothing but a set of statements which the Christian must carry around like a lot of useless baggage? Are they nothing but (arguably consistent) self-contained formulae? Are they, as some would put it, relevant to anything? These, I am sure, are questions which many readers are likely to want to raise at this point. Since this is not a work of systematic theology, and since I am not a theologian, I cannot hope to deal adequately with them. But I can see that they are pressing. In concluding this chapter, therefore, I would hazard the following replies, taking (as I have done throughout this chapter) the Incarnation and the Trinity as central Christian doctrines.

The doctrines and the language

People who feel that the doctrines are somehow irrelevant, or that they are simply formulae with which one can do little, frequently mean that they find it difficult to talk about God using the language associated with councils like Nicaea and Chalcedon. And one can see why this can be so. For one thing, the language can seem distracting in view of the way at least one of its common elements is now used. I refer here to the word 'person', which now suggests what was not meant by those who originally declared that Christ was one person having two natures and that the Trinity consists of three persons. Then again, it is not as if terms like *homoousios* and *hupostasis* are parts of the active vocabulary of modern people (except, perhaps, theologians). They are technical terms of an earlier age. But this does not mean that they cannot be read as helping to tell us something. Nor need we suppose that they are the only tools available for teaching what they were used to teach in the statements of Christian doctrine where we classically find them, i.e. in the texts of creeds such as those of Nicaea and Chalcedon. To those who are worried about the ability of the terms to convey anything, therefore, two things can be said. First, one can suggest that light may begin to dawn if some attempt is made to learn how the terms were originally used in expounding Christian doctrine. Second, if people can find a way of saying what was originally said by means of these terms, and if they can simultaneously manage not to deny what the terms were originally used to state, then let them go ahead and try. There can hardly be any objection in principle to new ways of stating old truths. Such ways are presumably what theologians are always trying to find. Such ways, it can be argued, are what those who formulated the doctrines of the Incarnation and the Trinity were themselves trying to find.

The doctrines and the Bible

Doubts about the significance of the doctrine of the Incarnation and the doctrine of the Trinity are often based on the conviction that they do not have a biblical basis. So it is probably worth noting that this conviction ought to be challenged and that someone who wishes to theologize in continuity with the Bible is not well advised to reject the doctrines on biblical grounds. It is, of course, true that the way in which the doctrines came to be expressed is not something we find in the Bible. The language of person, nature, hypostasis and so on is not biblical. But, as we saw in the last chapter, biblical writers do talk of Christ as of God. Taking the canon of the New Testament as it stands, we can certainly claim that the doctrine of the Incarnation is in continuity with what we find in the New Testament. And the same claim can be made with respect to the doctrine of the Trinity. It is not that the Bible highlights a doctrine of three persons who are equally divine. The Athanasian creed is not a biblical quotation. But, whatever else we find in the New Testament, we also find the Father distinguished from the Son, who is accorded equality with the Father. And we do find the Spirit distinguished from both Father and Son and referred to in passages where Father, Son and Spirit are both distinguished and brought together (cf. Mt 28:19; 2 Cor 13:14; Acts 2:33; 1 Peter 1:2). Here I agree with Alasdair Heron. As he puts it:

It must be admitted that the teachings of, say, the fourth and fifth centuries concerning the Father, Son and Spirit, cannot simply be read off the pages of the Bible. Yet . . . this does not mean that the development can properly be dismissed with an air of patronising superiority as 'unbiblical'. The trinitarian problem is posed by the New Testament itself, and the attempts of the fathers to rearticulate in debate with the questions arising in their day the profoundest implications of its witness must be measured by their adequacy to that purpose and not merely by the shallowness of a proof-text comparison with biblical statements (Heron 1983, p. 171).

Perhaps the word to emphasize here is 'problem'. Since we can deny that God is an explanation in the familiar sense, we can deny that the Trinity is an explanation. But nor is it something which pops into history during the fourth century like an extra-terrestrial. Insofar as this is so, therefore, the doctrine can hardly be anything other than significant for the Christian.

God and love

If the doctrines of the Incarnation and Trinity are true, then we are entitled to speak about God in a way which we cannot do apart from citing the doctrines. For with them we have grounds for affirming that God, as St John says, is Love (1 Jn 4:8). This is because the doctrines teach that God from eternity is no solitary individual. On the contrary, so they say, though single and undivided (though God, in short) God is related to another of equal status, an other from whom nothing that belongs to God by nature is withheld. God, we may say, has found himself in an equal, and his life from eternity is the sharing with an equal of what he is.

Some would reject this way of talking by means of the following arguments:

(1) God cannot love unless he somehow goes out of himself to establish a

relationship with human beings. So it is false that God is loving considered in himself, considered as what he is in himself from eternity.

(2) God cannot love unless he suffers. In their classical forms, however, the doctrines of the Incarnation and the Trinity deny that God suffers since they are tied to the view that God is impassible. Therefore, they do not license us to say that God is loving.

(3) Even if we knew nothing of the Incarnation and the Trinity it would still be justifiable to assert that God is loving. This is because we have solid independent grounds for that conclusion.

Yet none of these arguments is convincing.

(1) If God's ability to love depends on the existence of people, then what God is (the divine nature) depends for its existence on the existence of people. But if God is the Creator, the reverse is true. There being people will depend on there being what God is. Furthermore, since people have not always existed it follows that if God's ability to love depends on the existence of people then it was once true that God could not love (or did not love) and it subsequently became true that he could love (or did love). But this is incompatible with the fact that God is unchanging, for this means that there is nothing God could be but is not.

(2) Difficulties with (2) have already been discussed in Chapter 6. As I argued there, suffering is a limitation which we can refuse to ascribe to God, and there is no reason to suppose that love and suffering are inevitably bound up with each other. Nor need we ascribe suffering to God since that would make him passive, which, as Creator, he cannot be.

(3) Do we have solid grounds apart from the doctrines of the Incarnation and the Trinity for speaking of God as loving? Arguably not. We do have grounds for saying that God exists. But love presupposes at least two who love, and what independent reason (what reason apart from the truth of Christianity) is there for believing that God is two? Reason, indeed, would only seem to suggest that God is one, meaning that divinity is not something subject to multiplication. In reply to this some will say that God must be loving since he is good and since he has freely chosen to create. But something can be good without being loving, and to say that God has chosen to create is to say that God has created and that nothing compelled him to do so. Whether he loves his creation is another matter. The likely reply to this is that God must love since he is a person. But, for reasons which I have already given, we can challenge the formula 'God is a person'. And if we think of love, as we normally do, as something which two human beings can have for each other, there is positive reason for denying that God can love where the object of his love is supposed to be his creation. This is because love between human beings normally presupposes a relationship of equality between them,

and what is only created is not equal to God. A man may love his wife, but he cannot, in the same sense, love his overcoat. By the same token, so we might suggest, God cannot love his creation. If he is to love in anything like the sense in which a man can love a woman, the object of his love will need to be divine.

A large part of love is . . . a recognition of the other's existence as valid as one's own, a recognition that the other does not exist simply in function of you, but is *there* equally. . . . (So) it is evident that whatever relationship there may be between God and creatures it cannot be one of love. The relationship here is just as unequal as it is possible to be. There may be many other relationships; we can think of God as caring for his creatures and doing good for them, beginning with the primal good of bringing them into existence and sustaining them in existence. We can think of God as source of all the value that is in them. We can think of God rewarding them or ignoring their offences. We can think of him on the model of a kindly caring master instead of a frightening despotic master, but what we cannot do is think of him as giving himself in love to a creature (McCabe 1980, pp. 462f.).

This, of course, is putting things rather strongly, and the Christian may wish to qualify it by noting, for example, that according to the New Testament Christ, who is divine, loves his disciples as the Father has loved him. One might also add that in Christian thinking there is a long-standing tradition according to which people are to share in the life of God (cf. 2 Peter 1:4), from which one might infer that love between God and creatures is still possible. But this does not dispose of the main point now being made. It does not belong to our natural knowledge of God that God should be in love with a creature. From the philosophical point of view, the doctrine that God loves is a surprising one. But it is not surprising in terms of the doctrines on the Incarnation and the Trinity.

God and human beings

But this might now suggest that God and creatures are bound to be infinitely distant from each other, which brings me to my final point. For, in spite of what I have just said, if Christ was both truly human and truly God it follows that humanity is actually capable of the most intimate union with what is divine. Nobody seriously supposes that human beings are very glamorous when looked at outside the perspective of something like Christianity. People are all too evidently weak, fallible, capricious, and mortal. Not surprisingly, therefore, men and women have despaired when thinking about themselves and their future. But if Christ can be truly God and truly man, people also have cause to hope for themselves. For they can now say that the possibilities for humanity are greater than one might think when looking at people apart from the doctrine of the Incarnation. If God can be united to man as the doctrine of the Incarnation states that he was, then it cannot be impossible for man to be united to God. This, of course, is one of the reasons why Christians have insisted that Christianity is good news. On the surface, so they have said, the prospects for humanity look bleak. But great possibilities must be open to what is human if it was true that a man was God. And the same applies if the man in question invited others to enter into a relationship of fellowship with him. For if that man was truly God, then it follows that God has quite literally invited people into a relationship of fellowship with himself. In this sense, as Karl Rahner puts it, 'we see that Christology is at once beginning and end of anthropology, and that for all eternity such an anthropology is really theo-logy' (Rahner 1961, p. 185). The doctrine of the Incarnation may seem mysterious, but to take it seriously is certainly to be committed to entailments. And one of these is that man and God are able to be united whatever the appearances to the contrary. And to this one can add yet a further point. This is that, in spite of what I said above, if the doctrine of the Incarnation is true, then we are indeed licensed to say that God loves creatures, even if we cannot comprehend what exactly that involves. For we can certainly say that Christ loved other people. The evidence for this is not a matter of serious dispute even among those whose conclusions about our ability to discover the 'historical Jesus' are sceptical. This evidence, however, has an implication if taken with the doctrine of the Incarnation. We may be puzzled at the assertion that God has an object of love outside himself, but if Christ was God and if Christ loved people then it follows automatically that God loved people. In other words, though we may think of God as of something detached and remote, though we may think of him as in no way able to relate to human beings, we are entitled to balance such thoughts by other ones if the doctrine of the Incarnation is true. In terms of this doctrine, God is as near to people as Christ was to those who killed him. And the face of the crucified Christ is nothing less than the face of God.

CONCLUSION

So the upshot would seem to be not just that the Christian can defend himself in the light of a charge of contradiction. He can appeal to what is central in his Christian position in order to indicate that what he finds there is something with significance even if it is also something as mysterious as God himself. It is not just a matter of non-contradictory formulae. It is a matter, for example, of being able to say that God is love, that human nature is full of possibility, and that God loves not just God but people as well. In terms of the doctrine of the Incarnation and in terms of the doctrine of the Trinity one can say these things and mean them quite literally, and if that does not entail that the doctrines are significant, then it is hard to know what would. This is not to say that they are not significant for other reasons. But it is to say that if they are true they are significant for these reasons at least.

QUESTIONS FOR DISCUSSION

1 What is contradiction? How can one detect it? Is it the same as incoherence?
2 If I cannot prove that a proposition is not contradictory, does it follow that the proposition is subject to rational doubt?
3 'An argument with true premises and a heretical conclusion may be logically valid.' Discuss.
4 'Whenever a logical form is shown to be invalid by a theological counter-example, we could if we were clever enough construct a non-theological counter-example' (Geach, *Logic Matters*, p. 300). Discuss.
5 If Christian doctrines are true, does it follow that we must be able to make sense of them?
6 Is Christian theism more mysterious than theism?
7 Are the following statements true? (Cf. Aquinas, *Summa Theologiae* IIIa, 16)
    (a) God is a man.
    (b) A man is God.
    (c) The Son of God was made a man.
    (d) A man was made the Son of God.
    (e) Christ is a creature.
    (f) Christ began to be.
    (g) Christ existed always.
    (h) Christ, as man, is a creature.
    (i) Christ, as man, is God.
    (j) Christ, as man, is an independent subject or person.
8 Did Nicaea and Chalcedon offer a legitimate development of New Testament teaching? Does the doctrine of the Trinity (e.g. as in the Athanasian creed) offer such a development?
9 Can we state the doctrines of the Incarnation and the Trinity in new ways? If so, how?
10 Does belief in the Incarnation and the Trinity contradict what we can rightly believe about God by reason alone? Does it add to it significantly?

FURTHER READING

Readers who wish to follow up issues touched on in the preceding chapter might benefit from texts on the history of the development of the doctrines of the Incarnation and Trinity. Two indispensable and standard works are J. N. D. Kelly, *Early Christian Doctrines* (5th ed., London, 1977) and *Early Christian Creeds* (3rd ed., London, 1972). For a more philosophical discussion of the development of the doctrine of the Incarnation, see Christopher Stead, *Divine Substance* (Oxford, 1977). Another major text detailing the development of early Christology is Aloys Grillmeier, SJ, *Christ in Christian Tradition*, vol. I (2nd ed., London/Oxford, 1975). For a general account of Christian thinking about God in the early centuries, see also G. L. Prestige, *God in Patristic Thought* (London, 1936). For a brief and conservative exposition of the doctrine of the Trinity, together with a discussion of its biblical roots, see E. Calvin Beisner, *God in Three Persons* (Wheaton, Ill., 1984).

With respect to the question of contradiction in general, perhaps the best place to begin is with a good account of logical thinking on the subject. Useful material can be found in William Kneale and Martha Kneale, *The Development of Logic* (Oxford, 1962), which is a thoroughly admirable book. For a quick introduction to the topic of consistency, see P. T. Geach, *Reason and Argument* (Oxford, 1976), ch. 2. For a good beginner's guide to Gödel, see Ernest Nagel and James R. Newman, *Gödel's Proof* (London, 1959).

For a brief review of theories concerning the divinity and humanity of Christ one can recommend David F. Wells, *The Person of Christ* (London, 1984). Classical treatises on the Incarnation written by theologians who are also philosophers include St Anselm, *De Incarnatione Verbi*, and Thomas Aquinas, *Summa Theologiae* IIIa, 1–26. In talking about the person of Christ some have developed a theory (known as the kenotic theory) according to which the divine Word ceased to be God for the duration of the Incarnation and then became God again. I have said nothing of this view since it seems to me simply unworthy of discussion, except, perhaps, as a joke. But some who have tried to defend the consistency of the doctrine of the Incarnation have taken it seriously. See, for example, David Brown, *The Divine Trinity* (London, 1985).

For a discussion of different approaches to the doctrine of the Trinity, the following can all be recommended: Leonard Hodgson, *The Doctrine of the Trinity* (London, 1943); E. J. Fortman, *The Triune God* (London, 1972); John Mackey, *The Christian Experience of God as Trinity* (London, 1983); John J. O'Donnell, SJ, *Trinity and Temporality* (Oxford, 1983); C. Welch, *The Trinity in Contemporary Theology* (London, 1953). The volume by O'Donnell pays considerable attention to the Trinitarian views of Jürgen Moltmann. These are now conveniently found in *The Trinity and the Kingdom of God* (London, 1981). For two succinct expositions and discussions of the doctrine of the Trinity written by modern theologians, see Walter Kasper, *The God of Jesus Christ* (London, 1984) and Karl Rahner, *The Trinity* (London, 1970).

Recent philosophical discussions of the doctrine of the Incarnation and the doctrine of the Trinity are not very plentiful. But the following all contain useful and/or relevant material: David Brown, *The Divine Trinity* (London, 1985); Michael Durrant, *Theology and Intelligibility* (London, 1973), chs 2–5; P. T. Geach, 'Nominalism' in *Logic Matters* (Oxford, 1972); P. T. Geach, *The Virtues* (Cambridge, 1977), ch. 4; G. E. Hughes, 'The Doctrine of the Trinity', *Sophia* II (1963); H. D. Lewis, *Jesus in the Faith of Christians* (London, 1981); Herbert McCabe, OP, 'God: II – Freedom', *New Blackfriars* 61 (1980); Gareth Moore, OP, 'Incarnation and Image of God', *New Blackfriars* 64 (1983); H. P. Owen, *Christian Theism* (Edinburgh, 1984), chs 2 and 3; David Wiggins, *Sameness and Substance* (Oxford, 1980), ch. 1; C. J. F. Williams, 'A Programme for Christology', *Religious Studies* 3 (1968).

11
God and Prayer

We have now considered whether or not it is reasonable to believe in God. We have also considered what God is or is not, and how we may respond to beliefs about him which are unique to Christianity. Yet much of what I have said may seem far too theoretical or academic. Suppose that there is a God. Suppose that what Christians typically say about him is true. What follows from this? Is there anything one can do about it? Can belief in God make any difference to one's conduct?

Christians, of course, have not been short of answers to these questions. But one response has been especially popular or influential and it is to this that I want to turn by way of rounding things off. When asked what should be done in the light of belief in God, Christians from the beginning have said that one should *pray*. 'Rejoice always, pray constantly, give thanks in all circumstances; for this is the will of God in Christ Jesus for you' (1 Thess 5:16–18). Let us therefore conclude by reflecting on the practice of prayer. Should one engage in it? If so, why? And what would one be doing if one did?

'PRAYER' AND 'PETITION'

An initial problem is one of terminology, for 'prayer' is hard to define and the word seems to mean different things to different people. For the moment, however, we can ignore this difficulty since one thing, at any rate, is clear enough. This is that a good case can be made for thinking of prayer chiefly in terms of petition. When the gospels report that Jesus taught about prayer they tell us that he spoke about people making requests (cf. Lk 11:1–13; Lk 18:1–14). The Lord's Prayer, supposedly a model for Christian prayer, is quite simply a string of petitions (cf. Mt 6:9–13; Lk 11:1–4), and for many centuries 'prayer' and 'petition' were taken to be equivalent (cf. Dupuy 1982, pp. 832f.; cf. also Tugwell 1984, chs 9–11). According to a classic definition of St John Damascene (*c.* 675–*c.* 749), 'Prayer is a request to God for those things that are fitting' (*De Fide Orthodoxa*, Book 3, ch. 24). Not surprisingly, therefore, when Aquinas turns to the topic of prayer in the *Summa Theologiae* it is petition that he is talking about. 'It is in this sense', he writes, 'that we are speaking of prayer now as a kind of entreaty or request. It is, as Augustine says, "a kind of request"; or in Damascene's words "a request to God for things that are fitting" ' (*Summa Theologiae* IIa IIae, 83, 1). So let us at this point focus our concern more sharply. What can we make of petitionary prayer?

Problems with petitionary prayer

For some people the only honest answer to this question is 'Very little'. Why? Because, so it has been suggested, there is something misguided in the whole idea of asking for things from God. A number of different and sometimes related arguments have been given for this conclusion. Basically, however, they reduce to seven.

(1) The first is simply the objection of the atheist or agnostic. As Karl Rahner has said, 'the question of God and the question of prayer are not properly two questions that must be answered consecutively, but *one* question' (Rahner 1975, p. 52). In other words, prayer derives its sense from the belief that God is real. But what if he is not? Or what if his existence is more doubtful than otherwise? Then it would seem that the practice of petitionary prayer, at any rate, is rather futile. How can one sensibly ask for things from a non-existent God?

(2) But some would say that petitionary prayer is a questionable matter even though God does exist. This brings us to the second argument according to which God is not the sort of thing it is proper to address by means of petition. Here again we can quote from Rahner who alludes to the present argument in the following way.

There are certainly many people today who find prayer difficult even though they are prepared to confess the unnameable, nameless God as the one ground of all, as the all-permeating mystery. They are under the impression that because this nameless God is an as it were faceless and ineffable mystery he cannot be addressed. They think, more or less explicitly and reflexively, that he who bears and embraces all should not be turned by prayer into an 'object' of thought and speech, addressed and separated from all he bears.

Because he can be correctly thought of only when he is strictly understood as the all-overwhelming and incomprehensible mystery, these people think one cannot name him without turning him into an idol. They think they may not reach out in prayer to one who has no name, who as mystery cannot be 'clearly' expressed. They prefer to keep silent with averted face before this God and resignedly make for those regions of existence in which lie before one's mind and heart the individual surveyable realities with which one can really deal knowing what one is about and what is to be expected (Rahner 1975, pp. 52f.).

In other words, according to argument (2) the mystery and otherness of God ought to leave us reluctant to ask him for things. We can ask for things from people around us, but God is not like these. And to address him as if he were is to indulge in idolatry.

(3) The third argument also proceeds from the nature of God. For is it not true that God is unchanging or immutable? On the assumption that he is, some have concluded that nothing of significance can be gained by petitionary prayer. If God's will is unchangeable, so the argument goes, then the future is already decided. It is decided by the eternal decree of an immutable God. In that case, however, why bother to pray? In the words of an objection cited by Aquinas: 'Prayer is a way in which we bring someone round to our own view, so that he will do what we ask him to do. But God's mind is unchanging and immovable. . . . So again it seems inappropriate to pray to God' (*Summa Theologiae* IIa IIae, 83, 2 obj. 2).

(4) The fourth argument derives from the belief that God is omniscient and good. The idea here is that if God is both these things then we do not need to tell him what we need. For will he not know about our needs even before we express them? And will he not be moved in his goodness to deal with them without our asking him to do so? The general problem here is stated as follows by Origen (*c.* 185–254):

God knows all things before they come into being and there is nothing that becomes known to him from the fact of its beginning for the first time when it begins, as though it were not previously known. What need then is there to send up prayer to him who knows what we need even before we pray? For the heavenly Father knoweth what things we have need of before we ask him (Matt. 6.8). And it is fitting that he, being Father and Maker of all, who loves all the things that are, and abhors nothing which he has made (Wisd. 11.24), should order in safety all that has to do with each one, even without prayer, like a father provides for his little children, and does not wait for them to ask, either because they are quite unable to ask, or because through ignorance they often want to receive the opposite of what is of use and help to them. And we men fall short of God more than those who are quite children fall short of the mind of those who begot them (*Treatise on Prayer*, p. 94).

(5) According to the fifth argument, petitionary prayer is misguided since it proceeds from a failure to acknowledge that it is addressed to God as Creator. On this view, someone who believes in the value of petitionary prayer must somehow suppose that prayer can force or coerce God in some way. But this, so the argument continues, is false. Considered as Creator, God is not like something in the world which we can turn to and manipulate. He cannot be pushed around by people. So if we think of petitionary prayer as a way of getting things done, then we are in error. As some would put it, we are subscribing to a belief in magic, not to belief in God. Thus, for example, according to Hubert Richards, petitionary prayer (which Richards often calls 'intercessory prayer'), 'taken literally'

presupposes a God who is able to provide magically what we are unable to provide for ourselves. . . . All intercessory prayer is, at one level, an attempt to put pressure on God. It assumes that, given a formula which is liturgically or psychologically appropriate, God can be bribed or blackmailed, manoeuvred or manipulated, coaxed, cajoled or controlled. And it is a God of this kind that many people find they can no longer accept. The God they wish to worship must be more worthwhile than that. If intercessory prayer causes difficulty to many in today's world, it is because the God it presupposes is not God-like enough (Richards 1980, pp. 72f.).

(6) The sixth line of argument against petitionary prayer can be illustrated by citing some objections presented by H. P. Owen in chapter 4 of his book *Christian Theism* (Edinburgh, 1984). Basically, Owen's point is that while it is right to offer petition to God, only certain sorts of petition should be made. Owen begins by insisting that prayer cannot be a matter of us informing God about things or of us changing God's will or mind. On the other hand, says Owen, prayer for material gifts is enjoined by the New Testament and by subsequent Christian tradition. We must therefore, Owen concludes, think of petitionary prayer as a way of lining ourselves up with God's will, whatever that may be. Some would reply that prayer can be more than this since we can in prayer ask God for specific things like the welfare of others, events in the world around us, or events depending on the volition of other people. But Owen rejects this reply. 'The difficulty', he says, 'is to see what difference the prayer can make' (p. 78). If the welfare of others is spiritual, says Owen, God always wills this anyway. 'I therefore suggest that we interpret such intercessions as ways in which we identify ourselves with God's will for other people and offer ourselves, where this is possible, as means through which his will can operate' (p. 79). With respect to prayers for events in the world or events which depend on the will of others, Owen has this to say. First, he denies that God can 'adjust uniform and necessitated sequences in any significant way to the vast multiplicity of persons and the even vaster multiplicity of their requests' (p. 79). Second, he denies that we can 'expect God to violate another person's freedom or suddenly change that person's disposition in order that the person should act according to our requests' (p. 80). Owen's verdict, therefore, is that 'we ought to be very reluctant to pray for the occurrence or non-occurrence of particular events' (p. 80).

(7) The final main argument against petitionary prayer is as simple as can be. It holds that petitionary prayer is questionable or not worth believing in because, as a plain matter of fact, people do not always get what they ask for in prayer. We are urged to persevere in prayer and we are assured that our prayers will be answered. As C. S. Lewis puts it: 'The New Testament contains embarrassing promises that what we pray for with faith we shall receive. . . . Whatever we ask for, believing that we'll get it, we'll get' (Lewis 1964, p. 60). But, as Lewis goes on to say:

Every war, every famine or plague, almost every death-bed is the monument to a petition that was not granted. At this very moment thousands of people in this one island are facing as a *fait accompli*, the very thing against which they have prayed night and day, pouring out their whole soul, and, as they have thought, in faith. They have sought and not found. They have knocked and it has not been opened. 'That which they greatly feared has come upon them' (Lewis, p. 61).

And in the light of such facts many have simply concluded that petitionary prayer is vain. What is the point of praying when experience suggests that our prayers make no difference?

Comments on these arguments

But do these arguments oblige us to conclude that it is wrong to believe in petitionary prayer? To begin on a positive note, it seems to me that the following points can be made in their defence.

(1) If there is no God able to answer prayer, then petitionary prayer does seem to be open to question. In this sense, argument (1) is correct. Some would deny this on the ground that one can still engage in petitionary prayer even though one does not think of it as a matter of asking God to bring things about. According, for example, to Hubert Richards, the practice of petitionary prayer is intrinsically valuable for its effects on those who pray. 'Praying', says Richards, 'can relieve the tension of the person who prays' (Richards 1980, p. 62). It can also, he adds, be a practice in which one changes one's attitudes and behaviour. 'The prayer that one's enemies be forgiven is answered in the very act of saying such a prayer. . . . The very act of praying is its own answer' (pp. 64f.). For Richards, we may say, prayer is very much a form of self-therapy. It is also a way of acknowledging what we should be doing and how things stand with us. And others have taken much the same sort of view. In *Religion within the Limits of Reason Alone*, Kant suggests that prayer is a useful means of stirring ourselves up to a proper disposition with respect to moral goodness. In *Religion and the Scientific Outlook* (London, 1959), T. R. Miles describes it as a way of determining and expressing one's attitude to events. ' "Thy will be done" ', says Miles, 'is not a request at all. In using these words (and similar ones) we are committing and dedicating ourselves, not trying to persuade an unknown agency to influence the course of nature' (p. 186). But, though there is doubtless truth in all of this, it is also somewhat dubious. Prayer might indeed be such that considered on its own it is truly something desirable. And one might well deny that it involves persuasion and the influence of 'unknown agency'. Perhaps we can make the point by saying that there can be an 'internal' connection between prayer and the thing prayed for. As D. Z. Phillips puts it:

If a person asks that his devotional life be deepened, the prayer is not external to the way in which such deepening comes about.... Or again, a man may ask for God's help in overcoming his envy.... One cannot distinguish here between the asking for and the receiving, as one can between the asking for, and the receiving of, a loan. To ask God for something in the above examples is already to have begun receiving (Phillips 1965, p. 125).

Yet this does not mean that the practice of petitionary prayer can be sensibly retained without any belief that God is able to bring about something for which he is asked. For the whole notion of petition presupposes one who is asked and who is able to provide what he is asked for. In other words, if God does not exist as something distinct from people and their petitions, and if he is not there as able to grant what the petitions request, then why engage in prayer which takes the form of petition? Why suppose that one should behave as though one were asking God for something? Some will reply that though one may seem to be making a petition the appearance can be misleading while the apparent petition can still be significant. And this can be true. One can, for example, mutter 'Help!' under one's breath without there being any oddity in doing so and without any belief that there is someone to help and assist one. But it is surely implausible to suppose that this is the sort of thing that is happening when people address petitions to God. According to Miles, we can say things like 'Thy will be done' without making a request. But that suggestion involves a gross violation of English usage. For 'Thy will be done' just *is* a request. And if we do not believe that we should make such requests, if we do not believe that we can literally ask for things from God, then it would presumably be best simply to avoid saying things like 'Thy will be done'. And in this sense, at any rate, argument (1) is right. If there is no God to hear our prayers, then the practice of offering them is open to question. They may be of some value psychologically or morally, but they can hardly be what they appear to be. Nor can they be what most of those who offer them clearly suppose that they are – viz. requests offered to a God who really exists.

(2) A number of points can be made in defence of argument (2), but the important thing to note is that the argument is surely right to suggest that in the case of God we are dealing with something which is bound to be mysterious to us. I have emphasized this point at several stages in this book and all that I have said about it seems to me relevant again here. And the point, of course, is one that has been firmly taken up by various notable Christian authors. Thus it is that, for example, the author of *The Cloud of Unknowing* can write:

But now you put to me a question and say: 'How might I think of him in himself, and what is he?' And to this I can only answer thus: 'I have no idea'.... For a man may, by grace, have the fullness of knowledge of all other creatures and their works, yes, and of the works of God's own self, and he is well able to reflect on them. But no man can think of God himself (ch. 6).

This is not to say that we have no knowledge of God, *period*. But the author of the *Cloud*, following a clear biblical tradition and echoing as well as anticipating numerous Christian writers, is stressing the hiddenness of God and the fact that 'we cannot in this life know God as he is in himself, though we can know his works' (Tugwell 1984, p. 173). And, insofar as argument (2) can be read as agreeing with this emphasis, then the argument is of value. Rahner makes the point as follows:

Prayer can be itself only when it is understood as the last moment of speech before the silence, as the act of self-disposal just before the incomprehensibility of God disposes of one, as the reflexion immediately preceding the act of letting oneself fall, after the last of one's own efforts and full of trust, into the infinite Whole which reflexion can never grasp (Rahner 1975, p. 53).

And to all of this we can, perhaps, add a subsidiary point. For someone who is impressed by argument (2) may simply be struck by the differences there must be between talking to God and talking to other people, while a case can be made for holding that there must indeed be differences here. For one thing, if we assume that God is omniscient there can be no question of us informing him of anything by what we say or of us trying to get him to understand something. But in talking to other people we are quite commonly doing just these very things. Then again, when we address someone we direct our speech to some particular person in some particular place. Yet if God is omnipresent he is not to be simply located as here and not there. For reasons such as these one must surely say that talking to God or addressing him cannot be straightforwardly assimilated to talking to another as we commonly understand it. And, insofar as argument (2) is making that point, then we can again accept it.

(3) We can also, I think, see something worth accepting in argument (3). As we have seen, there are those who would deny that God is changeless. But, as we have also seen, we have good reason to reject this verdict. If God is the Creator, then he must indeed be changeless. And this would seem to mean that we cannot think of petitionary prayer as something that alters God in any way. It would also seem to mean that there must be a sense in which all that will happen is already decided. If God does not change, his will cannot be subject to alteration. There can be no sense in the notion of God first willing this and then changing his mind in order to pursue a different policy. If God does not change, his will cannot be subject to alteration and he wills what he does changelessly and from eternity. And in that case it would seem that whatever is taken as an answer to prayer is something willed by God changelessly and from eternity. Some would reply that this cannot be true since it would undermine the point of asking for things from God. As one writer puts it:

Not only would all events in the world be inevitable and therefore not the sort of things which could meaningfully be objects of petition, but God would not be the sort of being to whom petitions could meaningfully be addressed. If his intentions are immutably fixed from all eternity, he would not be able to *react* to what we do or feel, nor to the petitions we address to him. . . . We . . . have to presuppose that God is a personal agent who is capable of *real* responses to contingent events and to the free acts which human beings perform, as well as to the requests which they address to him (Brümmer 1984, pp. 35ff.).

But this is a line of argument which we are entitled to reject. For one thing, it seems to suppose that if God from eternity wills something created, then he does so of necessity and not by will. More importantly, however, there can be no question of God reacting or responding if that is taken to mean that he undergoes some change in himself. To suppose otherwise would be to picture God as something in the nature of a Zeus or an Apollo, as some kind of observer of the universe jogging along, albeit invisibly, through time and changes. And this, as I have argued, is something we ought not to do. In this sense we can deny that God reacts or responds and we can continue to insist that his will is unchanging. A likely objection to this is that it cannot be true since God must adjust himself to the free actions of people as they occur. And, in the light of this criticism it might be added that what is to come cannot be in any sense decided. If people are free, then, so it may be suggested, the future will be determined by what people freely do. And this, of course, seems true enough. If people are free, then not everything that happens does so because in some absolute sense it must. In this sense, so we may agree, the future is open and not determined. Yet, as I argued in Chapter 8, whatever we mean by 'freedom' we ought not to suppose that the free choice of creatures is something uncreated. My free actions must be caused by God as well as by me, and they are only caused by me because they are caused by God. And for this reason we can deny that the future is, as one might put it, absolutely open. If people are free, then the future is open since all that will come to pass need not be determined by the non-voluntary behaviour of things within the universe acting by virtue of natural necessity. But the future cannot be open if that means that it is not something owing all its reality to the creative will of God. And if that will is changeless, then the future must be contained in it. This is not to say that the future is somehow present as, for example, a foetus is present in the womb of a pregnant woman. Since the future is future, not present, one may simply deny that it exists. But insofar as anything is contained in God's will, then so is the future. In this sense, so one can argue, the future is already decided. That, perhaps, is not the best way of putting things for it could be taken to suggest that the future is something which is solidly determined or that everything that will happen must happen. And I do not wish to imply that. The theist is not committed to fatalism. But he is, I think, committed to holding that the whole history of creation is changelessly willed by God. This, of course, is part of the reason why Christians have appealed to the notion of predestination according to which God, as cause of his creation, must also decide the end of his rational creatures and must do so from eternity and with no threat of interference. To paraphrase St Augustine: 'At every stage it is God who makes the first move. And, in the last analysis, the whole mysterious and seemingly precarious process is rooted in the sheer determination of God to save those whom he wants to save, for no other reason than that he wants to save them' (Tugwell 1984, p. 66).

(4) So argument (3) is on to something. And the same goes for arguments (4) to (7). If God is omniscient, then it is surely perfectly true that our needs are known to him without our having to tell him about them. Any such telling would, in fact, itself proceed from him. Then again, how can we suppose that God is something which people can in any way manipulate or control? Some, indeed, have spoken as if people are able to induce some change in God analogous to the changes we induce in each other and on things within the universe. As we have seen, some would say that God is passive and that he is acted on or modified from outside (so to speak) by what people do. But we can reject this view in the light of the doctrine of creation. God, we may say, cannot be acted on. And, since it is God who makes creatures to be, the actions of creatures must in some sense be God's act. Insofar as argument (5) is taken as reminding us of this, then it is perfectly correct. Something has gone badly wrong if prayer is conceived as a matter of putting pressure on God. And something has also gone wrong if prayer is taken as an automatic or guaranteed way of ensuring what it asks for. For it is indeed hard to deny that, as argument (7) asserts, people have not always obtained exactly what they have asked for in prayer. Some would say that this is because the people in question have not really been praying – that their faith was not strong enough, for example, or that they did not pray hard enough. But, though there may be something in this response, the basic point remains. People may have prayed without conviction, but many have prayed as firm believers and with great fervour. This is C. S. Lewis's point and it would be silly to deny it. And it would be silly to deny that what such people have asked for has not always been granted. Nor need we suppose that everything people ask for *could* be granted. As Hubert Richards puts it, making a familiar observation:

It stands to reason that the farmer's praying for rain will clash with the prayer for fine weather arising from the Mothers' Union. It is impossible for both prayers to be granted. If the contestants in a race are all praying to win, only the prayer of one can be answered; those are the rules of the game. We live in a world where the principle of contradiction is in operation, that is to say, where mutually exclusive things unfortunately exclude each other. Many of the things people pray for cannot be realized simply because they are incompatible with the things other people are praying and working for (Richards 1980, p. 61).

Objections to the arguments

But is all of this to say that the practice of petitionary prayer is misguided? At this point we can return to the arguments against it in a more critical fashion.

(1) The first of them need not long detain us. The practice of petitionary prayer would indeed be open to challenge if there were no God, but we have reason to believe that God does exist and we do not need to give way on petitionary prayer in the light of agnosticism or atheism. And to this point we can add another – viz. that in the light of belief in God we can from the outset entertain the supposition that God can bring about what he is asked for in prayer. Here I refer the reader back to the earlier discussion of omnipotence (Chapter 7). It is true, as Richards says, that God may not be able to bring about everything which he is asked to bring about. But if what is asked for is something that could be created, then God can bring it about. In this sense the way is open for a more positive approach to the value of petitionary prayer. *A priori*, God can bring about what he is asked to bring about.

(2) But should he be asked at all? Not if argument (2) is accepted without criticism. But it need not, I think, be accepted in this way. For though we seem bound to acknowledge the mystery of God, and though there are differences between addressing God and addressing people, truths about God and people give one reason for supposing that asking for things from God is something which it is appropriate to do. In this connection, two points in particular call for notice.

(a) God may be mysterious and different from human beings, but he can still, as I have suggested, be described as personal. For we can think of God by analogy with human intention or intelligent agency, we can speak of God acting by will, not coercion, and we can ascribe knowledge to God. In the light of Christian theism, we can also speak of God as loving, and, insofar as we ascribe authority to the teaching of Christ as recorded in the Gospels, we are actually instructed to ask God for things. In that case, however, it seems appropriate to address God as personal, and since, in principle, God can bring about what he is asked to bring about, it also seems appropriate to ask him to bring things about. In other words, given that God is personal, given that the course of creation derives from his will, and given that Christians are instructed to ask for things from God, it would seem natural to turn to God as one who is able to bring about what one desires.

(b) We cannot view prayer as inaugurating a change in God, but it can still be important because of its connection with changes in us. For the practice of petitionary prayer is evidently one of the obvious ways we have of acknowledging that God is indeed the Creator and of making this acknowledgement more than something purely notional. 'At the most basic level, prayer of petition expresses our readiness to acknowledge that we stand before the face of God who searches out the heart of man; and that, on the other hand, God is very much at large in this world of ours' (Tugwell 1974, Vol. 2, p. 76). Someone may vaguely concede that everything comes from God, but in praying for things he puts this concession to work. And it is surely important that people should do this if God truly exists and if everything truly comes from him. For the result would be a fitting response to the way things are. Or, as Aquinas puts it, 'man pays God reverence in his prayer, in as much as he subjects himself to God and confesses, by praying, that he is in need of God as the source of all his good' (*Summa Theologiae* IIa IIae, 83, 3). In other words, if we are to respond to God at all, the practice of petitionary prayer is a natural way of setting about the job. For it reflects the recognition that creation is indeed God's work and it does so by using the mind. The response to things which most befits people is evidently a response which engages what they are by nature. Since people are rational creatures, therefore, it seems appropriate that we should respond to God as such. And petitionary prayer is evidently a way of doing this since it actually involves turning the mind to God and acknowledging him as Creator. In addition, of course, it can also be an expression of charity, as Aquinas goes on to observe repeating an ancient but obvious point. In his terminology: 'We are meant to desire good things not only for ourselves, but also for other people. This is part of what it means to love our neighbours. . . . Therefore, charity requires that we should pray for other people' (*Summa Theologiae* IIa IIae, 83, 7). If it is good that we should be concerned for others, and if it is true that the course of creation is God's effect, then it matters that we should ask him for the good of others. By doing so we would be actively charitable, we would be acknowledging how we stand in relation to the Creator, and we would be putting ourselves in the way of getting from God an answer to our requests.

(3) At this point, however, an objector might reply that God cannot answer requests if he is truly changeless. This brings us back to argument (3). In spite of its strengths, however, this argument also misses something of importance.

If God is changeless, then his creation is what he wills it to be from eternity, and prayer cannot be thought of as modifying the will of God. Since what we do is part of creation, our prayer will itself be something that springs from this will. Thus far argument (3) is correct, and we encounter yet another difference between God and human beings. When Bill asks Ben for an ice-cream, he may induce in Ben a new thought ('Why not give Bill an ice-cream!'). And the giving of the ice-cream to Bill may depend on the occurrence of this thought in Ben. But we cannot suppose that anything given by God comes about as a result of a process like this. If I get an ice-cream from God (and any ice-cream I get will, in the last analysis, be from God), then God from eternity has willed me to have it, and he has not been nudged into letting me have it by anything that I do or by anything that anyone else does.

But this does not mean that I would have been wrong to ask him for it. For if we ask God for something which we subsequently receive, if we ask for such and such to happen and if it happens, we are entitled to conclude that God has given us what we want and that our request has been met. For if God is the Creator, then anything that happens in the wake of our requests must be brought about by him. And if it is what we have asked for, then the conclusion must simply be that he has given us what we asked for. In other words, though God is changeless, prayers can be answered. They would be answered if they are offered and if what they ask for comes to pass.

And to this point we can add another. This is that prayers can also be necessary (i.e. needed), not in the sense that they make God do anything (that they act on him to force his action), but in the sense that if what they ask for comes to pass, then what comes to pass is what is asked for and is what is only truly described as such. In other words, prayers can be necessary since we can speak of what follows them as an answer to them only because they are offered. You may decide to give me money, and you may decide to give me the money whether I ask for it or not. Suppose I do not ask. What you then do is what you would have done had I asked. But you will not be doing something in accordance with my request, and you could not be said to be giving me what I ask for. By the same token, though God from eternity may have decreed to bring something about, the coming to pass of the thing will not be an answer to any request unless the request for it is made. In this sense, so we may say, prayer is needed before it can be answered, and it will be needed even though the will of God is not something open to modification by anything outside itself. As Aquinas once again observes:

We can shed light on the problem by realizing that divine providence not only arranges what results there are to be; it also arranges the causes that are to produce these results and the whole pattern of cause and effect. Amongst other causes, some things are brought about by human acts. So men have to perform certain acts, not with a view of changing God's purpose by what they do, but in order to bring about certain effects by what they do, in accordance with the pattern of causality laid down by God. The same applies also to natural causes. And the same thing must also be said of prayer. We do not pray with a view to changing God's purposes, but to win from God in prayer those things which God purposes to bring about through prayer (*Summa Theologiae* IIa IIae, 83, 2).

In other words, though nothing can cause God to will what he has not willed from eternity, God may will from eternity that things should come about as things prayed for by us. Some would reply that in that case prayer can make no difference, and there is a sense in which we can agree with this. Prayer cannot act on God as an exterior force making him bring about what he has not decreed from eternity to bring about. In this sense we can agree with argument (3) as well as with those who deny that we should think of prayer as a form of constraint. Yet what God has decreed from eternity may be what a person prays for, in which case the prayer will be part of what we need to mention in answering the question 'How has this come about?'. And in this sense prayer can be said to make a difference – not by doing something to God, but by being part of creation as willed by him, and an essential part at that. God from eternity decreed that the egg I had for breakfast this morning should be boiled in the water in which it was placed. For my breakfast today was a boiled egg produced in the usual way. But this does not mean that there was no point in putting the egg in the water and heating it. Nor does it mean that the egg did not boil because I put it in the water. In a similar way, so we may argue, God from eternity may have decreed that such and such should happen following my prayer, but this does not mean that there was no point in my praying. What it means is that the prayer is part of the history of creation leading to an answer to prayer. An objector might reply that if something only happens following my prayer, then the prayer is no cause of what happens after it. And on this basis he might deny that there is any need for my prayer. But why should we say that my prayer can be no cause of what happens after it? Could it be because it does not by itself necessitate what follows it? This is an answer that some would give. But if you can respond to me freely, then my asking you to do something does not make you do it though it can surely be a cause of your doing it. And, given the doctrine of creation, nothing that occurs in creation is necessitated by what precedes it, at least in one sense. Consider yet again the case of the boiled egg. Since the boiling of eggs is part of creation (since boiled eggs are created), eggs boil by virtue of God, and my putting an egg into water does not by itself guarantee a boiled egg. Nor does the action of any created thing. In spite of what an atheist might say, an egg needs God in order to get boiled. Yet no one would suppose that you do not need to put eggs into boiling water if you want a boiled egg. Nor would anyone suppose that my putting an egg into boiling water cannot be a cause of there being a boiled egg. Created causes can be true causes even though their effects are willed by God and even though their effects are therefore willed by God from eternity. And the same can surely be said with respect to prayer. This, if you like, can be as causal as the putting of an egg into water is causal with respect to the resulting boiled egg. God creates boiled eggs and we do not make him do so. But what we do can be needed if we are to have a boiled egg, and it is needed simply because God has arranged things that way. He has created a world in which boiled eggs come about in certain specifiable ways. And, as far as I can see, there is nothing to stop us saying that if our prayer is to be answered then it can also be needed because God has arranged it that way. Our prayer can be part of what God's changeless decree has determined as the means by which we receive things we ask for. And, as such, it can matter. As Herbert McCabe usefully puts it:

We should not say: 'In accordance with my prayer: God wills that it should be a fine day'; we should say: 'God wills: that it should be a fine day in accordance with my prayer'. God brings about my prayer just as much as he brings about the fine day, and what he wills, what he has willed from eternity, is that this fine day should not be, so to say, just an ordinary fine day, it should be for me a significant fine day, a sign, a communication from God. It should be a fine day that comes about through my prayer. Now what does that mean? It means that I can truly describe the fine day not just as a fine day but as an answer to my prayer, in other words, as a revelation to me of God's love, a sudden and privileged glimpse of the generosity of God (McCabe 1970, p. 417).

In other words, the changeless will of God need not be viewed as grounds for an objection to petitionary prayer. On the contrary. It can be seen as a necessary condition of there being an answer to such prayer. For a prayer that is answered will be answered by virtue of God's changeless will, and the answer can be seen as an expression of this.

(4) But could it, perhaps, be said that prayer is pointless in view of God's knowledge and goodness? Here we are again with argument (4), and, as I have said, we can concede that the argument has a point. If God is omniscient, then he knows what we want before we tell him and he knows our needs before we express them. And to this we can add that if God is good, it would also seem that he can will what is good without waiting for anyone to suggest that he does so. Insofar as we suppose that creation as such is good, we can actually suggest that he has already done this. So we cannot therefore suppose that prayer gives God information. Nor can we suppose that it is a necessary condition of God willing what is good.

But this again is not to say that prayer is not important. For while God may know what we want or need, and though he may choose in his goodness to give it to us, he cannot bring something about as an answer to our prayer unless we ask him for the thing. In spite of God's knowledge, therefore, for a prayer to be answered it has to be offered. Suppose I know what you want, and suppose I always provide for your needs. Suppose, in addition, that I do so without your knowledge and without your requesting me to help you. Then you get what you want and need, but you do not get answered. In the same way, so we may suggest, if God is to be said to answer our prayers, then we will have to offer them. This is not to say that God cannot or does not provide what we want or need without being asked. But it is to say that there is a significant difference between him providing these things without our asking him and providing them as things for which we have asked him. In

the first case something simply happens to us. In the second case we are
personally involved in what happens because it would truly be described as us
getting what we have asked for from God. It could also be described as us
getting what we want or need while acknowledging how, in the final
analysis, our wants and needs are met. 'God in his generosity does give us
many things which we do not ask for; but he wants some of his gifts to be
given to us in answer to our prayers, and this for our own good. He wants us
to acquire a certain confidence in running to him, and to acknowledge that he
is the source of all good for us' (*Summa Theologiae* IIa IIae, 83, 2 ad 3).

In response to points like this some would reply that there is something
rather distasteful in a God who waits for people to ask him for what is good
before they receive it. But here one can say at least two things. In the first
place, someone who believes in petitionary prayer is not bound to believe that
no good things come from God without prayer. He can, on the contrary,
hold that many good things come from God without being asked for. And he
can, in addition, observe that there is bound to be something wrong with the
suggestion that God waits for prayer before giving what is good. That
suggestion could be taken to imply that prayer is something which occurs
apart from God, as if God were saying to people 'It's all up to you. Give me
the nod and I'll provide what you want'. But we can sensibly deny that
petitionary prayer is anything like this. For if what we do is part of God's
creation, then so are our prayers. It cannot be that God stands back and gives
us what is good on condition that we ask him to do so independently of his
will. Our asking must itself be his action. 'God brings about my prayer just
as much as he brings about the fine day.' Our asking must itself be his action
in us, and his giving us what is good as an answer to our prayer must be a
giving us what is good as an answer to what we ask by virtue of him. And in
this sense we can deny that God waits for people to ask before he provides
them with what is good. Their asking for what is good will itself spring from
him.

But might it not still be argued that if God is good, then he will still bring
about what we want or need even if we do not ask for it? And does this not
mean that prayer is redundant? But how do we know that if God is good he
will bring about what we want or need without our asking for it? Think of
someone in need. Now say 'God will satisfy this person's needs whether
anyone asks him to do so or not'. How do you know what you say is true? If
you do know this, then you presumably know what will come to pass by
virtue of God. But how are you in a position to know this? The reply might
be that if God is good, then he is bound to bring certain things about. But
why should we suppose that God's goodness entails that he will bring
anything about, let alone something that we specify? Some, as we have seen,
say that God displays human virtues or that he is a person subject to duties

and obligations. And if this were true, then one might well be able to say what God can be expected to bring about. But, as I argued in Chapter 8, we ought not to think that it is true. God's goodness cannot lie in anything so creaturely. In that case, however, it is hard to see how we can know what God will bring about by virtue of his goodness. If God is good, then we might infer that he cannot will evil directly and for its own sake. In this sense we might be said to know what God will do. But it is really a case of what God will not do, and it is not the same as knowing that such and such will come to pass by virtue of God. And in this sense we may well take leave to doubt that God will bring something about without our asking him to do so. One might, of course, say that God *can* bring things about without our asking. But that does not mean that he always does so or that he will always do so. One might say that God *has* brought things about without our asking. But that does not mean that we should not ask for things now, nor does it mean that we should not ask for what God has decreed to bring about. People who say that God's goodness is an impediment to petitionary prayer sometimes suppose that God in his goodness will bring about certain things even though we do not ask him to do so. As I have already said, we may doubt that this is true for any concrete instance. But suppose it were true. Suppose that God in his goodness will bring about such and such without being asked to do so. Would it follow that prayer is redundant? It would not, of course, follow at all. All that would follow is that God in his goodness will bring about something without being asked to do so. And no one who believes in petitionary prayer has ever supposed otherwise.

(5) Nor have most of them thought that their prayers are a method for manipulating God, which brings us to argument (5). And here, once again, our verdict can be both positive and negative. Up to a point, the argument is correct. Prayer should not be seen as a way of manipulating God. But that does not mean that the practice of petitionary prayer is misguided.

Some, to be sure, do seem to have thought that prayer and manipulation amount to the same thing, as if offering a prayer and plugging the kettle in were basically equivalent. One can see this view at work in the presuppositions of people who have tried to test the efficacy of petitionary prayer in scientific terms. 'Can we report a significant correlation between, say, longevity and prayers for longevity? If we can, then maybe prayer works. If we cannot, then it does not work.' Something like this is the reasoning of Francis Galton. 'It is asserted', he writes, 'that men possess a faculty of obtaining results over which they have little or no direct personal control, by means of devout and earnest prayer . . . (This) . . . appears to be a very suitable topic for statistical inquiry' (Galton 1883, p. 277). Unfortunately, however, according to Galton the results are not very favourable for those who believe in petitionary prayer. Prayers are often offered for the welfare of the clergy, a 'far more prayerful class' than lawyers and medical men. But 'we do not find that the clergy are in any way more long lived in consequence ...(and)...the prayers of the clergy for protection against the perils and dangers of the night, for security during the day, and for recovery from sickness, appear to be futile in result' (cf. Galton, pp. 282ff.). And so on, together with the following conclusion: 'The civilized world has already yielded an enormous amount of honest conviction to the inexorable requirements of solid fact; and it seems to me clear that all belief in the efficacy of prayer, in the sense in which I have been considering it, must be yielded also' (cf. Galton, pp. 293f.).

But do we have to endorse this conclusion? If we think of petitionary prayer as an activity which guarantees that something or other shall happen, then maybe we should. But it would surely be silly to judge it on this basis since that would be to ignore what we might grandly refer to as the role that petitionary prayer plays in the life of believers. Generalizations in this area are admittedly dangerous, but it is still fair to say that within, for example, the Christian tradition, prayers have not been seen as forcing what they ask for from God. In the wake of New Testament parables like that of the widow and the judge (Lk 18:1–8), some have seemed to teach that prayer can be guaranteed effective simply by being prolonged, as if God, like the victim of a water-torture, is bound to give way if sufficiently irritated. But within the Christian tradition there are also grounds for distinguishing between prayer and manipulation or coercion. For Christians characteristically add to their prayers (specifically or by general intention) what is expressed by the formula 'Thy will be done'. As H. P. Owen puts it:

The aim of prayer is not to conform God's will to our wills but to conform our wills to his will. Hence whenever we ask him for something to happen we must always qualify our request with the words: 'if it is in accordance with thy will'. This qualification was added by Jesus himself in the prayer that he offered on the eve of his passion: 'Abba, Father, all things are possible to thee; remove this cup from me; yet not what I will but what thou wilt' (Mk.14.36) (Owen 1984, p. 78).

And even if all of this were false, that would still not mean that there is any objection to petitionary prayer. It would only mean that one can object to a view of it which confuses it with manipulating God. In reply to this one might say that if prayer and manipulation are not equivalent, then prayer gets nothing done. But not everything that gets done is the result of manipulation pure and simple. And for reasons which I have given we will have to deny that prayer and manipulation amount to the same thing. It cannot be that in prayer we put the screws on God. Since God is the cause of all that is created, it would, if anything, be more accurate to say that prayer is a matter of God putting the screws on us. This, in its own way, is just as misleading, of course. It suggests that our prayer is something determined by God so that those who pray are merely puppets. But at least it can be seen as displaying awareness that we do not act independently of God. More precisely, it can be seen as springing from the recognition that our actions are made to be by God and that the same is therefore true of our prayer. And this, I think, needs to be emphasized when it is said as an objection to petitionary prayer that we cannot manipulate God. The criticism, so one might argue, gets things the wrong way around. It can never be true that my prayer forces God to do anything, but it is always true that when we pray we are being moved to do so by God. Or, to put it more dramatically, 'it is God who prays. Not just God who answers prayer, but God who prays in us in the first place' (McCabe 1970, p. 416). Some will retort that if this is true then prayer cannot be free. But the objection rests on the view that God is a rival to human freedom, and that, as I have argued, is false.

(6) And with this point in mind we can now, I think, begin to see why we can also reject at least one of the conclusions about prayer offered by H. P. Owen. For there is one of them which precisely depends on the view that God might be a threat to human freedom. Owen, in fact, does not think of God as any such thing. Hence his suggestion that we cannot ask God for events depending on the volition of other people. But this suggestion only makes sense if someone's freedom is undermined by God causing him to act as he does. And the mistake lies there. Once it is recognized as a mistake, however, the way is open for supposing that God might act in people as we ask him to do. And if it makes sense to ask him for anything, it will make sense to ask him for this. And Christians, in fact, have done so throughout the ages. 'Therefore confess your sins to one another, and pray for one another, that you may be healed' (Jas 5:16). 'If anyone sees his brother committing what is not a mortal sin, he will ask, and God will give him life for those whose sin is not mortal' (1 Jn 5:16). Such sentiments are contrary to Owen's recommendation, but they are surely a better reflection of the belief that God is creatively present in all things. They also seem to make sense on grounds of charity. Owen would presumably think it right to suggest that we try to help others to be as good as they can or as happy as is possible. So why should we not ask God to correct the wicked or to lead them in the way of perfection? According to Aquinas, 'we should pray even for sinners, that they may be converted, and for the righteous, that they may persevere and make progress' (*Summa Theologiae* IIa IIae, 83, 7 ad 3). Why should someone who believes in God object to that? If everything comes from God, and if conversion, perseverance and progress are desirable, why not ask for God to bring them about?

And why not ask for him to bring other things about as well? Here we come to another of Owen's suggestions – that we ought not to pray for the

occurrence or non-occurrence of particular events. But why not? 'In everything by prayer and supplication with thanksgiving let your requests be made
known to God' (Phil 4:6). According to Owen, God cannot 'adjust' things
to comply with requests. But why talk of *adjusting* here? If God from eternity
has decreed the course of creation, then no answer to a prayer can involve any
adjustment. The prayer and the answer will be part of what God has changelessly decreed. Owen evidently supposes that this is not true, for he speaks of
God having to learn about prayers. God, says Owen, 'is ignorant of free
human choices (including, therefore, prayers) that are yet to be made' (p. 79).
But this we can deny. Our prayer, we may say, is itself God's action in us. It
is God who prays. In that case, however, what is to stop us asking for what
God has decreed to give us in answer to prayer? And what is to stop us asking
for particular things? This last question, of course, is one with a long history
in debates about prayer, and some have concluded that we should not ask
God for absolutely anything. It has been said, for example, that we should
not pray for what is evil or for what is damaging in some way. But it is one
thing to make this kind of proposal and another to deny that prayer can be
offered for particular things. And I can see no reason for supposing that it
should not be so offered. On the contrary, to ask for particular things is
precisely to acknowledge what God really is: not a distant figure vaguely
aiming at an abstract good, but the creator of absolutely everything from
poodles to philosophers. And that, presumably, is why petitionary prayer for
particular things is a prominent part of the Bible. Owen concedes that the
New Testament enjoins request for material goods, but the biblical clamour
for specified results is much more emphatic than the casual reader of Owen
might realize. In the Old Testament 'the object of petitions includes every
desirable good; but the OT reader notices that what he calls "spiritual"
goods are rarely asked. Most Israelite prayer asks the blessings of this life,
social and individual' (McKenzie 1975, p. 687). In the New Testament it is
said that we can ask for things like a safe journey (Rom 1:10), the salvation of
the Jews (Rom 10:1), deliverance from enemies (Rom 15:31), peace (1 Tim
2:1–4), and health (Jas 5:14). As Karl Rahner observes, though

attempts have been made to facilitate an apologia for prayer of petition by saying that one
can or should in genuine petitionary *prayer* ask for only 'heavenly' things, not earthly
things . . . the Old Testament Psalms, which Christianity too has regarded as authentic
models of prayer, are full of petitions. And we should not forget that Jesus's Our Father is a
prayer of petition and not a selfless glorification of God, and that as well as the heavenly gifts
asked for daily bread is mentioned (even in primitive Christianity there was a temptation to
interpret it as the bread of eternal life) (Rahner 1975, p. 56).

In other words, we may spiritualize the notion of prayer, but the biblical
tradition is one in which prayer involves knowing what one wants and
asking for it. And if petitionary prayer makes any sense at all, then that must

surely be right however we may subsequently wish to qualify the point. In this sense we can disagree with Owen. In this sense too we can also disagree with the assertion that, from the Christian point of view, petitionary prayer is some kind of low-grade prayer which we might even be encouraged to grow out of. This assertion is often made, and it is, in particular, commonly made in the name of Christianity (cf. Wakefield 1983, p. 311: 'Petition is the prayer of asking. It is often regarded as a "low level" of prayer like the mewing of a cat for milk'). But as a Christian judgement it is a non-starter. As I noted earlier on, for many centuries it was simply taken for granted that 'prayer' meant 'petition', and the Lord's Prayer is a string of petitions. Anyone who dismisses petitionary prayer in the name of Christianity will therefore be effectively sawing through the branch he sits on. He will be dismissing prayer as Christians understood it for centuries (and as many, of course, understand it today). As I have also noted, petitionary prayer can be an expression of charity, and this would seem to make it appropriate from the Christian point of view, unless we presume that true Christians are unconcerned about being charitable. Finally, and again as I have noted, the practice of petitionary prayer is an obvious way of acknowledging the creative presence of God. As Simon Tugwell puts it:

Petitionary prayer reminds us that God is not a God far off. He has come very close to us and is intimately involved in all the concerns of our human life. . . . Prayer of petition is always an act of faith in this immediacy of God's presence. And so, far from growing out of petitionary prayer as we mature spiritually, we are more likely to grow into it, as our awareness of God's presence becomes wider and more confident (Tugwell 1974, vol. 2, p. 76).

(7) Yet what about the fact that prayers are often unanswered? Does that mean that we should dismiss the practice of petitionary prayer? Our final objection to it says that this is just what it means. And I have already agreed that the objection has force because what people ask for in prayer does not always come to pass. With that observation, however, my agreement with the objection ends. It is not, I think, an objection to petitionary prayer that prayers are often unanswered. Here, it seems to me, the following points can be made.

(a) While we may suppose that prayers have been unanswered, we cannot conclude that this is an argument against petitionary prayer as such for we can also suppose that prayers have been answered. This is because people have prayed for things and what they have prayed for has come to pass. An objector might reply that things have come to pass without being brought about by God as an answer to prayer. But since God is the Creator we are entitled to say that what comes to pass does so by virtue of him. And, insofar as things have come to pass corresponding to what has been asked for in prayer, we are entitled to say that prayer has been answered.

(b) As I noted above, some prayers may conflict with each other. In that case, however, there can in principle be no objection to petitionary prayer on the ground that it is sometimes unanswered. Some would say that if God is omnipotent, then he could do what is logically contradictory and that it is therefore no reply to say that prayers may conflict with each other. But for reasons which I gave in Chapter 7 we need not suppose that omnipotence can stretch to performing feats which are logically impossible.

(c) It is often suggested that if someone prays for something in particular, and if what he asks for does not come to pass, then his prayer has been unanswered. But, as others have said, one can equally well observe that the prayer has been answered and that the answer is 'No'. Some have asserted that this is a silly point to make. As Hubert Richards puts it: 'It is silly to pretend that prayers to which the answer is no are "answered" ' (Richards 1980, p. 58). And one can certainly see what Richards is getting at. But it is also fair to note that 'No' is every bit as much of an answer as 'Yes'. Or are we to say that I can only answer you by giving you whatever you ask?

(d) While we may know that someone has not obtained what he asked for, it surely remains possible that the prayer offered may still have been answered in some way. This, again, is a familiar point, but it is still worth taking seriously. I can make a request, and I can formulate my desires in a specific way. What I ask for may not come to pass. But it may still be true that I have got what I have asked for. Can we therefore be sure that this has not happened in the case of prayers actually made? Can we be sure that it will not happen in the case of prayers to be made? At the very least, we should surely be cautious of supposing that we can. This is not to say that people have in some sense always obtained what they have asked for in prayer. But it is to say that we should be dubious about insisting that they never have simply because the description of what followed a prayer does not match the description of what was prayed for as given in the prayer. Some would reject this point on biblical grounds. They would say that according to the scriptures people will get whatever they pray for. But that would be to ignore the fact that the scriptures also insist that answers to prayer will always be in accordance with God's will, whatever that may be. Hence, for example, Christ is described as asking for one thing before his death and as accepting another (cf. Mt 26:39; Mk 14:35–36; Lk 22:42). It would be an odd sort of biblical fundamentalism which derived from the scriptures the conclusion that people are guaranteed what they ask for, no matter what.

(e) As Christians have said for a long time, requests in prayer that remain ungranted may be ungranted for a reason. It does not here matter what reasons there may be for requests being ungranted when offered in prayer; the point is just that there may be such reasons just as there are often such reasons when people refuse to yield what other people ask them. And this means that requests in prayer that remain ungranted cannot by themselves constitute an objection to prayer of petition as such. If we say otherwise, then for the sake of consistency we had better dismiss the practice of asking in general. If the fact that I do not get what I ask for in prayer today is a reason for asking for nothing in prayer, then the fact that I did not get what I asked Smith for today is a reason for asking nobody for anything.

(f) Even if we have no reason at all for supposing that a prayer has been answered, this does not mean that the prayer was futile. For, as I noted above, prayer can be regarded as intrinsically valuable since it is a natural way of acknowledging the dependence of creatures on God and since it can also be regarded as an act of charity. As others have also said, asking God for things can be intrinsically valuable if our concern is to stand before God as knowing ourselves before him. 'We should not be too impressed by the argument that if God has already heard our hearts, then there is no need to tell him in words what we desire. When God tested the heart of Abraham (*Gen 22:1ff*), it was not so that he could find out something he did not know already; it was to bring the whole situation out into the open, so that both God and Abraham would know what was in the heart of Abraham, and each would know what the other knew.... When we have desires in our heart, it is in the best interests of our relationship with God that we should be honest and open about them' (Tugwell 1974, vol. 2, p. 75).

Prayer of petition?

So my suggestion is that it does in fact make sense to ask for things in prayer. We can make something of petitionary prayer. On some views of it we can reject the practice of it as resting on some confusion. And standard objections to it are not without their merits. But in the wake of belief in God we are entitled to say that petitionary prayer can be necessary and that it can be something to which someone who believes in God can be rationally and inevitably drawn. And, as far as I can see, the practice is absolutely required of those who subscribe to Christianity, in spite of the fact that there are Christians who treat it as something second rate. 'If you then who are evil know how to give good gifts to your children, how much more will your Father who is in heaven give good things to those who ask him?' (Mt 7:11). As some have suggested, it may be true that Christians today are often struck by a sense of the difference between God and human beings, and that this is for them a chief obstacle to the practice of petitionary prayer. The difficulty might be expressed in terms of our argument (2). We can ask for things from persons, but how can we think of God as a person? Yet even though the Christian may reject the formula 'God is a person', he can still significantly assert that God is personal. And if he subscribes to the doctrine of the Incarnation, he can add to this point. For the doctrine certainly states that a man was God, that a person (in the everyday sense) is what the Christian can truly call God. In other words, reflection on Christology can also lead to an awareness of the significance of petitionary prayer. For if Christ is God, we can certainly approach God as a person because Christ is a person.

And, strangely enough, one might add to all this something which is often unnoticed. For would it not be rational for the unbeliever to pray?

The question may seem an odd one since the unbeliever presumably does not think that God exists and since it would therefore appear that he has no reason to pray. And one can see the force of this as an argument against the reasonableness of prayer as offered by the unbeliever. One might here repeat what I said above in response to T. R. Miles. If we do not believe that we can ask for things from God, then why ask?

But the unbeliever may not believe that we cannot ask for things from God. He may just not see why one should believe in God, which is compatible with supposing that if there were a God it would be reasonable to ask him for things in prayer. And if this is indeed the position of the unbeliever, then it is, I think, by no means unreasonable for him to pray. More specifically, it is by no means unreasonable for him to engage in prayer of petition.

Consider the following analogy.

A man is lost in the fog. He has no reason to suppose that anyone is near to help him. Possibly he has some reason for thinking that nobody is near. But if things go on as they have done, he has no hope of rescue. So he cries for help.

Cannot the unbeliever do something similar? If he takes himself to know that there could not be a God or that there certainly is no God, then presumably not. For if he asks for things from God while also believing that there is no question but that God does not exist, then he would contradict himself. Some would say that he is on the way to madness and should correct his course as quickly as possible. But it would surely not be unreasonable for him to ask God for what he needs if he thinks that there could be a God who could give him what he needs. The point is well made by Anthony Kenny.

There is no reason why someone who is in doubt about the existence of God should not pray for help and guidance in this topic as in other matters. Some find something comic in the idea of an agnostic praying to a God whose existence he doubts. It is surely no more unreasonable than the act of a man adrift in the ocean, trapped in a cave, or stranded on a mountainside, who cries for help though he may never be heard or fires a signal which may never be seen (Kenny 1979, p. 129; cf. Geach 1977a, p. 38).

This is not, of course, to say that petitionary prayer and religious scepticism are easy or desirable partners. But it is to say that they can be rationally united. The famous preface to prayer which runs 'O God, if there is a

God . . . ' will strike some as silly or irreverent. But it need be neither. On the contrary, if there could be a God, and if he could do what one asks, then it seems silly not to ask him and reverent to suppose that he could grant what one asks if he exists. Some will reply that where prayer is hedged around with 'ifs' and 'buts' it cannot really be prayer. But why not? It is easy, perhaps, to see how prayer can be a sham where the one who prays flatly rejects everything presupposed by the practice of prayer (cf. Phillips 1965, pp. 115ff.). But what of the prayer of someone who does not have such a settled or decided position? It may not spring from much that a believer would recognize as faith or trust in God. But it may be an honest expression of genuine need and a level-headed response to that need. And if someone who believes in prayer cannot think of it as being that, then one might well wonder whether he believes in prayer at all.

KINDS OF PRAYER

So again I suggest that petitionary prayer is something we can make sense of. Yet 'prayer', as I have noted, is a word which has been taken to mean more than just petition. Can we therefore add that sense can be made of it where it means more than simply asking for things?

This question, alas, is the programme for another book. For it cannot be adequately answered without a full examination of the way in which people have thought of prayer insofar as they have viewed it as more than petition. And that undertaking is a much more daunting task than people are commonly prepared to allow. The history of the word 'prayer' is a tangled maze. But with this point stated, let me just end with a few cursory observations.

(1) 'Prayer' is frequently taken to mean 'thanksgiving'. The idea here is that one can pray by thanking God. And if that is what prayer is taken to involve, then it is surely something which has a point. And the point is surely obvious. If God exists, then we have what we have by virtue of him. And nothing has constrained him to give it to us. So what could be more natural than to thank him for it? And to this, so we may say, the Christian, at any rate, can add something more. For it is part of Christian theism that God has not simply made us what we can know ourselves to be and what we can value without reference to Christian teaching. Insofar as the Christian is working on the basis of the New Testament (and it would be odd if he did not), he believes that God has made possible for people a union with himself which can be spoken of as a participation in the life of God himself. I take this to be the import of texts such as 2 Peter 1:3–4 and Jn 15:9–12. In that case, however, the Christian has additional reason for thanks. For he believes that by

virtue of God's will he is, so one may put it, more than merely human. He has been made a reflection of God.

(2) People sometimes say that there is something called 'mystical prayer'. Quite what this means is very much open to question, as readers will discover if they search through the literature for an agreed definition of 'mystical' and 'prayer'. But it often seems clear that by 'mystical prayer' is meant the desire for God by virtue of knowing him and the fulfilment (at least to some extent) of that desire. It has also been taken to include the conscious recognition that God in himself is supremely worthy of attention. This view of prayer has been criticized for many reasons (cf. Bouyer 1961, ch. XII), some of which are more cogent than others. But without going into details one can, I think, make at least this point regarding it.

As I noted earlier, human beings are rational by nature. I take this to mean that they are capable of knowledge and that they are therefore capable of being united to things in, for example, a way that a stone is not. According to Aristotle (*De Anima* III), the mind is in a sense all things – meaning that there can be a unique relationship between the knower and the known. A stone can make contact with things or be related to them by rubbing up against them materially or by being in such and such a physical location with respect to them. But the knower, on the other hand, can, as one may put it, have what he knows inside himself. If I know that Gibraltar is a rock, then I am simply capable of making a true judgement about Gibraltar. But in knowing Gibraltar, there can be a real sense in which myself and Gibraltar, though two, are also one. In that case, however, knowing something can be very much a way of being united to it. And, insofar as one desires union with God, one can therefore be said to desire knowledge of him. And one can be said to desire it as something which is appropriate to oneself as a human being. For knowledge is what people are capable of as people. Some would reject this view on the grounds that it seems too cerebral – as if the view were commending the joys of a more than usually difficult crossword puzzle. But this would be to miss the point. Knowledge is something natural to people. Stones do not have it. And, insofar as it is a union of the knower and the known, then knowledge of God is an obvious thing to seek if what we want is union with him. 'And this is eternal life, that they know thee, the only true God, and Jesus Christ whom thou hast sent' (Jn 17:3).

(3) 'Prayer' is sometimes taken to mean 'adoration' or 'worship', which, in turn, is understood to be the use of bodily gestures and behaviour (including singing) as a means of venerating God. Some have been decidedly scornful of this sort of thing on the assumption that God should be acknowledged in some kind of 'spiritual' sense. But the difficulty, of course, is to see why a piece of bodily behaviour should not be viewed as a perfectly obvious way of venerating God. For, as all of us know, our bodies are not an

optional extra to which we are yoked as someone in hospital is tied to his plaster-cast. That, for example, is why we can talk about sex as 'making love'. The love between spouses need not be thought of as something utterly different from what there is when the couple make love. The making of love can be part of what is meant by the love that is there between the couple, even though that love can be something more again. And the point carries over to the topic of adoration or worship. In some ways this can be made to seem utterly ludicrous. Someone who bows down before the Eucharist is bowing to God who is where the eucharistic species are. But people who bow nowhere in particular (as, for example, when reciting doxologies) are not prostrating themselves before God as a courtier may bow before his king. If God is omnipresent, one might flippantly observe that they are always pointing away from God whatever the direction of their bow. But this kind of observation would surely miss the point. As bodily creatures it is natural and proper for people to engage in bodily behaviour as a way of expressing what they believe about God. The result may be aesthetically unpleasing, as it doubtless often is. But that is not to say that it cannot be also appropriate. Think once again of bowing. The bow is a natural way of acknowledging superiority and of expressing dependence on the part of the one who bows. Given the nature of God as conceived by those who believe in him, and given the fact that people are God's creatures, what could be more natural than to bow as a gesture reflecting and living out one's belief in God? Some people will find the question utterly baffling. But some people would say that kissing is silly or puzzling.

In general, therefore, one may justly maintain that adoration or worship need not be pointless, though its point may be clear only to those who engage in it. But it is, perhaps, worth noting that it can be misguided. Here I am thinking of the claim sometimes encountered that all who assert in good faith that they worship God actually do worship the true God. The assertion has become popular since people are naturally anxious to unite religious believers even when they believe in different religions. 'We all worship the same God in the end.' But this view is questionable, as Peter Geach usefully indicates in an essay entitled 'On Worshipping the Right God' (Geach 1969, pp. 100–116). As Geach observes, someone may say that he worships God, but, like someone who says he supports a named politician but whose beliefs about the person are wildly false, he may do no such thing. His beliefs about God may in no way latch on to the truth. Here one seems obliged to say that, in spite of what he says, he does not worship God. 'A sufficiently erroneous thought of a God will simply fail to relate to the true and living God at all' (Geach, p. 111). And the upshot would seem to be that, though someone may conceive himself as worshipping God, it does not follow that he is doing so. It does not follow that he is worshipping the only true God. The reply might be that love can unite a person to God whatever he takes God to be. But though this sounds well enough, there is also a problem. 'A man's love for a woman, however much it means to him, scarcely latches on to her if his acquaintance with her is extremely slight, if she is for him a *princesse lointaine*, if he has fantastic misconceptions of her actual characteristics' (Geach, p. 111).

And I take that to mean that when we try to think about God it is important to get things right. In this book I have been trying to do that. In thinking about God for himself, may the reader fare better.

QUESTIONS FOR DISCUSSION

1 Consider the history of the word 'prayer' and its equivalents in other languages.
2 What are the major objections to the practice of petitionary prayer? How cogent are they?
3 Is prayer a form of magic?
4 Can one believe in the value of prayer without believing in the reality of God?
5 Does God answer prayer?
6 If Christ is God, can he pray?
7 Are there any limits to what one can properly ask for in prayer?
8 To what extent would different views of God yield different understanding of prayer?
9 Why worship God? Should anything other than God be worshipped?
10 Could there be such a thing as 'progress' in prayer?

FURTHER READING

For a brief survey of the word 'prayer', the reader can usefully begin with the article by Michel Dupuy on 'Oraison' in the *Dictionnaire de Spiritualité*, Tome XI (Paris, 1982). Two classic treatises on prayer (the second of which I am clearly much indebted to) are by Origen and Aquinas. For Origen, see *Treatise on Prayer*, trans. E. G. Jay (London, 1954). For Aquinas, see *Summa Theologiae* IIa IIae, 83 (*de oratione*). A modern translation of the Aquinas text can be found in vol. 39 of the Blackfriars edition of the *Summa Theologiae*, which also contains some helpful background material. The translation, unfortunately, is unreliable.

For recent, reflective discussion of prayer, the following will be found useful: Hans Urs von Balthasar, *Prayer* (London, 1961); Peter Baelz, *Prayer and Providence* (New York, 1968); Peter Baelz, *Does God Answer Prayer?* (London, 1982); Vincent Brümmer, *What Are We Doing When We Pray?: A Philosophical Inquiry* (London, 1984); Karl Rahner, *On Prayer* (New York, 1968); Karl Rahner, *Christian at the Crossroads* (London, 1975); Hubert Richards, *What Happens When You Pray?* (London, 1980); D. Z. Phillips, *The Concept of Prayer* (London, 1965); Ninian Smart, *The Concept of Worship* (London, 1972); Illtyd Trethowan, *Mysticism and Theology* (London, 1974); Simon Tugwell, OP, *Prayer*, 2 vols (Dublin, 1974).

Three books can be especially recommended as historical background to thinking about the history of views of prayer. These are: Louis Bouyer, *Introduction to Spirituality* (London,

1961); Simon Tugwell, OP, *Ways of Imperfection: An Exploration of Christian Spirituality* (London, 1984); Rowan Williams, *The Wound of Knowledge: Christian Spirituality from the New Testament to St John of the Cross* (London, 1979).

Among the many currently available short essays on prayer, the following should be found especially helpful; D. Basinger, 'Why Petition an Omnipotent, Omniscient, Wholly Good God?', *Religious Studies* 19 (1983); Brian Davies, OP, 'What Happens When You Pray?', *New Blackfriars* 61 (1980); Peter Geach, 'Praying for Things to Happen' in *God and the Soul* (London, 1969); Herbert McCabe, OP, 'Prayer', *Doctrine and Life* 20 (1970); H. Oppenheimer, 'Petitionary Prayer', *Theology* 73 (1970); H. H. Price, 'Petitionary Prayer and Telepathy' in *Essays in the Philosophy of Religion* (Oxford, 1972); E. Stump, 'Petitionary Prayer', *American Philosophical Quarterly* 16 (1979); R. Young, 'Petitioning God', *American Philosophical Quarterly* 11 (1974).

Bibliography

Note: All Scripture quotations are taken from the Revised Standard Version of the Bible, copyright 1946, 1956, 1957, and 1971 by the Division of Christian Education of the National Council of the Churches of Christ in the United States of America. Quotations from Aquinas are almost always from translations listed below, but I have sometimes preferred to use unpublished translations. I should note in particular that all the quotations from Aquinas in Chapter 11 have been translated by Simon Tugwell, OP. Quotations from Vatican I are taken from Vincent McNabb (ed.), *The Decrees of the Vatican Council* (London, 1907).

Anscombe, G. E. M., *Collected Philosophical Papers*, 3 vols (Oxford, 1981).

Anscombe, G. E. M., and Geach, P. T., *Three Philosophers* (Oxford, 1961).

Anscombe, Elizabeth, and Geach, Peter Thomas (trans. and eds), *Descartes: Philosophical Writings* (Open University, 1970).

Anselm, St, *Proslogion*, in *St Anselm's Proslogion*, trans. and intro. M. J. Charlesworth (Oxford, 1965/Notre Dame, 1979).

Anselm, St, *Cur Deus Homo*, trans. S. N. Deane, in *Saint Anselm: Basic Writings* (La Salle, Ill., 1962).

Aquinas, St Thomas, *Summa Theologiae*, Blackfriars ed., 61 vols, various translators (London, 1963–81).

Aquinas, St Thomas, *Summa Contra Gentiles*, trans. A. C. Pegis and others (New York, 1955–57).

Aquinas, St Thomas, *In Libros Peri Hermeneias*, ed. R. M. Spiazzi (Turin 1955); Eng. trans.: *Aristotle on Interpretation – Commentary by St Thomas and Cajetan*, trans. J. Oesterle (Milwaukee, 1962).

Aquinas, St Thomas, *De Potentia*, trans. L. Shapcote and others (Westminster, Maryland, 1952).

Aquinas, St Thomas, *De Ente et Essentia*, trans. A. Maurer (Toronto, 1949).

Aristotle, *Nicomachean Ethics*, trans. J. A. K. Thomson (Harmondsworth, Middx, 1955).

Athanasius, St., *Contra Gentes*, ed. and trans. Robert W. Thomson (Oxford, 1971).

Augustine, St, *Confessions*, trans. R. S. Pine-Coffin (Harmondsworth, Middx, 1961).

Augustine, St, *De Trinitate*, trans. A. W. Haddan (Edinburgh, 1873).

Augustine, St, *The City of God*, trans. John Healey (London, 1945).

Barnes, Jonathan, *The Ontological Argument* (London, 1972).

Barr, James, *Fundamentalism* (London, 1977).

Barth, Karl, *Church Dogmatics* I/1, trans. G. T. Thomson (Edinburgh, 1936).

Barth, Karl, *Anselm: Fides Quaerens Intellectum* (London, 1960).

Blehl, V. F. (ed.), *The Essential Newman* (New York, 1963).

Boethius, *The Consolation of Philosophy*, trans. V. E. Watts (Harmondsworth, Middx, 1969).

Bouillard, Henri, *The Knowledge of God* (London, 1969).

Bouyer, Louis, *Introduction to Spirituality* (London, 1961).

Brown, David, *The Divine Trinity* (London, 1985).

Brümmer, Vincent, *What Are We Doing When We Pray?: A Philosophical Inquiry* (London, 1984).

Burns, Paul, and Cumming, John (eds.), *The Bible Now* (Dublin, 1981).

Burrill, Donald R. (ed.), *The Cosmological Arguments: A Spectrum of Opinion* (New York, 1967).

Camus, Albert, *The Plague*, trans. Stuart Gilbert (Harmondsworth, Middx, 1960).

Clifford, W. K., 'The Ethics of Belief' in *Lectures and Essays* (London, 1879).

The Cloud of Unknowing, ed. James Walsh, SJ (New York/Ramsey, N.J./Toronto, 1981).

Coventry, John, *The Theology of Faith* (Cork, 1968).

Craig, William Lane, *The Kalām Cosmological Argument* (London, 1979).

Damascene, St John, *Expositio Fidei Orthodoxae*, ed. J. P. Migne, *Patrologia Graeca* XLIV (Paris, 1864).

Darwin, Charles, *The Autobiography of Charles Darwin*, ed. Gavin de Beer (Oxford/New York, 1984).

Davis, Stephen T., *Logic and the Nature of God* (London, 1983).

Delaney, C. F. (ed.), *Rationality and Religious Belief* (Notre Dame/London, 1979).

Descartes, René, *Meditations on First Philosophy* in *Descartes: Philosophical Writings*, trans. and ed. Elizabeth Anscombe and Peter Thomas Geach (Open University, 1970).

Dostoyevsky, Fyodor, *The Brothers Karamazov*, vol. I, trans. David Magarshack (Harmondsworth, Middx, 1958).

Dupuy, Michel, 'Oraison' in *Dictionnaire de Spiritualité*, Tome XI (Paris, 1982).

Eddy, Mary Baker, *Science and Health with Key to the Scriptures* (Boston, 1971).

Edwards, Paul, 'The Cosmological Argument', *The Rationalist Annual for the Year 1959*, ed. H. Hawton.

Edwards, Paul (ed.), *The Encyclopedia of Philosophy*, 8 vols (New York/London, 1967).

Evans, C. F., *Resurrection and the New Testament* (London, 1970).

Flew, Antony, *The Presumption of Atheism* (London, 1976).

Franklin, Eric, *How the Critics Can Help: A Guide to the Practical Use of the Gospels* (London, 1982).

Frege, Gottlob, *The Foundations of Arithmetic*, trans. J. L. Austin (Oxford, 1953).

Galton, F., *Inquiries into the Human Faculty and its Development* (London, 1883).

Garrigou-Lagrange, R., *God: His Existence and Nature*, 2 vols (St Louis, Mo./London, 1934 and 1936).

Gaskin, J. C. A., *The Quest for Eternity* (Harmondsworth, Middx, 1984).

Geach, P. T., *God and the Soul* (London, 1969).

Geach, P. T., *Logic Matters* (Oxford, 1972).

Geach, P. T., 'The Future', *New Blackfriars* 54 (1973).

Geach, P. T., *Reason and Argument* (Oxford, 1976).

Geach, P. T., *The Virtues* (Cambridge, 1977) (a).

Geach, P. T., *Providence and Evil* (Cambridge, 1977) (b).

Grisez, Germain, *Beyond the New Theism* (Notre Dame/London, 1975).

Haldane, Elizabeth S., and Ross, G. R. T., *The Philosophical Works of Descartes*, 2 vols (Cambridge 1911 and 1912).

Heron, Alasdair, *The Holy Spirit* (London, 1983).

Hick, John, *Evil and the God of Love* (2nd ed., London, 1977).

Hick, John, *Philosophy of Religion* (3rd ed., Englewood Cliffs, N.J., 1983).

Hick, John (ed.), *The Existence of God* (London/New York, 1964).

Hick, John (ed.), *The Myth of God Incarnate* (London, 1977).

Hughes, G. E., 'The Doctrine of the Trinity', *Sophia* II (1963).

Hume, David, *Dialogues Concerning Natural Religion*, ed. Norman Kemp Smith (Edinburgh, 1947; repr. Indianapolis, 1977).

Hume, David, *A Treatise of Human Nature*, ed. L. A. Selby-Bigge (Oxford, 1965).

Hume, David, *An Enquiry concerning Human Understanding*, ed. L. A. Selby-Bigge (3rd ed., Oxford, 1975).

Joyce, George Hayward, *Principles of Natural Theology* (London, 1923).

Kant, Immanuel, *Critique of Practical Reason*, trans. Thomas Kingsmill Abbott (London/New York/Toronto, 1909).

Kant, Immanuel, *Critique of Pure Reason*, trans. Norman Kemp Smith (London, 1964).

Kant, Immanuel, *Foundations of the Metaphysics of Morals*, trans. Lewis White Beck, ed. Robert Paul Wolff (Indianapolis, 1969).

Kant, Immanuel, *Religion within the Limits of Reason Alone*, trans. T. M. Greene and H. H. Hudson (New York, 1963).

Kelly, J. N. D., *Early Christian Creeds* (3rd ed., London, 1972).

Kenny, Anthony, *The Five Ways* (London, 1969).

Kenny, Anthony, *The God of the Philosophers* (Oxford, 1979).

Kenny, Anthony, *Aquinas* (Oxford, 1980).

Kenny, Anthony, *Faith and Reason* (New York, 1983).

Kittel, Gerhard (ed.), *Theological Dictionary of the New Testament*, Vol. 1 (Grand Rapids, Michigan, 1964).

Kretzmann, Norman, 'Omniscience and Immutability', *Journal of Philosophy* 63 (1966).

Lane, Dermot, *The Experience of God* (Dublin, 1981).

Leibniz, Gottfried, *On the Ultimate Origination of Things* in G. H. R. Parkinson (ed.), *Leibniz: Philosophical Writings* (London/Toronto, 1973).

Leibniz, Gottfried, *New Essays on Human Understanding*, trans. and ed. Peter Remnant and Jonathan Bennett (Cambridge, 1981).

Lewis, C. S., *The Problem of Pain* (London, 1940).

Lewis, C. S., *Letters to Malcolm* (London, 1964).

Lucas, J. R., *A Treatise on Time and Space* (London, 1973).

Lyons, J., *Introduction to Theoretical Linguistics* (Cambridge, 1968).

Mackie, J. L., 'Evil and Omnipotence', *Mind* 64 (1955).

Mackie, J. L., 'Omnipotence', *Sophia* I (1962).

Mackie, J. L., *Truth, Probability, and Paradox* (Oxford, 1973).

Mackie, J. L., *The Miracle of Theism* (Oxford, 1982).

Maimonides, Moses, *The Guide for the Perplexed*, trans. M. Friedlander (London, 1936).

Malcolm, Norman, 'Anselm's Ontological Arguments', *Philosophical Review* 69 (1960).

Mascall, E. L., *The Openness of Being* (London, 1971).

McCabe, Herbert, 'Prayer', *Doctrine and Life* 20 (1970).

McCabe, Herbert, and Wiles, Maurice, 'The Incarnation: An Exchange', *New Blackfriars* 58 (1977).

McCabe, Herbert, 'God: II – Freedom', *New Blackfriars* 61 (1980).

McCabe, Herbert, 'God: III – Evil', *New Blackfriars* 62 (1981).

McCloskey, H. J., 'God and Evil', *The Philosophical Quarterly* 10 (1960).

McKenzie, John L., *Dictionary of the Bible* (London, 1975).

Miles, T. R., *Religion and the Scientific Outlook* (London, 1959).

Moule, C. F. D., *The Origin of Christology* (Cambridge, 1977).

Nagel, Ernest, and Newman, James R., *Gödel's Proof* (London, 1959).

Neuner, J., and Dupuis J., *The Christian Faith in the Doctrinal Documents of the Catholic Church* (London, 1983).

Newton, I., *Newton's Philosophy of Nature*, ed. H. S. Thayer (New York, 1953).

Nietzsche, Friedrich, *The Genealogy of Morals* (1877), trans. Francis Golffing (New York, 1956).

O'Collins, Gerald, *The Easter Jesus* (London, 1973).

O'Collins, Gerald, *Interpreting Jesus* (London/Ramsey, N.J., 1983).

O'Hear, Anthony, *Experience, Explanation and Faith* (London, 1984).

Origen, *Treatise on Prayer*, trans. E. G. Jay (London, 1954).

Owen, H. P., *The Moral Argument for Christian Theism* (London, 1965).

Owen, H. P., *The Christian Knowledge of God* (London, 1969).

Owen, H. P., *Concepts of Deity* (London, 1971).

Owen, H. P., *Christian Theism* (Edinburgh, 1984).

Paley, William, *Natural Theology* in *The Works of William Paley*, vol. IV (Oxford, 1938).

Palmer, Humphrey, *Analogy* (London, 1973).

Parkinson, G. H. R., *Logic and Reality in Leibniz's Metaphysics* (Oxford, 1965).

Penelhum, Terence, 'Divine Necessity', *Mind* 69 (1960).

Penelhum, Terence, *Problems of Religious Knowledge* (London, 1971).

Phillips, D. Z., *The Concept of Prayer* (London, 1965).

Phillips, D. Z., *Faith and Philosophical Enquiry* (London, 1970).

Phillips, D. Z., *Religion Without Explanation* (Oxford, 1976).

Philoponus, John, *De Aeternitate Mundi Contra Proclum*, ed. H. Robe (Leipzig, 1899).

Pike, Nelson, 'Omnipotence and God's Ability to Sin', *American Philosophical Quarterly* 6 (1969).

Pike, Nelson, *God and Timelessness* (London, 1970).

Plantinga, Alvin, *God and Other Minds* (Ithaca, N.Y., 1967).

Plantinga, Alvin, *The Nature of Necessity* (Oxford, 1974).

Plantinga, Alvin, *God, Freedom and Evil* (London, 1975).

Plantinga, Alvin, and Wolterstorff, Nicholas (eds), *Faith and Rationality* (London/Notre Dame, 1983).

Prior, A. N., *Papers in Logic and Ethics* (London, 1976).

Quine, W. V., *Theories and Things* (Cambridge, Mass./London, 1981).

Rahner, Karl, *Theological Investigations*, vol. 1 (London, 1961).

Rahner, Karl, *Christian at the Crossroads* (London, 1975).

Rhees, Rush, *Without Answers* (London, 1969).

Richards, Hubert, *What Happens When You Pray?* (London, 1980).

Richardson, Alan, and Bowden, John (eds), *A New Dictionary of Christian Theology* (London, 1983).

Ross, James, 'Creation II' in Alfred J. Freddoso (ed.), *The Existence and Nature of God* (Notre Dame/London, 1983).

Russell, Bertrand, *Religion and Science* (London, 1935).

Russell, Bertrand, *Logic and Knowledge* (London/New York, 1956).

Sanders, E. P., *Jesus and Judaism* (London, 1985).

Sheehan, Michael, *Apologetics and Catholic Doctrine* (Dublin, 1962).

Sherry, Patrick, *Spirit, Saints and Immortality* (London, 1984).

Sobrino, Jon, *Christology at the Crossroads* (London, 1978).

Sorabji, Richard, *Time, Creation and the Continuum* (London, 1983).

Southern, R. W., *St Anselm and his Biographer* (Cambridge, 1963).

Stead, Christopher, *Divine Substance* (Oxford, 1977).

Strawson, Peter, *Introduction to Logical Theory* (London/New York, 1952).

Sutherland, Stewart, *God, Jesus and Belief* (Oxford, 1984).

Swinburne, Richard, 'The Argument from Design', *Philosophy* 43 (1968).

Swinburne, Richard, *The Concept of Miracle* (London, 1970).

Swinburne, Richard, *The Coherence of Theism* (Oxford, 1977).

Swinburne, Richard, *The Existence of God* (Oxford, 1979).

Swinburne, Richard, *Faith and Reason* (Oxford, 1981) (a).

Swinburne, Richard, *Space and Time* (2nd ed., London, 1981) (b).

Tennant, F. R., *Philosophical Theology*, 2 vols (Cambridge, 1928 and 1930).

Tugwell, Simon, *Prayer*, 2 vols (Dublin, 1974).

Tugwell, Simon, *Ways of Imperfection: An Exploration of Christian Spirituality* (London, 1984).

Wakefield, Gordon S. (ed.), *A Dictionary of Christian Spirituality* (London, 1983).

Ward, Keith, *Rational Theology and the Creativity of God* (Oxford, 1982).

White, Victor, *God the Unknown* (London, 1956).

Wiles, Maurice, *Faith and the Mystery of God* (London, 1982).

Wiles, Maurice, and McCabe, Herbert, 'The Incarnation: An Exchange', *New Blackfriars* 58 (1977).

Williams, C. J. F., 'A Programme for Christology', *Religious Studies* 3 (1968).

Wittgenstein, Ludwig, *Tractatus Logico-Philosophicus*, trans. D. F. Pears and B. F. McGuiness (London, 1961).

Wittgenstein, Ludwig, *Philosophical Investigations*, trans. G. E. M. Anscombe (Oxford, 1968).

Wittgenstein, Ludwig, *On Certainty*, trans. G. E. M. Anscombe (Oxford, 1969).

Index